The European Community
in Perspective

The European Community in Perspective

The New Europe, the United States, and the World

Gerhard Mally

Lexington Books
D.C. Heath and Company
Lexington, Massachusetts
Toronto   London

Library of Congress Cataloging in Publication Data

Mally, Gerhard,
    The European Community in perspective.

"Published for the Atlantic Council of the United States."
Bibliography: p.
    1. European federation. I. Title.
JN15.M24   341.24'2   72-10542
ISBN 0-669-85340-2

Second printing, October 1973.

Published simultaneously in Canada.

Printed in the United States of America.

International Standard Book Number: 0-669-85340-2

Library of Congress Catalog Card Number: 72-10542

Contents

List of Figures

List of Tables

Foreword

The 1970s hold the promise of becoming an exciting era in international relations as a result of the following historical developments.

1. Under the magnetic impact of the successful operations of the Common Market, six other nations (members of EFTA) decided to join the "New Europe" in a gigantic "European Free Trade Area"—the largest single commercial bloc in history, with the potential to emerge as a political superpower.
2. The traditional pro-European policy of the American government is in the process of transformation, hopefully toward a more enduring and more equal relationship of burdens, responsibilities, and opportunities.
3. The nations of the free world have committed themselves to begin negotiations on a reform of the international monetary system and on the problems of international trade in industrial and agricultural products, as well as on the issue of combined development assistance.
4. The member states of the Atlantic Alliance have agreed to meet with the Warsaw Pact countries in a European Security Conference to discuss the future of East-West relations, and a parallel negotiation will examine the question of mutual and balanced force reductions in Europe.

It is against the background of these momentous developments on the international scene that Professor Mally's study assumes greatest significance. *The European Community in Perspective* deals with the New Europe and its relations with the United States and the rest of the world and constitutes the most up-to-date and comprehensive treatment of the subject. Given the quality of Dr. Mally's book, and the timely and relevant nature of its analysis and conclusions for the European-American dialogue in the 1970s, the Atlantic Council is pleased to present this book to the public. The substantive views expressed are, of course, the responsibility of Dr. Mally.

Following a comparative examination of both the forces of integration and disintegration at work in Western Europe during the last decades, Gerhard Mally presents a balanced and objective picture of the European Community in transition from nationalism to regionalism. In the scholarly fashion of the political scientist, the author first evaluates the principal concepts and theories of international integration and then contributes his own original model of political unification.

Professor Mally also analyzes the phenomenon of European integration in terms of diplomatic history and foreign policy, comparative governmental structures and dynamics, international law and organization, and international politics and economics. Finally, the author presents a summary evaluation of the

European Community as a political system and sketches the alternative contours of a future united Europe.

For the scholar-diplomat and political practitioner as well as for the student on both sides of the Atlantic, the following major findings seem to be of greatest interest:

1. Integration-disintegration, being a dual syndrome in which centripetal and and centrifugal forces are simultaneously at work, results in the complex paradox that progress in economic integration may be accompanied by stagnation or regression in political unification, or vice versa.

2. Contrary to popular belief, many Europeans have refused to choose between nationalism and Europeanism. They choose both and are engaged in an unprecedented enterprise of seeking peaceful unification while maintaining their respective national identities. This phenomenon is referred to as "multiple loyalties." The question is, can this dualism be maintained?

3. *"Fédéralism à la carte"* seems to be the prevailing strategy of leaders of European political unification (rather than the architectonic approach), leading logically and inevitably, although not automatically, to the creation of the United States of Europe—a goal widely accepted as a *desideratum* by most Europeans. Thus European unity has become an *idée force*, and with the entry of Britain into the European Community, the movement has passed the point of no return.

4. The principal obstacle to the realization of a European federation is the persistent dichotomy between the "big power" aspirations of the people and the unwillingness of their governments to delegate sovereign powers to a single European authority.

5. Since solidarity in defense and the interdependence of postindustrial economies inevitably link Western Europe to the United States, the early realization of an Atlantic partnership of equals is in the enlightened self-interest of both Europe and America.

Ever since the end of World War II, the United States has been a champion of European unity. This desirable foreign policy approach has also been adopted by President Nixon and his secretary of state, who welcomed the enlargement of the European Community and expressed continued American support for the political unification of Europe. The rationale for this "European policy" of the United States has been succinctly stated by Henry A. Kissinger as follows: "There is no alternative to European unity, either for the United States or for Europe. In its absence the [Atlantic] malaise can only be alleviated, not ended."[1]

To be sure, the construction of Europe has some negative side effects on the United States which Dr. Mally believes are unintentional and transitory in nature. Secretary of State Rogers has declared that "we continue to be convinced that, with good will in accommodating mutual interests on both sides, the long-run economic and political benefits the United States will derive from European unity outweigh such temporary economic dislocations as may occur."[2]

Indeed, a "pro-European" attitude on the part of the American government is likely to assure cordial and mutually beneficial relations with the uniting Europe in the future. Conversely, a policy of opposition to European unity would only be counterproductive: it would cause great resentments across the Atlantic and might delay the building of the United States of Europe without preventing the achievement of this goal in the long run.

Undoubtedly, the transition from (European) dependence on, to equality with, the United States involves a delicate process of adjustment for both partners. Yet, there seems to be no reasonable alternative to this course of action. It serves a dual purpose: to forestall the establishment of an anti-American third force on the European Continent, and to counter neoisolationist tendencies in the United States. Greater European autonomy and the equitable sharing of political responsibility and financial burdens in NATO, the OECD, and other Atlantic agencies would contribute to harmonious trans-Atlantic relationships in the years to come. The leitmotiv for a Euro-American *modus vivendi* was once and for all defined by the "Three Wise Men" of NATO when they stated in 1956 that "moves toward Atlantic cooperation and European unity should be parallel and complementary, not competitive and conflicting."[3]

Given the interdependence of the United States and Western Europe in the fields of security (symbolized by NATO), in the economic realm (symbolized by OECD), and in the cultural area (symbolized by Western civilization), the consolidation of the Atlantic partnership has become a historical imperative.

January 1973

W. Randolph Burgess

Washington, D.C.

Preface

The enlargement of the European Community in 1973 marked the last in a series of momentous political events that signaled the beginning of a new era in international relations. With the expansion of the Common Market, which had been preceded by the admission of the People's Republic of China to the United Nations, and the rise of Japan as the world's third largest industrial power, the global political landscape has been substantially altered. In other words, the co-dominium of the United States and the Soviet Union, which had characterized world politics during the post-war period, was superseded by a more complex constellation of power centers. This systems transformation from bipolarity to pentagonal multipolarity occurred as three major powers—China, Japan, and Western Europe—joined the United States and the Soviet Union as principal actors in the international arena of the 1970s.

To be sure in terms of strategic-nuclear capability, the US and the USSR are still far superior to the other three major powers in this new oligopolistic setting. However, the advent of nuclear parity, the overkill syndrome, and the counter-productive nature of these ultimate weapons have clearly diminished their usefulness for both parties—as evidenced by the SALT accords and East-West détente. Paradoxically, the consequence of the reduced prospects for nuclear war and massive armed confrontations is an increased potential for international conflicts in the economic field. In other words, the Cold War between military adversaries is being replaced by the competitive co-existence between economic rivals.

It stands to reason that under these conditions the traditional concept of national power will be redefined and primary emphasis will be placed on such economic indicators as GNP, reserve assets, balances of payments and trade—rather than on atomic megatonnages and military hardware. It is in this pentagonal world of economic superpowers that the enlarged European Community can be expected to play a prominent role, given its vast politico-economic potential. With a population of over 255 million, the New Europe constitutes the world's third largest demographic unit. Its combined GNP amounts to about $630 billion and its total reserve assets exceed $40 billion. Finally, the total trade volume of the expanded Common Market is equivalent to that of the two superpowers taken together—thus making the European Community the largest trading bloc with a share of about 40 percent of the world market (see Table I-A).

Measured in these modern terms of "national power," the New Europe constitutes already an economic superpower with the potential of becoming a political entity before the turn of the century—provided that it succeeds in its efforts to define common policies implemented by a single political authority.

The preceding reflections regarding the on-going transformation of the

Table I-A
Comparative Data on the Major Economic Powers (1973)

	EC	USA	USSR	Japan	China
Population (in millions)	255	210	245	105	780
G.N.P. (in $ billions)	640	1,000	300	260	100
Reserve Assets (in $ billions)	45	12	10	17	2
Trade volume (percentage of world trade)	40	20	8	15	N.A.
Defense spending (in $ billions)	28	75	30	N.A.	N.A.

Sources: Statistical Office of the European Communities, *The Europa Yearbook 1971, The Statesman's Yearbook 1971/72*, The World Almanac.
Note: These 1973 estimates are based upon 1970 figures.

international system and the emergence of five leading actors provides the rationale for focusing on one of them, namely the European Community. Following the Summit Conference of Paris of October 1972, and the actual expansion of the Common Market from six to nine members in January 1973, the European Community stands at historical crossroads thus making an examination of the "state of the European union" an appropriate and timely study.

At this point it seems appropriate to identify this nucleus of any future united Europe as a regional organization composed of nine member-states, namely the six original nations (France, Germany, Italy, Belgium, the Netherlands, and Luxembourg), and the three new members (Britain, Denmark, and Ireland). Although technically, the "European Communities" consist of three component organizations—the European Coal and Steel Community (1952), the European Economic Community and Euratom (1958)—it will be treated as a single entity since its institutions were consolidated in the "Merger Treaty" of 1965. The above mentioned treaties were subsequently amended by the so-called "Acts of Accession" of 1972 which were ratified by all signatory states (except Norway which had signed the Acts but failed to ratify them following the negative outcome of a popular referendum on entry into the Common Market).

In this study the terms "European Community" will be used to refer to both the little Europe of Six (1952-1972) and the larger Europe of Nine (as of January 1, 1973); the former will also be called "Common Market" whereas the enlarged Community will usually be designated as the "New Europe."

In view of the continuing proliferation of regional groupings and/or recent changes in the membership of European organizations, epitomized by the expansion of the European Community and the *de-facto* replacement of the European Free Trade Association of 1960 by the European Free Trade Area of July 1972, an updated membership list for the principal European and Atlantic organizations is made available to the reader. (See Table I-B).

Table I-B
Membership in the Principal European and Atlantic Organizations (1973)

Organization Countries	OECD:	NATO:	Council of Europe	Western European Union	European Community	European Free Trade Association	European Free Trade Area
Austria	x		x			x	x
Belgium	x	x	x	x	x		x
Cyprus			x				
Denmark	x	x	x		x		x
Finland	x					A	x
France	x	A	x	x	x		x
Germany (West)	x	x	x	x	x		x
Greece	x	x	x		A		
Iceland	x	x	x			x	x
Ireland	x		x		x		x
Italy	x	x	x	x	x		x
Luxembourg	x	x	x	x	x		x
Malta			x				
Netherlands	x	x	x	x	x		x
Norway	x	x	x			x	C
Portugal	x	x				x	x
Spain	x						
Sweden	x		x			x	x
Switzerland	x		x			x	x
Turkey	x	x	x		A		
United Kingdom	x	x	x	x	x		x
Canada	x	x					
United States	x	x					
Australia	x						
Japan	x						
Total:	23	14	18	7	9	6	15

Note: A stands for associate; C stands for candidate.

The *purpose* of this study is to look at the European Community in perspective: to consider its successes and failures; to examine its internal structures and dynamics; and to evaluate its prospective role in the world of the 1970s. Moreover, the objective analysis of empirical data is complemented by subjective value considerations.

Given the political significance and timeliness of this study, it should be of interest to political analysts in both the United States and Western Europe. Whereas students of regionalism can be expected to look critically at the various propositions about political integration, pundits and government officials are likely to be interested in the prospects for the New Europe and its possible impact on the United States and the rest of the world.

For classroom purposes, this book may be used at both the undergraduate and graduate levels in the social sciences. For instance, juniors and seniors majoring in political science, economics, or history, could use it together with customary texts in the fields of international relations and comparative politics. Graduate students would find it useful in courses on international law and organization, comparative foreign policy, international economics, and in seminars on regionalism and international integration.

In order to facilitate the student's understanding of the complex structure and dynamics of the European Community, explanatory figures and tables complement the text. Furthermore, historical milestones in the development of the European Community are included in the Chronology. Finally, a selected bibliography and an appendix of significant documents complete this study of the European Community.

Acknowledgments

In the preparation of this book, the author has benefited from discussion with numerous scholars, diplomats, and friends on both sides of the Atlantic. Although the book was written in the early 1970s, my understanding of the dialectics of European integration and Atlantic cooperation developed gradually in the 1960s when I served on the staff of the Foreign Policy Research Institute and did field research in Western Europe under a Penfield Fellowship of the University of Pennsylvania. During this period of induction into the complexities of American foreign policy, I received valuable insights from Professors Robert Strausz-Hupé, Robert L. Pfaltzgraff Jr., Norman D. Palmer, William R. Kintner, Philip E. Jacob, Karl W. Deutsch, James E. Dougherty, and from the late Hans Kohn. These insights were complemented by European experts in the field during my association with the Atlantic Institute (Paris), and the Institut Européen des Hautes Etudes Internationales (Nice, France) where I benefited from the counsel of Messrs. Alexandre Marc, Pierre Uri, Jean Rey, Raymond Rifflet, Guy Héraud, Walter Dowling, and the late Pierre Duclos. In the early research-writing stage of the book, Inis L. Claude (University of Virginia) provided constructive criticism of conceptual designs for which I am very grateful. Subsequently, Bernice Williams (Southwestern at Memphis) checked the manuscript for "Germanisms" and supplied valuable editorial suggestions for which I am greatly indebted. I would also like to thank Miss Amy Kidd and Mrs. Nancy King for their splendid typing of the manuscript. Special thanks go to Mrs. Ella Krucoff, the Information Specialist of the European Community Information Service in Washington, D.C. for her effective assistance in providing me with all necessary documents and data. Needless to add that the contributions of the staff of D.C. Heath under its Director Geoffrey Gunn were quintessential in the efficient production of the book. Last but not least, I would like to express my appreciation to Ambassador W. Randolph Burgess and Mr. Joseph W. Harned for their offer to publish the book under the auspices of the Atlantic Council of the United States.

Finally, I am immensely grateful for the patient support of my wife and children to whom I dedicate this book.

Introduction

The contemporary international system is characterized by two major opposing trends, namely integration and disintegration. This complex dual phenomenon naturally commands the attention of many social scientists who recognize its saliency as a vital indicator of the relative degree of conflict and/or cooperation between the actors in the arena of international relations. In fact, both the likelihood and intensity of conflict are a function of the integration-disintegration syndrome, as is the potential and scope of cooperation between states. Usually, the notion "integration" is associated with beneficial results (such as peace, strength, and prosperity), whereas the term "disintegration" often has negative connotations (such as disunity and warfare). However, this "loaded" interpretation of the integration-disintegration continuum may not correspond to the actual political context in each instance and at all times. For example, integration may be regarded as a beneficial movement in one region (such as Western Eruope), while disintegration may be favored in another area (such as Eastern Europe). Depending on the vantage point—participant or outsider—integration may be looked at as desirable (on the part of small nations seeking strength in unity) or undesirable (on the part of a hegemonial power trying to divide and rule). Moreover, integration in one region may lead to disintegration of another (as in the case of the European Community attracting members of the COMECON), or may produce a "demonstration effect" in other areas (as in the case of LAFTA emulating the EEC). Finally, integration and disintegration may occur simultaneously (or consecutively) in the same region at different levels: transnational solidarity may grow while intergovernmental collaboration declines and vice versa.

Against the background of these considerations, the contrast between the process of disintegration in the former colonial regions of Africa and Asia on the one hand, and of the integrative movement in Western Europe which occurred simultaneously following World War II on the other is striking. The European willingness to experiment with novel approaches to intergovernmental cooperation should be understood in the light of three factors: first, Europeans have learned from experience that unification by force (à la Napoleon or Hitler) is ineffective and costly; second, they have recognized that there is no alternative to European unity in the twentieth century and that integration has to be accomplished by peaceful means; third, Europe previously invented the nation-state and could again serve as the laboratory of change and innovation—hopefully with more constructive results. Nevertheless, it seems paradoxical that the first significant movement toward regional unity should be launched by

The preface established the political rationale of the study; the introduction sets the stage for the following scientific inquiry.

European leaders whose predecessors had extolled the virtues of nationalism and had subsequently (or consequently) become notorious as the agents of internecine and global warfare.

In the light of the fact that European nationalism turned out to be at best a mixed blewwing—with both constructive and destructive features—a certain scepticism vis-à-vis Europe's new structural model, namely supranationalism, may be in order. In short, it seems advisable to analyze this model critically rather than to accept it without reservations as the panacea for future international relations.

To be sure, "the development of supranational institutions constitutes one of the most important and revolutionary features of the present age,"[1] and since this development has originated and subsequently progressed more rapidly and intensively in Western Europe, it is understandable that most theoretical treatments of the integration syndrome derived their data and propositions from the European context. This concern with the phenomenon of regional integration later extended to other areas of the globe affected by the "demonstration effect" of the European model, particularly Central and Latin America and Africa. But "virtually all investigators of the integration process approach their subject with a positive bias, accepting political integration as synonymous with progress. [Hence] there is a need for political scientists to examine the costs as well as the benefits of political integration through a mixture of empirical evidence and normative evaluations. [Consequently] integration theorists should expand their research horizons to include subjects of normative concern in order to ensure that new regional political systems do not duplicate or compound the problems of the nation-state."[2]

Indeed, many students of European integration have been overzealous in investigating the diverse aspects of the integrative process without sufficient regard to the actual or potential impact of its product for the rest of the world. Some of them have developed sophisticated models and refined approaches to integration at the international level, but few have approached the subject from a normative perspective.[3] Yet, this is precisely the task of the social scientist in general and of the political scientist in particular.

Contrary to the widespread belief that scholars should limit their investigation to empirical data (thus assuring scientific objectivity), the author of this study is convinced that a political scientist should not try to escape his intrinsic responsibility to evaluate and judge political phenomena critically. In other words, both empirical research and normative judgment are necessary ingredients for arriving at a comprehensive, honest, and truly objective conclusion.

The title of this book—*The European Community in Perspective*—indicates that an effort has been made to analyze this complex political animal in a balanced, objective fashion, both in terms of its internal achievements and its contributions toward the outside world, as well as its potential and prospects. For this purpose, all three basic types of scientific analysis—description, explanation, and conjecture—have been used in this study, with one or the other method being dominant in different chapters.

This book is divided into three major parts and subdivided into eight chapters, followed by a summary evaluation and conclusions. Part I examines the concepts and theories of international integration and raises inter alia the following questions: (1) Is the nation-state still a viable entity in the age of global interdependence, or have international organizations and transnational activities already perforated sovereign authority and undermined national independence? What is the role and impact of global and regional organizations, nongovernmental entities, and multinational corporations on the stato-national structures? Or, what is the ideal political unit in the nuclear age? (2) Furthermore, what are the relative merits of the major theories of regional integration? Is the "Gestalt model" the most comprehensive and balanced framework for the analysis of political unification at the international level?

Part II is concerned with the internal dynamics of the European Community and focuses on the following issues: (3) What are the salient external and internal forces that generated or blocked progress toward European unity since the end of World War II, and what were the motives of these federators? (4) How successful has the European Community been in implementing the policy objectives outlined in the constitutive treaties? Did the common institutions experience growth or decline and did the European organs achieve a viable degree of autonomy vis-à-vis national governments? (5) What are the "catalysts of integration" in the political, economic, social, and cultural sectors of the member states, and what is their centripetal potential? Conversely, which "catalysts of disintegration" are likely to delay progress toward European unity?

Part III evaluates the prospects for the New Europe and seeks to provide answers to the following important questions: (6) What are the implications of the enlargement of the European Community in terms of its internal development and the impact of the New Europe on the world? (7) Given the inherently discriminatory nature of a common market vis-à-vis outsiders, do the costs of economic integration to non-members exceed the benefits to the participants? (8) Does the European Community contribute effectively to the development of the Third World, or is it an inward-looking club of the rich? (9) What are the alternative contours for the "European Union" targeted for 1980: federation or confederation? (10) What are the attitudes of government officials, interest groups, and of public opinion on the crucial question of political unification? (11) What is the future role of a united Europe in the world and how will it cope with the "American challenge"? (12) Are the Nine going to be able to formulate a common foreign and defense policy and what would be its content? (13) Will "gigantism" inevitably foster big power ambitions, or will a sense of *noblesse oblige* compel the New Europe to act with wisdom and restraint in the interest of world peace? (14) What is the optimal seize of political units in the twentieth century in terms of providing maximum security and welfare for the people: the nation-state, the regional federation, the continental confederation, or a universal configuration? (15) What are the prospects for Atlantic cooperation: Is the European Community destined to evolve from tutelage to equality and will it become a partner or rival of the United States?

These are the principal issues of this study. In the following chapters an effort will be made to provide some answers and to stimulate further research on this challenging subject.

The European Community in Perspective

Part I:
Concepts and Theories of
International Integration

1

Universalism, Regionalism, Transnationalism: Actors and Forces in the International System

The contemporary international system is composed of numerous interacting units which can be classified into two categories: official and unofficial actors—a distinction based upon their respective status in the international arena. The two "official" actors are states and intergovernmental organizations; the two "unofficial" actors are nongovernmental associations and multinational corporations.

The sum total of interactions between official actors constitutes "interstate politics," whereas the interactions between the unofficial actors make up the remaining (mainly economic, social, and cultural) components of "international relations."

To the extent that the European Community structure permits and encourages regular and intensive interactions among these four types of actors in an important region of the international system, it can be considered as an almost ideal case study for the application of our model. In fact, the European Community forms a complex, interacting whole between official and unofficial actors contending for power and influence. However, the principal "battle" takes place between the proponents of the two overriding doctrines: the doctrine of "national interest" (supported by the defenders of the nation-state) and the concept of "international organization" (supported by regional supranationalists). Thus the European Community constitutes both an arena of diplomatic confrontation and a laboratory of peaceful conflict resolution.

The rationale for selecting the European Community for the study of progressive and original patterns of consensus formation is based upon the realization that "Europe gave the world the national state, and it may yet give the world the model for the larger unit to succeed the nation-state."[1]

With this perspective in mind, we will now turn to an examination of the modern (European) nation-state and its prospects: demise or resurgence.

The Nation State in the 1970s

Sovereignty

Traditionally, the state has been considered as the only subject of international law and the decisive factor in world politics. However, with the advent of the "age of global history"[2] and its corollary—interdependence—the quasi-monopoly of the state has been challenged as new forces emerged which eroded the

3

"sovereign independence" of the nation-state. In other words, the legal concept of sovereignty has been undermined by political and economic interdependence. The proliferation of international organization and other multinational bodies has resulted in the formation of a global network of interaction in the economic, social, and cultural fields, circumscribing the freedom of action of an increasing number of governments without, however, eliminating the state as the principal actor in world politics.

This transformation of the international system from one of monopoly of the state to one of oligopolistic competition with other actors is accompanied by a reappraisal of analytical concepts and a revision of scholarly terminology in the social sciences. It has become increasingly apparent that the traditional state-centric paradigm has partially lost its relevance and explanatory powers since it excludes important new factors of international life which codetermine world political events.

Scholars in both the United States and Western Europe began to question the validity of the state-national theorem following Raymond Aron's perceptive observation on the inherently temporary nature of the state. He noted that "all those who regard ideological and imperialistic units as transitory but national units as the only durable ones, put the seal of eternity on the historical philosophy of the nineteenth century without being aware of it."[3] Indeed, looked at from a historical perspective, the argument appears very plausible. After all, the Greek *polis* had been replaced by the Roman *imperium*, and the feudal principalities of the Middle Ages by the nation-states of the nineteenth century. There seems to be no logical impediment to the continuing evolution of societal structures in the future.

According to a prominent functionalist, "the immediate issue is nothing less than breaking away from a concept and practice which since the end of the Middle Ages had been inculcated as an ideal, the near worship of the national-territorial state."[4]

The principal academic apologist of the territorial state, however, insists that "there will be no 'superseding of the nation-state.' "[5] On the contrary, he argues that "nation-states—often inchoate, economically absurd, administratively ram-shackle, and impotent yet dangerous in international politics—remain the basic units in spite of all the remonstrations and exhortations. They go on *faute de mieux* despite their alleged obsolescence; indeed, not only do they profit from man's incapacity to bring about a better order, but their very existence is a formidable obstacle to their replacement."[6]

The most compelling argument in support of the hypothesis that the nation-state has become an anachronism is its apparent inability to fulfill its two primordial functions, namely to provide its people with military security and with economic prosperity. All objective observers have long recognized that most nation-states are no longer capable of defending their people effectively in the nuclear age, nor are governments autarkic in the economic field; yet national leaders cling to the empty shell called "sovereignty." As the nation-state is losing its *raison d'être*, "the conclusion now seems to impose itself on any unbiased observer that the small independent nation-state is obsolete or obsolescent."[7]

The dispute over the viability of the nation-state, opposing the proponents of its demise and its resurgence, finds an impressive illustration in the attempt of one scholar to reconcile his original appraisal of the nation-state as an anachronism in the nuclear age with his revised view of this traditional political unit as a self-sufficient and legitimate actor in international affairs.[8]

In support of the proposition that the nation-state is increasingly regarded as a transitory phenomenon, two eminent scholars conducted a survey and came to the conclusion that "Europe and America are moving from nationalism to regionalism (Gaullism having been a transient phase) . . . [and] postwar Europeans have renounced the traditional ideology of nationalism. A solid majority of our panelists in each country declare that the nation-state as a political form is obsolete (55% in Britain, 64% in France, 73% in Germany), and even larger majorities believe that its obsolescence is (or would be) a good thing (67% in Britain, 62% in France, 78% in Germany)."[9] Furthermore, they found that "political parties do not contest the consensus that the nation-state is obsolete" and "that European elites have been transformed from ideologues to pragmatists."[10]

These findings seem to support the audacious projections of an analyst who states that "the long-term trend toward integration seems to be . . . from smaller units to larger ones; from states to federations; from federations to supranational unions; and from these to super-systems."[11]

Notwithstanding these optimistic predictions, the nation-state seems to prosper, not only in the developing areas where "sovereignty" has become a status symbol for the newly independent countries entitling them to UN membership, but also in Western Europe. If the projection is correct that there will be no substitute for the nation-state during the remainder of this century,[12] it appears all the more appropriate to examine the contemporary meaning of the concept. The term "nation-state" suggests a symbiotic relationship between the sociological component of the nation (people) and the legal component of the state (organization), which have gradually been merged into a sovereign entity in Europe, beginning with the Treaty of Westphalia (1648). Jean Bodin first conceptualized "sovereignty" as supreme power of the state, thus legitimizing the ultimate authority of the state over its people. Originally, this concept of *de jure* sovereignty coincided with the *de facto* ability of the government totally to control its people within the respective territory, and largely to determine the degree of its involvement in international affairs. However, with the advent of the modern age of mass communication and intercontinental weapons, the independence of the nation-state (i.e., the external dimension of sovereignty) has been considerably undermined, although technology still permits governments to exercise adequate control over their population (i.e., internal sovereignty).

Hence, the right *of* became a claim *to* sovereignty; in other words, *de jure* sovereignty has been eroded by *de facto* interdependence.

The progressive loss of external sovereignty makes the nation-state an anachronism, but its increased ability to assert its power on the domestic scene justifies its continuing existence. It is this curious combination of obsolescence and resilience, symbolized by the government's inability to provide for national security and its ability effectively to impose "law and order" on the people, which characterizes the modern nation-state and explains in part why many scholarly writers differ in their assessment of its prospects.

Stato-Nationalism

Aside from the contradictory evidence concerning the future of the nation-state as a form of societal organization, the phenomenon "nationalism-statism" constitutes another significant focus of analysis. In its traditional sense, the term "nationalism" has both positive and negative connotations: nationalism served as a constructive ideology for the purpose of unifying diverse social groups both in Europe (Germany and Italy) and in the Third World in an effort to achieve nationhood.[13] However, nationalism became increasingly regarded as an evil force generating and maximizing conflict between nations, eventually leading to two world wars. Since this study focuses on the European political scene, we will distinguish between the "old nationalism" of the 1930s and the "new nationalism" of the 1960s. If the former emphasized oppression of the people at home and a xenophobic, chauvinist and expansionist policy abroad, the "new nationalism" is characterized by "domesticism"—a preoccupation with domestic affairs rather than with imperialist aggression—but with official spokesmen still stressing the national interest and demanding the loyalty of their people.[14]

Despite these obvious, significant differences between the old and new forms of nationalism, they have one element in common, namely "statism." This corollary of the ideology of nationalism constitutes its vital organizational infrastructure and permits its operationalization. In other words, statism is the leitmotiv and hallmark of national bureaucrats in charge of administering the affairs of the state. To the extent that their very existence depends upon the preservation of stato-national structures, they have a vested interest in the *status quo.* Even if some enlightened and honest government officials are aware of the fact that the *raison d'état* (the interest of the state to remain sovereign) no longer coincides with the national interest (the need for supranational integration),[15] the instinct of self-preservation tends to prevail over idealistic policies which would ultimately result in the replacement of the office holders themselves (e.g., neither a foreign minister nor a customs official is likely voluntarily to abdicate in favor of supranational consolidation). This understandable lack of enthusiasm on the part of national bureaucrats for commiting hara-kiri is compounded by the inertia[16] and apathy of the masses (rather than by their conscious loyalty toward the system), whose conservative tendencies have been reinforced by the *Wirtschaftswunder* and its beneficial impact on the standards of living in most nation-states. The fact that this favorable development was primarily the result of partial integration, rather than the achievement of national governments, is not sufficiently appreciated.

Consequently, it seems that people have given credit to the state for socioeconomic progress which had been achieved in spite of, and not because of, national governments. Thus the success of integrative measures apparently has counterproductive results, since it is the state which gets the credit for services initiated and implemented by extra-national organs. In the absence of a general sense of urgency, precipitated by an internal crisis or intense pressures from a common enemy, national self-abdication seems an unlikely prospect. In other words, bureaucracies might only be abolished when they are superseded, and a rapid, drastic metamorphosis of stato-national structures seems to be a remote possibility.[17]

As to the *status quo* argument of national bureaucrats that they are realists in defending statism, whereas internationalists allegedly propagate utopian ideas, one could reply that "there will always be those who say that the whole conception [of supranationalism] is utopian: that people who reach for the stars are likely to fall on their faces. But this was repeatedly said of the projects for the European Community; it was said, for that matter, of the federalist proposals of the Founding Fathers of the United States. It is liable to be said of any idea that may change the course of history."[18]

Finally, it should be pointed out that most major powers have opted for continental, federal structures (the United States, the Soviet Union, Brazil, Australia, Canada, India, with China being the exception), rather than for the pseudo-sovereignty of the nation-state, thus demonstrating true realism.

The Phenomenon of Interdependence

With the advent of the age of global history, nations have become increasingly interdependent and aware of their common destiny on this planet. This development has its origin in the eclipse of distance through rapid transportation, the perfection of communication permitting instant and vicarious participation in all major events throughout a shrinking world, and, last but not least, the development of weapons of mass destruction. The unprecedented and still accelerating technological revolution makes mankind an interacting whole—a global neighborhood coexisting on this spaceship earth, all being subject to potential annihilation by either thermonuclear weapons or environmental pollution.[19]

This *ridimensionamento*—a change of scale in the twentieth century accompanied by a population explosion and the intensification of interaction between nations—has both objective and subjective aspects. The rising *de facto* interdependence can be empirically observed as all states, including the superpowers, have become entangled in a "web of interdependence."[20] But apart from this objective aspect, interdependence has a subjective dimension because its existence can be acknowledged or ignored by governmental leaders depending on the imperatives of the national interest. Consequently, interdependence may be perceived to be present or absent by different governments at the same time. Ergo "existential" interdependence only becomes operational between nations when the leaders of two or more of them take actions that are mutually contingent (e.g., strategic or monetary policies). Therefore, it is necessary to determine in each instance whether a foreign policy decision tends to strengthen, break, or confuse the web of interdependence.[21]

If nations are horizontally connected through factors of objective interdependence such as defense and trade, each one of them is also linked vertically to the international system per se. This aspect of interdependence between domestic and foreign policies has been identified as linkage factor and the resulting interaction processes as linkage politics.[22] Such national-international linkages exist at various levels and intensity; some are more salient to policy decision-makers than others and vary according to their perceived importance.[23] Undoubtedly the crucial problem in the comparative analysis of the linkage syndrome is the relative potency of domestic and international factors in foreign policy decision; it is increasingly recognized as a vital area of study in political science (e.g., comparative foreign policies and linkage politics).

Notwithstanding the apparently widespread phenomenon of interdependence, social scientists differ in their evaluation of its significance in international politics, according to their background and *Weltanschauung*. For instance, Rosenau states unequivocally that "modern science and technology have collapsed space and time in the physical world and thereby heightened interdependence in the political world."[24] His view is corroborated by Oran Young, who believes that "the margin of action in external affairs is becoming narrower and the links between internal and external activities are becoming tighter. As a result, the level of interdependence among the component units of the world system has risen markedly not so much as a function of any increase in the volume of transactions among the units as because the units are becoming increasingly sensitive to the activities of each other as their internal freedom of action becomes more and more circumscribed."[25] In contrast, Karl Deutsch feels that the world is becoming more insulated and nations more self-preoccupied.[26] The likely reason for these divergent interpretations of global trends seems to be the different data base used and/or the diverse perspectives adopted by these investigators. In short, the selection of research foci (political, economic, cultural, etc.) or level of analysis (subregional, regional, continental, global) will determine the conclusions.

However, given the complexities of linkages between the national and international systems, it might be prudent to avoid generalizations and instead examine each case on its own merits. In other words, "we must first know whether these societies are becoming more independent or more interdependent; whether similarities in their domestic political processes and social structures are due to transnational forces of modernization affecting each society separately or to convergencies resulting from their mutual interpenetration; and whether the rates of convergence and interpenetration are increasing, decreasing, or remaining more or less constant."[27] These considerations are especially pertinent in the light of the dialectics of integration and disintegration which characterize the international system in the 1970s: as the "simple" bipolar constellation gives way to a much more complex polycentrism, "islands of regional cooperation" simultaneously increase (regional) and decrease (global) interdependence. With regard to institutions established to handle these interdependent affairs, it has to be recognized that "many of the international capabilities for dealing with problems that arise from these interdependencies have suffered a decline . . . [while] the burdens of interdependence have grown faster than the international capabilities for dealing with them."[28]

Undoubtedly, the dual threats of mass destruction and underdevelopment constitute the core elements of the global interdependence syndrome. But, man has not yet devised effective machinery to cope with a challenge that requires an inventiveness equaling the enormous advances in the technology of mass destruction. The situation is one comparable to that of the sorcerer's apprentice who unleashed the demon (of nuclear technology) prior to inventing a mechanism for its control. However, in the absence of such "perfect" institutions man has experimented with a series of limited-purpose organizations capable of dealing with specific problems of interdependence. Indeed, these diverse institutions have proliferated at an unprecedented rate within the last few decades in all parts of the globe. Hence, increased attention has been given to the analysis of the structural properties and political dynamics of these international entities.

The following sections will therefore deal with the alternatives to the state-centric model, particularly transnationalism, and with the international organizational environment of the 1970s.

The Emergence of Transnationalism

International interdependence has as its operational corollary transnational processes which affect mainly "unofficial actors" but may also involve an "official" actor. The notion of "transnational interactions" has been defined as "the movement of tangible or intangible items across state boundaries when at least one actor is not an agent of a government or an intergovernmental organization."[29] If one distinguishes between four major types of global interactions, namely communication (information, ideas, doctrines, and beliefs), transportation (war material, merchandise, and personal property), finance (money and instruments of credit), and travel (persons), transnational inter-actions take place whenever nongovernmental actors play a significant role, even if governments are involved.[30]

Consequently, *world politics* can be defined as "all political interactions between significant actors in a world system in which a significant actor is any somewhat autonomous individual or organization that controls substantial resources and participates in political relationships with other actors across state lines."[31]

This conception of world politics is undoubtedly unorthodox and takes into consideration all transnational forces without neglecting the important role of the state and intergovernmental organizations. The difference between this "world politics paradigm" and the traditional state-centric theorem consists in its attempt "to transcend the 'level-of-analysis problem' both by broadening the conception of actors to include transnational actors and by conceptually breaking down the 'hard shell' of the nation-state."[32]

The comprehensive "world politics paradigm" includes the following types of actors: (1) governmental (states and governmental subunits), (2) intergovern-mental (international organizations and their subunits), and (3) nongovern-mental (transnational organizations and their subunits, as well as certain individuals).[33] Placed in a diagrammatic context, the paradigm shows that interstate interactions cover only four of the thirty-six possible types of politically significant interactions across state boundaries identified by the world politics paradigm. Thirty-two types of interaction (which are not included in any state-centric paradigm) include the following: transgovernmental interactions (between governmental subunits), and transnational interactions (between trans-national organizations and their subunits).[34]

Naturally, the question arises as to which of these thirty-six types of interaction are the most salient and which have marginal impact. In other words, is there a need for distinguishing between *Grosspolitik* (concerned with foreign and security affairs) and domestic politics (economics and welfare matters), since questions of "high politics" are likely to be more important than those of "low politics."

Although this distinction still has some validity, it is of diminishing impor-tance as informal interpenetration occurs between modern political systems, linking foreign and domestic affairs in a web of interdependence. This trend is likely to accelerate in the atomic age since "high politics" has ultimately been conducted by military force, a counterproductive strategy for nuclear powers threatened by retaliation. Consequently, foreign policy has to be conducted without resort to force and has to emphasize peaceful means such as internation-al trade and finance, foreign aid and technical assistance, and cooperation through multilateral channels involving intergovernmental and nongovernmental organizations. In short, the importance of transnational relations increases while the significance of *Grosspolitik* diminishes as global interdependence becomes a reality.

Inevitably, the defenders of the state-centric model will bring up the argument that in direct confrontations between governments and nongovernmental actors, the former will win. This line of reasoning is supported by the assertion that modern technology enables states to better control the activities of their respective societies, including transnational relations. The counterargument stresses the fact that intergovernmental and transnational relations are becoming intertwined as the latter are being politicized. Moreover, any government prevailing in a direct confrontation with transnational actors may discover that it won a political "pyrrhic victory" which turned out to be economically costly. The best example would be the nationalization without compensation of a multinational firm, an action that may cause diplomatic reprisal and may prove costly in terms of lost capital, technology, and employed labor.

The "American" world politics paradigm has been reinforced and complemented by the "European" concept of transnational relations, or "multinational politics." It refers to "processes which cannot be assigned unequivocally to politics between states and in which states are not the sole actors.... Within multinational politics bureaucracies allocate values either jointly in decision-making frameworks that are intermeshed across national frontiers or separately as a result of transnational interaction at the societal level."[35] Three types of multinational politics can be distinguished: (1) multibureaucratic decision-making, which takes place when structures of different national governmental and international bureaucracies intermesh within specific issue areas for the allocation of values (e.g., an international agency implements an aid program in a developing nation); (2) transnational politics, which consists of political processes between national governments that have been set in motion by transnational relations (e.g., the free movement of investment capital or labor across frontiers); and (3) multinational integration, which takes place between states when the preparation, formulation, and implementation of political decisions shift from an exclusively national to a joint, multinational framework on a regional basis in which governments, societal actors, and, if necessary, international organizations participate (e.g., decision-making on agricultural policy in the EEC).[36] Thus both models of transnational relations show that the exclusive state-centric perspective in international politics is inadequate and unrealistic.

Nevertheless, it is true that, in extremis, the state is still the superior force capable of mustering the necessary popular support, economic means, and military arsenal to "win" in a direct confrontation with nongovernmental actors.

The seeming paradox of the frequently mentioned "loss of control" over the external environment on the part of modern governments which are, reinforced by their technological apparatus, supposedly more capable of controlling events, has been explained as follows: "the impact of transnational relations creates a 'control gap' between the [state's] aspirations for control over an expanded range of matters and the capability to achieve it. The problem is not a loss of legal sovereignty but a loss of political and economic autonomy. Most states retain control over their policy instruments and are able to pursue their objectives. They are just less able to achieve them."[37]

Furthermore, it is true that "while the range of relevant issues has been greatly broadened by the introduction of the welfare state, technology has increased the mobility of factors and the sensitivity of markets, and societies, to one another. Advances in transportation and communications technology are destroying the fragmentation of markets that is a necessary condition for autonomous national policies; ... [in short] complexity and frustration in foreign affairs are among the consequences of the modern capitalist welfare state."[38] In the final analysis the argument between the defenders of the state-centric model and the promoters of the world politics paradigm can be settled as follows: both are partially right, depending on the original perspective of the observer; it is analogous to the dispute between two persons looking at a glass of water which appears half-full to one and half empty to the other (water symbolizing sovereignty).

Typology of International Organizations

If "international organizations" constitutes the generic term for interaction processes in the universal organizational environment, the following quadruple typology can be constructed:

Type I: the criterion of distinction being "membership" (governments or
          private groups)
Species term: 1) Intergovernmental organizations (IGOs): e.g., UNESCO
               2) Nongovernmental entities or transnational
                  associations or nongovernmental organizations
                  (NGOs): e.g., International Political Science
                  Association

Type II: the criterion of distinction being "geographical scope"
Species term: 1) Global or universal organizations: e.g., United
                  Nations
               2) Regional organizations: e.g., Organization of
                  American States

Type III: the criterion of distinction being the "nature of function" (in the
          quantitative sense)
Species term: 1) Unifunctional organizations: e.g., Universal
                  Postal Union
               2) Multifunctional organizations: e.g., Organization
                  for Economic Cooperation and Development

Type IV: the criterion of distinction being the "essential purpose" (in the
qualitative sense)
Species term: 1) Military organizations (alliance): e.g., NATO
2) Nonmilitary organizations (cultural, social,
economic): e.g., Council of Europe

When we apply these criteria to the *European Community*, the following
profile emerges: it is an intergovernmental, regional, multifunctional, nonmilitary organization.

In the following section we will first examine transnational nongovernmental
entities, and subsequently deal with global and regional intergovernmental
organizations.

Nongovernmental Entities

In view of the fact that the nation-state, albeit declining in influence, is still the
ultimate repository of authority, it may be unrealistic and premature to accord
equal status to nongovernmental entities or supranational bodies. Nevertheless,
to the extent that the powers of governmental actors are being circumscribed in
the twentieth century, the significance of certain transnational groups is rising as
their functional scope and autonomy expands (usually at the expense of the
national actors). Hence, some nongovernmental entities have ceased to be passive
components of the international environment; they have become active participants in the shaping of foreign (economic and cultural) policies of national
governments and thus genuine actors in the international system.

These nongovernmental entities can be grouped into two categories: nongovernmental organizations and multinational organizations. Nongovernmental
organizations (NGOs) or transnational associations transcend national boundaries both in terms of (private) membership and operational capacity, and are
not established by intergovernmental agreement. In numerical terms, NGOs are
far more important than IGOs: for instance, in 1971 there were 2296 NGOs and
only 242 IGOs.[39] The growth pattern of NGOs compared with IGOs during the
period from 1860 to 1968 shows that a phenomenal rise in the number of NGOs
occurred in this century: from 135 in 1901 to 2188 in 1968, a spectacular
increase over six decades.[40]

The geographical scope of NGOs may be universal, as in the case of the
International Red Cross, or it may have regional character, as in the case of the
European Movement. In this context it is noteworthy that approximately
one-quarter of all NGOs, namely 454 in 1968, are operating exclusively in
Europe.[41] Furthermore, it is interesting to find that the nations of the Atlantic
region (Northwest) are interconnected by the largest number of NGOs, or 53
percent of all NGOs in 1966.[42]

The range of activities of NGOs is virtually unlimited. A breakdown according to functions performed shows that most professional categories are represented in NGOs: the economic sector clearly dominates with 233 NGOs in commerce and industry (as of 1969), followed by health-medicine (214), science (152), and international relations (125); among the other groups represented are education (105), professions (105), and religion (103). Business and professional groups in the European Community and EFTA are represented in 273 additional NGOs.[43]

Among the better known NGOs are the following: the Roman Catholic Church, the World Council of Churches, the International Commission of Jurists, the International Olympic Committee, the World Federation of Trade Unions, the International Air Transport Association, Interpol, the Salvation Army, Lions International, the Experiment in International Living, and the Ford Foundation.[44]

This random selection of NGOs illustrates their wide range of concerns and their scope of activities in all sectors of society. Furthermore, "the NGO world is growing and changing in many ways. New organizations are added and old ones disappear. New countries become represented and others see their relative share of influence reduced. New functions are performed, new procedures adopted, and more channels of information established."[45]

There are two essential causative factors in national societies that are conducive to interest-group participation in NGOs, namely, a high degree of technological and economic development and a pluralistic ideology. Assuming that these factors will continue to promote transnational interaction processes, the number of NGOs is expected to increase vastly within the next thirty years: "With a modest growth rate of 5 percent per year from 1968, there will be 9,049 NGOs in the world in the year 2000."[46]

As to the impact of NGOs on the international system, it can be described as "undramatic, diffuse and slow."[47] Some of them play the role of lobbies before governments (such as the European Movement), others exert influence in their capacity as observers—often with consultative status—on intergovernmental organizations such as ECOSOC, UNESCO, FAO and ILO (e.g., with the International Confederation of Free Trade Unions). However, European NGOs serving as regional pressure groups within the European Community have the most significant political influence.[48]

Multinational Corporations

If NGOs are more numerous, multinational corporations (MNC) have undoubtedly a more spectacular impact on nation-states in the twentieth century. Not only are there more than twice as many of them as "sovereign" states—about 300 MNCs versus 140 odd states—but their budgets sometimes exceed those of smaller states. The MNCs operate freely across national borders, frequently manage to bypass state regulations, and escape controls of national governments.

Given their productive capacity, financial resources, and mobility in terms of investment, establishment and distribution, they constitute genuine transnational actors in the economic domain.[49]

The MNC has been authoritatively defined by Raymond Vernon (who calls it "multinational enterprise") as "a cluster of corporations of diverse nationality joined together by ties of common ownership and responsive to a common management strategy."[50] Their structures differ in detail, but the basic features are similar. "From the headquarters company (and country) flow direction and control, and from the affiliates (branches, subsidiaries, joint enterprises) flow products, revenues and information."[51]

There are three different types of MNCs, according to their "sphere of influence" and management structure:[52] (1) ethnocentric companies (like PanAm or Air France), which are firmly controlled from the national headquarters and whose overseas offices are mostly staffed by their own countrymen; (2) polycentric companies (like Philips or Unilever), which still have national headquarters but whose subsidiaries abroad are run by local managers; and (3) geocentric companies (like Shell or IBM), whose headquarters could be anywhere and who recruit managers from any country and place them in charge of subsidiaries anywhere.

All of them, but particularly the geocentric type, have become industrial leviathans that constitute both a political challenge and an economic opportunity for the states which have acknowledged both the power and the potential usefulness of MNCs. Usually, "the dialogue between the corporation and the state consists largely of a simple assertion by the former: 'anything you can do, I can do better.' "[53] Moreover, these new giants are multiheaded and stateless, making it difficult for any national government to control them effectively. Therefore, a supranational *lex mercatoria* has been proposed, the essence of which is "that world corporations should become quite literally citizens of the world."[54] This international effort to regulate MNCs would, however, give them official status and freedom, thus enhancing rather than diminishing their already enormous influence.

The rapid growth of MNCs has given rise to widespread complaints about industrial imperialism, usually directed against the United States because four out of five MNCs are controlled by an American firm.[55] These complaints are sometimes compounded by anti-American sentiments: "there is nothing a European dislikes as much as an expert from overseas."[56] The most dramatic description of this "American challenge" to Western Europe has been that of a French journalist-politician who consciously exaggerated the actual danger of US economic might in order to incite former President de Gaulle to permit and facilitate intra-European company mergers.[57] Although these claims may not be totally accurate, "many governments view the MNCs with a sense of acute discomfort, basing their reaction on an amalgam of fact, fear and fancy ... [since] the increasing intimacy of [their economic] ties presents challenges of a new order to the individual nation-state."[58] Fear of a gradual loss of control over economic sovereignty is accompanied by a dilemma regarding possible countermeasures. The dilemma consists of the government's understandable desire to "tie down Gulliver" and to curtail the operations of such powerful MNCs in the host country by an all-out attack ("nationalization") or to discourage them by severe legal restrictions (rules of establishment or taxation). However, such political measures are frequently nothing but an exercise in futility; even worse, they turn out to be counterproductive because they have an unintended by-product in the economic sector, where the departure of a MNC may cause severe dislocations through loss of vital investment capital, industrial technology, and even rising unemployment. The ineffectual nature of these countermeasures is compounded in the case of the Common Market because MNCs, harassed by a nationalist government, can simply transport their facilities across the border into another member state and preserve access to the market of the country from which its subsidiary has been expelled (an experience that frustrated de Gaulle who, in trying to arrest inevitable developments, sometimes appeared as the Don Quixote of modern times).

If the exponential growth of MNCs continues unabated and "foreign" investments increase faster than domestic expansion, "the world economy may be more than half internationalized by the end of the century."[59]

Although there is little doubt that national economic sovereignty is gradually being eroded and reduced by the dynamism of MNCs, it is too early to assess their impact upon the political sovereignty of nation-states. Thus evidence that MNCs are already contributing to a transformation of the international political system is inconclusive.[60] Nevertheless, it can be argued that to the extent that sovereignty is lost in the economic realm, the nation-state suffers at least a partial loss of sovereign control. Consequently, MNCs join NGOs as "subversive" agents of transnationalism, promoting and increasing interdependence between nations and thus contributing to the advance of international organization.

Intergovernmental Organizations

If nongovernmental organizations promote transsocietal links, intergovernmental organizations establish and promote cooperation between national governments. In many instances, the activities of the "unofficial" actors complement and reinforce the efforts of the "official" actors since most NGOs and IGOs attempt to substitute peaceful and mutually beneficial relationships between nations for armed conflict between states. However, they differ widely in terms of their respective purpose and functions, as well as in their political influence in the world community. If their positive common denominator consists of facilitating international integration, their common deficiency often lies in the fact that both NGOs and IGOs aim at once too high horizontally (for universal membership) and too low vertically (cooperation rather than integration).

The United Nations

In the intergovernmental category, the largest and most influential group is in the UN Organization, composed of the "principal organs" (Security Council, General Assembly, Secretariat, International Court of Justice, Trusteeship Council, and Economic and Social Council) and its "specialized agencies," which are affiliated with the UN through treaties and report to ECOSOC. Among the best known and most effective IGOs associated with the UN are the International Labor Organization, the World Health Organization, the Food and Agriculture Organization, the International Monetary Fund, the Universal Postal Union, and the World Meteorological Organization, as well as such institutions as the International Atomic Energy Agency, the General Agreement on Tariffs and Trade and the UN Conference on Trade and Development.[61]

Whereas the principal organs, especially the Security Council and the General Assembly, usually "make the news" because of their conspicuous function as the world's supreme crisis-management agencies, the specialized agencies are frequently ignored.[62] Indeed the degree of news coverage frequently stands in inverse ratio to the success of the organization concerned; it is a truism that only "bad news" makes the headlines and successful routine operations are hardly ever mentioned in the news media. Moreover, if the major organs in charge of global peace and security are frequently criticized for being ineffective, it is usually for the wrong reasons. After all, the UNO is the product, and reflects the shortcomings, of its creators—national states unwilling to delegate sovereignty to the UN institutions which are officially in charge of preserving international peace and security. Therefore, it is not only unfair but also unrealistic to expect the UNO to fulfill obligations without having the necessary instruments to do so. In other words, it is the decentralized international system, the absence of enforcement machinery, and the principles of "domestic jurisdiction," as well as the veto powers of the permanent members of the Security Council, that handicap the most competent UN civil servant and paralyzes the entire UN operation. Notwithstanding several successful peace expeditions (e.g., in the Congo and the Middle East), the inability of the UN organs to deal effectively with global crises involving major powers is well known. Some observers cite the pathetic spectacle of inaction on the part of the UN in the 1971 crisis in East Pakistan as an illustration for their "case" (the ineptitude and uselessness of the UN, even in situations in which no superpower is directly involved). Unfortunately, the United Nations Organization is not a world government; it is but the sum of its parts (i.e. "sovereign" nation-states) and consequently reflects their policy attitudes and diplomatic interactions. Unable to determine the actions of their members, the UN organs can merely pressure them to "yield to world opinion" and to defer voluntarily to the authority of the Security Council.

The operations of the UN are also handicapped by the well-known fact that the patients brought before the UN organs are usually in a coma (to paraphase Secretary-General Kurt Waldheim) and the world unfairly expects the UN to succeed in a "mission impossible." This is a problem of cardinal importance, since the patient's chances for survival largely depend on his preoperative condition. If conflicts are submitted for UN consideration only "five minutes before twelve," it is inevitable that the outcome of the surgical intervention will be unsatisfactory to all involved.[63]

If the activities of the United Nations were reduced to "peace-watching,"[64] the organization's *raison d'être* could indeed be questioned. However, conflict resolution takes place on various levels and in different phases. Apart from the obvious decision (or nondecision) to restore international peace and security in a conflict situation in the form of a "resolution" of the Security Council or the General Assembly, the United Nations operations have indirect, long-term effects which are usually ignored or underestimated. Among these subtle "nonresolution consequences" of political socialization at the international level are the following: (1) the impact of the participation in sessions of the UN organs on the national representatives of member nations (exposure to the multinational UN atmosphere tends to increase their tolerance of diversity and improves their sense of perspective); (2) the development of personal friendships among delegates across national lines (informal social interactions among official delegates facilitate and often replace formal diplomatic contacts); (3) the emergence of peer groups (experts who sit on specialized committees); (4) the formation of shifting majorities or voting alignments (depending on the nature of the issues); (5) the extension of national concern to additional geographic areas and subject matters (as a result of the scope of the UN agenda); and (6) the opportunity to realistically compare states and policies on the basis of objective, comprehensive data (the UN Secretariat has a virtual monopoly on complete and accurate information).[65]

Although the effect of these interpersonal behavior patterns and multi-national experiences is not quantifiable, they may well ultimately have a more enduring and decisive impact on international relations than the short-term and dramatic "official" operations of the principal organs. In short, the role of the United Nations as an educational institution (the learning process involves the gradual acceptance of the rules of the game of parliamentary democracy) and as a "decompression chamber" for the ventilation of interstate grievances is unique and cannot be duplicated. Indeed, the significance of the very existence of the UN becomes evident as soon as the following question is raised: "What would happen if there were no UN?" The logical answer imposes itself: "The organization would have to be invented." Even if the UN is constitutionally unable to intervene decisively in big-power conflicts, its functions as a forum for "preventive diplomacy," as an initiator of "cooling off" operations in crisis situations, and as a neutral fact-finder alone justify its existence. After all, the UN has so far succeeded in its ultimate mission—the prevention of world war III, an accomplishment that cannot be denied; even if the UN has not been the only or decisive inhibiting factor of global warfare in the nuclear age, no compelling argument has been advanced to invalidate UN achievements in this regard. To be sure, the UN has been less successful in preventing local or regional conflicts and in restoring lasting peace to certain areas, particularly if one or both of the superpowers were directly involved.

Needless to add, the reluctance of many members to pay their "fair share" of assessed UN budgets also reduces the effectiveness of the organization and threatens it with the specter of bankruptcy.[66]

An expert scholar on international organization in general and on the United Nations in particular placed the issues in perspective:

International organization is an attempt to minimize the conflictual and maximize the cooperative aspects of international relations. The philosophy of international organization is idealistic—not in its view of the facts, but in its hope for changing those facts; not in the sense that it promises a panacea, but in the sense that it expresses an optimism sufficient to justify a reformist effort. It does not deny the reality of conflict, but asserts the conviction that it is necessary, and may be possible, to reduce that aspect of reality to manageable proportions. [However] in the final analysis, both the possibilities and the limitations of international organization are set by the political forces operative within and among member states. The deficiencies of the United Nations indicate a greater need for review and revision of national policies than of the Charter itself. [Furthermore], there is more to be seen than unsolved problems, unresolved conflicts, and unparalleled dangers of chaos and destruction. Fallibility is not the same as futility; limited achievement is not the same as unlimited failure; danger is not the same as doom.[67]

Yet despite its obvious deficiencies, the UN is a vitally important IGO inasmuch as it symbolizes an incipient world government and constitutes the only universal body and global forum potentially capable of maintaining international peace and security in the world. What is needed is therefore not more criticism of the imperfect nature of the UN, but the political, moral, and financial support of its members and their willingness to play by the rules of the game outlined in the Charter. In short, in the absence of a more perfect universal organization (such as a world government), the UN is the only such organ available and should be utilized by all members since no alternative organization is on the horizon.

Regional Organizations

If global international organizations are based upon such noble and ambitious expectations as world peace through universal membership in the United

Nations, regional groupings seem to have less grandiose but possibly more realistic designs. In contrast to the "maximalist" approach of the universalists à la Kant, the regionalists base their "minimalist" rationale on the convergence of interests similar to the philosophy of Thucydides.[68]

The philosophical dichotomy between the universalist and the regionalist approach has been aggravated rather than alleviated by the UN Charter, which legitimized regionalism by authorizing "regional arrangements" (Chapter 8) without defining the term "region."[69] This unfortunate lack of conceptual clarity precipitated political controversies over the legal interpretation or Article 51, which permits both restrictive and liberal interpretation. The rapid proliferation of regional organizations around the globe seems to indicate that the liberal version prevailed: today, 53 percent of all IGOs are of a regional type, and the number of newly created regional organizations rose constantly during the past quarter century, now making up 73 percent of all IGOs founded in the period 1956-65.[70]

Regional organizations are as diverse in their purpose, scope, and structure as their universal counterparts. They can be categorized according to the following criteria: (a) formal function (political-diplomatic, strategic-military, socioeconomic); (b) actual scope of activity (monofunctional or multipurpose); (c) size of member states (egalitarian or nonegalitarian); (d) degree of geographical continuity of the members; and (e) areas covered (micro- or macro-region).[71] Obviously, no regional organization corresponds to an "ideal type." Nye also introduced the useful distinction between international regionalism in the *descriptive* sense (i.e., the formation of interstate associations or groupings on the basis of regions), and in the *doctrinal* sense (i.e., the advocacy of such formation).[72]

Another scholar of the subject alerted academicians to the pitfalls of partisanship for a political cause when he stated that "sound scholarship involves a commitment to study rather than to support, to analysis rather than advocacy . . . [and] both global and regional organizational developments are important enough to deserve serious study. They are not antithetical or mutually exclusive. Both types of institution exist in the real world, and global and regional specialists should be capable of academic coexistence."[73] Nevertheless, the writer recognized that there is a history of controversy over the regionalism-universalism issue.

An internationalist-activist has stated the case succinctly: "Typically, regionalist thinkers conceive of globalism as either premature or altogether unworkable. Internationalists, on the other hand, have developed an image of regional arrangements as harmful roadblocks on the path to world order. Neither perception leaves room for what the record demonstrates: that frequently globalism has served as a second line of defense for regionalism and that regional arrangements have served as backstops for the world organization. Certainly, there is ample room for both types of political order-building on the world scene."[74]

The case for regionalism has been presented in a balanced fashion by a student of this subject:

To the extent that regional cooperation provides for an increase on regional stability by removing historical rivalries, settling intra-regional disputes, and facilitating economic and social cooperation, it serves as a useful organizational mechanism for regional peace and order by sublimating regional power politics into constructive channels. But in and of itself regionalism as an approach to world order is incomplete. Regional entities cannot isolate themselves and hope to survive in a world rendered drastically small by modern communications and technology and awesomely threatened by the specter of nuclear war. In a world of increasing interdependency, regionalism is only a parial solution to problems whose ramifications if not their origins are universal.[75]

In contrast, a strong indictment of regionalism (both in its Communist and free world versions) came from another student of international organization who "holds a dim view of both past performance and potential future of most regional institutions" and observes that "their segmental character tends to disqualify them from coping with interregional problems. The nature of regional perspectives, instead of facilitating the process of negotiation and consensus-building across regions, has more often hardened irreconcilable positions. The firmer and more comprehensive their regional ties, the less likely are countries to be sensitive to interests of states outside the region."[76] He identified the following Achilles heel as cause for the "illusions of regionalism": the refusal of member states to delegate sovereign powers to regional authorities, just as they are unwilling to permit UN organs to interfere in matters of domestic jurisdiction. The writer concludes that "regionalism has not replaced nationalism as the dominant force in the political organization of the world. The nation-state, not the region, remains the pivot of action. Meanwhile regionalism has done nothing to change the essentially global dimension of most of the problems that have to be solved. Interdependence operates within regions, to be sure; but it is just as powerful a reality across regions."[77]

Undoubtedly, interdependence exists at various levels. The question, however, is its degree and intensity, which definitely vary with the dimension of interaction. In other words, it can safely be assumed that intraregional cohesion is substantially stronger than global interdependence. This may be unfortunate but it is nevertheless true. Hence a prominent scholar argued convincingly that "from the viewpoint of democracy, genuine freedom and development within a limited block of countries should be preferable to stagnation within a larger area or under inadequate or premature world government. The larger the area, however, in which genuine integration and development can be carried on successfully, the greater will become the probability that eventually the challenge of world order and world government will be mastered."[78]

In view of the fact that both regionalists and universalists are fighting a common "enemy" in the form of national sovereignty, the artificial dichotomy between the two concepts is indeed the prototype of a *faux problème*; both are combating the fragmentation of the global community and attempt to unify it on different but complementary levels. In any case, the "theoretical debate as to the superiority of the regional or the universal approach to international organization for the handling of political and security problems is a rather sterile exercise, for experience suggests that statesmen need not, and do not, choose one of these approaches to the exclusion of the other."[79]

In fact, the theoretical proposition that cooperative efforts at the regional level contribute to global peace has become a fundamental principle of foreign policy in the West. This doctrine was again confirmed for the United States by President Nixon when he stated that "regional cohesion contributes to world stability."[80]

The complementary nature of the two concepts can also be described in terms of the two principal features of international relations, namely conflict and cooperation. Whereas universalism is essentially trying to cope with the cleavages existing in the multistate system, regionalism exploits and expands the actual similarities and solidarities within a limited group of nations. Thus universal organizations are mainly areas for conflict between states, whereas regional institutions function as "workshops for collaboration among states."[81]

The case for complementarity is best illustrated in the area of human rights: On December 10, 1948, the General Assembly of the United Nations adopted the "Universal Declaration of Human Rights," a *resolution* of good intentions but of merely hortatory value which is by definition (unfortunately) unenforceable: the UN Commission on Human Rights can only make recommendations which have no binding force. However, given the universal value of this important resolution adopted by a global body, the Council of Europe, a regional organization, sponsored the "European Convention for the Protection of Human Rights and Fundamental Freedoms" two years later (signed in Rome on November 4, 1950).[82] Although the substantive rules embodied in this *convention* are largely based upon the UN resolution, it has one decisive advantage: it can be implemented through two organs: the European Commission of Human Rights and the European Court of Human Rights. This example demonstrates that regional organizations can and do serve as subsidiary and complementary structures to the global organizations in effectively realizing common goals.

Notwithstanding the widespread success of regionalism, it should, however, be remembered that "integration of a regional bloc is not necessarily a step toward integration of the world community and may, in fact, tend to create a cleavage."[83] To be sure, the potential danger of the replacement of a number of medium-sized nation-states by a powerful, ambitious region-state cannot be discounted. After all, "exclusive regional integration and the substitution of inter-regional conflict for international conflict is no improvement at all since larger units can engage in larger wars."[84] Considering the potentially nefarious effects of regionalism, an expert in this field observed that "the future, then, may be such as to force us to equate peace with nonintegration and associate the likelihood of war with successful regional integration. This is possible, not certain, and perhaps not likely. But we ought to inquire about the degree of possibility or likelihood . . . because the stakes are too high."[85]

Obviously, this caveat applies to all integrative ventures on all societal levels in all parts of the globe. Therefore, it seems wise to avoid doctrinaire affirmations and to evaluate the performance of particular regional groupings empirically in terms of their conflict reducing (or increasing) propensity.

In a recent comparative analysis of the contributions of regional organizations to world peace, one of the expert scholars on regionalism found that although "the number of regional organizations has grown rapidly (and will probably continue to grow in the future) . . . micro-regional economic and macro-regional political organizations have made modest contributions to the creation of islands of peace in the international system, and their costs for world peace in terms of conflict creation have been less than their modest benefit to the world in conflict diversion."[86] Nevertheless, Nye admits that "micro-regional economic organizations (such as the European Economic Community) have helped to create a web of functional links, which has improved the nature of relationships among the members. And macro-regional political organizations (such as the OAS or NATO) have been able to control certain types of conflicts among their members and prevent them from spreading. In short, contrary to its doctrines, regional organization does not provide a master key to a peaceful world order. Regional organizations merely contribute small but useful pieces to the puzzle of peace."[87]

A balanced evaluation of regionalism would have to include the following considerations:

1. Regionalism is one legitimate and complementary approach to international organization; it constitutes a partial substitute and constructive step toward (rather than an alternative to) world government. Indeed, regionalism appears to be the (second) best method of counteracting the Balkanization of the international system—until and unless a global community of peoples emerges.

2. Regionalism derives its theoretical justification and practical utility from several unifying factors, namely geographic proximity, a common sociocultural background, a similar state of economic development, and compatible political objectives. These centripetal forces are opposed by the centrifugal ideology of stato-nationalism.

3. Most regional IGOs by definition suffer from a common congenital defect, namely the unanimity rule and its corollary, the paralyzing veto principle of sovereign nation-states. However, having a limited membership, regional organizations stand a better chance (mathematically) of arriving at a

consensus since the number of possible vetoes cast is necessarily much lower.

4. Regionalism is not a panacea for conflict resolution but a useful means of reducing the number of potential combatants in an international dispute, thus minimizing the chances and risks (without completely eliminating the possibility) of global warfare.

5. The effectiveness of regional organization increases commensurately with the greater willingness of its participants to delegate sovereign power to common organs. The tendency to share sovereignty with like-minded nations may give regionalism the decisive advantage in terms of future growth potential.

The main purpose of the first chapter was to identify the various actors in the international system—states, IGOs, NGOs—and to analyze the terms interdependence, transnationalism, and regionalism. The next chapter deals with conflicting propositions about the interaction processes between these actors, i.e., regional integration.

2

Approaches to the Study of Regional Integration

The substance of international integration is theoretically of concern to all social scientists, and governmental officials in all parts of the globe. However, in practice, the study of this truly interdisciplinary phenomenon has been virtually monopolized by American political scientists specializing in the analysis of regional integration. The original works of the two pioneers in this field of study, Karl Deutsch and Ernst Haas, have been criticized, amplified, and refined by both epigones and young turks from other schools, as well as by the "founding fathers" themselves. Consequently, a wide variety of paradigms, models, approaches, and methodologies have been proposed by a number of scholars during the last two decades, demonstrating the vitality of the discipline. Notwithstanding this intensive scientific cross-fertilization, the relentless search for the "dependent and/or independent variables" continues, thus indicating that the study of regional integration is still in the stage of pretheorizing. Hence, further research on this subject is warranted, especially since "one major normative utility of the study of regional integration is its contribution as a conceptual, empirical, and methodological link between work on the future of the international system and the future of the nation-states whose interrelationships make up the system."[1] In this chapter a number of approaches to regional integration will be examined and grouped under the following concepts: federalism, functionalism, neofunctionalism, communications theory, the configurative approach, and the "Gestalt Model."

Federalism

Federalism is a multidimensional concept of principles, doctrines, institutions, and processes dealing with the problems of concentration, diffusion, and sharing of power in political systems.

The *federal principle* has been authoritatively defined as "the method of dividing powers so that the general and regional governments are each, within a sphere, co-ordinate and independent."[2] This principle became the basis for "territorial, institutional federalism" which manifests itself in its federal or confederal form. The former, vertical type of (legal) federalism involves political integration; the latter, horizontal type, only policy coordination. In the global integration—disintegration continuum, federalism is situated in the center—between unitarism and internationalism. The following typology will cover the total spectrum of organizational schemes and is based upon the criterion of concentration of powers in a central authority:

1. Unitarism: a. Centralized unitary system: e.g., Peoples Republic of China
                                      b. Decentralized unitary system: e.g., United Kingdom
2. Federalism: a. Federation: e.g., United States
                                      b. Confederation: e.g., American Confederation (1777)
                                      c. Supranational Community (functional, administrative federalism): e.g., European Community
3. Internationalism: a. Union of States: e.g., Commonwealth of Nations
                                      b. Intergovernmental organizations: e.g., UN

Given the focus of this study, we will be concerned with federation, confederation, and supranationalism. The criteria of distinction used are the nature of the constitutive act, the location of sovereignty, and the type of jurisdiction given to the respective organs.

A *federation* (Bundesstaat) can be defined as a system of government based upon a constitution which divides powers between interdependent authorities—a sovereign central government, and autonomous provincial and local governments. The central government represents the federation externally, and its decisions are directly applicable to all citizens internally.

A *confederation* (Staatenbund) is an association of sovereign states based upon a treaty (according to international law) which gives the common authority certain powers of policy coordination subject to unanimous approval by all members (who have veto power). A confederation has only limited external sovereignty, and all decisions are carried out indirectly through the member states.

A *supranational community* is a hybrid system of administration with federal, confederal, and international features, a dual-voting procedure (unanimous and majority voting), and direct jurisdiction on the part of partially autonomous common organs over individual citizens of the member states.

These relatively legalistic-institutional interpretations of federalism have been complemented by a modern, dynamic version, namely, the *process* of "federalizing a political community, that is to say, the process by which a number of separate political organizations, be they states or any other kind of associations, enter into arrangements for working out solutions, adopting joint policies, and making joint decisions on joint problems."[3]

This "functional federalism" is both pragmatic and evolutionary in nature and engenders the presence of a "federal spirit" in the socioeconomic communities involved in this federalizing process.[4] In other words, the dynamic concept of federalism is a method of travelling (presumably toward a common goal), rather than a destination. This process version of federalism has the advantage of being flexible in terms of strategy, but it does not answer the question, how can we travel together toward a nonspecified goal? This problem has been settled (in theory) by the representatives of the third type of federalism: "integral federalism."[5] This *Weltanschauung* is comprehensive in that it concerns society at large (not just its political institutions) and aims at a total transformation of societal structures. Integral federalism calls for the centralization of certain functions in a federal government and for decentralization at regional and local levels in order to provide for the maximum participation of the individual. In this ideal federalist society, power would be distributed in an elaborate framework of sociopolitical institutions which would virtually guarantee participatory democracy. Integral federalists consider such a new polity as the ideal compromise between totalitarianism (as exemplified by the Communist world) and particularism (exemplified by the anarchical international system). This dialectical model has been justified on the grounds that the needs for solidarity and autonomy have developed at the same time in postindustrial societies, calling simultaneously for larger supranational units and smaller intranational entities.[6]

The result of the application of this model would be a "federation of small units" in which the federal government acts on behalf of all provinces which have their own autonomous authorities, according to the principle of convergence of interests in foreign affairs and optimum diversification in the domestic sphere.

As far as the realization of the federalist design is concerned, two possible avenues are available: the first (minimalist) strategy is that of the "federal pact" (*foedus*), which involves the conclusion of a federal bargain between (hitherto sovereign) governments to join in an overarching political system (federation or confederation). The second (maximalist) strategy is that of a "constituant assembly," either convened by the existing legislative bodies of the potential partners or by the people at large (a rather academic option, since it would amount to a quasi-revolution). It can be assumed that the success of both strategies depends on the existence of widespread *animus integrandi*, although an emerging will to unite might suffice in the case of a covenant between governments.[7]

There is no doubt that a successful implementation of federalism in any part of the globe is an extremely difficult undertaking for all participants. Applied to Western Europe in the form of a "Europe of Regions",[8] it would radically alter its traditional political landscape.

Functionalism

Whereas federalism emphasizes the legal-political dimension of interstate relations, functionalism concentrates upon the socioeconomic and welfare functions of sovereign governments. Their ultimate objective is the same: superseding the sovereign nation-state by peaceful means, with an international organism better equipped to assure peace and prosperity for the people. But they differ in their respective strategy: orthodox federalists launch a frontal attack on national sovereignty; functionalists attempt to by-pass this obstacle by a "backdoor approach" of penetrating the stato-national framework through gradual erosion of independent prerogatives with international functional activities. The basic assumption underlying traditional functionalism is that politics and economics are separate functions of the state and thus can be "internationalized" without disturbing the sleeping lion of national power and sovereignty, who, upon awakening, realizes that he has become obsolete and has been replaced by a new order. The principal exponent of this theory, David Mitrany, refers to it as "federation in installments" and as a method which would "overlay political divisions with a spreading web of international activities and agencies, in which and through which the interests and life of all the nations would be gradually integrated."[9]

Referring to functionalists like Mitrany and Merton, an observer noted that they "are interested in identifying those aspects of human needs and desires that exist and clamor for attention outside the realm of the political. They believe in the possibility of specifying technical and 'non-controversial' aspects of governmental conduct, and weaving an ever-spreading web of international institutional relationships on the basis of meeting such needs. They would concentrate on commonly experienced needs initially, expecting the circle of the non-controversial to expand at the expense of the political, as practical cooperation becomes coterminous with the totality of interstate relations. At that point a true world community will have arisen."[10]

Despite the pragmatic nature of the two basic assumptions—the separability of *Grosspolitik* from welfare issues and the potential of international organizations—there appear to be two fallacies. Pointing at what is probably the most crucial fallacy of functionalism, namely its assumption that peace can be automatically achieved through economic and social internationalization, a perceptive critic raised the question "whether states can in fact be induced to join hands in functional endeavor before they have settled the outstanding political and security issues which divide them. Functionalism's insistence upon putting first things first does not settle the matter of what things are first."[11]

In addition to the "priority fallacy," there is the problem of the ultimate shift of loyalty and sovereignty from the states to international organizations. The functionalist strategy consists of strengthening international agencies and increasing their tasks in an effort to demonstrate to the people and their leaders (through direct contact with them) that these agencies are better equipped than national governments to handle matters of common concern. The functionalists, then, hope that under the impact of the impressive performance of these functional universal agencies, people will eventually shift their loyalties from the state to international organizations. *Helas*, the performance of most specialized agencies (and for that matter of the major UN organs as well) has been less than spectacular. International organizations have been especially unsuccessful in generating popular support within states for an incremental delegation of functions to international organs. Yet this is precisely one of the assumptions of functionalism. Hence, the second fallacy consists in the belief that people are willing and capable of pressuring their governments to transfer powers to international bodies.[12]

In addition to these two substantive fallacies, there is a fallacy of scope in the sense that functionalism has global ambitions. Its proponents expect that their strategy can be implemented on a worldwide basis simultaneously and regardless of the different nature and degree of interdependencies in various parts of the globe. These universalist aspirations have been widely regarded as the principal cause for the failure of the functionalist strategy, especially by the neofunctionalists. Although their common objective is the same—namely, the replacement of the nation-state by non-coercive means—neofunctionalists are less ambitious in that they concentrate on specific regions rather than on the international system at large. It is through this selective attempt to transcend the nation-state in areas where its hard shell shows some signs of erosion due to increased transnational linkages that they hope to build islands of peace and cooperation which will serve as building blocks toward a system of universal peace.

Both functionalists and neofunctionalists differ from the federalists in that the latter try to defeat the nation-state by replacing it with federal-type structures while the former propose a gradual approach designed to transcend the nation-state.

Neofunctionalism

The neofunctionalist approach to regional integration assumes that actor behavior in a regional setting is analogous to that in a modern pluralist nation-state and takes for granted that these actors are motivated by self-interest. Its central proposition can be summarized as follows: There exists a continuum between economic integration and political union; the two areas are linked by an automatic politicization process ("spillover"). Actors are involved in an incremental process of decision-making, beginning with economic and social matters (welfare maximization) and gradually extending to the political arena (*Grosspolitik*). Ernst Haas, the founding father of this school, puts it this way: "Under modern conditions the relationship between economic and political union had best be treated as a continuum. . . ."[13] Moreover, "the superiority of step-by-step economic decisions over crucial political choices is assumed as permanent. . . ."[14] Having identified the "political community" as his terminal condition, Haas defines "integration" as the "process whereby political actors in several distinct national settings are persuaded to shift their loyalties, expectations, and political activities toward a new and larger center, whose institutions possess or demand jurisdiction over the pre-existing national states".[15]

He expanded on this definition later when he stated that "integration can be conceived as involving the gradual politicization of the actor's purposes which were initially considered 'technical' or 'noncontroversial'. Politicization implies that the actors, in response to miscalculation or disappointment with respect to the initial purposes, agree to widen the spectrum of means considered appropriate to attain them. This tends to increase the controversial component, i.e., those additional fields of action which require political choices concerning how much national autonomy to delegate to the union. Politicization implies that actors seek to resolve their problems so as to upgrade common interests and, in the process, delegate more authority to the center."[16] However, under the impact of President de Gaulle's nationalist policies in 1965, Haas amended his concept of automatic functional integration by allowing for the possibility of charismatic leaders temporarily blocking the movement: "Pragmatic interests, simply because they are pragmatic and not reinforced with deep ideological or philosophical commitment, are ephemeral . . . and a political process which is built and projected from pragmatic interests, therefore is bound to be a frail process, susceptible to reversal."[17] At that time, he also proposed to distinguish between "dramatic-political" and "incremental-economic" actors, suggesting that integration depends on their respective influence, which might result in smooth (or impossible), erratic and reversible, or gradual and automatic types of integration.[18] Once the actors are involved in decision-making at a regional level, Haas proposes three modes of accommodation facilitating conflict resolution, namely accommodation on the basis of the minimum common denominator; by splitting the difference; and by upgrading the common interest.[19]

Integration can be considered successful (in terms of institutionalization) if the common institutions increase their autonomy, authority, and/or legitimacy. Indeed, the effective transfer of "authority-legitimacy" has become the master concept of neofunctionalism since this "multiple dependent variable . . . enables us to specify to whom the authority and legitimacy have been transferred."[20]

In order to illustrate possible temporary results of integration processes, Haas proposes three types of configurations: the "regional commune," described as "an anarchoid image of a myriad of units which are so highly differentiated in function as to be forced into interdependence. Authority is involved primarily in the sense of having been taken away from previous centers without having found a new single locus. Legitimacy . . . would not take the form of loyalty akin to nationalism." The third type, called "asymmetrical overlapping," has various patterns of interdependence, with authority partially withdrawn from the units without being symmetrically vested in the center, and with legitimacy linked to multiple loyalties. These three types differ in how legitimate authority is diffused.[21]

In an effort to list the independent variables of economic unions, Haas and Schmitter decided on the following categories. *Background conditions*: (1) size of unit, (2) rate of transaction, (3) pluralism, (4) elite complementarity; *conditions at the time of economic union*: (5) governmental purposes, (6) powers of union; *process conditions:* (7) decision-making style, (8) rate of transaction, (9) adaptability of governments.[22] The chances of automatic politicization depend on the number of conditions met in a given case. This initial list has subsequently been modified and expanded to take political developments and scholarly criticism into consideration. Thus Haas and Barrera added "perception of dependence" to the four background conditions; and placed "external pressure" among both the "conditions at the time of union" and under "process conditions." The resulting twelve variables were then used to test the performance of EEC, EFTA, LAFTA, CACM, and COMECON. It was concluded that the Central American Common Market and the EEC rated highest among the five groups in terms of integration potential.[23]

Currently, several students of integration are engaged in an effort to further refine and operationalize these independent variables. Referring to his and Haas's original list of nine variables as a "successful failure" (because it had been inadequately conceptualized but still served as an attractive target for respeculation), Schmitter proposed to revise it by focussing on relations between well-defined variables and by considering different integration outcomes.[24] Calling his dependent variable "actor integration strategies," he proposed a model that focusses on predicting the policies of national actors with regard to expanding or contracting the scope and/or the level of regional authority. Then he identifies the following seven types of actor strategies:

1. Spillover: i.e., to increase both the scope and level of his commitment concomitantly
2. Spillaround: i.e., to increase only the scope while holding the level of authority constant
3. Buildup: i.e., to increase the decisional autonomy or capacity of joint institutions but deny them entrance into new issue areas
4. Retrench: i.e., to increase the level of joint deliberation but withdraw the institution(s) from certain areas
5. Muddle-about: i.e., to let the regional bureaucrats debate, suggest, and expostulate on a wider variety of issues but decrease their actual capacity to allocate values
6. Spillback: i.e., to retreat on both dimensions, possibly returning to the *status quo ante*
7. Encapsulate: i.e., to respond to crisis by marginal modification within the zone of indifference[25]

The same author had previously offered three interesting hypotheses relating to the process of integration. First, the "spill-over hypothesis" suggests that "the greater the policy scope and the higher the level of the initial commitment to collective decision-making, the greater the propensity for task expansion." Second, the "externalization hypothesis states that "once agreement is reached . . . members will be forced to hammer out a collective external position." Third, the "politicization hypothesis" postulates that, "faced with this cumulation of commitments, national actors find themselves gradually embroiled in ever more salient or controversial areas of policymaking." Ultimately, as a result of this automatic process, "there will be a shift in actor expectations and loyalty toward the new regional center."[26]

Another neofunctionalist scholar, Leon Lindberg, has been extremely successful in bringing order into the chaos of independent variables. In an effort to relate David Easton's concept of the political system to the European integration phenomenon, Lindberg adapted William Riker's categories of governmental functions and came up with a comprehensive classification scheme to be used for the purpose of testing the degree of integration in the European setting.[27] This model subsequently became the basis for the sophisticated and balanced evaluation of the performance of the European Community by Lindberg and Scheingold.[28]

In addition to this device for measuring the scope of the European Community system, the authors also proposed a "scale of the locus of decision-making" which is very useful. The scale ranges from low to high integration and covers the following five types of decision-making: (1) all policy decisions by national processes; (2) only the beginnings of community-decision processes; (3) policy decisions in both, but national activity predominates; (4) policy decisions in both, but community activity predominates; and (5) all policy decisions by joint community processes.[29] This device can be used to determine the relative amount of decision-making power vested in the institutions of the community as compared to the authority remaining in the hands of the national governments. In the same study, Lindberg and Scheingold suggested a list of indicators dealing with demand flow and leadership in the community. Considering the power, influence, and resources of actors making demands, they distinguished between dramatic-political and incremental-economic actors and between those whose responsibilities or constituencies or authority were system-wide rather than limited to a region, category, industry, or interest group. They listed five conditions for demand flow and two for leadership which, to the extent that they were fulfilled, would indicate the chance for growth.[30]

Later, Lindberg refined his model considerably and added another concept, namely that of resources, which he proposes to operationalize. It contains five components: (1) prior agreement on what can be decided collectively—existing level; (2) decision-making norms; (3) supranational structures—supranational structural growth, resources of supranational structures, national-supranational transactions; (4) financial resources; (5) support resources—expectations of future gain, belief in legitimacy, belief in a common interest, and sense of mutual political identification.[31] On this occasion, he also updated his concept of "political integration," now defined as "the emergence or creation over time of collective decision-making processes, i.e., political institutions, to which governments delegate decision-making authority and/or through which they decide jointly via more familiar intergovernmental negotiation."[32] In sum Lindberg differs from his mentor essentially in the emphasis he places on decision-making styles and the role of supranational leadership as decisive factors of integration, whereas Haas focuses on functional, cross-sectorial spillover and politicization; moreover, Lindberg is almost exclusively concerned with the European theater, whereas Haas attempts to construct models with universalistic application.

The original neofunctionalist approach, represented by the writings of Haas, Schmitter, Barrera, Lindberg, Scheingold, and Scheinman, were criticized by other students of integration on several counts.[33] The first point dealt with the alleged neglect of exogenous factors as contributing variable to regional integration. Although Haas and Schmitter corrected this deficiency later, Lindberg and Scheingold are primarily interested in the internal dynamics of the regional (European) political system (which is most certainly an adequate parameter of scholarly research).

The second point concerns the "Europe-centric" nature of most neofunctionalist research and propositions, which are allegedly tailored to the European setting and stage of development and are often nonconsequential, or merely peripherally germane, to integration processes in developing regions or to the Communist countries. This criticism is again somewhat unfair since every empirical theory has to "take-off" initially in a limited setting in order to be tested under relatively homogeneous conditions (later to be exported into different political landscapes for the purpose of determining its "universalistic" validity).

The third point of criticism centers on the basic neofunctionalist assumption that there is a continuum between the economic and political sectors of nation-states permitting functional integration to spill over from the welfare area into the domain of *Grosspolitik* in an automatic, deterministic fashion, resulting in the emergence of a new regional unit. This is obviously a historical, *status quo* argument which does not take evolutionary forces working in each society into consideration. Thus Haas modified his paradigm to allow for the interference of the idiosyncratic variable (to use Rosenau's term) when he conceded that "dramatic-political actors" can block the integrative process (without being able to halt it indefinitely).

In conclusion, it can be stated that the premises of neofunctionalism have not yet been sufficiently tested in order to make a final judgment on its value for promoting international integration. However, inasmuch as the European Community can be considered as an almost ideal laboratory for the testing of the major propositions ("neofunctionalism in operation"), this strategy has been demonstrated to be at least partially successful in the political arena.

Communications Theory

This approach to international integration derives its basic premises from Wiener's cybernetic model and assumes that social processes follow the causal logic of cybernetics. Using as its principal indicator transactions between people, the communications theorists postulate that an intensive flow of transactions will establish the mutual relevance of political actors and will create a pattern of interaction between groups that will eventually lead to the emergence of "security communities." Under the condition that loads and capabilities remain balanced, the theory suggests that there is a cause-effect relationship between mass communication—mutual elite responsiveness—and community formation. This, in turn, presupposes the possibility of using quantitative indices (transactions) to explain qualitative factors (perceptions). To be sure, there is great validity in the proposition that a high level of transactions is unlikely to be associated with a state of tension and conflict.

The logic of the theory is acceptable if one accepts the inherent deterministic element and ignores the possibility of the "missing link syndrome." In the words of a skeptic, "The trouble with [this theory] is that it attempts to reduce the explanation of the political phenomenon of joining together to an explanation of the social and economic condition of the population. In bypassing the political, in bypassing the act of bargaining itself, it leaves out the crucial condition of the predisposition to make the bargain."[34] This commentary of an analyst with the federalist perspective points at the dilemma involved, consisting in the attempt to explain integration in terms of background variables.

In the "classic" study, Karl Deutsch and his associates identified nine essential conditions for an "amalgamated security community," of which federalism is a subclass: (1) mutual compatibility of main values; (2) a distinctive way of life; (3) expectations of stronger economic ties or gains; (4) a marked increase in political and administrative capabilities of at least some participating units; (6) unbroken links of social communication, both geographically between territories and sociologically between different social strata; (7) a broadening of the political elite; (8) mobility of persons, at least among the politically relevant strata; (9) a multiplicity of ranges of communication and transaction. In addition, they found that three other conditions may be essential: (10) a compensation of flows of communications and transaction; (11) a not too infrequent interchange of group roles; (12) considerable mutual predictability of behavior.[35] However, the authors attached a caveat to this list: "None of these conditions, of course, seems to be by itself sufficient for success; and all of them together may not be sufficient either. . . . Nonetheless, it does seem plausible to us that any group of states or territories which fulfilled all the essential conditions for an amalgamated security community . . . should also be at least on a good part of the way to successful amalgamation."[36] The term "amalgamation" is defined as "the formal merger of two or more previously independent units into a single larger unit; with some type of common government after amalgamation. This common government may be unitary or federal."[37]

One of Deutsch's epigones, Bruce Russett, who is best known for his collection of cross-national transaction data,[38] identifies the following salient conditions for political integration at the international level: a degree of cultural similarity or at least compatibility for the major politically relevant values; economic interdependence; the existence of formal institutions with substantial spillover or consensus-building effects; and geographical contiguity.[39] He is mainly concerned with the notion of *responsiveness* as a crucial variable (a point Deutsch emphasized in his *Political Community at the International Level*). Russett therefore defines political integration as "the process of building capabilities for responsiveness relative to the loads put on capabilities. The degree of integration at any time would be the current ratio of capabilities to loads. Thus we are concerned with behavior, and with the community ties underlying behavior."[40] He adds that "social community is a necessary, though not sufficient, condition for voluntary amalgamation . . . and in non-coercive political communities social community must develop first or simultaneously."[41] His insistence on this latter point is perfectly consistent with Deutsch's "order of priorities"; however, Russett demands a higher level of capabilities than Deutsch, but a lower level than Haas. We conclude, then, that communication theorists differ from the neofunctionalists in that they do not focus on "institutionalization" as the principal indicator of integration. Instead, Russett emphasizes *capabilities* as a means to improve responsiveness: "by capabilities I mean facilities for attention, communication, and mutual identification. The first two are essential but clearly insufficient. . . . Essential bonds of the social fabric between groups or especially nations are such ties as trade, migration, tourism, communication facilities like mail and telephone, and cultural educational exchange. . . . They serve to strengthen the sense of mutual identification with the entire collectivity, and to promote a readiness to respond sympathetically to the needs of others within the collectivity."[42]

Russett is sensitive to the vexing problems of priority, causation and circularity in theorizing about regional integration. He frankly admits that "we can never prove causation . . . [but] some highly plausible assertions can still be made in combination with the elimination of certain other causal possibilities."[43] In the light of these reflections, Russett concludes that "probably each social element has the capacity to initiate the process (of integration) under some circumstances, and certainly each plays a crucial role in maintaining it. Naturally, it is not a simultaneous process of reciprocal causation, although it is sometimes presented that way and it may be difficult or impossible empirically to identify which precedes which."[44] Notwithstanding these extremely appropriate reservations about integration theory, he contends that transactions, under favorable circumstances, can either "describe or predict or make possible or cause integration."[45] Incidentally, Russett has been criticized for inadequately conceptualizing his key term "region."[46]

Another of Deutsch's epigones, Donald Puchala, who limited his transaction analysis almost exclusively to Franco-German interaction data, repeatedly theorized about the similarities and differences between the models of his mentor and that of Ernst Haas. Thus he makes a fundamental distinction between the two major dimensions of international integration: "*International community formation* or the linking of peoples in bonds of mutual confidence, amity, identification, economic and information exchange, and social assimilation and *international political amalgamation* or the linking of governments in international or supranational institutions and policymaking processes."[47] According to Deutsch, community formation (or, as he often calls it, "nation-building") and amalgamation may occur separately, producing either a pluralistic security community or an empire, or simultaneously producing an amalgamated security community. Puchala prefers to treat his two dimensions as sets of subprocesses, conceptually and operationally, as follows:

Community formation . . . includes 1) the growth of 'we feelings' and mutual deference and esteem between peoples; 2) the development of mutual trust, confidence, and predictability; 3) economic integration or the growth of communities of exchange; 4) the disappearance on international communication barriers; and 5) the heightening of mutual awareness, attentiveness, and responsiveness at all societal levels in merging societies. In the same manifold way *International political amalgamation* includes: 1) the emergence and expansion of international and supranational institution linking governments; 2) the emergence and increasing efficacy of political interest articulation and aggregation in a supranational arena, and 3) increasing frequency, ease, and efficacy in intergovernmental accommodation in an international 'consensus finding' or 'conflict resolving' process.[48]

In contrast to Haas (and like Nye), Puchala treats international integration not as a single, composite dependent variable, but rather as a matrix of several subprocesses. He concludes that "international community formation is not directly related to international political amalgamation . . . [and] that neither transactional theories of integration which predict amalgamation . . . to follow from community formation, nor functional theories which predict the reverse are wholly accurate. . . . [Instead, their relationship] is an indirect, by no means determined, three-cornered linkage between community bonds linking peoples, capabilities for cooperative interaction between governments, and subsequent progress toward political amalgamation."[49] Nevertheless, Puchala remains attached to his favorite approach, transaction analysis, which suggests that "whenever it is the case that a population shares values, preferences, life-styles, common memories, aspirations, loyalties, and identifications, it is also the case that people within this population communicate clearly, and effectively, in balanced manner, over multiple ranges of social, economic, cultural and political concerns." Consequently, international community formation" would be indicated by increasing volumes of multiple-ranged transaction between potential community members."[50] Puchala, however, adds the caveat that "transaction flows reflect . . . [but] do not cause regional integration."[51]

Given his membership in the behavioralist camp of the discipline, it comes as a genuine surprise when Puchala suddenly injects the concept of political "will" into his analysis. This unusual allowance for an essentially nonquantifiable variable in integration theory by a (former?) quantifier par excellence is all the more astonishing since he apparently selects it as the decisive criterion when he states that "emotional and identitive affinities between peoples create conditions within which governments can work toward mutually accommodating conflict resolution as well as toward more positive international cooperation . . . , [but] none of this is to argue that community formation eventually must lead to political amalgamation . . . , [since] the initiative toward international political amalgamation remains an *act* of elite or governmental *will*, probably influenced but certainly not determined by community ties between peoples."[52] (Emphasis added.)

With this sign of emancipation from the original "Yale group" consisting of Deutsch, Russett, and Puchala, the latter apparently joined earlier modifiers of the communication school, namely Philip Jacob and his associates at the University of Pennsylvania.[53] In his special contribution to this study, Jacob examined the *acts* of politically relevant individuals who make "the political decisions which either trigger or jam integrative relationship."[54] In his perceptive analysis, Jacob stresses the point that apart from, and in addition to, social and economic prerequisites (transaction indicators), integration requires conscious decisions by policy-makers willing to engage in transnational community building. His analysis rests upon the "assumption that political behavior is fundamentally a process of decision. It is the resultant of a complex of human choices. Hence it must be understood in terms of, and traced back ultimately to, the determinants of the *personal* behavior of all those who in one way or another have a hand in 'politics,' that is, in the process of directing or controlling the collective actions of the society."[55] If political decisions are rooted in human behavior, he contends, the examination of *values* is of paramount importance. Hence, Jacob defines values as "the normative standards by which human beings are influenced in their choice among the alternative courses of action which they perceive."[56]

Having underlined the normative component of values as a determining factor for decision-making, Jacob distinguishes between social norms (community standards of legitimacy), role values (related to the individual's function), the interests of special groups (loyal to the policy-maker), and personal values (of the policy-maker).[57] The author is on safe grounds when he stresses that *people* decide to integrate or not to integrate. He concludes with a rather unconventional observation involving the role of deviant values in integration which is supposed to "come about on a broad scale as a result of a kind of conspiracy of deviators within existing political communities."[58] These traitors must be united in their purpose and must skillfully outmaneuver the power holder with the goal of creating a new integrated polity.

Another scholar interested in the psychological aspects of integration isolates identification with political units, inducements to cooperation, and similarities in experience, values, and attitudes as salient indicators of integrative potential and attempts to explain how people acquire the disposition favorable to integration.[59] In his approach to social learning, shared values, and elite responsiveness, the author shares many of Haas's concerns, without accepting his "spillover" concept.

Jacob and Teune also joined forces in an attempt to construct a comprehensive conceptual framework for the analysis of political integration.[60] Initially, they raised the most fundamental issues in integration, namely the definition of the concept, the identification of the variables, and their interrelationships, presenting the crux of the matter as follows: "We need to know not only that a particular condition or factor *has* some influence upon political behavior, but *how much* influence it has, in what *combination* it functions with other determinants of interaction, and in what *sequence* of circumstances it must occur to be influential."[61] Subsequently, they note that integration is a *relative* term because communities are *more* or *less* integrated, and go on to define "political integration" as "a state of mind or disposition to be cohesive, to act together, to be committed to mutual programs."[62]

Having defined their key concept, they identify the following ten factors that may exert integrative influence upon people: 1) geographical proximity; 2) homogeneity; 3) transaction or interactions among persons or groups; 4) knowledge of each other; 5) shared functional interests; 6) the character or motive pattern of a group; 7) the structural frame or system of power and decision-making; 8) the sovereignty-dependency status of the community; 9) governmental effectiveness; 10) previous integrative experiences.[63] This "grand design" was conceived as a model capable of accommodating integration at the international and subnational levels. But the authors are careful to note that before arriving at a composite assessment of the integrative process, answers to the following questions must be found: What is the threshold or critical mass? What is the mix of variables and the integrative syndrome? What is the political relevance of each variable? And what is the necessary sequence of steps leading to integration (time-process analysis), as well as the costs and benefits (price of merger)?[64] These are most certainly the pan-ultimate questions troubling all students of the phenomenon of integration, regardless of their respective intellectual background or allegiance to a "school," and as of today there is no consensus on any of these issues. Recent attempts to theorize on some of these issues were made by several scholars without any spectacular results.[6 5]

The Configurative Approach

This approach to the study of integration at the international level is the most comprehensive one for the analysis of regional sociopolitical systems because it takes a *vue d' ensemble* by considering both internal and external factors of integration. Moreover, most scholars who adopted this approach engaged in cross-regional comparative analysis. The principal representative of this "school" is undoubtedly Amitai Etzioni, a political sociologist, whose *Political Unification: A Comparative Study of Leaders and Forces* can be regarded as the contemporary classic in this field.[6 6]

Etzioni constructed a paradigm featuring the entire spectrum of significant independent variables necessary to study the phenomenon of integration in different regional setting. In contrast to Haas, he uses "integration" to refer to a condition (rather than to a process), explaining that "a *political community* is a community that possesses three kinds of integration: a) it has an effective control over the use of the means of violence (though it may 'delegate' some of this control to member units); b) it has a center of decision-making that is able to affect significantly the allocation of resources and rewards throughout the community; and c) it is the dominant focus of political identification for the large majority of politically aware citizens."[6 7]

Etzioni's emphasis is on political integration (he calls it unification) and the threshold of his political community is higher than that of both Haas and Deutsch in that it requires the ability of the decision-making institution to significantly affect the allocation of resources through the community. Furthermore, he makes a useful distinction between *political communities* that are integrated and systems that are interdependent. Thus integration becomes the more inclusive term since all units that are integrated are also interdependent, but not vice versa. In his comparative analysis of the success or failure of unification movements in four regions (the Federation of the West Indies, the United Arab Republic, the Nordic Union, and the European Economic Community), Etzioni seeks to establish *who led* a particular unification effort, under what *conditions*, by what *means*, and with what *results*. In order systematically to examine the integrative processes at work, he devised a three-dimensional framework consisting of the *preunification state* (including unit, environmental and system properties); the *unification process* (divided into integrating power and sectors); and the *termination state* (involving the level, scope, and dominant function of the political community).[6 8] Using this comprehensive scheme of salient variables, Etzioni tried to determine under what conditions unification efforts succeed or fail. He isolated three kinds of internal and external powers affecting the unification process: coercive, utilitarian, and identitive. Each of these powers depends for its effectiveness on three facilitating factors: adequate communication, representation, and responsiveness.[69]

The second most significant contribution to the examination of external factors in the evolution of regional organizations was made by a European scholar, Karl Kaiser. Focusing on the interaction between regional subsystems and the superpowers, he proposed the following definition of an international subsystem: "a pattern of relations among basic units in world politics which exhibits a particular degree of regularity and intensity of relations as well as awareness of interdependence among the participating units."[70] Then he distinguished between an "intergovernmental regional subsystem" in which the authority rests exclusively with the governmental elites (e.g., NATO, OECD), and a "comprehensive regional subsystem" in which both governmental and nongovernmental elites participate in the decision-making process (e.g., the European Community).[71] Furthermore, Kaiser makes a useful distinction between "overlapping" (e.g., OAS and LAFTA) and "nonoverlapping" regional subsystems (e.g., EEC and COMECON).[72] Finally, he establishes a series of hypotheses concerning the interaction processes between nonoverlapping regional subsystems. For example, do they stimulate, induce, or contribute to the formation of other subsystems? (Do alliances breed counteralliances?) Or, do certain comprehensive regional subsystems serve as models for other regional efforts (demonstration effect)?[73] In other words, is there a tendency to restore equilibrium or to establish symmetry between regional integrative efforts?

Another student of comparative regional integration is Joseph Nye, who established himself as a persistent critique of the allegedly "Europe-centric" neofunctionalist school. Although he acknowledged the contributions of its principal representatives (particularly the "Haas-Schmitter paradigm"), Nye consistently felt that most neofunctionalist generalizations are based upon assumptions derived from a strictly West-European setting with little relevance to developing (and Communist) regions. In his attempt to compare integration movements in Central America, East Africa and Western Europe, Nye paid attention to both the internal and external forces at work in these areas, thus following the "configurative approach." His theoretical framework differs from Etzioni's but is equally comprehensive and balanced. Having defined "integration" as "forming parts into a whole or creating interdependence," Nye insists on disaggregating his dependent variable into a tiers concept: economic integration (the formation of a transnational economy), social integration (the formation of a transnational society), and political integration (the formation of a transnational political interdependence).[74] He prefers "to develop separate indicators for various types of integration so that relationships can be compared more accurately and lags determined,"[75] given the regional differences in "infrastructure, market mechanisms, external dependence, administrative resources, political group structure, interdependence of social sectors, ideology and national consciousness."[76]

Furthermore, Nye advocated this approach because of the frequent discontinuities occurring in integrative processes in the sense that they are often accompanied simultaneously by disintegrative forces. This is one of the reasons why he rejected the neofunctionalist dogma of functional spillover (from the economic to the political sector) since it is dependent upon the postindustrial European conditions. In other words, he challenged the notions of the continuum of welfare and politics, as well as the automatic nature of actor politicization.[77] Instead, Nye introduced the concept of "cultivated spillover": "In contrast to pure spillover in which the main force comes from a common perception of the degree to which problems are intrinsically intertwined in a modern economy, problems are deliberately linked together into package deals not on the basis of technological necessity but on the basis of political and ideological projections and political possibilities."[78] In addition he proposed a revised list for the comparative analysis and measurement of common markets composed of two groups of variables: (1) *process mechanisms*, including functional linkage of tasks, rising transactions, deliberate linkage and coalition formation, elite socialization, regional group formation, ideological-identitive appeal, and involvement of external factors; and (2) *integrative potential*, including structural conditions (symmetry of units, capacity of member states to adapt and respond, pluralism, elite value complementarity), and perceptual conditions (perceived equity of distribution of benefits, perceived external cogency, and low visible costs).[79] Nye also hypothesized that four dynamic outcomes characterize a regional integration process over time: politicization (growing controversy among an increasing number of participants), redistribution (of benefits in phases of growth and equally among sectors), reduction of alternatives (open to decision-makers as integration proceeds), and externalization (pressure to hammer out collective policies toward third countries.)[80]

Another useful model was designed by Louis J. Cantori and Steven L. Spiegel,[81] who examine five different regions in terms of "subordinate systems" (the Middle East, West Europe, Latin America, Southeast Asia, and West Africa). They distinguish between the dominant (global), subordinate (regional), and internal (nation-state) political systems, and select four pattern variables: (1) cohesion—social, economic, political and organizational; (2) communications—personal, mass media, elite exchanges, and transportation; (3) power—material, military and motivational; and (4) structure of relations—spectrum, causes, and means of relations. The distinction between core and periphery is of direct relevance to integration theory in terms of the interaction processes between the old and new centers of power.

Robert A. Bernstein also follows the configurative approach when he looks at integration in terms of common action of a system in relation to the outside world.[82]

The "Gestalt Model"

Methodological Considerations

The rationale for the construction of the Gestalt model of regional integration is threefold:

1. "Integration" is an interdisciplinary phenomenon in the state of "pretheorizing" and no finite paradigm has yet been devised which includes and/or identifies all salient (dependent and independent) variables and also solves the vexing enigma of causation
2. Knowledge in the social sciences expands as a result of a reciprocal, cumulative process of formulating, and redefining concepts, testing hypotheses and criticizing propositions advanced by other scholars in the field
3. This study of regional political integration, focusing on the European Community as the most advanced of all integrative movements, constitutes an ideal experimental laboratory for the testing of various propositions on community formation at the international level

Definitions

Integration (in the sense of regional, political integration) is a complex, dialectical *process* involving pluridimensional, multisectorial interactions between various societal groups engaged in gradual, transnational consensus-formation on procedures and policies, aiming at the creation of a common political community.

- The integrative process is *complex* since it progresses in a nonlinear fashion (like ebb and flow), albeit within a continuum of time and space;
- It is *dialectical* in the sense that centripetal and centrifugal forces are simultaneously at work;
- It is *pluridimensional* since it affects all levels of society: individuals (through intermarriage, migration, etc.), groups (parties and interests), and private and public organizations (including the governments);
- It is *multisectorial* since it involves all four sectors of the polities concerned, namely the political, economic, social, and cultural sectors;
- Consensus formation involves ultimately agreement on both the common *institutional framework* (including the *procedural code*) and *common policies* on the principal issues.
- The common goal of the participating groups is the creation of a new superstructure (a political community) in incremental stages.

Political community (as the *product* of an integrative process) is a pluralistic, sociopolitical unit characterized by shared values, mutual responsiveness, compatible objectives, a significant amount of transactions, and loyalty toward common institutions of authority. The political community, the product of the integrative process, would be the dependent variable.

The Gestalt model features the following elements of the syndrome of regional integration.

The Conceptual Framework

I) The integrative context:
    A) External factors (nature of):
        1) The geophysical setting
        2) The geopolitical environment
        3) The legal-organizational framework
    B) Internal factors (degree of):
        1) Cultural homogeneity
        2) Social assimilation
        3) Economic interpenetration
        4) Political unification
II) The substance of integration: people and things
III) The object of integration:
    A) Community formation
    B) Institution building
IV) The process of integration:
    A) Background conditions:
        1) Properties of separate units
            a) ecology (territory and people)
            b) geopolitics (location and power)
            c) development (stage)
            d) polity (nature of political system)
        2) Elements of interdependence:
            a) proximity (common borders)
            b) interaction (goods, people, services)
            c) constraints (external pressures)
            d) purpose (common objectives)
            e) communication (transnational elites)
            f) organization (nature of common organs)
    B) Process conditions:
        1) Cooperation of national units
        2) Capacity of common institutions
        3) Procedural code (style of decision-making)
        4) Influence of supranational elites

  5) Support of the masses
  6) Rate of transactions
  7) Systemic restraints

V) The participating actors in the integrative movement (federators and inhibitors):
  A) Internal actors:
    1) Governmental leaders
    2) Supranational elites
    3) Transnational groups
    4) Mass of people
  B) External actors:
    1) Direct federators or inhibitors
    2) Indirect federators or inhibitors

VI) The societal forces involved in an ongoing integration process—an aggregate list of independent variables including all potential catalysts of integration and disintegration:

Objects	*Subjects*
Political Sector: Legal framework	Executive officials
Structure of political system	Technocrats
Scope of authority	Parliamentarians
Composition of bureaucracy	Party members
	Pressure groups
Diplomatic functions	Judiciary
External relations (trade, aid)	Military, police
Economic Sector: Fiscal sources (budget, taxes)	Bankers
Monetary system (currency, exchange rates)	Businessmen
Trade relations (internal, external)	Workers
Movement of goods, services, capital	Professionals
Competition policy (monopolies, etc.)	
Industry (production, distribution, management)	Miners
Energy resources and exploitation	Tax collectors
Agriculture	Farmers
Business	Customs officials
Patents and licenses	
Transportation	Transport personnel
Research and development (technology)	Scientists
	Engineers
Countercyclical policy	
Planning	
Military procurement	

Social Sector:	Public health	Physicians
	Social welfare	Technicians
	Tourism	Nurses
	Migration	Welfare administrators
	Intermarriage	Tourists
	Foreign labor	
	Jumelages	
Cultural Sector:	Education	Faculty
	Basic research	Students
	Human rights	Administrators
	Recreation and leisure	Lawyers
	Exchange of persons	Judges
	Communications	Journalists, editors
		Artists

VII) The products of integration (political community):
      1)   Confederation
      2)   Supranational community
      3)   Federation

VIII) Measurement of degree of integration:
     A)   Formal indicators (institution building)
        1)   Legal competence
        2)   Political control
        3)   Budgetary authority and planning function
     B)   Informal indicators (community formation)
        1)   Transactions:
           a)   communication
           b)   tourism
           c)   trade
           d)   exchanges
        2)   Attitudes:
           a)   government officials
           b)   elites
           c)   people

Propositions about Integration

1. In contrast to coercive integration by an imperialist dictator, there is no monocausal factor that can bring about peaceful, voluntary integration of pluralistic societies by *fiat*

2. Environmental challenges (such as a threat from outside) and widespread dissatisfaction with the *status quo* within nation-states constitute the breeding ground for integrative movements

3. Pressures from hostile and/or benevolent "external federators" facilitate

the definition of collective policies on the part of "internal federators"

4. The perception of complementary objectives and compatible interests on the part of governmental leaders in various countries are essential for the launching of integrative movements

5. A successful takeoff and sustained growth of an integrative movement depends on the cumulative interplay between three actors: statesmen (who have the power to make political decisions), designer-advocates (who have a vision of the ultimate goal and/or the courage to call for the immediate realization of the maximum objective), and technocrats (who have the expertise to coordinate integrative measures)

6. The chances for the successful implementation of the common strategies defined by the "official" internal federators are enhanced by the operations of transnational pressure groups

7. The creation of common institutions permits the people to shift their loyalty to new supranational organs whose effective performance, in turn, generate widespread satisfaction over the increasing benefits

8. The successful operations of common organs in one societal sector results in disequilibria in others, thus generating demands for adjustment in hitherto unaffected areas

9. New integrative steps per se provide a momentum ("spillover") which may result in vertical integration (increase in the level of joint intrasectorial activity) and/or horizontal integration (expansion of the scope of joint intersectorial endeavors)

10. This "expansive logic of sector integration" is reinforced by the natural interdependence of functional tasks ("process linkages") and the controversial nature of common policy issues

11. The "spillover" tendency is accelerated by technocrats who "cultivate" successive disequilibria thus giving impetus to a further perforation of the stato-national structures ("creative destruction")

12. The superior performance of supranational institutions in limited fields induces national governments (for reasons of enlightened self-interest) to delegate additional powers to those (or other complementary) regional authorities

13. As a result of increased tangible benefits distributed among the participating nations, the new institutions acquire a "myth of success" which in turn, gives them prestige and status in the eyes of the people and maximizes their *animus integrandi*

14. The widespread popular recognition of the competence of regional organs in the economic and social fields (growth and welfare) may induce elite groups to pressure their national leaders into agreeing to joint efforts in the field of security (*Grosspolitik*).

15. The formal transfer of authority in the two vital areas of welfare and

defense to common institutions will give them legitimacy in the eyes of the people and cause them to shift their aspirations and loyalties to the new regional polity.

Given the dialectical nature of the integrative process which involves the simultaneous or consecutive interaction between centripetal and centrifugal forces within a given region, it is necessary to complement the preceding propositions by a number of countervailing arguments.

Propositions about Disintegration ✺

1. Integration and disintegration are rival dialectical processes in the sense that centripetal and centrifugal forces are simultaneously or consecutively at work within a nascent political community
2. No single political leader or socioeconomic agent is capable of permanently blocking an integrative movement once it has taken off, although a determined nationalist can temporarily prevent progress toward political unity through brinkmanship and unilateral policies
3. An optimal combination of centrifugal forces, joined in a "negative alliance," may bring an integrative movement to a halt or reverse it
4. The perceived absence or diminution of an external threat tends to slow down an integrative movement as it reduces the sense of urgency and generates complacency among the participating units
5. The very success of limited sector integration may produce inertia as people no longer see the obvious need for additional sacrifices on the altar of supranationalism
6. The superior performance of supranational institutions may prove counterproductive as many people credit their national governments for the improvements in the standards of living and for economic growth
7. The bureaucratic nature and technical functions of supranational organs tends to alienate people who may favor integration but feel that popular participation in the operations of these bodies is technically infeasible and makes democratic control impossible
8. Disintegrative impulses in one sector have a propensity to spill over into other sectors, resulting in a cross-sectorial spillback and eventual stalemate or possible reversal of the integrative movement

In conclusion, we hope that the Gestalt model is both comprehensive and realistic in the sense that it contains most salient elements of the complex integrative syndrome. However, in view of the fact that integration theory is still in a phase of "pretheorizing," the Gestalt model lends itself (like any scholarly paradigm) to criticisms of all sorts.

In full awareness of the imperfections of our model, an attempt will nevertheless be made to use it for the purpose of this study. Thus Part II deals with the external and internal factors of the integrative process, as well as with the catalysts of integration and disintegration in the four societal sectors. It is expected that this comprehensive approach to, and analysis of, the process of European integration will yield a balanced result, and permit a better assessment of the prospects for an authority-legitimacy transfer in the European region.

Part II:
The Internal Dynamics of the
European Community

Whereas Part I dealt with the general concepts and theories of international integration, Part II will focus on the internal dynamics of the European Community, including the past, present and future leaders and forces that determined or could influence the balance of integration-disintegration in the European Community. The first chapter in Part I identified the principal actors and trends in the contemporary international system.

Chapter 2 grouped the major contemporary approaches to international integration in five categories, and then presented our comprehensive approach of choice, the "Gestalt model," which disaggregates all salient variables and includes both indigenous and exogenous factors as important aspects of the integrative process. This "Gestalt model" provides the conceptual parameters for Part II.

3 Federators and Inhibitors

The term "federator" identifies the principal political actors (governmental officials and leaders of supranational bodies) who contributed significantly to progress in European unification in general and/or to the internal consolidation of the European Community in particular, either as internal or external pressure groups, ever since the end of World War II. This integrative support may have been intentional or incidental, direct or indirect, benevolent or the result of aggressive policies.

The term "inhibitor" (suggested by Inis Claude) refers to actors who made a conscious, direct, and purposeful attempt to undermine the basic rationale of political unification and to sabotage the operations of supranational organs in charge of promoting integrative measures.

External Federators: The Soviet Union and the United States

The Soviet Union: A "Hostile" External Federator

One of the principal variables, if not the most cogent exogenous factor, in regional integration movements is the presence of an external threat, actual or perceived as such by the candidates for integration.[1] In the case of Western Europe, the Soviet Union served as a powerful galvanizing agent of the integrative movement at its take-off stage, a service rendered unintentionally but nevertheless of decisive importance.[2] Indeed, the irony of this impetus to European unification was that the Kremlin leaders desired the exact opposite: the isolation of Germany and Soviet hegemony in Europe.

Moscow's opposition to the European unity movement has always been based upon the dual components of Russian national interest and Communist doctrine. The former, a geopolitical factor, found (and still finds) its expression in the latent drive of the USSR to dominate the Eurasian continent from the Atlantic to Vladivostok. The latter, an ideological element, derives its rationale from the dogma of Marxism-Leninism which holds that Communism has to be spread around the world, with the Soviet leaders serving as chosen missionaries. The second task was apparently facilitated by the existence of a "fifth column" in Western Europe—the strong Communist parties in France and Italy which controlled about one-third of the respective electorates. Moreover, the Kremlin leaders disregarded the possibility of integrative efforts in the West since capitalist nations were by definition incapable of peaceful cooperation. Hence, the dogmatic Marxist view of internal Western contradictions as a permanent variable of their ideology, prevented the Soviets from seeing the counterproductive nature of their foreign policy. This wishful thinking of "what should not be, cannot be," not only blinded Stalin but continues to handicap Soviet foreign policy, as demonstrated by Moscow's reluctance to recognize the European Community by establishing diplomatic relations.

The promotion of the Russian national interest, however, was recognized as dependent on future developments in Europe in general, and on the fate of Germany in particular. It cannot be overemphasized what a disproportionate role Germany has played, and still plays, in Soviet policy-making. To be sure, this concern is based upon historical experience, but the danger of German militarism and revanchism has been conveniently used for many years as a bogeyman to keep Soviet satellites under subjugation. The use of an alleged foreign archenemy to consolidate domestic control had been reinforced by the strategic doctrine of "imperialist encirclement," which holds that aggressive capitalists, led by the United States, are constantly menacing the "peaceful, brotherly" Communist nations.

Against the background of these considerations, the European policy of the USSR took shape following the end of World War II. Its leitmotiv has been and still is the traditional Roman rule of *divide et impera*, which makes European unity without Soviet domination a political anathema to Moscow. In other words, the Soviet Union wants to lay down the law as the hegemonial power on the continent.

The pattern of the Kremlin's European policy became apparent soon after the Yalta Conference of February 1945, at which Stalin had joined Roosevelt and Churchill in the "Declaration of Liberated Europe," pledging the formation of democratic regimes in the newly liberated countries. In direct defiance of the spirit and letter of the Yalta Agreements, Stalin began the "russification" of Eastern Europe despite vehement protests by the Western Allies. The same happened with regard to the Potsdam Agreement of July 1945 (which dealt with the German question), when Stalin violated the procedures for joint occupation and four-power collaboration in Germany.

The first European statesman to recognize the "handwriting on the wall" and its implications for the West was Winston Churchill. Speaking at Westminster College in Fulton, Missouri, in March 1946, Churchill warned that an "iron curtain" had fallen from Stettin to Trieste, dividing Europe territorially and ideologically. He concluded that since the USSR was intent upon indefinite expansion of Soviet power and ideology and since Stalin respected only force, the Western nations had to forge a close political and military union in order to prevent the extension of the Soviet orbit to the Atlantic. Demonstrating his realism and the need for urgent and effective political measures, Churchill drew the conclusions from his "iron curtain speech" at the University of Zurich on September 19, 1946. On this occasion, Sir Winston deplored the lamentable economic and political conditions prevailing in postwar Europe and called for the creation of a "United States of Europe" patterned after the Swiss model.[3]

However, Churchill's warning was taken seriously only after the cold war had intensified as a result of growing Soviet hostility, intransigence, and self-imposed isolation. The isolationist aspect of Soviet foreign policy became evident when Molotov declined to accept the generous American offer to participate in the Marshall Plan. Not only did the USSR refuse to join in this proposed pan-European recovery program, but Moscow prevented other East European nations from participating in the work of the Committee on European Economic Cooperation (July 1947). Instead, the Soviet Union pressured its satellites into joining the *Cominform* (September 1947) and the *Comecon* (January 1949). This Russian-inspired polarization between the "people's democracies" in the East and free Western Europe reached a crisis stage in 1948: In February Stalin instigated the *coup* of Prague which resulted in the formal incorporation of Czechoslovakia into the Communist camp. This ruthless display of Stalinist tactics not only shocked the West but "helped to crystallize the idea of European unity by dramatizing the need for collective security measures."[4] In response to the challenge and under British leadership, France, the Benelux countries and the United Kingdom reached agreement within two weeks on the creation of the Brussels Treaty Organization, signed on March 17, 1948, which provided for automatic mutual, military assistance. In addition to common defense policies, the signatories also agreed "to strengthen ... the economic, social, and cultural ties ... [and] coordinate their efforts to create in Western Europe a firm basis for European economic recovery."[5] This major stepping-stone toward European unity was followed the next day by a "Motion on European Union" presented to the House of Commons by more than a hundred members, calling for a long-term policy "to create a democratic federation of Europe," and proposing the convocation of a "constituent assembly ... to frame a constitution for such a federation."[6] Although this ambitious project failed to materialize, the nucleus of the European unity movement had been established in Brussels.

As if Stalin wanted to accelerate this momentum, he imposed a blockade on Berlin in June 1948. Under the impact of this event, the United States decided to abandon its policy of neutrality and join with its European allies in the formation, in April 1949, of the Atlantic Alliance which in turn provided the essential umbrella of security under which the European unity movement could flourish.

In view of the rapid sequence of these events, there is little doubt about the positive feedback between Stalin's maneuvers, compounded by the specter of overt Soviet aggression, on the one hand, and the successful beginnings of the European unity movement on the other.

During the interregnum following Stalin's death in March 1953,[7] the collective leadership in the Kremlin attempted to de-Stalinize its rule, only to seek refuge in "traditional" means of oppression at the first opportunity, the impromptu uprising in East Berlin in June 1953.

This neo-Stalinist operation, performed by Russian tanks attacking unarmed civilians in the Communist sector of the former German capital, not only shocked the people of free Berlin but precipitated West Germany's rearmament and its admission to both the Western European Union (October 1954) and NATO (May 1955). Inasmuch as the *non plus ultra* of Soviet foreign policy consisted in the attempt to prevent the resurgence of the "revanchist" German Federal Republic, Germany's accession to Western organizations as an equal partner had to be considered as a severe setback to Moscow's ambitions in Europe and as a decisive step forward in European integration.

With the subsequent establishment of the Warsaw Pact (May 1955), the (ideological) cold war was complemented by two (military) camps in Europe, each dominated by a superpower.

When Khrushchev came to power in 1956, he denounced Stalinism and pronounced the scheme of "separate roads to socialism," a courageous but unrealistic attempt to liberalize Communist regimes. The inherent contradiction between limited freedom and totalitarian dictatorship manifested itself sooner than expected, namely in Poland and Hungary. Again Soviet *Realpolitik* triumphed over ideological polycentrism when Russian tanks mercilessly suppressed the anti-Communist uprisings in Poznan (June 1956) and Budapest (October 1956). Having restored order in the Soviet empire, Khrushchev mounted a spectacular peace-offensive toward the West, designed to extricate Germany from the Western entanglement and sabotage the *relance* of the Common Market. When it became apparent that this attempt had failed and West Germany enjoyed an unprecedented *Wirtschaftswunder*, the Soviets constructed the Berlin Wall in 1961 to prevent East Germans from escaping to the West which had become an attractive alternative to the regimented life in the Communist empire. Ironically the Kremlin leaders continued to preach peaceful coexistence with the capitalist nations.

However, as soon as West Germany, frustrated over the impasse on the question of German reunification, began to respond to the Kremlin's seductive proposals for reunification and rapprochement with Eastern European nations, Brezhnev decided to stage an encore of the *coup* of Prague in the summer of 1968. This flagrant violation of Czech sovereignty was justified in a surprisingly frank imperialist credo[8] and caused consternation among many people in the West who, inspired by Moscow's policy of peaceful coexistence, had engaged in wishful thinking about an impending East-West *détente*. Under the impact of China's rise in the East and in an effort to revive the seriously shaken *détente* policy, the Soviet Union launched an orchestrated peace-offensive designed to undermine the common sense of purpose of Western nations and to lull them into a feeling of false security. This divisive strategy began with the signing of a nonaggression treaty with the former archenemy, the German Federal Republic, in August 1970 and was followed by a Four-Power Accord on the status of Berlin (August 23, 1971). Simultaneously, Moscow advocated the convocation of a European Security Conference, allegedly designed to bring about a rapprochement between the Warsaw Pact and NATO through mutual, balanced force reduction. In reality this was an ill-conceived attempt to stabilize the *status quo* of Soviet control over Eastern Europe and hegemony on the European Continent, since US troops would have to retreat 3000 miles while the Red Army would move back only 300 miles, thus creating an obvious asymmetry of power. Most important, however, the pious expressions of peaceful *intent* by the leaders of the USSR hardly squared with the unprecedented military build-up of the Soviet armed forces which took place simultaneously and was aimed at achieving strategic superiority over the West.[9]

However, despite this apparent defect, the proposal has some attractive features for West Europeans, in general, who are eager to terminate the cold war, and for Germans desiring reunification in particular. The Soviet leaders are aware of this fact and use the ESC as a bargaining tool to prevent the consolidation of Western Europe. For instance, in his address to the 24th Congress of the Communist Party, Mr. Brezhnev declared that the USSR refuses to recognize the European Community since its existence only perpetuates the division of Europe; instead, he proposed a European Security Conference in which all Western nations (separately, rather than as a cohesive entity) would negotiate with the Soviet Union.[10] Among the experienced statesmen in Western Europe to reject the Soviet offer to convene a ESC was the new President of the European Movement, Walter Hallstein, who argued that such a meeting held prior to the enlargement and strengthening of the European Community would have a disintegrative effect on it.[11] Therefore, West European governments (with the support of the United States) appointed a common spokesman in the person of Signor Manlio Brosio (the former secretary-general of NATO) to represent them in future negotiations with the Soviet Union on European security issues. Hence, the Soviet attempt to divide the West actually resulted in the adoption of a common Western front toward the USSR, certainly an unintended result of Soviet policy.

Soviet opposition to the European Community is not so much directed against it as an economic bloc (from which the USSR stands to benefit commercially) as against its serving as the nucleus of European political unity. For instance, the Soviets have tried hard (if unsuccessfully) to deter Britain and the other EFTA countries from joining the Common Market (and consequently promoting unity) by sybilline warnings about each nation's losing its independence and prejudicing its vital interests. Furthermore, Soviet propaganda depicted the community as an economic arm of NATO, while stressing the differences between Europe and the United States. Radio Moscow also opposed

British entry on the ground that London insisted on expanding military cooperation within the framework of the community by favoring a joint nuclear arsenal—a plan to give the German Bundeswehr access to nuclear weapons.[12]

An additional reason for Soviet fears about European unification is that "Moscow considers a politically integrated Western Europe a major threat to the cohesion of its alliance system in Eastern Europe. Western Europe's economic, cultural, and political contacts have always been stronger with Eastern Europe than with the Soviet Union. Thus political unity in the West would be regarded as an intensely disturbing factor for the loyalties of East Europeans. One reason for the Soviet invasion of Czechoslovakia may well have been fears of closer economic links between that country and Western Europe. . . . [In short], although the Soviet Union accepts the status quo in Europe, disruption of the Western Alliance remains a high priority."[13]

Therefore, the Kremlin offers pan-European cooperation as an "alternative" to West European integration. Politically, it would bring about a *détente* between East and West and end the cold war; economically, it would open up the vast Soviet market. However, the Russian leaders definitely prefer an arrangement similar to COMECON, in which the Soviet Union is the dominant economic power and expects to exercise political control over the other members sooner or later. Since a strong European Community would present a permanent obstacle to the implementation of such an ambitious imperialist design, the Soviet government is determined to undermine its structures and try to block any further unifying measures. The negative reaction of the members of the enlarged European Community substantiated this proposition. Prior to the formal signing of the treaties, the Soviet press had already shown great irritation and launched a virulent attack against the project of building a ten-member bloc in the West. But once the formal ceremony in Brussels had established a *fait accompli*, the official organ of the Communist Party, *Pravda*, accused Britain of being the Trojan Horse of the United States and stated that "Europe today does not need any new closely associated political groups, but a policy of realism oriented towards the creation of an atmosphere of security, trust and cooperation between all States of the Continent."[14]

Since most enlightened European leaders recognize that the ultimate aim of Soviet policy is to prevent unification in the West in order to facilitate Soviet hegemony over Europe, the USSR serves as a negative external federator *par excellence*.

The United States: A "Benevolent" External Federator

If the Soviet Union served as an unintentional, coercive external federator, the United States served as a purposeful, benevolent external federator. Indeed, American support and advocacy of European unification have been among the most consistent elements of US foreign policy ever since the end of World War II. According to Jean Monnet's principal associate, "from the beginning the United States spurred Europe to unite."[15] In fact, "four Administrations [prior to Nixon's] have been committed to the recovery and to political integration of Europe."[16] Moreover, the United States "supported the goal of a united Western Europe of the kind contemplated by Monnet and Schuman."[17] To be sure, this policy had no precedence in diplomatic history, the paramount and persistent theme of which had been the *Realpolitik* of "divide and rule." Hence, the "European policy" of the United States since the end of the war could have been regarded as an exercise in altruism and idealism. Although an element of morality in terms of genuine concern for people in distress was undoubtedly present, it was overshadowed by a number of very concrete and realistic considerations.

First of all, Western Europe faced a "clear and present danger" of falling under Soviet domination unless immediate measures were taken to strengthen its defense posture; therefore, the principle of "unity makes strong" became the dominant aspect of the rationale of US diplomacy.

In order to assure the necessary economic base for military defense, the United States had to provide the means for the reconstruction of the national economies, a task that was greatly facilitated by the existing infrastructure of sophisticated manpower ready to apply its talents to the effective use of American resources. Apart from this immediate objective of assisting the European nations in the recovery effort, it was in the long-term national interest of the United States to promote the emergence of a viable economic partner across the Atlantic, capable of comanaging the international economic system and contributing its fair share to the development of the Third World. Finally, many American officials were understandably concerned about the problem of peace in Europe, an area notorious for its historical rivalries. After all, the United States had been forced to intervene twice against its will to restore democracy in the old world and had no desire to settle intra-European disputes in the future. However, the American government applied a lesson learned from previous experience when it wisely decided (in another unprecedented policy) to include the defeated powers in the recovery program, rather than repeating the counterproductive policy of vindictiveness through forced reparations and other means of retribution.[18] This generous gesture on the part of the principal victorious power vis-à-vis the victims of the war may have been the most lasting (although largely intangible) and impressive sign of the American commitment to European reconstruction.[19]

At this point it seems appropriate to note that the United States did not drift into supporting the European cause but consciously rejected the other option. When the United States decided to make support for European unification a principle of its foreign policy after the Second World War, it took the conscious risk of facilitating the rise of a rival power across the Atlantic, the scope and structure of which could not be predicted from Washington. Whereas the attractive features of the future European entity were identified quite easily— European political unity would eliminate the danger of both regional conflicts and create a bulwark against Communism—the potentially obnoxious traits of this US-sponsored unit were less clearly foreseen (or conveniently ignored). Yet it was inevitable that the emerging European grouping would sooner or later become an economic competitor of the US and an independent center of power in the international arena. The obvious strategy to control the structural development and external policy of this new Western power would have consisted in an American decision to organize an Atlantic community, involving the US, Canada, and Western Europe. Naturally, this course of action would have entailed a pooling of sovereignty with the other nations, an approach advocated by Clarence Streit and other Atlantic unionists.[20] However, the US government never considered this approach seriously and refused to take the initiative to build an "Atlantic Union now." Instead, the United States followed Winston Churchill's policy of noninvolvement with the Continental nations, a policy based upon the principle that "Europeans should unite—but without us" or that "integration is good for them but we do not want to participate in this endeavor."

Following the exposition of the complex rationale of the "European policy" of the United States since 1945, we shall now examine the "ways and means" by which it was implemented. The first illustrious spokesman for the benevolent external federator was Secretary of State George C. Marshall. Speaking at Harvard University on June 5, 1947, he described the seriousness of both the physical destruction and the dislocation of the entire fabric of the European economy and stressed the need for massive American assistance. However, he added, "before the United States Government can proceed much further in its efforts to alleviate the situation and help start the European world on its way to recovery, there must be some agreement among the countries of Europe as to the requirements of the situation and the part those countries themselves will take in order to give proper effect to whatever action might be undertaken by this Government. It would be neither fitting nor efficacious for this Government to undertake to draw up unilaterally a program designed to place Europe on its feet economically. This is the business of the Europeans. The initiative, I think, must come from Europe."[21] The European reaction to Mr. Marshall's challenge was prompt and enthusiastic: the people saw in the United States a kind of *deus ex machina* capable of providing material assistance, and political leaders and elites were inspired to take concrete action in an attempt to realize the ideal of European unity—at last. Following careful deliberations in the US Congress and frantic diplomatic activity in Europe, President Truman signed the Foreign Assistance Act (April 3, 1948), which authorized a sum of $5.3 billion for the European Recovery Program.

However, prior to the distribution of Marshall Plan aid to Western Europe, the sixteen participating countries had to draw up a joint program of resources and requirements according to the "Marshall formula." To this end they set up the Committee for European Economic Cooperation under Sir Oliver Franks and met in Paris on July 12, 1947. By September they had completed their mandate and traansmitted a comprehensive list to Washington. In addition to this "joint European inventory," Congress made foreign aid conditional upon "the continuous effort of participating countries to achieve a common program of recovery ... and to set up a permanent organization to this end."[22] Partially in response to this clause, the sixteen European governments involved signed the Convention of European Economic Cooperation (establishing the OEEC) in Paris on April 16, 1948. With the United States and Canada as associate members, the principal accomplishment of the OEEC was the liberalization of intra-European trade; it was complemented by the European Payments Union (sponsored by OEEC in 1950), which paved the road toward full convertibility of currencies. Despite these important achievements, the OEEC failed to promote political integration because the Marshall formula of "friendly aid" was not sufficient to overcome the reservations of certain governments (especially the British) to the idea of pooling sovereignty. Nevertheless, the OEEC and EPU made an indispensable contribution to the cause of European unity by serving as the first institutional vehicle for joint political efforts to deal with common economic problems, thus providing a training ground for "Euro-socialization"—the prerequisite for unification. Its qualified success was mainly due to the initiative and financial support of the United States, the benevolent external federator. However, American support for the concept of European unity in general, and of economic integration in particular, did not cease with the expiration of the Marshall Plan aid, which formally came to an end in December 1951, after having contributed about $11 billion dollars to European reconstruction.

Concurrently, the United States had sponsored NATO, which served not only as another instrument for European military cooperation (particularly through its integrated command structure), but provided the necessary protection for other joint endeavors by European nations. Among the organizations that were established in this formative period were the Council of Europe (1949), and the European Movement, which emerged from the Congress of Europe in the Hague (May 1948). At that time, the US State Department issued a declaration that "favored the progressively closer integration of the free nations of Western Europe,"[23] and was designed to give moral support to the cause of the Congress. *Hélas*, the first official "European" organization, the Council of Europe, was merely designed to promote greater political unity through a "closer association" between the member states, i.e., through traditional intergovernmental cooperation as favored by the British government.

This regression from the limited form of joint action achieved in OEEC greatly disappointed European federalists and dramatized the need for another, more ambitious undertaking. The first step in the direction of forming a

European federation was taken on May 9, 1950, when the then French Foreign Minister proposed his ambitious "Schuman Plan," which called essentially for peace through functional integration. The result of a genuine European initiative, it became operational when France, Germany, Italy, and the Benelux countries signed the Treaty of Paris, which took effect in 1952, creating a "supranational authority." The new European Coal and Steel Community immediately gained the official support of the United States,[24] although Americans had to reconcile unconditional support for regional integration with the desire for global trade liberalization. However, the argument that European unification was in the interest of the United States prevailed, as symbolized by the strong language used by the US Congress in the Mutual Security Act of 1952, which read as follows: "The Congress welcomes the recent progress in political federation, military integration, and economic unification in Europe and reaffirms its belief in the necessity of further vigorous efforts towards these ends as a means of building strength, establishing security and peace in the North Atlantic area."[25]

This favorable response to the creation of ECSC prompted another bold French initiative, namely the proposal for a supranational European Defense Community. Based upon the "Pleven Plan" (after the then French Prime Minister), this project aimed at the formation of an integrated European army with a unified command. It was logically linked to the proposal for a European Political Community that would have perfectly complemented the existing ECSC.

The Eisenhower administration's strong support of the EDC project facilitated its acceptance by the six governments concerned, and the treaty was signed in Paris on May 27, 1952. But the process of ratification was noticeably slow and came to a virtual standstill when the Korean War ended in the summer of 1953. At that point, the United States took the initiative in an effort to prevent what was considered to be a potential catastrophe. It was Secretary of State John Foster Dulles who pointedly warned the European opponents of the EDC regarding the consequences of its failure. Speaking in Paris in December 1953, he threatened an "agonizing reappraisal" of US foreign policy in the event of nonratification of the Treaty.[26] Notwithstanding intense American diplomatic pressure, the French Parliament rejected the EDC in August 1954, thus bringing the European unity movement to an abrupt halt. Following the vote in the French Parliament,[27] Dulles issued a bitterly worded statement calling it a "tragedy."[28] This term is not inappropriate in view of the relatively small parliamentary majority against the treaty which was nevertheless capable of frustrating the official will of the six governments concerned. The French deputies apparently rejected the treaty out of the dual fear of German militarism and of the need for a surrender of sovereignty, compounded by their inability to cope with the dilemma of wanting a German army bigger than that of the Soviet Union, but smaller than that of France.

This turn of events came as a shock to both Europeans and Americans—to the former because it demonstrated a lack of common purpose at a crucial time in the European unity movement, and to the latter because many Americans had hoped that Europeans would follow their example and build a federation patterned after the political system of the United States.

Nonetheless, the brusque criticism of Secretary Dulles (directed particularly against the French and the British, who had disassociated themselves from the EDC venture) did have some positive effects: immediately following the *débacle* of August, the British government proposed an alternative to the EDC, an initiative which resulted in the creation of the Western European Union in October 1954. Although this new organization was devoid of the supranational features of the EDC project, it nevertheless served as a useful arena for intra-European military cooperation within the framework of NATO.[29]

The collapse of the EDC affected the tactics of the "European policy" of the United States but not its strategy, which remained committed to the cause of European unity. The test came the following year when the six members of the ECSC decided on a *relance* of European integration at the Conference of Messina (June 1955). In a favorable response to this auspicious development, Secretary Dulles welcomed moves "toward a United States of Europe on terms of economic and political unity."[30] However, the tone of American policy statements had changed from fervent advocacy to quiet support or tacit approval.

At this juncture in European diplomacy, the United Kingdom proposed the establishment of a Free Trade Area for Western Europe, a barely disguised attempt to sabotage the project of a Common Market which was drafted at the Messina meeting. In an effort to win American support for this purely intergovernmental arrangement, Prime Minister Eden visited Washington in 1956. But his mission apparently failed since he declared, with a certain resignation, that "The U.S. Government entertained for the proposals resulting from the Messina Conference the same enthusiasm as they had shown towards the ill-fated EDC."[31] In fact, as soon as the EEC and Euratom were established in 1957, President Eisenhower formally welcomed "the efforts of a number of our European friends to achieve an integrated community to develop a common market . . . and a cooperative effort in the field of atomic energy."[32] By giving preference to the creation of a smaller but more cohesive entity (the European Community) over a larger but loosely organized group (the Free Trade Area), the United States again demonstrated its belief in the intrinsic value and potential of European political unification as compared to economic cooperation. However, in order to mitigate the split between the Six and the newly established British-sponsored European Free Trade Association (1959), the United States decided to join with Canada and West European nations in a new Atlantic organization, OECD, which replaced OEEC in December 1960. Furthermore, OECD was to become an enlarged forum for dealing with common economic problems and coordinating expanded development assistance programs.

American support for European integration reached a new high when the Kennedy administration assumed power in 1961, by which time Britain had decided to apply for membership in the Common Market. In an effort to find an imaginative and realistic formula for future Atlantic relationships, the partnership concept emerged as the "grand design" of the US government. Unofficially referred to as "operation dumbbell"—symbolizing a relationship of two powers with comparatively equal weight—the new policy was designed to give formal recognition to both the "New Europe" and Atlantic interdependence. It was officially formulated by President Kennedy on Independence Day, July 4, 1962, in Philadelphia. On this historic occasion, the American president called upon the European Community to join the United States in an "Atlantic Partnership" of equals. President Kennedy first emphasized the fact that his administration would continue to pursue the same policy toward Western Europe which had been initiated by the Marshall Plan after World War II and expressed his satisfaction with the progress achieved by the Common Market since 1958. He said:

The nations of Western Europe . . . are joining together . . . to find freedom in diversity and unity in strength. The United States looks on this vast new enterprise with hope and admiration. We do not regard a strong and united Europe as a rival but as a partner. To aid its progress has been the basic objective of our foreign policy for seventeen years.[33]

Stressing the need for close cooperation between the European Economic Community and the United States in the future, the American president sketched the "grand design": "We believe that a united Europe will be capable of playing a greater role in the common defense, of responding more generously to the needs of poorer nations, of joining with the United States and others, in lowering trade barriers, resolving problems of currency and commodities, and developing coordinated policies in all other economic, diplomatic, and political areas. We see in such a Europe a partner with whom we could deal on a basis of full equality in all the great and burdensome tasks of building and defending a community of free nations."[34]

He then urged the European nations to increase their efforts in order to achieve political unity: "It would be premature at this time to do more than to indicate the high regard with which we view the formation of this partnership. The first order of business is for our European friends to go forward in forming the more perfect union which will some day make this partnership possible."[35] Finally, the American president stated that the United States is ready for a Euro-American partnership: "But I will say here and now that the United States will be ready for a 'Declaration of Interdependence,' that we will be prepared to discuss with a United Europe the ways and means of forming a concrete Atlantic partnership, a mutually beneficial partnership between the new union now emerging in Europe and the old American Union founded here one hundred and seventy-five years ago."[36]

The entire "grand design" reflected the convictions of Jean Monnet and his unofficial "liaison Officer" in Washington, US Under-Secretary of State George Ball. In fact, the new policy was so perfectly orchestrated that it is plausible that Kennedy and Monnet arrived at a consensus on the "declaration of interdependence" during the latter's visit to the White House in the spring of 1962. This assumption is reinforced by the similarity in the wording of a declaration of the Action Committee for the United States of Europe, issued on June 26, 1962, which stated:

While the economic unity of Europe is being consolidated and a start made on its political unification, the cooperation that has already grown up between the United States and European countries should gradually be transformed into a partnership between a United Europe and the United States . . . a relationship of two separate but equally powerful entities, each bearing its share of common responsibilities in the world. This partnership is natural and inevitable because the peoples of Europe and America share the same civilization based on freedom, and conduct their public life in accordance with democratic principles.[37]

This dramatic meeting of the minds—coincidental or orchestrated—of an American President and "Mr. Europe," demonstrated clearly that the United States firmly supported the dual concepts of European integration and Atlantic cooperation as compatible and mutually reinforcing policies. The "official" European reaction came from the Commission of the European Economic Community in a statement hailing the American partnership proposal. It read as follows: "The declaration made by President Kennedy on Independence Day was received with real satisfaction in the Commission of the European Economic Community. In President Kennedy's reference to the historic significance of European progress toward unity and the need to build a free world under just and orderly conditions, the Commission sees more than a renewed affirmation of the European undertaking. President Kennedy's words are also a challenge to accept great opportunities of our age—to move forward swiftly and directly to the achievement of full European unification and thus to lay the foundations of an Atlantic partnership, a partnership which takes into account a responsibility to the entire free world."[38]

Addressing the European Parliament on June 26, 1963, Commission President Hallstein referred to President Kennedy's "Declaration of Interdependence" when he said, "What do these words mean basically? They mean nothing less than a recognition that the United States is prepared to share, and is already sharing, the position of world power—which it is the only nation in the free world to possess—with a Europe which is increasingly assuming economic and political proportions comparable to its own, is ready to accept the principle of equality in this partnership, and wishes to collaborate with an organized Europe in mastering common problems and world problems. Our answer to this can only be in the affirmative."[39]

A prominent European analyst and one of the drafters of the Rome Treaty welcomed the American partnership proposal because it "contains three essential elements. It recognizes that the United States is no longer the sole great power in the Western world in the full sense of that term. It recognizes that another power is being born—still far behind the United States in terms of volume of production, but nevertheless of comparable size. It accepts the principle of equality, of responsibility and of joint authority for making decisions, accompanied by an equitable sharing of burdens."[40]

In conclusion, the same analyst stated that what makes Atlantic partnership particularly palatable to Europeans is, in fact, that it would "start with the recognition that Europe as such has begun to exist. It would acknowledge the growing reality of this Europe already on its way toward unity. It would call for a reinforcement of this European unity so as to establish between two groupings of comparable weight the basis of coordinated action."[41] Most importantly, the partnership proposal assumes that Europe would be united and that this united Europe would constitute a positive element in trans-Atlantic relations, since the balance of power would be redressed. In fact, an American observer suggested, "if Western Europe can become a political, military and economic unit, both Europe and the United States may put an end to a problem which has plagued their relations throughout the postwar period: Europe's sense of inferiority to and dependence on American power. A united Europe will be able to deal with the United States on equal terms . . . [and henceforth] a trans-Atlantic bond of equality will prove more enduring than one of dependence."[42]

One of the fathers of the "dumbbell" concept expressed the official position of the State Department when he stated that "a strong partnership must almost by definition mean a collaboration of equals. When one partner possesses over 50% of the resources of a firm, and the balance is distributed among 16 or 17 others, the relationship is unlikely to work very well. . . . It was in recognition of this fact that since the war we have consistently encouraged the powerful drive toward European integration."[43]

However, General de Gaulle emerged as a serious obstacle to the realization of the "grand design," particularly with his veto of Britain's admission to the EEC, expressed at a news conference in January 1963. Even though de Gaulle's nationalist policies blocked substantial progress toward the achievement of the Atlantic partnership, thus providing the United States with a good reason to follow up on John Foster Dulles's threat of an agonizing reappraisal of American policy toward Europe, Washington remained calm and determined to resist the temptation to retaliate against this vexing and obstinate "ally."

Commenting on the enduring value of the ideal of European unity and

Atlantic cooperation, Paul-Henri Spaak, a true *homo atlanticus*, recommended the "outlasting" of General de Gaulle when he declared that "these ideas are still held today by the overwhelming majority of European statesmen. They are shared by the overwhelming majority of European people. Let us not, then, be dismayed. . . . The dissident element constituted by current French policy may be a cause of delay, but it cannot prevent the ultimate success of the great undertaking to which Europe and the United States have set their hands."[44] In fact, his advice was followed by all Western statesmen.

The Johnson administration also affirmed its belief in the validity of the "grand design" and remained faithful (though not ardent) in its support of the European cause. President Johnson declared in January 1964 that the American government "welcomed the emergence of a Europe growing in unity and strength. For we know that only a uniting Europe can be a strong Europe and only a strong Europe will be an effective partner."[45]

Again, on April 4, 1964, the American president, speaking on the occasion of the fifteenth anniversary of NATO, declared that "the union of Europe is her manifest destiny . . . [and] we welcome the new strength of our transatlantic allies . . . [and] are eager to share with the new Europe at every level of power and responsibility."[46] Johnson's Secretary of State Dean Rusk, commenting on the widely expressed feeling that de Gaulle's frontal attack on the concept of Atlantic Partnership had completely undermined or rendered obsolete the basic principles of US foreign policy, admitted that de Gaulle has temporarily halted the evolution, "but this has not, as some commentators have dramatically asserted, left our Atlantic policy in shambles. On the contrary, the main lines of that policy have become more than ever valid and urgent."[47]

However, when de Gaulle vetoed British accession to the EEC for the second time (1967) and severed French ties with NATO (1966), it appeared as if the partnership idea had evaporated and that European integration would be blocked for a long time to come.

Under these circumstances it was not surprising that criticism arose concerning the validity of the traditional European policy of the United States. One of these critics was Henry Kissinger, who argued that "in the recent past, the United States has often defeated its purposes by committing itself to one particular form of European unity—that of federalism. . . . In the next decade the architestonic approach to Atlantic policy will no longer be possible. The American contribution must be more philosophical; it will have to consist more of understanding and quiet, behind-the-scenes encouragement than of the propagation of formal institutional structures."[48] On another occasion, the same analyst warned that in the future "the passionate commitment of so many American policymakers to a single formula of European integration, that of supranationality, could in fact bring about results quite contrary to those intended. The United States should therefore leave the internal evolution of a united Europe to the Europeans and use its ingenuity and influence in divising new forms of Atlantic cooperation."[49]

Another line of criticism in the United States developed as it became increasingly clear that the Common Market had become an economic giant, thus fulfilling the expectations of those who saw in it a partner as well as of those who feared that it would emerge as a rival. Hence, some critics not only recommended reduced urgency in American advocacy of European integration but actually questioned the very assumptions of the traditional "dumbbell theory." Claiming that the European unity movement had entered a period of stagnation, they argued that American economic sacrifices have begun to outweigh political advantages of potential European unity. In the words of one of these critics, "There is no longer any reason to pay a commercial prize for non-existent political unity in Europe."[50]

Although this argument has some validity and is understandable in the light of certain protectionist features of the EEC, it does not invalidate the basic principle of traditional US policy. After President Nixon assumed office in 1969, he set the record straight in an unmistakable tone: "We favor a definition by Western Europe of a distinct identity, for the sake of its own continued vitality and independence of spirit. Our support for the strengthening and broadening of the European Community has not diminished. We recognize that our interest will necessarily be affected by Europe's evolution, and we may have to make sacrifices in the common interest. We consider that the possible economic price of a truly unified Europe is outweighed by the gain in the political vitality of the West as a whole."[51]

In his "State of the World" message of February 25, 1971, the American president stated that "the evolution of a mature partnership reflecting the vitality and independence of Western European nations" had priority on his agenda. Mr. Nixon added that "our partnership, once a vehicle for our underwriting of Europe's defense and recovery, has grown into a more balanced, dynamic and complex coalition. We welcome this success of our postwar policies. . . . The United States has always supported the strengthening and enlargement of the European Community. We still do."[52]

The American president, however, refrained from recommending a formula for European unification. He said that "Western Europe is uniting, and will soon be in a position to forge an identity of its own, distinct from America within the Atlantic world. . . . Our friends must soon decide, then, how they see Europe's role in the world and its relationship with us. The form and degree of its unity is for the Europeans to settle."[53]

In his foreign policy report to Congress of February 9, 1972, President Nixon commented on the emergence of the New Europe of Nine and its potential impact on Atlantic relationships. He stated that

the United States is realistic. This change means the end of American tutelage and the end of the era of automatic unity. But discord is not inevitable either. The challenge to our maturity and political skill is to establish a new practice in

Atlantic unity—finding common ground in a consensus of independent policies instead of in deference to American prescriptions. This essential harmony of our purposes is the enduring link between a uniting Europe and the United States. This is why we have always favored European unity and why we welcome its growth not only in geographical area but also into new spheres of policy. We continue to feel that political and defense cooperation will be the fulfillment of European unity. European and American interests in defense and East-West diplomacy are fundamentally parallel and give sufficient incentive for coordinating independent policies. Two strong powers in the West would add flexibility to Western diplomacy, and could increasingly share the responsibilities of decision.[54]

The Secretary of State also reaffirmed the continuity of the European policy of the United States in the 1970s when he declared that "the Administration firmly and unequivocally supports this process of European integration. We support it because we are confident that the people of Western Europe and the people of the United States share the same values and that European and American strength can only supplement each other. We support it even though we recognize that the process of integration may produce some economic dislocations and disagreements between us as Europe develops new economic policies and as our economies adjust."[55]

Secretary Rogers also welcomed the enlargement of the European Community "as a major step toward realization of the full constructive potential of Europe."[56] He added that "as the Common Market enlarges a production and consumption area comparable to the United States will be created, Europe's economic growth will be further accelerated and the prospects of closer European political cooperation will be enhanced. An already strong western Europe will become an even more powerful and self-confident participant in the political, economic, and security affairs of the world. . . . [Hence] it is axiomatic that the United States desires close cooperative relations with our friends and allies. . . ."[57]

The Secretary of State reiterated American support for the enlargement of the European Community in his official report and added that "we are aware that, as Western Europeans develop collective policies, their views and ours, particularly on economic issues, will not always coincide. . . . But we have never ceased to believe that Western Europe's growing economic and political strength can only reinforce our own and thus be of mutual benefit."[58]

The proposition that the United States served as the benevolent external federator for the uniting Europe after World War II has been corroborated by "Mr. Europe" himself in the following statement: "Ever since the Marshall Plan, and Schuman Plan, American support for European unity has never faltered. I can testify from my own experience that this support has been invaluable in bringing European unity to the point where it is today. For once, the most powerful country in the world has helped others to unite instead of adopting the old principle of divide and rule."[59]

Having recognized the historically unprecedented American policy of consciously contributing to the rise of a potential rival power across the Atlantic, Jean Monnet expressed his belief in the interdependence of the West when he declared that "Europe and America must both acknowledge that neither of us is defending a particular country, but that we are all defending our common civilization."[60]

The same proposition has also been supported by a European federalist who stressed the unique friendship and efforts on the part of a dominant power, the United States, since the end of World War II in facilitating unification (instead of exploiting disunity) and promoting the emergence of a United States of Europe.[61]

The United States as an Indirect External Federator

As shown in the preceding section, the American government has officially supported the concept of European unity ever since the end of World War II. However, American support has not been expressed only in this fashion. Naturally, the formal declarations on the part of administration spokesmen in favor of European unification were the most obvious demonstrations; however, this important *political* support was complemented by a series of less spectacular but equally significant cultural expressions of solidarity with the European cause. For instance, Americans usually and unconsciously refer to "Europe" as an entity, rather than to its individual components. This is true for government officials,[62] as well as American businessmen (who run multinational companies) and ordinary tourists, who feel an instinctive attraction to the "old world" and an urge to go to "Europe" (instead of announcing a visit to Italy, Germany, Britain, etc.). It is therefore not surprising that many people on the Continent feel that "Americans are the best Europeans." Of course, this feeling has been reinforced by the US-sponsored "partnership" idea which was congenial to most Europeans because "there is a natural affinity among West Europeans vis-à-vis the Americans, which is why the idea of a united Europe acting as a complement to the United States has been so attractive."[63]

Apart from these largely subconscious sociopsychological elements of American support for the European cause, there are powerful American pressures in the economic field which often produce unintended (although not necessarily unwelcome) results in Western Europe. The following examples for the United States serving as "indirect external federator" can be given. First, the United States proposed the "Kennedy Round" of trade negotiations which inevitably forced the West European governments to adopt a common platform and harmonize their commercial policies.[64] This pattern of pressure continues in the 1970s as the United States urges the European nations to negotiate new trade agreements with Washington within the framework of GATT, and to adopt a common position in the monetary field within IMF. Second, the United States is in the process of gradually reducing American forces in Europe which, in turn, provides a powerful incentive for Western Europeans to unite politically in order to be able to defend themselves militarily. This incentive is accompanied by formal American requests for greater European "burden-sharing" in NATO, a legitimate demand which requires cost reduction through integration of European defense establishments. In fact, the "Nixon Doctrine" gave new impetus to the European unity movement as it called for increased "self-help" on the part of American allies around the world through the development of regional political cooperation and indigenous defense capabilities. This doctrine applied to Western Europe took the form of requests on the part of the administration for an enlarged contribution of the European members of NATO to Atlantic defense costs. It was significantly reinforced by rising pressures in the US Senate for a substantial reduction of American troops in Europe. It was in direct response to this dual pressure that ten West European NATO nations organized the so-called Eurogroup in 1970. This European nucleus within the Atlantic Alliance subsequently adopted a five-year "European Defense Improvement Program" which provides for increased European defense contributions in terms of collective financial and technological efforts. Thus the United States serves— albeit because of domestic political considerations—as a real promotor of European defense cooperation.

All these examples illustrate the role of the United States as an indirect external federator that *nolens volens* advances European unity.

Internal Federators: The European Commission and the Action Committee for the United States of Europe

An integrative movement is propelled by both external pressures and internal forces which interact and are, in turn, subject to the negative influence of inhibitors intent upon preventing further progress toward political unity. In the preceding section we identified the two external federators which facilitated European integration through complementary initiatives—the Soviet threat to Europe's security and American support for European unification.

In the following section we will identify the two principal "internal federators" of the European unity movement, namely the European Commission (the "official" internal federator) and the Action Committee for the United States of Europe (the "unofficial" internal federator).

The European Commission

The European Commission is an organ *sui generis* which derives its powers from the treaties establishing the European Community.[66] Although a creature of sovereign states, its authority transcends national jurisdiction in certain specified functional areas. The commission has supranational attributes in the sense that its members are independent international civil servants ("Eurocrats") and that it is the only truly "European" body, representing the common interests of all members of the community.

The commission's principal mission is the implementation of the objectives of the Treaties of Paris and Rome. However, the commission has substantial latitude *within* the legal framework of the treaties to accelerate integrative steps and to expand its tasks to related functions not specifically defined in the "constitution." In its effort to achieve economic integration, the commission, in effect, promotes political unity since the former constitutes a *sine qua non* for the latter: it predisposes the participants to political cooperation beyond the sphere of successful economic integration. Hence the commission serves as an internal federator to the extent that it facilitates *policy harmonization* within the European Community; it cannot, however, expand its own jurisdiction beyond the treaty parameters.

Among the "supranational" powers of the commission is its *right of initiative* to submit new proposals to the Council of Ministers for decision. This function as the "engine of the Community," together with its comprehensive planning authority, permits the commission to provide the ferment of change to serve as a dynamic internal federator of the European Community. Since virtually all policy proposals originate from the commission, and since the council can reject its proposals only by unanimous vote, "no one has a veto power on progress, and everyone has a veto against regression."[67]

The official mandate of the commission enables it to act on behalf of the community through bold policy initiatives and effective administrative measures, designed to advance the cause of integration.

With a view to ensuring the functioning and development of the Common Market, the Commission shall: ensure the application of the provisions of this Treaty and of the provisions enacted by the institutions of the Community in pursuance thereof; *formulate recommendations or opinions* in matters which are subject to this Treaty, where the latter expressly so provides or where the *Commission considers it necessary*; under the conditions laid down in this Treaty dispose of a *power of decision of its own* and participate in the preparation of acts of the Council and of the Assembly; and exercises the competence conferred on it by the Council for the implementation of the rules laid down by the latter.[68] (Italics added)

The scope of these powers gives the commission an unprecedented influence over the destiny of the community and differs qualitatively from those given to traditional international administrative organs. Indeed, "one can scarcely find a better example of political dynamism in the whole world of international organization."[69]

Despite its collegiate nature, the commission soon became an energetic and innovative body under the able leadership of Professor Walter Hallstein, the first President of the European Commission.

To demonstrate the crucial role of the commission as internal federator in the European Community the following three case studies have been selected: the proposals for the creation of a common agricultural policy; the establishment of an autonomous budget; and the formation of an economic and monetary union.

A Common Agricultural Policy (CAP). Whereas the Rome Treaty was very specific with regard to the modalities for achieving a customs union through the elimination of trade barriers among the members and the erection of a common external tariff vis-à-vis nonmembers, its provisions on agricultural policy were extremely vague. Indeed, the treaty contained a specific timetable for the progressive reduction of tariffs on manufactured products, but it set forth only general goals for agricultural goods: "member states shall gradually develop the common agricultural policy during the transitional period and shall establish it not later than at the end of that period."[70] If the treaty itself served as a potent instrument to achieve a customs union (a goal completed ahead of schedule on July 1, 1968), the commission had to assume the difficult task of translating the general objective of a CAP into specific policy measures. This mission was complicated by a number of structural problems in the agricultural sectors of the six economies: a comparatively large part of the work force (between 20 and 40 percent) was engaged in farming; governments protected small farmers against foreign competition and assured their incomes through massive subsidies; and finally, the divergent demands of surplus food producers (e.g., France) and importers of agricultural goods (e.g., Germany) had to be reconciled.

Hence, "to work out a common policy that would require all countries to change their established practices and policies indeed seemed a herculean task. . . . [It was] the hardest area of all to integrate."[71] Despite these obstacles, which were compounded by the emotional and nationalist attitudes of the peasantry, the commission, under the skillful leadership of Vice-President Sicco Mansholt, took up the challenge of formulating a CAP. In November 1959, the commission issued its first draft proposal, which led to an agreement in principle on the CAP in 1962. This was followed by a series of proposals which resulted in an agreement on a common farm policy for rice, beef, and dairy products in December 1963. Constant prodding by the energetic vice-president, the vital support of specialized "management committees," and extended marathon sessions with the Council of Ministers, as well as Gaullist pressure, resulted in the adoption of a common price for grains (December 1964) and for milk and dairy products, fats, oils, beef, veal, sugar, and rice (July 1966). Consequently, by 1967 "the scope of the common agricultural market was extended to 90 percent of the total production."[72] As a "reward" for its successful efforts, the commission was later given the power of administering the European Agricultural Guidance and Guarantee Fund (FEOGA), an important financial instrument for regulating the market mechanism. With the decisions of the Summit Conference of the Hague, complemented by the council decisions of February 1970, the CAP had come into being in accordance with the Rome Treaty provisions and against all odds.

The successful implementation of the first "Mansholt Plan" was primarily due to the tenacity of the commission and its dynamic vice-president. To be sure, the series of steps leading to the CAP "were taken at the initiative of the Commission. The policy adopted by the Community conforms quite closely to that desired by the Commission. Indeed, the CAP is in a real sense the creation of Commissioner Mansholt, . . . a veritable European minister of agriculture."[73]

An Autonomous Budget for the Community. Although agreement on a CAP for many important products had been achieved by the summer of 1965, there was still disagreement on its financing. Since the French government was extremely eager to settle this question (in the interest of the French farmers who were surplus producers), Commission President Hallstein concocted an ingenious plan, containing desirable and undesirable elements from the French point of view. Elaborated by the commission and officially presented to the European Parliament on March 31, 1965, the "Hallstein Plan" contained three interlaced elements: the first part dealt with the "carrot" for de Gaulle—a formula for the financing of the CAP in accordance with French recommendations. However, Hallstein also included "escalated demands" for transferring the power of the purse over a common fund (composed of both the levies on agricultural imports and the proceeds of industrial tariffs), to the commission. Finally, he proposed that, given the large amount of money involved, this independent community budget be placed under the democratic control of the European Parliament, which would have to be strengthened in order to fulfill this responsibility.[74]

This loaded, radical proposal was subsequently placed on the agenda of the Council of Ministers in a modified form, but it proved unacceptable to de Gaulle, mainly because of its highly political overtones. The French president recognized the potential of the "Hallstein Plan" as a potent means of political integration and used the pretext of a discord in the council over the financing of the CAP on June 30, 1965, to suspend French participation in the operations of the community institutions for six months. During this "constitutional crisis," de Gaulle questioned the good faith of France's five partners and attacked the "political pretensions of the federalist Commission" at a press conference. He stated that "this embryonic technocracy, in large part foreign, which was to trample over French democracy and settle problems crucial to our existence, obviously did not suit us. . . . The Commission suddenly abandoned its political reserve and formulated terms . . . whereby it would have a budget of its own . . . that would be submitted to the Assembly for consideration . . . which is essentially an advisory body."[75] De Gaulle's anger and outrage over the audacity of the "Hallstein Plan" and his vitriolic attacks on the commission indirectly attest to its effectiveness in formulating far-reaching proposals in the interest of the community. "What is perhaps most striking in de Gaulle's speech was his decision to do battle with the Commission. He would almost certainly have preferred to ignore the Eurocrats as beneath his concern out of the consideration that a direct confrontation could only close 'the prestige gap.' Thus, the direct attack should probably be viewed as a left-handed sign of respect and as an indication that de Gaulle felt himself threatened by the Commission in some significant ways."[76]

The French boycott lasted until January 1966 when French representatives resumed their regular functions in Brussels following a special meeting of the Council of Ministers in Luxembourg which modified procedures in the European Community.[77] The unfortunate casualty of the bold "Hallstein Plan" turned out to be its sponsor, who resigned under heavy Gaullist pressure (only to become the outspoken president of the European Movement). However, the "moribund" proposals of the commission, first announced by Mr. Hallstein in Strasbourg in 1965, were accepted in their entirety by the leaders of the six countries at their summit meeting at the Hague in December 1969. The final communiqué stated:

As regards the completion of the Communities, the Heads of State or Government reaffirmed the will of their Governments to pass from the transitional period to the final stage of the European Community and accordingly to lay down a definitive *financial arrangement* for the *Common Agricultural Policy* by the end of 1969. They agreed progressively to replace, within the framework of this financial arrangement, the contributions of member countries by their own resources, taking into account all interests concerned, with the object of achieving in due course the *integral financing of the Communities' budgets* in accordance with the procedure provided for in Article 201 of the Treaty establishing the EEC and of *strengthening the budgetary powers of the European Parliament.*[78] (Italics added.)

This case study of the development of the community budget from the initial proposal in 1965 to its adoption four years later demonstrates the effectiveness of the European Commission in launching audacious proposals which gradually gained acceptance. Following the "planting of the seeds" in the minds of the participants in integrative venture, this plan ripened in an evolutionary process because of its compelling, objective logic and finally became official community policy.

"Planning" for an Economic and Monetary Union. The achievement of an "economic community" is the principal goal of the EEC Treaty. It is the last phase of the process of economic integration which involves—in ascending degrees—a customs union characterized by free trade among the members and a common external tariff; a common market characterized by the free movement of goods, labor, and capital; and an economic union. The latter involves a complete harmonization of national economic and monetary policies—in other words, some kind of central planning. However, the signatories of the Rome Treaty, in establishing this "European Economic Community," failed to provide it with the necessary planning organism to implement this ambitious goal. The basic reason for this serious neglect was ideological: the French economic doctrine of "dirigism" was incompatible with the German belief in a "freie Marktwirtschaft," and this dichotomy was built into the Rome Treaty. Naturally, it became the cause for frequent "ideological" confrontations between the two camps.

Under these circumstances, the European Commission had to serve as an arbiter by interpreting the doctrine of the treaty as one of a "mixed economy" involving as much free-market liberalism as possible and as much planning as necessary. The compromise concept was labelled "programming," a type of limited, indicative planning patterned after the French model but avoiding the terminology to which the Germans were traditionally allergic.

The commission's first attempt to launch a comprehensive scheme for arriving at an "economic and monetary union" in gradual phases was its Memorandum on the Action Program for the Second Stage. Submitted to the Council on October 24, 1962, this "Action Program" called for specific actions within a four-year period to promote an economic union. The commission argued for the formation of a "Community short-term policy into which national policies will merge":[79] in other words, they advocated "planning." The "Action Program" came immediately under attack by the German Minister of Economics, Dr. Ludwig Erhard, who criticized the memorandum on the grounds that "two different [economic] systems cannot exist side by side. It is impossible to pursue, on the one side, competition and, on the other, planning, planification or programmization."[80]

Despite continued German opposition to the principle of planning, the council accepted the rationale of the commission on April 15, 1964, when it established the so-called Medium-Term Economic Policy Committee and charged it with the drafting of a five-year economic policy program under the supervision of the commission.[81] Encouraged by this breakthrough, the commission submitted a complementary memorandum to the council on September 30, 1964; in this so-called Initiative 1964, the commission stressed the urgent needs for an early harmonization of monetary policies.[82]

Having submitted its dual package-plan for an economic and monetary union through concerned planning efforts, the commission drafted its first "Medium-Term Economic Policy Program," which was accepted by the council on February 8, 1967, and marked a milestone in the development of the European Community.[83]

Working in cooperation with the "Medium-Term Economic Policy Committee" and the "Monetary Committee," the commission was remarkably successful in its challenging task of overcoming ideological differences and mastering the difficult problem of making economic projections without having comprehensive aggregate data. The subsequent acceptance of the commission's second and third Medium-Term Economic Policy Programs (the latter covering the period from 1971 to 1975) by the council[84] seems to indicate that "programming" has become an accepted part of the community method. It also suggests that the (albeit limited) planning function entrusted to the commission has elevated it to a potentially powerful apparatus with far-reaching oversight over the economic policies of the European Community.

Subsequently the commission continued to press for further action toward achieving a genuine economic and monetary union. In its "Memorandum to the Council on the Co-ordination of Economic Policies and Monetary Cooperation within the Community" of February 12, 1969, the commission called for the "fuller concerting of the short-term economic policies, and Community machinery for monetary cooperation."[85] This initiative was followed up by the so-called Communities' Work Program, submitted to the council on March 29, 1969, in which the commission outlined the major tasks facing the community in the 1970s: (1) the creation of a genuine Common Market, necessitating the complete removal of all barriers to the free movement of goods, persons, services, and capital and the elimination of distortions and impairments of competition within the community; (2) the establishment of a common economic policy, a goal of increasing urgency because as national barriers fall, the risk grows that isolated economic policies will conflict and, unless coordinated, will threaten the already integrated sectors. Therefore, the commission proposed the harmonization of general economic policies (medium-term economic policy, anticyclical, financial and monetary policies), commercial policy, agricultural policy, industrial policy, policy on research and technology, energy policy, transport policy, regional policy and social policy; (3) the enlargement of the community; (4) the merger of the communities; and (5) the creation of a sound financial base for the community.[86]

These two commission documents became the basis for the agenda of the Summit Conference of the six Heads of State at the Hague in December 1969. On this occasion the governmental leaders of the six member states of the European Community reaffirmed their will to promote an economic and monetary union "on the basis of the memorandum presented by the Commission on February 12, 1969, and in close cooperation with the Commission."[87] Moreover, the final communiqué of the Summit Meeting reflected the issues outlined by the commission in its Communities' Work Program, issues that can be summarized under three headings: consolidation, strengthening, and enlargement.[88]

The commission's proposal of February 1969 also served as the basis for the "Interim Report on the Establishment by Stages of Economic and Monetary Union," an elaborate document drafted by an *ad hoc* group chaired by M. Pierre Werner from Luxembourg. This "Werner Report" was submitted to the six governments on October 15, 1970, and affirmed that the goal of an economic-monetary union "can be reached during the present decade, providing the governments maintain constant political support. Economic and monetary union means that the main economic policy decisions will be taken at Community level and that the necessary powers will be transferred from the countries to the Community. The ultimate goal could be the adoption of a single currency, which would ensure that there was no going back on the decisions taken."[89]

The principal conclusions of the "Werner Report" were adopted in modified form in the "Resolution of the Council and of the Representatives of the Governments of the Member States" on February 9, 1971. On this occasion, the council expressed its "political will to set up, during the next ten years, an economic and monetary union according to a phased plan."[90]

This agreement in principle was elaborated on in detail in the "Resolution of the Council and the Representatives of the Governments of the Member States concerning the gradual realization of Economic and Monetary Union in the Community" of March 22, 1972.[91] The decision on the implementation of the first phase of this union was hailed by the French Minister of Finance M. Giscard d'Estaing, as "the most important since the Summit at the Hague; the unanimous will to achieve real Economic and Monetary Union is from henceforth plain. From now on Europe will constitute an independent monetary whole...."[92] M. Malfatti, the president of the commission, pointed out that this decision had [also] matured at the initiative of the Commission and was taken on the basis of Commission proposals."[93]

In the light of its success in the adoption of these three crucial proposals sponsored by the commission—the creation of an economic and monetary union, a common agricultural policy, and an autonomous budget—the European Commission can be justly referred to as the "official" internal federator. Without its collective initiatives, courage, expertise, and perseverance, the European Community would hardly be the new economic superpower of the 1970s.

The Action Committee for the United States of Europe

The process of community formation involves both "official" internal federators, such as the European Commission, which operate on the basis of a legal mandate; and "unofficial" internal federators, such as the Action Committee for the United States of Europe, which promote the same cause through informal contacts between national power elites.

Any examination of the role of the Action Committee must initially focus on its sponsor-president, Jean Monnet, and his "European strategy." Monnet felt that the geopolitical *ridimensionamento* following World War II necessitated a redefinition of the traditional role of the sovereign European nation-state. It was only within an enlarged organizational framework that the major problems in postwar Europe could be resolved effectively. However, given the conservative nature of national bureaucratic structures, the objective necessity to unite was insufficient to bring about integrative steps. People had to be given the opportunity to rally around new institutions capable of realizing the imperative goal of European unity through promoting *de facto* solidarity and through visible achievements in their sphere of competence. By redefining the issues in an enlarged context, these supranational institutions would be able to identify and gradually upgrade the common interest of all participants in a limited sector. "By putting old problems in a new framework, one forces the parties to confront them together. This idea has probably been the central contribution of Jean Monnet, whose bold concepts and driving initiatives lay behind the creation of all three European Communities. Once set up, institutions have a way of becoming common interests in themselves, capable of carrying the members beyond their original objectives into a new sense of community and common achievement. [Hence] one of the best cases for new institutions and common programs is that they are educational."[94] In other words, the new institutions of the European Community became genuine agents of "Euro-socialization"—the sociological corollary of political unification.

However, these supranational institutions had to be created in the first place. Thus Monnet persuaded the then French Foreign Minister Robert Schuman to give his name and support to the establishment of the European Coal and Steel Community in the early 1950s. During this formative period in European integration, Monnet emerged as the champion of supranationalism and as the resolute head of the High Authority of the ECSC. Unfortunately, this phase of "creative opportunism" ended with the debacle of the EDC in 1954. But Monnet was immune to transient disappointments and remained undismayed: "What has happened, has happened, but it does not affect anything fundamental. The important point is for us not to be deflected, not to lose momentum. We must go forward. We may alter our tactics but never lose our main objectives."[95] Consequently, Monnet resigned from his post in recognition of the fact that the constraints imposed by the legal parameters of the Treaty of Paris did neither allow for an expansion of the ECSC's authority from inside, nor permit him to take political initiatives outside the institutional arena. As he explained in his farewell address to the Common Assembly in 1954, "The indispensable contribution which the ECSC has made and will continue to make towards European federation consists in progress and success in the areas entrusted to it. However, the institutions of our Community exercise only those powers delegated to them. It is not for them to extend them. The decision to transfer new powers to the European institutions belongs entirely to the national parliaments and governments. The impulse must, therefore, come from without."[96]

In order to provide this "impulse from without" the institutional arena,

Monnet organized the Action Committee for the United States of Europe. Created on October 13, 1955, its purpose was to "conduct a collective and concrete campaign directed at the governments and in the parliaments with a view towards the realization of the United States of Europe."[97] There has never been any doubt in Monnet's mind about the inevitability of European unity and the existence among Europeans of a "permissive consensus" (to borrow a phrase from Lindberg and Scheingold). But he recognized that there was a missing link between the aspirations of the people and the creation of federal organs for a united Europe, a link that the institutions of the community could not effectively establish without outside intervention. In view of the apparent reluctance of the six national governments to delegate additional powers to supranational bodies, and to share sovereignty in other than the economic fields, Monnet proceeded to select prominent European leaders to join him as "constructive conspirators" in a common cause. Convinced that "the mode whereby the inevitable comes to pass is effort" (to quote O.W. Holmes), President Monnet selected a small elite group of thirty-odd accomplices who recognized that "integration comes about on a broad scale as a result of a kind of conspiracy of deviators within existing political communities."[98]

Jean Monnet's personal mode of operation is based upon his optimistic, realistic, and determined approach to the challenge of European unification. His method is essentially one of persuasion—"to induce and cajole men to work together for their own good"—in short, "Jean Monnet is the supreme practitioner of the art of personal diplomacy. And he practices that art with unfailing perception of the loci of power and with an extraordinary singlemindedness. Optimism works for him because he accepts opponents but not defeat."[99] Monnet's skillful behind-the-scenes tactics made him the *éminence grise* of European diplomacy. His personal style and effectiveness in dealing with people constantly increased his influence with political leaders throughout Europe (including Britain). Even in the United States, Monnet's pragmatic and realistic approach to the European and Atlantic problems was widely acclaimed.

In an effort to revitalize the stagnant unity movement in Western Europe, Monnet therefore established a tight network of informal channels of communication with and between the six national governments and parliaments through the formation of a national lobby composed of prominent elite members on the political, economic, and social sectors of the six states. This supranational pressure group was appropriately called "Action Committee for the United States of Europe," its name being indicative of its mission. The criteria for selection to this august body were the following: (1) agreement on the ultimate objective of European federation; (2) willingness to persuade, influence or pressure national decision-makers to implement the joint resolutions of the committee; (3) capacity to serve as "multiplier," given one's membership in multiple national organizations (public and private); (4) being representative of the major political parties and interest groups. In the light of these criteria

Monnet chose high officials; among them were outstanding "Europeans" such as former Italian President Guiseppe Saragat and recent or incumbent Prime Ministers such as Willy Brandt and Kurt G. Kiesinger of Germany; Guy Mollett, Pierre Pflimlin, René Pleven, Antione Pinay, and Maurice Faure of France; Aldo Moro and Mariano Rumor of Italy; Theo LeFèvre of Belgium and Max Kohnstamm of the Netherlands. However, these political leaders did not represent their respective states but participated as members of one of the following national parties or trade unions: the Socialist Parties were (and/or still are) represented by such officials as Herbert Wehner and Pietro Nenni; the Christian Democratic Parties by Rainer Barzel and Mario Scelba; the Conservative Party by Sir Alex Douglas-Home; and the Liberals by Walter Scheel and Ugo La Malfa; together with the members of the trade unions, the party officials, President Monnet and Vice-President Max Kohnstamm, these political leaders made up the Action Committee in 1971.[100]

Despite the substantial increase in the number of committee members (from thirty-four in 1955 to sixty-four in 1971, including Monnet), the turnover rate was relatively low, the rationale being that regular members become progressively "Euro-socialized"—an interpersonal aspect of Monnet's *engrenage* concept. In fact, in many cases "long service . . . [has] converted lukewarm participants into ardent supporters of the supranational community."[101] The potential impact of vicarious involvement in the European enterprise was also expected to modify the intellectual context of British party members, who were invited to join the committee on October 25, 1968, in anticipation of and preparation for British entry into the Common Market.

The invitation of British party officials to join the Action Committee prior to the *fait accompli* of British accession to the European Community epitomized Monnet's doctrine of the "self-fulfilling prophecy" in operation. Indeed, from the very beginning, Monnet had acted on the assumption that the energetic, consistent advocacy of the desirable objective by prominent personalities including himself would actually advance the cause of unity.[102] Although the political value of Monnet's version of the dictum that "the past is prelude"—it would have to read "the future has arrived"—is hard to demonstrate empirically, its psychological momentum cannot be ignored, as will be shown later.

Prior to the examination of the activities of the Monnet group since its inception, it should be stressed that the Action Committee has never been intended as a substitute for, or competitor of, the European Commission. On the contrary, Monnet envisaged the official and unofficial internal federators as a tandem, operating in a complementary and mutually reinforcing manner. This synchronized attack on national sovereignty was to yield concrete results within a short period of time. Immediately following its creation in 1955, the committee acted to assure the success of the *reliance* (generated by the Messina Conference of June 1955) by intervening constructively in the process of ratification of the Rome Treaties. Monnet and his associates were able to coordinate the sequence of action in the German and French parliaments during the crucial phases of deliberation and voting, an effort that resulted in the early ratification and subsequent signature of the Rome Treaties, followed by the creation of the EEC and Euratom in 1957. This successful intervention clearly established the committee's credentials as an effective internal federator.[103]

Yet, this was only the beginning of the committee's operations. "As soon as the EEC and Euratom Commissions were established, the Action Committee began to function in close cooperation with them. This was made easier since a number of the new Commissioners were old friends and allies of Jean Monnet."[104] It was therefore not surprising "that many ideas, whether later advanced by the Action Committee or the Commission, did in fact emerge out of the constant interchange of views within this enlarged group, and that officials of the Commissions and members of the purely private Action Committee were able to coordinate their activities well enough to play assigned roles in support of an agreed course of action."[105]

From 1956 onwards, the Action Committee began to meet in regular intervals at different locations and pronounced its policy options—designed to produce maximum spillover in the form of joint declarations on the actual problems of the European Community at a given point in time. To be sure, "Action Committee resolutions and official policy declarations by the EEC executive have generally complimented one another . . . [and] the Action Committee has also been of value to the Community executives as a convenient place for first launching controversial ideas."[106] This constructive interplay between the "official" internal federator in Brussels and the "unofficial" federator in Paris greatly facilitated the operations in the early phase of the Common Market. During this period, "Monnet watched (he insists, without much surprise) his principles put into practice, change begetting change. The early results (helped by the crest of a boom) were spectacular. . . . People not only adjusted themselves, but anticipated changes that actually took place. 'The history of European unification,' he said in 1962, 'shows that when people become convinced that a change is taking place that creates a new situation, they act on their revised estimate before that situation is established.' "[107] Monnet's crucial role in this development cannot be overemphasized. Indeed, "the personality and mode of operation of Jean Monnet are to a significant degree responsible for the inauguration of this gradualist strategy [of the community, since] he combines enthusiastic leadership with the tactics of an astute politican who learned to recognize the limits within which unification can progress."[108]

The second opportunity for the Action Committee to intervene on behalf of the European Community arose in the context of the dispute over the future of OEEC in the late 1950s. At that time, the British government had proposed the creation of a "free trade area" for all members of the OEEC as an alternative to the supranational European Community. Still unwilling to join the Common Market, Britain instead organized EFTA in 1959, while the OEEC was superseded by OECD in 1960. The failure of the "Maudling mission" to organize an intergovernmental free-trade zone was mainly due to the sophisticated behind-the-scenes manipulations of the Action Committee, which played the "American card" against the British for the benefit of "Little Europe." Undoubtedly, "the Monnet Group played an important role in determining the strategy which led to the formation of a new organization replacing OEEC and thereby accomplished its primary aim which was to prevent a dilution of the supranational Community for the sake of accommodating the United Kingdom and other European countries eager to share in the commercial advantages of the Common Market without assuming any of the obligations and burdens of membership."[109]

This apparently anti-British attitude on the part of the Action Committee (to be explained only in terms of insistence on priorities, i.e., consolidation before enlargement of the European Community) was more than compensated for by its persistent efforts to bring Britain into the Common Market. In fact, the committee urged the United Kingdom to seek membership in the EEC one year prior to Britain's first application in the summer of 1961. In its Joint Declaration of July 11, 1960, the committee commented on the irreversible centripetal nature of the European Community and stated that "the acceleration of the Common Market [through tariff reductions] has shown the United Kingdom and other European countries that there is now no going back on European integration, that it is profitable, and also open to all."[110] Following Prime Minister Macmillan's official request for negotiations on British membership in the EEC of August 9, 1961, the Action Committee very specifically stated its policy on this matter in a Joint Declaration of June 26, 1962: "The entry of the United Kingdom into the European Community on a basis of equality under the conditions laid down by the Rome Treaty will reinforce the unity of Europe.... Britain's participation in the beginnings of a European political union will increase the influence Europe can exert on the world's affairs ... [and] as a member, the United Kingdom will want to contribute to the effectiveness of a Community, which confers such a role on Europe...."[111] This pronouncement reinforced the European Commission's difficult position during the Brussels negotiations in 1962, which had almost succeeded when President de Gaulle vetoed their continuation. However, Monnet did not give up; instead he affirmed that "the process of change will go on: de Gaulle cannot stop it."[112] In an interview with the *Corriere della Sera* on April 7, 1963, Monnet regretted the breakdown of the Brussels Round and blamed its failure on intergovernmental diplomacy, asserting that the problem could have been solved by employing the community method. He was optimistic about the eventual entry of Britain because of the lack of other realistic alternatives for Europe and expressed his conviction that, once a member, Britain will become Euro-socialized and adhere to the rules of the game.[113] On this occasion, Monnet admitted that de Gaulle's action of January 1963 had caused a crisis of confidence in Europe, but expressed his conviction that the process of *engrenage* will continue: "Since 1950, the six countries of the European Community have ... [been] acting as a Community. They accept the same rules and have created common institutions. ... This is the beginning of the future European federation. ... By asking to enter the Common Market, Britain shows that she is now ready to do what we have been doing for twelve years."[114] The following year, Monnet continued to advocate British membership in the EEC in defiance of de Gaulle. Speaking in Bad Godesberg, Germany, on February 25, 1964, the president of the Action Committee said, "The United States of Europe have begun to be built. Today, the European Community is limited to the six countries of the Common Market. It must be extended to all democratic countries of Europe which accept the Community's aims, rules, and institutions. Here, we all have Great Britain particularly in mind. Her place is with us. ...."[115] The Action Committee echoed their leader in its Joint Declaration of June 1, 1964, and May 9, 1965.[116]

During the latter part of 1966 and in early 1967, Prime Minister Wilson toured several European capitals (including Paris) in order to explore with European leaders the chances for British entry into the Common Market. Reactions by the German, Italian, and Benelux governments were extremely favorable, whereas de Gaulle remained noncommital. At that juncture, the Action Committee moved to encourage Wilson to reapply for British Common Market membership. In a communiqué issued on March 15, 1967, it announced that its members were unanimously in favor of British accession to the EEC.[117] On May 2, 1967, the United Kingdom decided to apply under art. 237 of the Rome Treaty for full membership in the European Community. Only two weeks later, speaking at another press conference (May 16), the French president in effect postponed negotiations until Britain was "converted to the European ideal."[118] Refusing to accept another Gaullist *diktat*, Monnet decided to permit Britain to "symbolically enter Europe" by inviting the representatives of Britain's three political parties to join the Action Committee on October 25, 1968. Commenting on this revolutionary step taken by his group (the Action Committee had been strictly limited to representatives from the Six), President Monnet declared, "I consider the fact that the three main political parties have joined the Action Committee for the United States of Europe as an important new factor which should facilitate British participation in the Common Market and in the unification of Europe."[119] Six months later, in March 1969, the Action Committee admitted representatives from the French Independent Republicans (a coalition partner of the ruling Gaullist UNR Party), thus making the committee representative of eighty million voters and twelve million labor union members (except the Communists).[120] With the inclusion of several prominent "Europeans" such as Sir Alex Douglas-Home and Mr. Roy Jenkins of Britain, and M. Valéry Giscard d'Estaing of France, the Action Committee proceeded to push for British membership, convinced that the informal communication network of personal contacts thus created between London and

Paris will ultimately yield beneficial results. In order to underline the committee's position, it decided to meet in London on March 11, 1969. On this historic occasion, the committee expressed its solemn support for British membership in the EEC and resolved unanimously to "seek solutions to the problems of British entry in the monetary, agricultural, technological and institutional fields. . . . [And in order] to assist it in working out the solutions which it will propose to the governments," the committee appointed the following prominent experts: Dr. Guido Carli, governor of the Bank of Italy; Professor Robert Triffin, Yale University; M. Edgar Pisani, former French minister of agriculture; Lord Plowden, a former British official; and Professor Karl Winnacker of the German Hoechst Chemical Company; former Commission President Professor Walter Hallstein. The five reports were subsequently presented and discussed at the Brussels meeting of the committee on July 16, 1969. After hearing them, the committee declared that its conviction had been confirmed that the problems raised by Britain's entry into the Common Market could be solved.[121] Having outlined the basic solutions to these important problems, the Monnet committee reinforced the position of the European Commission by recommending "that the Six . . . decide . . . to enter into negotiations with Great Britain and prepare their common position for these negotiations. . . . The Committee finds it surprising that the Commission's opinion on the enlargement of the Community has not yet been discussed by the Council; this should be done without delay."[122] This admonition by the Action Committee seemed to have had salutory effect: six months later, the leaders of the Six, meeting in the Hague (in de Gaulle's absence), supported the concept of enlargement in their final Communiqué of December 2, 1969.[123] Meeting in Bonn, on December 16, 1969, the Action Committee "noted with satisfaction the results of the summit meeting" and urged the resumption of negotiations between the Six and the United Kingdom on the basis of the Committee's earlier proposals.[124] This resolution of the Action Committee was "implemented" on June 30, 1970, when negotiations between the European Community and Britain (plus the three other applicant countries) began in Luxembourg.[125] During this crucial phase in European diplomacy, the unofficial internal federator again stepped into the political arena on February 23, 1971. Reinforced by the presence of government officials (Chancellor Brandt, Foreign Minister Scheel, and Sir Alec Douglas-Home), the Action Committee met in the *Bundeshaus* in Bonn, Germany. Jean Monnet presided over the meeting, which was attended by most if its members (among them were Messrs. Barzel, Schmidt; Nenni, Scelba; Jenkins, Healey; Faure, Pinay) and the Rapporteurs Messrs. Hallstein, Marjolin, Rey, Vetter and Werner. After an address by M. Monnet, the committee adopted several resolutions, among them one on enlargement. Specifically, the committee demanded that the principal issues of the negotiations between Britain and the European Community "be resolved before the summer holidays."[126] This resolution was promptly "adopted" by the Council of Ministers on June 23,

1971, in Luxembourg, when it concluded an historic agreement with the British delegation laying the foundations for British entry into the Common Market.

There is no doubt that the "unofficial internal federator" had substantially contributed to the formation of this consensus by providing channels for informal contacts between key actors in the seven countries concerned, by proposing realistic and specific solutions to the principal questions involved in the negotiations, and by publicly pressuring the national governments to make concessions and come to a compromise agreement on the issue of "Britain and European Unity."[127] The committee had accomplished its mission as an unofficial federator for the European cause; the decision "to go or not to go into Europe" was now up to the British Parliament. Faced with widespread public opposition, Prime Minister Heath, a convinced "European," conducted a vigorous public relations campaign in support of his government's policy of Common Market membership. This campaign ended with a triumph on October 28, 1971, when Parliament voted for British membership in the European Community by a large majority.[128] Jean Monnet, the "optimistic realist," had become the father of the enlarged European Community.

Internal Inhibitor: Gaullism

France has always held the key to the success or failure of the European unity movement. In the early 1950s, Robert Schuman provided the decisive impetus to European unification with his ingenius plan for the creation of a supranational European authority, conceived as a first step in the direction of a European federation. In the early 1960s, Charles de Gaulle became the grave-digger of supranationalism and the new hero of stato-nationalism, determined to promote French grandeur and independence at all cost. Thus General de Gaulle, an outstanding historical personality, and undoubtedly the most controversial statesman of his time, played the unfortunate role of "inhibitor" of the European unity movement.

Upon his return to power, President de Gaulle immediately began to implement his cherished notions of France—a glorious nation with a manifest destiny, and a powerful state with an important role in world politics. Although Charles de Gaulle was neither the inventor of nationalism nor the original architect of the state,[129] he made a conscious effort to revitalize the anachronistic dual concept of stato-nationalism and to spread this contagious doctrine of *égoisme sacré* at a most inappropriate period in history. His political philosophy found expression in his brilliantly written memoirs and through his inimitable, impressive pronouncements at carefully staged press conferences. De Gaulle was convinced that charisma was an essential quality of the successful leader and had to be enhanced through personal aloofness and the skillful use of paraphernalia.

Charles de Gaulle's ambitious concept of French nationalism found its most eloquent expression in the opening paragraph of his memoirs:

All my life I have thought of France in a certain way. This is inspired by sentiment as much as by reason. The emotional side of me tends to imagine France . . . as dedicated to an exalted and exceptional destiny. . . . But the positive side of my mind also assures me that France . . . cannot be France without greatness.[130]

This idealistic-romantic vision of France had to be implemented; hence de Gaulle devised the following strategy:

I intended to assure France primacy in Western Europe by preventing the rise of a new Reich that might again threaten its safety; to cooperate with East and West and, if need be, contract the necessary alliances on one side or the other without ever accepting any kind of dependency; . . . to persuade the states along the Rhine, the Alps, and the Pyrenees to form a political, economic, and strategic bloc; to establish this organization as one of the three world powers and, should it become necessary, as the arbiter between the Soviet and Anglo-American camps.[131]

Upon his return to power as president of the Fifth Republic, de Gaulle immediately began to undertake the necessary measures to realize his plans. However, prior to pursuing foreign policy designs, he had to deal with urgent domestic problems; after all, he had been recalled from retirement to save France (for the second time) from internal chaos.

In an effort to restore France's greatness, de Gaulle terminated the war in Algeria, granted independence to this former colony, and established internal stability through the creation of new, effective and popular political institutions, and through revitalizing the economy and strengthening the currency. Together with the nuclear *force de frappe*, the new *franc* became the symbol and pillar of French sovereignty.

Once the conditions of French independence had been established, de Gaulle, the new hero and savior of France, could finally concentrate on his real mission: to restore France's rightful place as a major power in world politics. He realized that in the age of *grandes ensembles* France needed Europe as a necessary power base from which de Gaulle could play his desired role as spokesman for this "third force." Therefore, de Gaulle proclaimed himself an ardent supporter of the cause of a united Europe which had already begun to take shape during his retirement. While de Gaulle believed in the ultimate objective of this new Europe as promoted by the community institutions in Brussels, he completely disagreed with the strategy and means by which this desirable goal—a united Europe—should be implemented. The reason for this opposition to the neofunctionalist approach of supranationalism was his axiomatic belief in the permanence of the nation-state as the ideal type of societal organization.

De Gaulle expressed his credo as follows: "What are the realities of Europe? What are the pillars on which it can be built? The states are certainly very different from one another, each of which has its own spirit, its own history, its own language, its own misfortunes, glories and ambitions; but these states are the only entities that have the right to order and the authority to act. To imagine that something can be built that would be effective for action and that would be approved by the peoples outside and above these states—this is a dream."[132] Therefore de Gaulle declared that "only states are valid, legitimate and capable of achievement . . . [and] there cannot be any other Europe than a Europe of States."[133]

The goal of a Europe of fatherlands became the foreign policy platform of the French president promoted under the so-called Fouchet Plan, which essentially contained proposals for a confederation of states. De Gaulle's adamant refusal to make concessions to the proponents of supranationalism, compounded by his veto of British entry into the Common Market, led to increasing opposition to de Gaulle's European policy both in France and abroad. Thus five ministers in the cabinet of Premier Pompidou resigned in protest against their president's nationalist foreign policy; in their joint communiqué, they declared that "between General de Gaulle's conceptions on the direction and objectives of the European policy and the ideas to which they are attached, the press conference [of May 15, 1962] revealed essential differences which do not permit them to remain in the government."[134]

Not only was de Gaulle opposed by members of his own cabinet, but also by the governments of France's five partners in the European Community. In the light of this confrontation between the Gaullist version of a European confederation and the principle of supranationalism supported by the majority, negotiations on the Fouchet Plan were suspended *sine die* in May 1962.

This complete failure to convince France's partners of the virtue of the Gaullist design and the validity of French diplomacy disappointed and frustrated the French president. His *revanche* came eight months later at another press conference in which de Gaulle vetoed British entry into the Common Market—an objective that was close to the hearts of the other five members of the European Community. Speaking in Paris on January 14, 1963, the French President formally pronounced Britain unfit to join the Common Market. This unilateral French decision resulted in the suspension *sine die* of the negotiations between the United Kingdom and the Six and produced shock waves in all of Western Europe. The atmosphere of despair was aptly described by Paul-Henri Spaak, who spoke of a "day of defeat [when] a severe, if not mortal blow has been dealt at the Community spirit [because] as soon as one member of a Community seems to force all the others into decisions of capital importance for its life, the Community spirit ceases to exist."[135] Moreover, he stated that "it reveals General de Gaulle's open contempt for the views of his partners and at the same time a will to make his own views prevail. . . . What we are witnessing is an attempt by one partner, who regards himself as the strongest, to impose his own will on the others . . . . [however] the partners have no intention of accepting such treatment."[136]

The principal motive behind de Gaulle's opposition to British entry into the

EEC was his belief that the United Kingdom, an Anglo-Saxon power linked to the United States by a "special relationship," would play the role of a "Trojan horse" and represent American interests in the European Community. This specter was entirely incompatible with de Gaulle's ambitious long-range plan to construct a pan-European grouping comprising all nations on the Continent. Based upon a Franco-German axis, this continental confederation would be built according to the strategy of "détente-entente-coopération" between Western and Eastern Europe, and eventually extend from "the Atlantic to the Urals."[137] Having eliminated British influence on the Continent, de Gaulle persuaded the aging Chancellor Adenauer to sign a Franco-German Treaty of Friendship and Cooperation on January 22, 1963. This treaty was to provide a model for the other European nations "to organize themselves in order to conduct together a policy which is European."[138] However, prior to the ratification of the treaty, the German Parliament inserted a preamble which in effect repudiated the exclusivist spirit of the document and placed it within the context of Germany's traditional European and Atlantic policies which explains why the Treaty subsequently remained largely "on paper" only.[139]

If de Gaulle's expectation that he could get German support at the expense of the Federal Republic's friendship with the United States proved unrealistic, the second assumption behind his concept of a "European Europe from the Atlantic to the Urals" turned out to be even more illusionary. The mistaken Gaullist inference was that "Russia," a traditional European nation-state, would sooner or later abandon both its Communist ideology and its Asian territories (to China) and join France in coadministering an idyllic pan-European confederation. The fantastic and completely unrealistic assumptions of de Gaulle's chimera—an independent Europe run by two coequal powers, France and "Russia," containing between them a weak Germany and excluding the "Anglo-Saxons"—are the reason for the total failure of this project.[140]

With this long-range goal out of sight, de Gaulle concentrated on the realization of his short-term objective, namely the building of a "European Europe" of states West of the Elbe, dominated by France. However, he soon discovered that not even this limited goal was acceptable to the other European nations, essentially because it would imply the severing of ties with both Britain and the United States and would result in an exchange of American for French "protection"—a profoundly disquieting prospect in terms of national security. Against the background of these obstacles to de Gaulle's European policies, the genuine irony of his position becomes even more evident.

An increasing number of political analysts in the West came to realize that "the French President rejects any hegemony over Europe except his own. Yet his own arrogance and imperious, high-handed methods make the Gaullist image of Europe unattractive to all his prospective partners. Short of conquest, a 'Gaullist European Europe' cannot be organized. The only possible basis for creating a powerful Europe, truly independent of the United States, fully capable of pursuing independent action, is by renouncing the nationalist and imperialist molds of the past and integrating the separate states in a new supranational community."[141] Notwithstanding the compelling nature of this argument, de Gaulle remained obstinate in his defense of the nation-state. In fact, he made it categorically clear that France had "no desire to be dissolved in a federation called 'European' (which would actually be 'Atlantic') since . . . any system that would consist of handing over our sovereignty to august international assemblies would be incompatible with the rights and duties of the French Republic."[142] There is no doubt that "de Gaulle . . . had nothing but contempt for supranationalism."[143]

But de Gaulle not only defended French sovereignty, he attacked the custodians of supranationalism by referring to them as "apatrides, anonymous and irresponsible technocrats"[144] intent upon increasing their power by undermining French sovereignty. Paradoxically, however, de Gaulle needed the Eurocrats for the purpose of promoting French national interest, particularly in the field of agriculture where the common policy of the community coincided with de Gaulle's domestic concerns. Thus de Gaulle found himself frequently in the unlikely role of champion of *economic* integration while remaining a foe of *political* unification. However, inasmuch as he contributed, albeit involuntarily, to political unity by supporting selective integrative measures in the economic realm, Charles de Gaulle actually served as a *fédérateur malgré lui*.

Notwithstanding his incidental contributions to European integration, the French president almost succeeded in destroying the institutions of the European Community when he first boycotted its meetings and subsequently demanded a *révision générale* of its constituent treaties in 1965. Although he eventually agreed to France's return to Brussels, the result of this unilateral intervention—the Luxembourg Protocol—still testifies to the detrimental influence of his aboriginal nationalism.[145] Even more important than de Gaulle's tangible legacy was the negative psychological impact of his diplomacy of brinkmanship, blackmail, and ultimata on the community spirit. Since de Gaulle's only guideline was the French *raison d'état*, his actions amounted to flagrant violations of the unwritten code of behavior—the so-called community method of consensus formation by compromise and respect for the views of the partners. Indeed, de Gaulle's unwillingness to play by the rules of the game and to join the other five governments in the institutionalized habit of seeking and upgrading the common interest created an unfortunate precedent and induced France's partners to insist on their respective prerogatives as well. If the community became increasingly "rediplomatized" (rather than integrated), "certainly de Gaulle's negative attitude toward the Community and toward its underlying aim of political unification has contributed to this state of affairs."[146]

Apart from de Gaulle's reintroduction of the traditional preoccupation with national interest into the institutions of the community, he also "succeeded" in fanning the fires of latent nationalism in Western Europe, particularly in Germany, where he addressed crowds on several occasions using the phrase "das grosse deutsche Volk" and reminding his audience of the greatness of their nation. The danger of unabashed French nationalism for the future of Europe was recognized by perceptive observers in France and abroad. Thus the former French ambassador to the German Federal Republic voiced a solemn warning when he stated that "it may well happen that the example of French nationalism becomes contagious and revives the nationalisms of the neighbors, particularly that of Germany." He complemented his ominous remarks about the "sirens of nationalism" with an attack on de Gaulle's proposal for a European confederation when he stated that "it is not without regret and astonishment that one sees the French Head of State . . . march against history [since] the policy to which the General remains attached is that of alliances of the classical type which have been practiced in the 19th century."[147]

The validity of this criticism was also recognized by a distinguished political philosopher, who warned of the cumulative danger of nationalism when he wrote that "if the chief inspiration of French policy is going to be *la grandeur de la France* there is no reason why the chief inspiration of German policy should not be *Deutschland über alles*."[148]

Once Konrad Adenauer, who had been mystically attached to General de Gaulle as a historical personality, had left the political scene, signs that the above predictions were correct became apparent.

The example of "Gaullism" (a species term) inevitably generated neonationalism (the generic term), especially in Germany, where the so-called German Gaullists under the leadership of Franz-Josef Strauss emerged as a vocal political group. This potentially dangerous development was, however, not the result of an unfortunate *faux pas* by the French president but the logical by-product of the foreign policy of General de Gaulle, who took the calculated risk of "awakening the sleeping lion" across the Rhine in the pursuit of his anti-American policy of forging a "European Europe," which necessitated German cooperation.

This undisguised attempt to establish French hegemony in a "third force" Europe did not appeal to France's partners, however. Faced with the option of choosing between a distant powerful protector and the questionable *force de dissuasion* of an ambitious neighbor, the other European nations realistically preferred the United States. This, in turn, prompted de Gaulle to sever French ties with NATO's integrated command in 1966, a unilateral step based upon the argument that military integration is coterminous with political subordination—a position which no independent state such as France could tolerate. Interestingly, de Gaulle chose not to abrogate the Treaty of Washington so that France, still a formal member of the Atlantic Alliance, could continue to benefit from the American nuclear umbrella.

The preceding analysis demonstrates that de Gaulle's nationalist policy was counterproductive, given his intention to promote European independence: "because they believed that de Gaulle wished to dominate Europe, the Germans, the Italians, the Dutch, and to a lesser degree the Belgians, reinforced their ties with the United States. Thus their dependence grew."[149]

To be sure, it was just a matter of time until the other European nations would realize that de Gaulle's "European policy" was a French policy camouflaged under European rhetoric. In other words, de Gaulle's France was sailing under a European flag and its president used Europe as an "elevator" to enhance French national interest. As one observer put it, "The General, whenever he speaks of Europe, thinks less about Europe with France than about France in Europe. In this particular concept the nation does not give way to unity designed to create a larger ensemble. On the contrary, it [the nation] has to maintain and even accentuate its own personality."[150]

Despite these handwritings on the wall, de Gaulle persisted in the pursuit of his nationalist policies since he was determined to incarnate France and to reestablish its *grandeur*—an ephemeral, unrealistic concept in an age of continental superpowers. His insistence on taking the façade of French sovereignty seriously gradually exacerbated even France's best allies, who contemplated the question: "with such an ally—who needs an enemy?"

Yet Charles de Gaulle was too infatuated with his own vision of French glory to recognize all the implications of his policy. If he did, he ignored the risks involved. In fact, he believed that the French "national situation"[151] justified his emphasis on the national interest; after all, France had been among the victors of World War II, whereas Germany was defeated. Hence, it behooved France to resist the appeals of the "apostles of self-abnegation" who were resigned to the demise of the nation-state. Instead of listening to these "sirens of doom," de Gaulle felt the need for rekindling the *sentiment national* in the French population, which, in turn, was expected to generate a "European nationalism," and to a degree it actually did.

In view of the fact that Charles de Gaulle had been an experienced student of European history, this reckless play with the fires of nationalism amounted to an irresponsible, risky, and Machiavellian policy with an enormous boomerang potential. After all, in the past Germany's superiority has been amply demonstrated, and West Germany (only a part of divided Germany), had already emerged as Europe's industrial giant, a development that prompted de Gaulle's successor to welcome Britain into the Common Market as a countervailing force. The disintegrative feature of de Gaulle's diplomacy consisted in the attempt to appeal to latent reactionary instincts among the European people by proclaiming the need for preserving the historic states—and by deliberately sabotaging political integration. Hence, it has been widely recognized that "the French President's policies undoubtedly helped bring to consciousness, and make respectable, national interests and attitudes inconsistent with the European idea."[152] What is worse, "he has contributed to the resurgence of nationalism

when there were prospects for European cooperation and he has sown in Europe
the seeds of national rivalries when there was for the first time a genuine hope
for political unity."[153]

In the light of the preceding considerations, it can be argued that to the
extent that de Gaulle served as the self-appointed apostle of a discredited and
contagious ideology by preaching the virtues of nineteenth century nationalism
in France and abroad, he contributed decisively to a decline of the European
cause.

Admirers of Charles de Gaulle—the charismatic statesman—often claimed that
the French President was a man of the twenty-first century, but he was
misunderstood by most of his contemporaries. Empirical evidence seems to
indicate the contrary, namely that he was a quasi-monarchical representative of
the nineteenth century who refused to accept the challenge of European
unification. This argument is based upon de Gaulle's interpretation of reality and
the *Zeitgeist*. For him, nation-states, the remnants of the nineteenth century,
were "reality," and supranational entities were "dreams and myths." However,
according to the most prominent French planning expert and futurologist,
"realism is not on the side of those who want to maintain the structures and
compartmentalization of the past. The time has come for the organization of a
political society on a scale which transcends even that of nations."[154] In fact, it
is this progressive interpretation of realism that would have permitted de Gaulle
to pursue his ambitious plans. Yet the French president insisted on a *status quo*
definition of realism. But "how can a 'Europe' be built that would assume full
responsibility for its own destiny and play the role of arbiter between the 'two
hegemonies,' when the only real political entities in Europe are the separate
national states? What in fact would this 'Europe' accomplish, except to
perpetuate the classic nationalist strivings in which 'the small want to become
great, the strong to dominate the weak, the old to live on? What magic,
automatic harmony of interests would bind together a conglomeration of
separate states that were caught up in their traditional power rivalries and
squabbles?"[155] In short, how can one reconcile the pursuit of twenty-first-cen-
tury goals with the use of nineteenth-century means? A true leader would have
recognized the *ridimensionamento*, advocated structural renewal, and facilitated
political integration. But instead of assisting the supranational organs in their
historic task of overcoming national rivalries, de Gaulle castigated the Eurocrats
as members of an "Areopagus" who were by definition disloyal to their six
governments (despite the fact that they often advanced the political goals of the
French president). A prisoner of the past, de Gaulle accepted *les choses comme
ils sont* and argued that politics is nothing but the "art of the possible." A
genuine *homme politique* (in contrast to a *politicien*) would have practiced the
"politics of making possible what is necessary" to meet the changing needs of
the time. Unfortunately, de Gaulle chose only to disrupt the efforts of the true
realists on both sides of the Atlantic. "By the same token, this strident

nationalist . . . demonstrated his total inability to construct a 'European Europe,' or, indeed, any kind of Europe."[156]

Undoubtedly, the most tragic aspect of the figure of Charles de Gaulle was his failure to fulfill a historic mission, that of the European "federator with sufficient power, authority and skill."[157] When de Gaulle assumed the presidency of France, Europeanism had just received a new impetus from the creation of the Common Market and Euratom, although supranationalism was slowly declining but far from moribund.[158] Thus a unique opportunity presented itself to a potential federator, particularly to one of the stature, prestige and influence of General de Gaulle. By restoring the momentum of supranationalism and advocating concrete steps toward political integration, de Gaulle could have become the first president of a United States of Europe. It is quite likely that most European statesmen, particularly Chancellor Adenauer (the decisive one), would have been prepared to grant the French President the privileged position of *primus inter pares* and would have accepted him as Europe's spokesman. But, *hélas*, Charles de Gaulle failed to see and/or was unprepared to accomplish his historical mission. Instead, he chose the role of the hero of a pseudosovereign nation-state by accepting the consolation prize of "savior of France"—a sad substitute for the first presidency of a united Europe. Thus General de Gaulle, the potential federator, became Europe's foremost inhibitor.

In retrospect, it must be stated that Gaullism failed to reverse the tides of European integration but "succeeded" in producing temporary stalemates and considerably slowing the integrative steps. The transitory nature of this "spillback" is evidenced by the rapid progress achieved following de Gaulle's departure from the political scene, symbolized by Britain's accession to the European Community and the decisions of the Hague Conference in 1969. However, the most destructive legacy of Gaullism may well be his "success" in making nationalism respectable again by giving "aid and comfort" to all latent and prospective nationalists in France and abroad, and serving as the most illustrious and eloquent spokesman for this discredited cause in the West.[159] The widespread flirtation with the idea of a "Europe of Fatherlands" among Europeans attests to the prevailing influence of his anachronistic political theories and models. If the only available test case for the confederal formula in operation, the Franco-German Treaty of 1963, is taken as a measure of the success of this intergovernmental form of cooperation, the prospects for the future of Western Europe are indeed dim.[160] The juxtaposition of policies formulated by the governments of states that are roughly equal in power is bound to produce a sterile cacophony rather than creative harmony.

Unfortunately, the European past could become its prologue as the contours of the Gaullist design of the 1960s begin to appear in the 1970s. Conjecturally, there are chances for the establishment of *l'Europe des patries*, but with a significant *retouche*: "Should a reunified Germany emerge in a Gaullist Europe, it would be stimulated by the toxin of Gaullist nationalism and freed of the restraints that weigh upon the present generation. A new generation of leaders would by then have come of age, no longer feeling the stigma of the Nazi past and eager to reassert German power on the stage of world politics by emulating the egoistic, nationalistic behavior of de Gaulle. When viewed from this perspective, the Gaullist dream becomes a nightmare."[161]

As to the Gaullist visions of a "European Europe" (i.e., liberated from American hegemony, to use Gaullist parlance) or of a "Europe from the Atlantic to the Urals" (including the USSR, since no sane observer can foresee a truncated European Russia superseding the Soviet Union), they may materialize with a fatal modification: "If such a Europe ever comes to pass, it would leave either a divided Germany or a Germany that would be reunited on Soviet terms. This version of Europe from the Atlantic to the Urals would surely not be dominated by Paris, or even by Paris and Moscow, but by Moscow alone."[162] It is therefore not surprising that the leaders of the Kremlin have become the spiritual heirs to de Gaulle's fantasies, with one difference: they have a reasonable chance to implement them, given a minimum amount of friendly cooperation from naive politicians in Western Europe.[163]

In this chapter an attempt was made to test a number of propositions advanced in the Gestalt model, the pretheory of international regional integration elaborated in Chapter 2. Given the lack of quantitative approaches with meaningful explanatory power, no attempt was made to determine the relative potency of the centripetal and centrifugal forces at work in the process of European unification. However, an effort was made to show the causative impact of external and internal federators, as well as the negative influence of the inhibitor, on the initiation and evolution of the European Unity Movement which had been launched by determined governmental leaders after World War II. This comparative analysis of the policies pursued by both direct and indirect *external*, and official and unofficial *internal* federators, and the "counterpolicies" of the inhibitor (including the effect of the *fédérateur malgré lui*) covered an extended period (1945-72). The findings suggest that the cumulative interplay of threats, support, pressure, and policy initiatives on the part of the actors in the arena of European politics resulted in gradual—albeit frequently interrupted—but *constant progress* toward the ultimate goal of European unity, permitting the organizational development of the European Community from a supranational nucleus of six nations to the New Europe—the world's largest commercial power.

4

Policy Harmonization and Institutional Development

In the preceding chapter an effort was made to identify the principal actors in the European unity movement since its inception following World War II. The purpose of this chapter is to determine the relative success or failure of the European Community in terms of both policy harmonization and the strengthening of common institutions. This performance evaluation covers the period from 1952 to 1972; projections are made up to 1980 (see Figure 4-1).

The standards against which this performance evaluation has been undertaken consist of the following legal-political documents: the Treaties of Rome establishing EEC and Euratom; the Treaty of Paris, creating ECSC; the "Merger Treaty" (1965); the Final Communiqué of the European Summit Conference at the Hague (December 2, 1969); the Resolution of the Council on Economic and Monetary Union (Brussels, 1971); and the Communiqué of the European Summit Meeting (Paris, 1972).[1]

The criteria for measuring the relative amount of progress or regression are the following (letters in parentheses refer to the scoreboard shown in Table 4-1):

Accomplishments (A): all actual achievements (total or better than 75 percent complete implementation of the goal).

Progress (B): agreement in principle and partial implementation (less than 50 percent) of the proposed measures.

Stagnation (C): agreement on the principle but no major decisions on detailed measures taken.

Regression (D): prior agreements on the principle suspended or declared void.

Prospects (P): projections for future integration: favorable, unfavorable (F,U) based mainly on decisions of the Paris Summit.

The matrix reflects the findings of Chapter 4, except for section IV (external relations) which is dealt with in Chapter 6. The data used to interpret the findings reflected on the score board are based upon the following sources (official or semi-official publications of the European Communities): *The Facts* (1971), *The Anatomy of Enlargement* (1972), *European Community* (monthly) and Agence *Europe* (daily). The articles and titles referred to in the following section (I) are those of the Treaty establishing the EEC, unless other sources are mentioned. The articles referred to in section II (institutional development) are those of the EEC Treaty as modified by the Acts of Accession of 1972, taking into consideration Norway's failure to ratify these Acts.

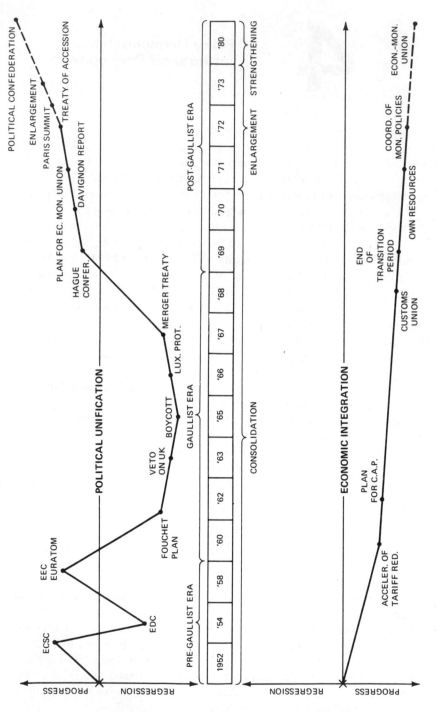

Figure 4-1. The Political and Economic Development of the European Community (1952-1980).

Table 4-1

Matrix for Performance Evaluation: Scoreboard (1952-1980)

Objects \ Results	Accomplishments (A)	Progress (B)	Stagnation (C)	Regression (D)	Prospects (P)
Internal Policy Harmonization					
Common Market:					
Free movement of goods	x				F
Free movement of labor	x				F
Free movement of services		x			F
Free movement of capital		x			F
Rules governing competition		x			F
Economic and Monetary Union:					
General economic policy		x			F
Monetary policy		x			F
Fiscal policy		x			F
Agricultural policy	x				F
Commercial policy		x			F
Industrial policy		x			F
Research & technology policy		x			U
Energy policy			x		U
Transport policy			x		U
Regional policy		x			F
Common social policy		x			F
Common cultural policy		x			F
Institutional Development					
Council of Ministers				x	U
Commission	x				F
Permanent Representatives		x			F
European Parliament			x		F
Court of Justice		x			F
Economic and Social Committee		x			F
Special Advisory Bodies		x			F
Ancillary Institutions		x			F
Legal/Financial Bases					
Consolidation of Treaties			x		U
Merger of Institutions	x				F
Accession Treaty	x				F
Community budget		x			F
External Relations					
Enlargement of Membership	x				F
Association Agreements	x				F
Trade Agreements	x				F
International Organizations (nature of relationships)			x		F

Performance Evaluation of the European Community

Internal Policy Harmonization—The Common Market

Free Movement of Goods (Part II, Title I): A. One of the principal objectives so far reached by the European Community (EC) is the establishment of a customs union among the six member states. This involved the removal of all tariff barriers by July 1, 1968, and the elimination of quota restrictions by January 1, 1962, as well as the adoption of a common external tariff on July 1, 1968. This CET is lower than the average tariff of the six national tariffs prior to 1968 and became the lowest (6 percent) of all industrial countries in 1972 after the final cuts agreed upon at the GATT negotiations in 1967 (Kennedy Round) were made. Some remaining nontariff barriers are being gradually abolished.

Free Movement of Labor (Title III, 1): A. A common market requires—in addition to the creation of a customs union—the free flow of factors within the territory of the member states. Thus the EC provided for the legal freedom of workers to take up jobs in any one of the six countries, and to be entitled to social security benefits, family allowance, sickness, maternity and unemployment benefits.

Free Movement of Services (Title III, 2 and 3): B. In addition to the free movement of labor, a common market implies the freedom of establishment of firms, agencies and professionals, and the freedom to supply services (banking, insurance, building, whole-sale and retail distribution, and the exercise of liberal professions). By the end of the transition period, the Six had only removed restrictions against nationals from other member states in certain areas including mining, real estate, re-insurance, petroleum exploration, gas and electricity production, whole-sale and retail trade, movie production, and cinema exhibition.

Free Movement of Capital (Title III, 4): B. The third factor supposed to flow freely in a common market is capital: it complements the free flow of persons and services. Although numerous restrictions on capital movement remain, a substantial number of exchange controls were removed unconditionally by directives (1960, 1963).

Rules Governing Competition (Part III, Title I,1): B. Because of the ideological differences between Germany (which believed in the *freie Marktwirtschaft* principle) and France (which insisted on democratic planning), the Treaty of Rome does not provide for "free" competition but rather calls for "fair" or "workable" competition: i.e., prevention of distortions to free trade. Thus both the ECSC and the EEC treaties prohibit agreements or practices such as price-fixing, market-sharing, restriction of production, investment, or technical development, and discriminatory supply conditions. However, agreements with an overall beneficial effect on the economy and negligible restraints on effective competition were authorized to improve production, distribution or development of firms. Thus the EC tolerates "desirable" cartels and mergers, but insists that state monopolies adjust business practices to the requirement of fair competition, a demand that has only been partially fulfilled.

Internal Policy Harmonization–The
Economic and Monetary Union

General Economic Policy (Title II): B. Whereas the rules governing competition were included at the insistence of the Germans, the concept of medium-term and short-term economic planning reflects the French practice of "dirigism." This planning function (euphemistically referred to as "programming" to appease sensitive German free traders) is exercised respectively by the Short-Term and Medium-Term Economic Policy Committees, which engage in "indicative planning" rather than in compulsory legislation. These expert-groups forecast general economic trends, set guidelines and make recommendations to the six governments. Specifically, the Medium-Term Economic Policy Committee projects population trends, gross national products, and trade figures over five-year periods. Although the three treaties do not officially call for the creation of an "economic and monetary union," the six members committed themselves to this objective on the occasion of the Hague Conference of 1969. In February 1971, the Six formally launched a three-stage plan for the establishment of a complete and monetary union by 1980. In view of this objective, the Six had agreed in 1970 to coordinate their medium-term economic policies by jointly setting target figures for the main economic indicators (growth, prices, unemployment, and the balance of payments). The monetary union is being promoted through the creation of a currency reserve pool to support members suffering from serious balance-of-payments difficulties; through the holding of regular meetings of the six finance ministers and central bankers; and through the approximation of exchange rates for the purpose of creating a single currency by 1980. Given the interdependence of economic and monetary affairs, the Commission favors a strategy of "parallelism" in promoting an EMU.

Monetary Policy (Title II, 2): B. In view of the political sensitivity of all measures concerning the harmonization of monetary policies, it is not surprising that progress in this direction was extremely slow. It took a series of severe monetary crises, beginning with the unilateral devaluation of the Franc (August 8, 1969) and Germany's unilateral decision to "float" the DM (September 1969), followed by the rapid influx of "hot money," resulting from a wave of speculation against the US dollar (May 1971), and culminating in President Nixon's decision to suspend the convertibility of the dollar (August 15, 1971), to induce the Six to initiate common monetary measures. Although the heads of state had agreed on the need for a monetary union already in 1969, and although the finance ministers had approved of this goal in principle in February 1971, definitive progress was not made until March 22, 1972. At that time, the six ministers of finance, in cooperation with officials from prospective member states, adopted a far-reaching compromise on a community exchange system based on fluctuation margins reduced to 2.25 percent for all currencies involved (effective April 24, 1972). Subsequently, at the European Summit in October 1972, it was decided to create a "European Monetary Cooperation Fund" by April 1, 1973, initially endowed with $1.4 billion. This EMCF is considered to be the forerunner of a European Reserve Bank in charge of managing a future "Euro-currency".

Fiscal Policy (Title I, 2): B. The approximation of the diverse tax systems within the six countries constitutes a *sine qua non* for the creation of an economic union. Despite the complexity of the problem—some members prefer direct taxation, others rely more on indirect taxes—the Six succeeded in 1967 in introducing a common value-added tax (VAT or TVA), a turnover tax levied successively on products as they move from the producer to the consumers and enabling goods to cross national borders without being subject to taxes and refunds. Although the Six were able to agree on the harmonization of this indirect tax (effective 1972), no consensus has been reached as to other fiscal charges such as direct income taxes, excise taxes, finance charges, and company taxation.

Agricultural Policy (Part I, Art. 3 and Title II): A. Apart from the "declaration of intent" to inaugurate a common agricultural policy (CAP), the Rome Treaty does not make any specific provisions on this subject, thus permitting the commission to fill in most details. The lack of precision on this matter was due to the sensitive nature of the agricultural sector within the six countries: each member state had its own formula of massive government intervention through a variety of internal support measures (subsidies) as well as protective devices against food imports. Given the enormous complexity of the issue, it did not lend itself to gradual harmonization measures (as in the case of industrial products) but required radical solutions. Therefore, the Six decided to abolish national agricultural policies and create a CAP, centrally financed and with a common policy towards outsiders.

This CAP was implemented in stages, beginning in January 1962, when the Six adopted a procedural framework for the marketing of agricultural products during the transition period. At that time the Six also established the "European

Agricultural Guidance and Guarantee Fund" for the purpose of gradually taking over the cost of implementing the CAP, especially through support buying and export refunds. These initial steps were followed by a decision of the council of December 1964 to adopt a common price structure for basic agricultural products. In July 1966, agreement was reached on extending the scope of the single market to 90 percent of the total food production, and on the principle of financing the entire CAP by July 1, 1968. This decision was complemented by an agreement of the council on December 22, 1969, which involved an arrangement for the gradual financing of the total CAP with autonomous community resources (effective January 1, 1971). Notwithstanding this extraordinarily successful integrative step, the European Community still faces an enormous challenge in the agricultural field because of the existing structural diversity among the six members. In an effort to cope with this challenge, Commissioner Mansholt proposed a drastic reform plan—called "Agriculture 1980"—designed to achieve the following objectives: raise the living standards of farmers, reduce the agricultural labor force and the total farmland, and assist farmers to find jobs in industries through retraining and financial support. The expected result would be a reduction of small farms, a more efficient production by large enterprises, and reduced costs for the CAP, as well as a significant reduction of surplus products. The first decision on the principles of this long-term program was made by the council in March 1971. It was followed up by the overall agreement on the program for the modernization of structures over a period of ten years (March 24, 1972).

Commercial Policy (Part III, Title II, 3): B. Although the treaty required the implementation of a common external trade policy between the Six and the rest of the world by the end of the transition period, the community only succeeded in adopting common rules for trade with Eastern European countries. A common commercial policy implies that trade negotiations and general import and export policy are handled by the commission rather than through bilateral agreements between the national governments. This principle was agreed upon in December 1969, but the commission does not yet have total control over all trade negotiations with noncommunity countries. However, the commission has already demonstrated its ability to serve as common spokesman and actor for the six member states when it successfully negotiated the multilateral tariff-cutting agreement under the Kennedy Round of 1967 and during the third UNCTAD Conference in Santiago, Chile, in May 1972.

Industrial Policy (Part II, Title III and Part III, Title I; Treaty of Paris, Title I): B. Whereas the treaties do not explicitly refer to a common "industrial policy," many provisions are in fact designed to achieve such a goal. They can be divided into two basic categories: one dealing with the creation of a legal fiscal and financial framework favorable to promoting a common industrial policy; the other one involving structural reform and modernization of industries, as well as the establishment of European corporations capable of competing with global, multinational companies. For instance, legal action includes the adoption of a European company statute and more flexible arrangements for encouraging cross-national industrial mergers, as well as the conclusion of a European patent accord; among the necessary fiscal measures are the harmonization of taxes, industrial property laws, regulations for subsidiary companies, bankruptcy laws etc.; in the financial field the creation of a genuine capital market is essential for a common industrial policy. In the legal field some progress has been made on a European Patent Accord, and on a European company statute, but only sporadic measures were taken in the fiscal and financial areas. A series of specific steps to promote structural reform were agreed upon in principle by the Council in June 1970, and by the European Summit in Paris in 1972.

Research and Technology Policy (Title II, 1 Euratom Treaty and Final Communiqué, the Hague, 1969): B. The objective in this area is to promote coordinated scientific research and technological development in the European Community. Since Euratom's jurisdiction is limited essentially to the field of nuclear energy, the Six decided in 1967 to expand the scope of technological cooperation to include the following other areas: computers, telecommunications, new means of transport, noise and pollution control, meteorology, oceanography, and metallurgy. An expert group (the Maréchal Committee, subsequently known as Aigrain Group) was charged with the identification of projects suitable for cooperative ventures. In 1969 the six governmental leaders reaffirmed their readiness to continue more intensively the activities of the community with a view to coordinating and promoting industrial research and development in the principal sectors concerned, in particular by means of common programs, and to supply the financial means for the purpose. They further agreed on the necessity of making fresh efforts to work out in the near future a research program for Euratom, designed in accordance with the exigencies of modern industrial management, and of making it possible to ensure the most effective use of the Joint Research Center. This JRC, originally set up to conduct research on the peaceful use of atomic energy for Euratom, was reorganized in 1969 to coordinate national research in nonnuclear fields such as data processing and environmental protection. The research budget for the 2500 scientists working directly for the JRC amounts to less than $400 million for the projected multinational research program from 1970-1975.

Energy Policy: C. The treaties of the European Community, while not providing for a "common energy policy," deal with the basic forms of energy in a compartmentalized fashion. Therefore, the responsibilities are divided between ECSC (for coal), EEC (for natural gas and oil), and Euratom (for nuclear energy), resulting in three segmented energy markets with different price structures. The built-in lack of coordination in this field has been mitigated by the institutional merger of July 1967, when the single commission became responsible for the promotion of a common energy policy. Whereas ECSC, through the coordination of coal and steel production, and Euratom, through the creation of a common market for nuclear materials, were instrumental in promoting a common energy policy, EEC failed to coordinate policies with regard to oil and natural gas. Despite frequent attempts on the part of the commission to "Europeanize" the energy market for the purpose of assuring optimum internal production and minimum dependence on external supply, these efforts have not yielded significant results. However, faced with the increasing demand for energy (especially oil) on the one hand, and the growing proportion of imported energy on the other, the Six became keenly aware of their almost total dependence on outside energy supplies. Consequently, the council decided in November 1969 to approve the principal guidelines for a common policy for all sources of energy (proposed by the commission in 1968.)

Transport Policy (Part II, Title IV and Chapter IX of ECSC Treaty): C. Progress in this field has been very slow because of the differences in the transport systems of the six countries and because of the various modes of transportation involved in this area (road, rail, inland waterway; air and sea transport are excluded). To provide the community with a modern transport network, a common transport policy would have to be implemented, entailing the unrestricted supply of transport services, harmonized conditions of competition between national systems and different modes of transport, and an equal treatment for all forms of transport as regards taxation, social charges, and subsidies. It was not until December 1968 that the council set itself a specific timetable affecting primarily road transport and the harmonization of competition. No progress had been made on the questions of railroad transportation and the allocation of infrastructure costs when the transition period ended in 1969.

Regional Policy (Title IV): B. One of the principal goals of the Rome Treaty is the harmonious development of the underdeveloped regions within the community: they include southern Italy, the southern and southwestern areas of France, northern Holland, and parts of Germany along the Eastern frontier. These regions are either predominantly agricultural areas, or older industrial areas with a stagnant economy or declining production (e.g., coal mines, steel mills, and textile firms). Regional policy also has to cope with the problems of large concentrations of people and industry in urban zones and attempts to promote a more balanced economic growth between regions. A common agricultural policy naturally complements other harmonization measures in the economic and social fields. The principal instrument charged with implementing the common regional policy is the European Investment Bank, which is to contribute, by calling on the capital markets and its own resources, to the balanced development of the Common Market. The other two bodies involved in the promotion of a common regional policy are the European Social Fund and the European Agricultural Fund, which assist backwards regions through grants for the retraining of labor and structural improvement in farming. The commission's medium-term economic programs consistently emphasized the need for co-ordinating regional policies in order to prevent the widening of gaps between the most industrialized and the least developed areas. At the European Summit in October 1972 it was decided to set up a "Regional Development Fund" by December 31, 1973, to be financed from the Community's own resources.

Common Social Policy (Part III, Title III): B. The ultimate purpose of building an economic and monetary union is to serve human and social needs. Therefore, the main objective of a common social policy is to prevent or mitigate harmful consequences of economic development by assisting the working population in adapting to technological progress through occupational retraining and assuring full employment. The Rome Treaty calls specifically for the approximation of measures relating to employment, working conditions, occupational retraining, social security, industrial safety and hygiene, and equal remuneration as well as minimum wages. The main organism in charge of coordinating social policy is the Committee on Employment (set up in 1970), whereas the European Social Fund gives financial assistance to the member states as they assure the reemployment of workers through vocational retraining and resettlement. Given the crucial role of the European Social Fund in the creation of an economic and monetary union, the Six, meeting in the Hague, agreed on the principle of reforming this institution. In July 1970, the council therefore agreed on extending the jurisdiction of the Fund and increasing its budget, which is to be based on the community's own resources, beginning 1975.

Common Cultural Policy: (Euratom Treaty Art. 9, 2; Final Communiqué, The Hague Summit, Item 11): B. Although the treaties establishing the European Community do not extend to the cultural field—their focus being on the economic and social sectors—European leaders have increasingly become aware of the importance of this third dimension of political integration. Thus the heads of state, meeting in the Hague in 1969, reaffirmed their interest in the creation of a European university and charged the national ministers of education of the council to implement this objective. After years of debate over the formula for financing this international postgraduate institution, a compromise was reached on March 29, 1972, which apportioned expenditures for the European University as follows: 28 percent each for France, Germany, and Italy; 7.9 percent for Belgium and the Netherlands; and 0.2 percent for Luxembourg. Italy is supplying the site (Florence) and the curriculum includes the humanities, social sciences, and law; the official languages are German, French, English, and Dutch.

To complement the European University, the commission proposed the establishment of a "European Research and Development Fund" patterned after the Social Fund and the Agricultural Guidance Fund. However, no action has been taken on this important proposal. The commission also recommended the creation of a "Consultative Committee on Youth" to give its opinions on questions concerning the problems of the young. Furthermore, the commission suggested large-scale community action in the field of tourism and the setting up of a permanent body in charge of facilitating travel across frontiers and drafting a "European charter" for travel agencies. However, the only substantial progress toward a "common cultural policy" was the accord on the new European University, undoubtedly an important step.

Institutional Development

The Council of Ministers (Merger Treaty, 1965, Chapter 1): D. Following its consolidation in 1967, the "Council of the European Communities" became the supreme decision-making organ on all matters of concern to the EEC, ECSC and Euratom. The council derives its legal authority from the three treaties, but its political powers emanate from the national governments. The council's jurisdiction is vast since it serves in a dual capacity—as legislature and executive ("fusion of powers"). Furthermore, the council was given the "power of the purse," an authority that it will share with the European Parliament after 1975. It is composed of national government officials. Each member state is normally represented by its foreign minister, but council sessions are frequently attended by the ministers of agriculture, economics, finance, industry, or transport, depending on the subject matter under discussion. The office of the president of the council is held by each member in turn, in alphabetical order of the nine States, for a period of six months.

In its preeminent role as legislator, the council makes "European law": *Regulations* have the effect of legislation, are binding on all member states, and become automatically part of municipal law without having to be ratified; *directives* are binding only on the states to which they are addressed, leaving the enforcement procedures to the discretion of the national authorities; *decisions* may be addressed either to a government, an enterprise, or a private individual and are binding on the parties involved. The treaty provides for a dual voting procedure: by unanimity and by majority. Virtually all basic policy decisions are taken unanimously: the decision to admit new members (art. 237); the size and membership of the commission (articles 157 and 158); the appointment of judges on the Court (art. 167); the election of the European Parliament by direct universal suffrage (art. 138); the extension and revision of the treaty (articles 235 and 236); and the association with other states or international organizations (art. 238).

However, in contrast to the charter provisions of traditional international organizations, the treaty established the principle of *majority voting* as the *rule*, effective upon the completion of the transition period in 1969, with unanimous votes being the *exception* (art. 148). When a qualified majority is required, the votes of the nine members are weighted as follows: Germany, France, Italy and United Kingdom, ten each; Belgium and Netherlands, five each; Denmark and Ireland, three each; and Luxembourg, two—a total of fifty-eight. The qualified majority in the case of a decision on a proposal by the commission, is forty votes. If the council deliberates without the commission proposal, a decision is possible if the forty votes express the favorable vote of at least five members. A simple majority consists of five members.

The introduction of majority voting as a principle of law to govern interstate relations was a revolutionary attempt to abolish the paralyzing veto power of national governments and replace it by the doctrine of shared sovereignty on a common cause. According to the treaty, the rule governing majority voting was to become operational in gradual phases: During the first stage (1958-61) decisions by qualified majority were applicable in twelve cases.[2] During the second stage (1962-65), the principle of majority voting was extended to six additional cases.[3] Upon entering the third stage (January 1966), most decisions were to be taken by majority.[4]

The principle of majority voting still stands as the innovative maxim of the Rome Treaty and was confirmed in the Accession Treaty. However, its application has been suspended *sine die* by a council compromise called the Luxembourg Protocol. Formally referred to as the "Texts on which agreement was reached at the Extraordinary Session of the EEC Council of Ministers" in Luxembourg on January 26, 1966, this document deals with two major issues: first, the application of the majority voting rule by the EEC Council of Ministers; and second, the cooperation between the council and the commission.[5]

This "amendment" was the result of an "agreement to disagree" between France and the other five members of the European Community over the interpretation of art. 148-150 of the EEC Treaty. These articles provided for the principle of majority voting by the council as of January 1, 1966 (the end of the transition period). The uneasy compromise reached by the Six over the disputed principle was phrased as follows: "When issues very important to one or more member countries are at stake, the members of the Council will try, within a reasonable time, to reach solutions which can be adopted by all members of the Council, while respecting their mutual interests and those of the Community, in accordance with Art. 2 of the Treaty.[6] The French delegation, having failed to achieve a *revision générale* of the Rome Treaty, a revision that would have led to the abolition of the crucial majority voting principle, insisted that discussion must be continued until unanimous agreement on all important issues is reached—a statement with which the other five delegations disagreed.[7] The second issue of the Luxembourg Protocol concerned the interplay between the intergovernmental council and the European Commission. The French government (i.e., President de Gaulle) had submitted a "decalogue" of demands aiming at "clipping the wings" of the Hallstein Commission, which had allegedly abused its powers under the Rome Treaty by a series of unwarranted initiatives and by its claim to represent the Six. Although the final text of the protocol only listed seven rules of cooperation between the council and commission, it gave the council, in effect, oversight over the activities of the commission.

The adoption of the Luxembourg Protocol certainly constituted a step in the direction of increased national control over the European Community organs and was thus an indication of a trend toward intergovernmental cooperation (rather than supranational integration). However, in legal terms, this "agreement to disagree" did not alter the basic philosophy of the Rome Treaty since the principle of majority voting is still intact. What has been decided upon, at least temporarily, was to suspend its application pending the projected merger of the three treaties or their revision (art. 236 of the EEC Treaty). In effect, it amounted to an official recognition of the practice of seeking unanimity on council decisions during marathon sessions by "stopping the clock," if necessary.[8]

The Luxembourg Protocol only emphasized one of the cardinal features of the European Community, namely the interdependence between the "executives." This internalized code of collective decision-making between the council and the European Commission has been referred to as "community method." It describes the constant and intensive interaction between these two organs, comparable to a dialogue between two Janus heads. However, if there had been any doubt as to which of the two was "more equal" than the other, the Luxembourg Protocol settled the debate in favor of the council (see Figures 4-2 and 4-3).

Since the Council of Ministers is ultimately responsible for the success or failure of the European Community enterprise, its performance over the last twenty years deserves careful attention. Thus it has been argued that "the Council has done more to unify Europe than any other institution in the history of the Continent."[9] This judgment is undoubtedly correct if one compares the output of the council with that of traditional intergovernmental organizations. However, if one chooses the standards set by the Rome Treaty which outlined the council's goals in terms of policy harmonization through the gradual use of majority voting, the judgment will differ considerably. Not only has the council failed to adopt majority-voting as a rule (with unanimity being the exception), but it has also shelved hundreds of proposals submitted by the commission for action on a variety of subjects.[10] On a number of other items, the council procrastinated for years until it finally dealt with the backlog that had accumulated and when inaction could no longer be justified. In short, the council (of national) ministers was usually reluctant to act and on the defensive against the dynamic "Eurocrats" of the commission, the second most important organ.(see Figures 4-2 and 4-3).

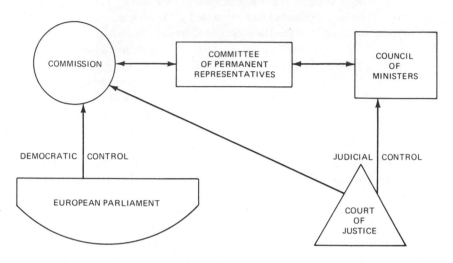

EXECUTIVE–LEGISLATIVE
INTERACTION

Figure 4-2. The Institutions of the European Community.

The Commission (Merger Treaty, 1965, Chapter II): A. The European Commission is the nexus of the community's institutions and serves as the only genuine spokesman for the emerging united Europe. It is an organ *sui generis* with no counterpart in other regional organizations. Its nucleus was established in the form of the supranational High Authority under President Jean Monnet in 1951. Its composition varied in numbers from nine to fourteen; originally, the EEC Commission under President Walter Hallstein had nine members; the number was temporarily increased to fourteen by the Merger Treaty in 1967 (it was reduced to nine in 1970). Finally, the Accession Treaty of 1972 established the new commission of thirteen members, distributed among the nine countries as follows: France, Germany, Italy, and the United Kingdom, two members each; the other five states have the right to nominate one member each (effective as of January 1973). The membership of the commission also varied over the years, as did its presidents and vice-presidents.[11] The responsibilities of this collegiate body are divided into nine general areas: the president is in charge of the Secretariat, the Legal Service, the Spokesman's Group, and the Security Office. The three vice-presidents are responsible for agriculture, economic and financial affairs, and the Statistical Office; and for the Internal market, the harmonization of laws, energy, the supply agency, and safeguard and controls. The other commissioners are responsible for the following areas: social affairs, transport, credits and investments, budgets, financial control; coordination of enlargement negotiations, development aid; competition; regional policy; press and information; dissemination of scientific information; external relations; external trade; industrial affairs; general research and technology; joint research center.[12]

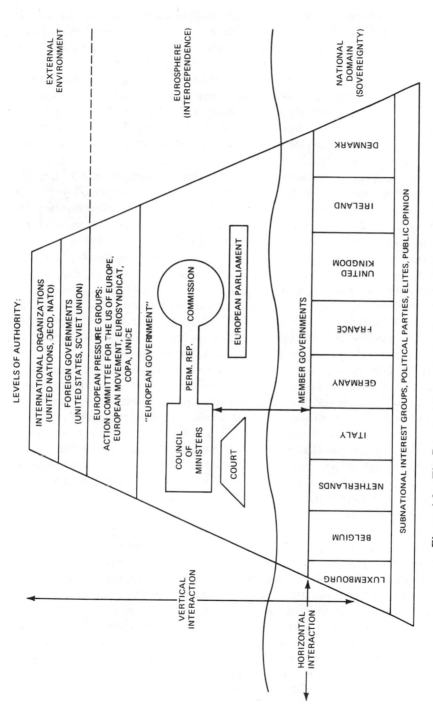

Figure 4-3. The Principal Actors in the European Community System.

The administration of this "Eurocracy" is divided into departments known as "Directorates-General," each responsible to a commission member. Commissioners hold office for a period of four years; presidents and vice-presidents are appointed for two years (as of 1973). The difficult preparatory work on any commission initiative is performed by the Directorates in cooperation with various national interest groups as well as transnational pressure groups such as the Union of Industries of the European Community (UNICE) and the Committee of Professional Agricultural Organizations (COPA). Subsequently, the commission consults with the Committee of Permanent Representatives; finally, the council has to decide on the matter.

The European Commission has many vital missions to fulfill; like the president of the United States, it "wears a number of hats." First, the commission is the *guardian* of the treaties in its task of overseeing the application of "European law" in the community. Second, the commission is the *initiator* of policy-proposals[13] which are decided upon by the council and subsequently implemented by the commission (the "community method"). Third, the commission serves as the official *mediator* between the member governments in policy disputes arising out of common policies. Hence, the commissioners are expected to be at once administrators, politicians, and diplomats. Furthermore, the commissioners have to reconcile their legal obligation to preserve the treaties with their political mandate to expand the "Eurosphere" (the prototype of a conservative-progressive dilemma).

In the light of these unprecedented demands on the ingenuity, competence, skill, courage and, last but not least, on the stamina of the commissioners, they are carefully chosen and given complete independence from national supervision and control. The commission arrives at decisions by simple majority votes, and all members are collectively responsible for them. The commission's task is facilitated by the fact that it is the only community organ with a "European" perspective. Its unique, comprehensive view of complex technical problems is possible because the commission has a virtual monopoly on "objective data" (national governments have necessarily a biased tunnel-vision, distorted by their respective national interest). This "Euro-perspective," in turn, permits the commission to make sound and fair proposals based upon anticipated counter-arguments likely to be presented by the national governments.

Moreover, this superior perspective, based upon objective, comparative evaluations, enables the commission to launch a two-pronged attack on the integrity of national structures and to fragment the national interest on certain issues. Indeed, "the Commission, by its existence, sharpens the awareness of alternative courses of action [not only *between* governments but also] among groups *within* the state; and when it enters into relationships directly with these groups, the Commission effectively highlights the extent to which the views of governments and the views of some internal groups differ. Governments are on the defensive insofar as they now have to make a deliberate effort to preserve an appearance of state interest in the face of the Community. The integrity of national decision-making structures is challenged from without and erosion from within."[14]

The methods used by the commission to advance the "European cause" can be defined as *goal articulation* (of the common interest), *coalition-building* (with national bureaucracies or pressure groups), *brokerage* (serving as an "honest broker" or facilitator between national governments), *package dealing* (arriving at compromises that optimize joint gains), and *expansion of tasks* (through redefinition of national objectives in the direction of greater need for Community action).[15] In order to enable the commission to be fully effective in these delicate operations, two essential conditions are necessary: a cooperative attitude on the part of the council and the willingness of the national leaders to respect the "community spirit." As long as these two conditions were met, the commission has been an effective internal federator. In fact, "whether it is in its growth in policy-making power or in administrative responsibility that one measures the early achievements of the Commission, one can scarcely find a better example of political dynamism in the whole world of international organization."[16] It may well have been due to this spectacular success in the early 1960s that the commission under its first president developed excessive zeal in the pursuit of political goals. Thus Professor Hallstein used to refer to the European Community on several occasions as a "federation in the making," with its principal institutions having prefederal character.[17] He also referred to the community as a phenomenon *sui generis* and a new legal order, a new corporate entity, and a new personality in international law and international politics.[18] Considering himself as the true spokesman of this new European body politic (particularly during his frequent visits to the United States), Dr. Hallstein encouraged the creation of diplomatic missions to the community and received foreign emissaries with all the paraphernalia usually reserved for leaders of sovereign states. Therefore, it was not surprising that General de Gaulle, who was extremely sensitive to what he considered the *malapropos* pretensions of stateless technocrats, eventually insisted not only on the dismissal of the president of the EEC Commission, but also on the elimination of all traces of its sovereign prerogatives.[19]

Despite de Gaulle's all-out attack on the very existence and *raison d'être* of the commission, it refused to retreat from the political arena. Indeed, Hallstein's successor, Jean Rey, immediately set the record straight when he assumed office in 1967. In an address to the European Parliament, President Rey compared the evolution of the European Community to that of the American federation and declared that "we are perfectly aware that our task is to achieve not only the economic unification of Europe but also political progress. . . . We do not see ourselves merely as administrators of the Community; we are also there to provide inspiration."[20]

President Rey also succeeded in obtaining the first mandate as official spokesman for the European Community at the Kennedy Round negotiations in 1967, thus giving substance to Professor Hallstein's claim that the community is a legal personality in international law.

The third president of the commission, Signor Malfatti, also pressed for greater recognition of the commission as an actor in international politics. He urged the national governments to grant the commission an official status in the ongoing negotiations on European political cooperation. He argued that "we are directly and immediately faced with the problem of the roles played by the Commission, which cannot be excluded from participation in the process of building political union in Europe, since it is itself the main protagonist of the construction of the Community. . . . The Commission's participation [would also] improve the efficacy of the role assigned to our institution [since] it is obvious that the process of economic unification and the process of political unity are nothing but two sides of the same coin."[21] Although the president usually serves as its official spokesman, the European Commission did on several occasions collectively go on record in favor of closer political unity. For instance, in its INITIATIVE 1964, the commission used the terms "federation" and "political union" and affirmed that "there can be no disputing the fact that the way towards European federation lies through the existing Communities . . . [because] as long as the Communities survive and remain a life-blood, there is a real chance that a full-scale federation will come about."[22] The commission further noted that the community is concerned with both elements of "political union," namely "the extension of the process of European unification beyond the mere pooling of economic and social policies [and] the improvement of the European institutional structure."[23] This theme was reiterated in the "Statement of the Commission to the European Parliament" on the significance of July 1, 1968. In this formal declaration, the commission referred to this date as a "milestone in the history of Europe" and stated that "Europe must have the institutions it needs to become a politically organized continent—not only economic institutions, which are already well on the way to completion, but also political institutions through which it can act to become . . . a European federation."[24] In its General Report of 1970, the commission again projected its future in optimistic terms when it pointed out that "the Community is already political in essence and in the very form of its institutions. But it is destined to become even more political, to increase the powers of its institutions, to align the policies of its Member States and to work out step by step a foreign policy at Community level."[25]

On June 30, 1971, the commission took a major political initiative on the question of institutional reform of the community organs and their respective powers. Prompted by the council decision to increase the authority of the European Parliament during the 1970s, the commission appointed a group of independent experts on constitutional law to study the implications of this important development. The mandate of this group of "wise men" chaired by M.

Vedel was: to look into all the implications of widening the powers of the European Parliament, (1) from the point of view of transferring certain responsibilities from national authorities to the community institutions, (2) with a view of providing the community with effective institutions, (3) with a view of guaranteeing that community decisions will be democratic and legitimate, and (4) taking account of the constitutional practices and principles of the member states. Within these general guidelines the group of "wise men" was to analyze the following specific topics: (a) the participation of the European Parliament in the continuing *constitutional* role of the community—allotting new powers, reform of the institutions, political union; (b) the participation of the European Parliament in the *legislative* process of the community—relationships between community law and national laws, the nature of council decisions, sharing of legislative powers and the parliament's right of initiate action; (c) the budgetary powers of the Parliament; (d) its political control over community actions: (e) modifications of relations between community institutions; and (f) the link between strengthening the powers of the European Parliament and its direct election by universal suffrage.[26] The "Vedel Report" was submitted to the commission in March 1972.[27]

Notwithstanding these constant efforts on the part of the commission to participate as a significant political actor in debates and negotiations on European political unification, it has been increasingly attacked for its alleged ineptitude, lack of courage and initiative, and preoccupation with trivial routine administration. Thus it has been argued that the commission failed to fulfill its essentially political role and has become a mere administrative organ, characterized by progressive bureaucratization and unable to provide supranational leadership.[28] Surprisingly, this criticism by an outsider was corroborated by a member of the commission itself when he referred to it as an "inefficient bureaucratic colossus animated by a mania for harmonization."[29] Undoubtedly, Parkinson's Law of the inherent tendency of bureaucracies to proliferate applies to the commission as much as to any other large-scale organization with a vested interest in self-preservation and an inclination to engage in "empire-building." The commission could refute this argument and justify its emphasis on the rapid approximation of national laws as being part of its mandate. But there appears to be evidence that some of its members have developed "Euro-myopia" in the sense that they are exclusively concerned with the welfare of the community ("inward-looking") and neglect or ignore the legitimate interests of nonmember nations. If "Euro-centrism" would in the future prevent the commission from recognizing the worldwide responsibilities of the European Community, such criticisms would indeed be justified and necessitate a radical re-orientation of its policies in the 1970s.

The actual powers of the European Commission have frequently been misinterpreted along two lines: some analysts have looked upon it as an embryonic European government; others have regarded it as a mere variation of traditional international administrations. In reality, the truth lies somewhere in between these two optimistic and pessimistic extremes. The judgment has been rendered more difficult as a result of the merger between the "supranational" High Authority of the ECSC and the "extranational" commissions of EEC and Euratom in 1967. Although art. 9 of the Merger Treaty states that the consolidated commission shall exercise the powers given to the High Authority in the Paris Treaty, its mandate is undoubtedly more limited, especially because the Luxembourg Protocol considerably circumscribed its freedom of action. Against the background of these preliminary considerations, the actual and potential powers of the commission can be described as follows: (1) The *supranational authority* of the commission is limited to its jurisdiction under article 15 of the ECSC Treaty, which gives the High Authority the power to take decisions that are *directly* binding on individuals and enterprises throughout the community *without* the intervention of national governments; (2) the *extra-national influence* of the commission (or its *potential* supranational powers) consists of the following attributes: (a) commissioners are *independent* European civil servants and completely free from national controls or supervision; (b) decisions are taken by *majority votes* in the *common interest* of all members; (c) its policy *proposals* are the *prerequisite* for council action; (d) its balanced, objective *European perspective* gives it the monopoly in planning new programs; (e) the *political neutrality* and *technical competence* of its members makes the commission the crisis management agency *par excellence* and the most effective arbiter in intergovernmental disputes over community policies.

In summary it should be noted that the European Commission is bound to remain the subject of political controversy in the years to come because of the unique nature of its structure and mission. In fact, should the debate over the *raison d'être* and performance of the commission subside, it would signal the demise of the European unity movement since conflict is endemic as long as there is progress. In its function as the supreme crisis management agency in the European Community, the commission has the responsibility to produce a European synthesis whenever a national thesis confronts a national antithesis. This vital role as the acknowledged facilitator of conflict resolution, and as the dynamic driving force in European integration, makes the commission the "official internal federator" of the European Community.

Whether the commission of the New Europe will be primarily concerned with administrative tasks or with political action will depend on its composition during the next decade: if it consists exclusively of international civil servants, its style will be "technocratic"; if the majority of its members are political leaders, they will make the commission a political actor in its own right.

The Committee of Permanent Representatives (Merger Treaty, 1965, Chapter I, 4): B. Whereas the Treaties of Rome and Paris did not give *de jure* recognition to the Committee of Permanent Representatives, the Merger Treaty accorded official status to this subsidiary body of the council. Composed of high level officials from the member governments (usually with ambassadorial rank), the committee serves as a crucial liaison organ between the intergovernmental council and the European Commission. Its chairman is the permanent representative of the member state whose minister presides over the council (on a rotating basis). The committee assures continuity—since the council meets only at certain intervals—through continuing contacts with the staff of the commission and through the preparation of the council's agenda. The role of the permanent representatives is necessarily characterized by ambivalence because a premium is placed on the successful balancing of the defense of the national interest against the promotion of common policies. This dual responsibility tends to create a "split personality syndrome" which has been aptly illustrated by the German reference to the permanent representatives (or *Staendige Vertreter*) as "*Staendige Verraeter*" (or permanent traitors). Notwithstanding this criticism, these "Euro-Ambassadors" have been surprisingly successful in their delicate task of blending multiple loyalties while preserving personal integrity. Thus the permanent representatives have become a vital link between their respective national capital and Brussels and have served as congenial partners of, and intermediaries between, the national bureaucracies and the "Eurocracy," composed of the commissioners, their staff, and the experts of the various Management Committees. The interaction and intermingling of national and international bureaucrats in various committees and working groups within the decision-making context of the European Community has been called "bureaucratic interpenetration."[30] Its two principal purposes are to secure the maximum amount of data from all available sources (national administrations, interest groups, and community data), and to present the most balanced version to the council, and subsequently to generate support for the "European version" of the proposal in the six capitals. Both technical experts and political generalists are locked in this complex process of drafting symbiotic proposals and "condemned to succeed" in arriving at equitable solutions (which already anticipate national reactions) by the time the council meets in regular session. It appears that the success of bureaucratic interpenetration involves three elements: the specificity of the treaty provision regarding a given subject; the psychological orientation of Eurocrats; and the constellation of political forces vis-à-vis the issue at the crucial moment. To be successful, bureaucratic interpenetration has to proceed pragmatically and in an atmosphere of dispassionate deliberation, giving the optimum version of a proposal the chance to materialize. This "internalized" form of decision-making (typical for the European Community and atypical for other international organizations) is of course characterized by a constant tension between two ideologically opposed parties: the conservative national representatives inclined toward preserving the status quo, and the progressive Eurocrats concerned with system transformation.[31]

The permanent representatives obviously hold the key position in this process of bureaucratic interpenetration as they may opt for lubricating or blocking interaction between Brussels and their respective capitals. As virtual alter egos of their foreign ministers, permanent representatives serve as a two-way channel of influence: as spokesmen for their national cause in Brussels during "prenegotiations" on new commission proposals, and as advocates of the optimum European compromise with their domestic bureaucracies. The value of the committee has always been recognized by the commission. In fact, "from the inception of the Community the great majority of Eurocrats have considered the need to cultivate close relations with the national bureaucracies not simply important but virtually axiomatic . . . [since] one cannot integrate against the national administrations."[32]

In recognition of the services rendered by the permanent representatives as "go-betweens" and screening organs, a number of proposals have been made by leaders of the national governments aiming at the upgrading of "Euro-ambassadors" to secretaries of state for European affairs or even European ministers.[33]

The European Parliament (EEC Treaty, Part V, Title I, 1, 1): C. Notwithstanding its futuristic name, the European Parliament[34] is not a supranational legislature but a consultative assembly composed of delegates from the national parliaments of the member states of the European Community. Originally, the total membership of this body was 142, but the number was increased to 198 by the Accession Treaty of 1972, which apportioned the seats as follows: France, Germany, Italy, and the United Kingdom, 36 each; Belgium and the Netherlands, 14 each; Denmark and Ireland, 10 each; and Luxembourg, 6. The method of selection varies from one country to another, usually reflecting the respective strength of the parties in the national parliaments, as well as the expressed desire of delegates to represent their nation in Strasbourg (the seat of the European Parliament). Its most original feature, without precedent in the history of international assemblies, is its organizational structure. Instead of being grouped along national lines or in alphabetical order (as are the assemblies of the Council of Europe and the Western European Union), delegates to the European Parliament sit according to party affiliation. Originally, three such transnational political parties existed: in order of strength, the Christian Democrats, the Socialists, and the Liberals. They were joined by the European Democratic Union (French Gaullists) in 1965, and by the Italian Communists in 1969. The three major "European Parties" frequently achieved cross-national consensus on political issues and served as transnational advocates of "European solutions." The Parliament is further organized in thirteen standing committees in each of which all six national parliaments are represented. Whereas most "European political parties" in the parliament organize informal working-groups on the basis of ideological denomination, the main criterion for membership in a standing committee is expertise in the area covered by the committee: political affairs, foreign trade, agriculture, labor affairs, internal market, economic and financial affairs, relations with developing countries, transport, energy, research and cultural affairs, health protection, administration and budget, and legal affairs. Each committee has a rapporteur who prepares reports and draft resolutions which are subsequently debated in the annual plenary sessions. Representatives of the commission attend "hearings" of committees, deliver an annual report to the Parliament, and reply to both written and oral questions posed during the plenary sessions.[35] Occasionally, representatives of the Council of Ministers participate in the debates of the European Parliament, but the council is never bound by its "recommendations."[36]

Lacking the three essential attributes of a genuine legislature (i.e., a popular mandate, legislative powers, and budgetary control) the European Parliament is a mere consultative body, although it has the power to force the commission to resign by a vote of censure with a two-thirds majority (art. 144). According to the treaty, the assembly was to exercise powers of deliberation and control (art. 137); it was also supposed to draw up proposals for the direct election of its members by universal suffrage (art. 138, 3). However, "the Council, acting by means of a unanimous vote, shall determine the provisions which it shall recommend to Member States for adoption in accordance with their respective constitutional rules" (art. 138, 3). In accordance with its mission, the assembly proceeded to study the possibility of direct elections by creating a "Working Group for European Elections" on October 22, 1958. Under the chairmanship of the Belgian Senator Fernand Dehousse, it elaborated a draft convention which was adopted by the assembly in May 1960 and submitted to the council for consideration in June of that year.[37] The council assured the assembly in October 1960, and again in July 1961, that it was "studying" the draft convention on direct European elections, but the council did not take any action. Since this "political" attempt to increase its authority had failed, the parliament decided to take a "legal" initiative on March 12, 1969, by adopting a special resolution based upon art. 175 of the EEC Treaty. This article gives each community institution (and each member state) the right to refer the matter to the Court of Justice if the council (or the commission) violates the treaty by failing to act. Faced with the potential threat of judicial action, the council referred the project to the Committee of Permanent Representatives, which studied it during the fall of 1969. Continuing French opposition, however, prevented the adoption of the draft convention, and the six heads of state simply noted in the final communiqué of the Hague Conference (December 1969) that "the problem of the method of direct elections is still being studied by the Council of Ministers." But in the same communiqué, the six governments decided to strengthen the budgetary powers of the European Parliament in accordance with art. 201 of the Rome Treaty, beginning in 1975. In an effort to put new pressure on the national governments to undertake the necessary steps toward the creation of a genuine European legislature, the president of the

European Parliament demanded that this body should be given legislative powers and the right of investiture of the commission, and that uniform regulations for the direct election of the members of the European Parliament be formulated before January 1, 1975.[38] However, the Parliament remained unsuccessful in promoting its just cause. (See also Appendix D, item 15.)

In sum, the past performance of the European Parliament has been characterized by a great deal of motion but little action—not because its members were incompetent but because of their lack of legislative powers.

The Court of Justice (EEC Treaty, Part V, Title I, 1, 4): B. The court of the enlarged European Community is composed of nine eminent judges appointed for six years by agreement among the member states. All decisions of the court are joint opinions; there are no "dissenting opinions," a provision that ensures noninterference of national governments (they are unable to determine as to whether a national judge has been "loyal" in a given case). The Court of Justice is comparable to a federal "supreme court" since it preserves the rule of law within the political system of the community, serving at once as a constitutional court, an international tribunal, and an administrative court. In its role as a *constitutional* court, it ensures the observance of law and justice in the interpretation and application of the treaties.[39] In its role as an *international* tribunal, the court settles disputes between the member states.[40] In its role as an *administrative* court, it decides in cases between the community and its personnel.[41] In addition to this triple role, the Court of Justice is entitled to "make [community] law": constitutional, administrative and private law. This judicial control over the "new legal order" of the community is reinforced by the doctrine that community law is superior to municipal law, a principle that is recognized in the constitutions (or amendments) of all member states and confirmed by rulings of their highest courts.

The court's jurisdiction not only extends over the national governments and the community institutions, but permits individual firms and private citizens to bring suit directly to the Court of Justice, whose rulings, in turn, are binding on all parties concerned. This right of appeal on the part of private citizens constitutes a truly innovate feature of the legal order of the community, underlining the proposition that the Court of Justice is already a quasi-federal organ within its sphere of competence. In terms of accomplishments over a period of about fifteen years, the court has been quite effective: by 1970, 717 cases had been submitted to the court, 518 of which had been decided on, while 121 were settled at an earlier stage; the rest is pending.[42]

However, the court has been less effective in promoting *political* unification since it abstained from any involvement in doctrinaire controversies between the apostles of federalism and the defenders of national sovereignty.

The Economic and Social Committee: (EEC Treaty, Part V, Title I, 3): B. This consultative body consists of representatives of the following groups: producers, farmers, workers, transport operators, merchants, artisans, the liberal professions, and the general interest. The role of the committee—a kind of "supranational interest group"—is to advise the council and the commission on all major policy issues affecting the economic and social sectors of the member states. In turn, the committee must be consulted before decisions on certain matters involving the EEC or Euratom can be taken (e.g., arts. 43, 49, 54 EEC). The members of the committee are appointed for a four-year term by the council, acting unanimously, after consultation with the commission. According to the Rome Treaties, the members serve in a personal capacity and are not bound by any instructions. France, Germany, Italy and Britain are represented each by 24 members; Belgium, the Netherlands, Denmark and Ireland send 12 delegates each and Luxembourg sends 6, making a total membership of 143. Although the ESC has constant rapport with several hundred pressure groups headquartered in Brussels, its influence on the decision-making process is marginal since its functions are advisory only.[43]

The Consultative Committee. Established by the ECSC Treaty, it is composed of seventy-odd representatives from various economic and social groups and fulfills the task of advising the commission and the council on matters concerning ECSC, thus serving in a complementary role to the Economic and Social Committee (which is in charge of EEC and Euratom affairs).

Special Advisory Bodies: B. Whereas the "consultative bodies" discussed in the preceding section deal with general policy issues affecting the three community organizations in the economic and social fields, the role of the "special advisory bodies" consists in providing expert advice to the commission and the council on specific subjects such as monetary, transport, or scientific and technical affairs.

The Monetary Committee. In accordance with art. 105 of the EEC Treaty, the Monetary Committee consists of fourteen members (two from each member state and two appointed by the commission); they are usually central bankers or high civil servants capable of advising the community organs on monetary affairs. Their mission consists in keeping under review the monetary and financial situation, including the balance of payments of all members, and in submitting periodic opinions to the council and the commission. In the event that one member state experiences a serious disequilibrium of the balance of payments, the commission, after consultation with the Monetary Committee, may recommend that the council take steps in the direction of granting mutual assistance to the government concerned.[44]

The Transport Committee. Established by the EEC Treaty (art. 83), it is composed of thirty experts appointed by the governments and attached to the commission, which may consult it on transport questions whenever the need arises.

The "113 Committee." Created by the EEC Treaty (art. 113), this committee consists of senior officials appointed by the council and is charged with assisting the commission in tariff negotiations with nonmember states.

The Scientific and Technical Committee. Together with the Nuclear Supply Agency (created by the Euratom Treaty), and the Nuclear Research Consultative Committee (set up in 1961), it advises the commission on problems of nuclear energy and research.

The Short-Term Economic Policy Committee (set up in 1960) and the *Medium Term Economic Policy Committee* (set up in 1964). These are composed of national representatives and commission members. The task of the first is to assist the member states in coordinating their day-to-day economic policies; the latter's task is to chart the probable trend of the community's economy over a five-year period.

The Special Agricultural Committee (or Management Committee). It was established in 1960 and consists of senior officials from the national Ministries of Agriculture and commission experts who are charged with preparing compromise solutions for the implementation of the Common Agricultural Policy.

The Administrative Commission for the Social Security of Migrant Workers. Set up in 1959, it is made up of national officials and Commission members who are to protect the interests of community citizens working in another member country.

The Budgetary Policy Committee. Set up in 1964, it consists of national officials responsible for drawing up the budgets of the member states.

The Committee of Central Bank Governors. Set up in 1964, it meets to discuss credit, money-market and exchange matters, with a member of the commission attending.

Industrial Policy Group. It purports to promote a favorable climate for intra-European industrial cooperation.

Permanent Committee on Employment. This committee is concerned with assuring the highest level of employment throughout the community.

Ancillary Institutions B: Internal Institutions. These bodies assist mainly in the implementation of internal economic, social and regional policies.

The European Investment Bank. Established by the EEC Treaty (arts. 129-130), the bank is an autonomous organ headed by a Board of Governors composed of the Finance Ministers of the member states. This body, in turn, appoints the Board of Governors, which consists of nine members, one from each member state. An Administrative Council compromises eighteen administrators and their substitutes. France, Germany, Italy, and Britain are represented by three administrators each; and the smaller countries by one each. The daily administration is carried on by a Management Committee comprised of five members. The bank was set up with a subscribed capital of $1 billion to aid capital investment in the underdeveloped regions of the community and to help finance projects of modernization of enterprises and innovative programs. The three new members also contribute proportionately to the statutory reserves of the bank.

The European Social Fund. Administered by the commission, the fund was set up under the EEC Treaty (arts. 123-128) to aid employment and labor mobility within the community by reimbursing member states for half the cost of retraining and resettlement of workers affected by economic changes in the Common Market. The fund's expenditures from 1960 to 1968 averaged about $10 billion a year to assist 960,000 workers. In the 1970s the fund is to become a dynamic instrument of modern employment policy with an annual budget of $250 million to help 150,000 workers per year.

The European Agricultural Guidance and Guarantee Fund. Created in 1966, the so-called FEOGA is administered by the commission and finances the common agricultural policy (CAP) of the EEC. Its central budget was approximately $2.7 billion in 1970. Financed out of levies on agricultural imports into the member-states and transferred to a community budget, the fund assists European farmers through subsidies in the modernization of agricultural production and distribution.

Ancillary Institutions: External Institutions. In addition to the ancillary bodies set up to assist in the organization of the internal European Common Market, the following institutions are designed to provide for improved development aid to African nations.

European Development Fund. Created in 1958, the EDF finances economic and social development projects in the associated overseas countries by direct grants. The fund is administered by the commission and distributes development aid of approximately $100 million annually, the budget being composed of contributions by the member states.

Councils of Association. In an effort to provide for a joint machinery between the community and its associated member states, Councils of Association were created by the following agreements:

1. Agreement of Association between the EEC and Greece (October 9, 1961).

2. Agreement of Association between the EEC and Turkey (September 12, 1963).
3. The Yaoundé Convention between the EEC and eighteen associated states in Africa and Madagascar (July 20, 1963); the Convention was su'sequently renewed on July 29, 1969, and the Association Council continues to function for the period ending January 1975.
4. The Arusha Convention between the EEC and three East African countries (Kenya, Uganda, and Tanzania) was signed on July 26, 1968, and renewed on September 24, 1969; it is in force from January 1, 1971 to January 31, 1975.

Legal-Financial Bases

Consolidation of Treaties (Merger Treaty, 1965, Preamble): C. Although the member states are on record as expressing their determination to proceed with the unification of the three communities, no progress has been achieved on this fundamental issue. The only solution to this problem would consist in a consolidation of the three treaties establishing the three organizations, namely the Treaty of Paris (signed on April 18, 1951; entry into force on July 25, 1952) establishing the ECSC, and the Treaties of Rome (signed on March 25, 1957; entry into force on January 1, 1958), creating respectively EEC and Euratom. In addition the provisions of the Treaty Establishing a Single Council and a Single Commission or Merger Treaty (signed on April 8, 1965; entry into force on July 1, 1967) will have to be taken into consideration. Finally, the Accession Treaties with the new member states of January 22, 1972, would have to be included in such a fusion agreement. The consolidation of the treaties is complicated by the fact that they were signed at different stages of the European integration process. Consequently, the Rome Treaties lack the supranational provisions of the Paris Treaty. Furthermore, the Paris Treaty is a normative legislative document (a *traité loi*), whereas the Rome Treaties are essentially programmatic in nature, leaving the elaboration of the principles to the competent institutions (*traités cadres*). It is also noteworthy that the EEC Treaty was concluded for an unlimited period (art. 240) and created a new legal personality (art. 210). These two points are underlined by the fact that over eighty states have accredited diplomatic representatives to the community at Brussels (its *de facto* capital).

The preceding considerations concerning the legal nature of the European Community demonstrate that its parameters were originally determined and have subsequently been modified by treaties according to international law. But the community is not only born of law; it also creates law. The three treaties plus the amendments have given the European Community an autonomous legal order—a *personnalité juridique*—enabling its organs to make laws that are directly applicable in the member states.[45] These unorthodox socioeconomic powers of the community are exercised by a legislative body (the council) and a judicial organ (the court) in cooperation with an executive-administrative institution (the commission) and an assembly (the Parliament). In view of the unprecedented control given to this international organization in its areas of jurisdiction, the European Community has been referred to as a prefederal system or as an incipient federation—the assembly being the quasi-legislature, the court the embryonic judiciary, and the council and commission symbolizing the future executive-administration. Although this analysis may still appear futuristic and optimistic, there is no doubt that the European Community is an original, innovative phenomenon *sui generis*. Its complex political system could be analyzed in terms of four dimensions:

1. The international level (intergovernmental cooperation between the member-states).
2. The supranational level (internalized decision-making and dialogue between council and commission).
3. The infranational level (direct vertical applicability of community law to states).
4. The transnational level (horizontal community formation across national borders).

Merger of Institutions (EEC Treaty, Convention and Merger Treaty): A. On the occasion of the signature of the Rome Treaties, the six governments expressed their concern over the multiplicity of institutions responsible for the achievement of similar aims within the European Community and decided therefore to create certain single institutions to perform these tasks. The problem was essentially one of semantics. Whereas the Treaty of Paris referred to a "Common Assembly," a "Special Council," a "High Authority" and a "Court of Justice" (art. 7), the Rome Treaties referred to an "Assembly," a "Council," a "Commission," and a "Court of Justice" (art. 4 of the EEC Treaty and art. 3 of the Euratom Treaty). These terminological inconsistencies were eliminated by the following amendments providing for a merger of the four bodies. In the convention, signed by the six governments together with the treaty establishing EEC in 1957, the signatories had combined two of the four institutions provided for respectively in the three treaties; thus a single assembly and a single Court of Justice were created.

The other two organs were consolidated ten years later when the six member states of the European Community signed the "Treaty Establishing a Single Council and a Single Commission of the European Communities" on April 8, 1965, an agreement that entered into force on July 1, 1967, with the creation of a new Commission, composed of fourteen members (reduced to nine after three years); and a single council.[46] This "Merger Treaty," while creating a single council and commission, did not alter their respective powers and responsibilities under the three treaties. In other words, the council and the commission continue to exercise their functions in accordance with the provisions of the Treaties of Paris and Rome. Furthermore, the treaty gives the Committee of Permanent Representatives (hitherto an informal liaison group between Brussels and the six capitals) formal status as an institution. In addition, the treaty calls for the fusion of the three administrations (the European civil servants in Brussels and Luxembourg) and the three budgets (of ECSC, EEC and Euratom). Although the "Merger Treaty" only formalized a state of affairs that existed in practice when it amalgamated the councils (since the same national ministers had been represented in these bodies ever since 1958), it did enhance the prestige of the unified commission—the embryonic European executive—by giving it control over the three administrative services (about 5000 Eurocrats).

The Treaty of Accession: A. On January 22, 1972, the United Kingdom, Denmark, Ireland, and Norway signed the Treaty of Accession to the European Community in Brussels. The treaty entered into force, following its ratification by the nine national parliaments concerned, on January 1, 1973. From that date on, the European Community's membership expanded from six to nine states: the original Six plus the three new signatories, all of which (except Norway) accepted the basic principles and amendments of the three original treaties, subject to modifications agreed upon in the Accession Treaty.

The Community Budget (EEC Treaty, Part V, Title II, Merger Treaty, Chapter III): B. According to the Paris Treaty, the High Authority had the power to raise funds for the operations of ECSC (art. 49), but the EEC Treaty and the Merger Treaty gave the council (and thus the governments) almost complete control over the budget of the community. This common budget consists mainly of financial contributions of the member states on a scale roughly proportionate to their economic strength (GNP): thus France, Germany, and Italy contribute 28 percent each, Belgium and the Netherlands 7.9 percent each, and Luxembourg 0.2 percent.

Starting on January 1, 1973, the new member states will contribute to the Community budget. They will pay their receipts from agricultural levies and customs duty as well as a proportion of value-added tax (VAT) revenue. During the five-year transition period, however, total contributions from the new member states will be subject to limitations expressed as percentages of the total community budget:

	1973	1974	1975	1976	1977
Denmark	1.099	1.382	1.698	2.040	2.408
Ireland	0.272	0.342	0.421	0.505	0.596
UK	8.640	10.850	13.340	16.020	18.920

Beginning on January 1, 1978, the new member states will make full contributions, subject to the following conditions: in 1978 the increase in contributions from the new members may not total more than two-fifths of the difference between their respective contributions in 1977 and what would have been their full contributions for 1977 had they not benefited from reduced payments during the transitional period; in 1979 the increases in the contributions from the candidate countries (expressed as a percentage of the community budget) may not exceed those of the previous year.

This concludes our comparative analysis of the European Community's performance over the last twenty years in terms of "policy harmonization" and "institutional development" (including the legal/financial bases). Reflecting the "grades" given to the Community for the 33 categories listed on the scoreboard (Table 4-1) in the preceding investigation (pp. 98-125), the aggregate "grade-sheet" looks as follows:

Nine As (for accomplishments); eighteen Bs (for progress); five Cs (for stagnation); and one D (for regression).

Whereas the "external relations" (last section on the scoreboard) are dealt with in Chapter 6, the results of our analysis are "pre-recorded" in this chapter: three As for accomplishments in enlargement, association, and trade agreements; and a C for insufficient efforts to establish closer relationships with other international organizations.

The prospects (P) were rated favorable (F) in 28 cases, and unfavorable (U) in five cases (see Table 4-1).

5 Catalysts of Integration and Disintegration

In the preceding chapter we evaluated the performance of the European Community in terms of its achievements and failures in both policy harmonization and institutionalization against the standards set by the constitutive treaties of the community.

In the following chapter an attempt is made to project the future of European unification by a *realistic* survey of all major societal forces that appear to have the greatest potential for growth or decline. For this purpose, we divided the emerging European polity into four sectors: the political, economic, social, and cultural sector; then we identified the most likely centripetal forces as "catalysts of integration" in each of the four sectors. This effort was complemented by an identification of the most potent obstacles to further progress toward political unity, namely the "catalysts of disintegration." For the purpose of our analysis we grouped these actual or potential centrifugal factors into two categories: in the first one, we will focus on the forces of transnational interdependence and global systemic constraints. The second category will deal with the national elements of diversity in Western Europe and the pockets of resistance to European integration.

This ambitious and risky exercise in conjecture seems justified because the ultimate *raison d'être* of political scientists consists in making predictions as to the most likely outcomes of ongoing political processes in both the domestic, regional, and global systems. Thus we projected the evolution of the European Community during the next decades (see Table 5-1). These projections are supported in the following section.

Catalysts of Integration

The Political Sector: The European Parliament

One of the crucial decisions made at the Summit Meeting of the Hague in 1969 was "to progressively replace . . . the contributions of member countries by the Community's own resources, taking into account all the interests concerned, with the object of achieving in due course the integral financing of the Communities' budgets in accordance with the procedure provided for in Article 201 of the Treaty establishing EEC and of strengthening the budgetary powers

Table 5-1
The Evolution of the European Community (1958-1980)

	Achievements and Prospects					
	No Tariffs or Quotas	Common External Tariff	Free Flow of Factors	Common Economic Policy	Common Monetary Policy	Common Foreign Policy
Free Trade Area (1968)	x					
Customs Union (1968)	x	x				
Common Market (1970)	x	x	x			
Economic Union (1975)	x	x	x	x		
Monetary Union (1980)	x	x	x	x	x	
Political Union (1980)	x	x	x	x	x	x

of the European Parliament."[1] This momentous decision by the six leaders of government was complemented by an amendment to the Rome Treaty, creating a common budget for EEC, ECSC, and EURATOM which was signed by the council on April 22, 1970, and came into force on January 1, 1971, as part of the package completing the merger of the three communities.[2] At the same time, the council decided to increase the European Parliaments' powers of control over this common budget and agreed on the means for financing that budget. Until 1975 a draft budget will be drawn up by the commission from the budget requests of the three communities, subject to review by the council. Subsequently, the council may accept or reject the amended version, again by the same voting procedure, whereupon the budget becomes law (see Figure 5-1). Although the post-1975 procedure for determining the common budget has not yet been decided upon, it is expected that the European Parliament will be given the final authority for enacting it after the council has had an opportunity to modify it.[3]

Under the impact of both enlargement and economic growth, the common budget of the European Community is expected to double by the end of the decade. As substantive revenues are progressively removed from the control of national parliaments and placed under the supervision of the European Parliament, the latter will have to become representative of the people at large. In other words, the exercise of the "power of the purse" will require the possession of a popular mandate based upon the direct election by universal suffrage of the European Parliament.

Ostensibly, the highly political issue of direct elections involves a legal

PHASE I:

THE THREE COMMUNITIES

Budget requests   *(By July 1)*

COMMISSION

Draft proposals and suggestions   *(By September 1)*

COUNCIL OF MINISTERS

Proposed budget   *(By October 5)*

EUROPEAN PARLIAMENT

(1) Budget becomes law if within 45 days the parliament approves the proposed budget or takes no action.

(2) Budget returns to council if the parliament suggests modifications.

PHASE II:

Budget Returned to Council

(1) Proposed modifications that do not increase the total budget must have a weighted majority council vote to be rejected.

(2) Proposed modifications that would increase the budget must have a weighted majority council vote to be accepted.

The president of the council then declares the budget to be law.

Community Budget—1971

Receipts	(in millions of dollars)	Expenditure	(in millions of dollars)
Euratom research	7.9	Research and investment (Euratom)	66.6
Miscellaneous (e.g. publications)	12.4	European Social Fund	55.0
ECSC levies allocated to administrative expenditure	18.0	European Agricultural Fund	2,346.5
Payments by member states for Euratom "complementary programs"	26.7	Administrative costs of community institutions	149.2
Subtotal		Food aid	20.0
Community resources and direct payments by the member states	2,699.0	Reimbursement of member states' costs of collecting levies and duties	126.7
Total	**2,764.0**	**Total**	**2,764.0**

Figure 5-1. The Budget Process (1971-1974).

dilemma that has separated the advocates from the opponents of direct elections for years: the former have insisted that only a duly elected parliament should have prerogatives such as the "power of the purse"; the latter have argued that direct elections by universal suffrage can only be justified for a genuine legislature possessing real powers.

In an effort to cut this Gordian knot, a group of "wise men" submitted a realistic proposal to the commission in March 1972 concerning the extension of the legislative competences of the European Parliament.[4] The report suggests the fixing of two stages during which the powers of the Parliament would be increased *parallel* with the direct elections of its members by universal suffrage. In the first stage, beginning in 1974, the parliament would be given the power of *codecision* on a series of important matters (List A), such as the revision of the treaties (art. 236 EEC), in which case the ratification would take place after the Parliament's approval; the power of codecision would also apply to art. 235 (extension of community jurisdiction), art. 237 (admission of new members), and art. 238 (international agreements). This power of codecision would be supplemented by strengthened *consultative powers* ("suspensive veto") consisting of the right to demand new deliberations within the council on a series of subjects (List B).[5] In the second stage, beginning 1978, all matters (Lists A and B) would be the objects of powers of codecision.[6] Concurrently with this extension of powers, a *timetable* for the direct election of the European Parliament would be adopted.[7] The "Vedel Plan," however, did not preclude the direct election of the European Parliament in incremental stages through *unilateral* procedures. The first promising initiative in the direction of organizing direct European elections was undertaken by a number of national parliaments, based upon art. 138, 1 of the EEC Treaty, which provides for the selection of delegates to the European Parliament.[8] For instance, in a draft bill of May 14, 1970, laid before the Belgian Parliament, M. Nothomb-Chabert recommended that "the Belgian Parliament shall hold elections by direct universal suffrage in order to nominate from among its members . . . Belgian representatives to the European Parliament" (art. 1).[9] Similar bills have also been introduced in the parliaments of Italy, the Netherlands, Luxembourg, and Britain.[10] A bill for the direct election of German delegates to the European Parliament was approved by the Bundestag after its first reading in March 1972. It provides for the first direct election of German members on the occasion of the 1973 legislative elections.[11]

The various proposals introduced in the Belgian, Dutch, German, Luxembourg, Italian, and British parliaments defining the most appropriate procedures for a direct election of their respective delegations to the European Parliament have been strongly supported by the national organizations of the European Movement and orchestrated by its central organs in Brussels.

Speaking in his capacity as president of the European Movement, Dr. Walter Hallstein (the former president of the European Commission) declared that "the draft legislation produced in the various member countries of the Community relating to direct, universal election of the national delegates to the European Parliament . . . deserves the categorical support of all political quarters which are in favor of the principle of European elections. . . . [However] these efforts should be better coordinated . . . [and] should form part of a genuine campaign to inform the people in order to bring about a democratization of the European Communities and in particular the election of the members of the European Parliament by direct universal suffrage."[12]

Although this decentralized approach to the direct election of the European Parliament is cumbersome, it may well be the only realistic forward strategy until France reverses her position; this moment may arrive as soon as the European Parliament assumes control over a significant portion of the community budget. Once elected by universal suffrage, the European Parliament would carry a genuine mandate from the people and could serve as a "constituent assembly" and the political catalyst of a European federation.[13]

This argument has been corroborated by a perceptive student of European politics who predicted that "by 1978 the EEC will have at its disposal a major independent source of funds accruing from levies on farm products imported into the Community. With financial resources totaling several billion dollars annually, the Community is likely to face pressures for control, perhaps from the national governments but more likely from those who seek to increase the representative nature of European institutions. Thus, another force will be generated for the strengthening of the European Community as a political institution."[14]

The potential significance of the European Parliament has also been recognized by a European scholar who foresees a loss of control over international bureaucracies. He believes that, "due to the limited prerogatives of the European Parliament and the inefficacy of the efforts of national parliaments to assert themselves in European affairs, many activities of the Commission of the European Community are de facto removed from democratic control."[15] Ergo, as the functions of the commission increase in scope and importance, the need for democratic controls over the European technocracy will become increasingly obvious and demands will be made to place them under the control of a genuine European Parliament. (See Appendix D, item 15.)

The "Vedel Report" may well have broken the ice on the thorny issue of increasing the authority of the European Parliament while assuring its popular mandate through direct elections by universal suffrage. It can therefore be argued that, regardless of the degree to which the recommendations of the "Vedel Group" will be implemented, the report, complemented by unilateral steps toward direct elections of national delegates, has already provided the necessary ferment of change. Thus it appears as if the European Parliament, progressively endowed with the prerogatives of a genuine legislature, could play the role of "catalyst of integration" in the political sector.

The Economic Sector: Structural Reform

The concept of economic integration consists of two interdependent dimensions: the harmonization of economic *policies* between the participating nations, and the formation of cross-national *structures*. The former necessitates the coordination of governmental regulations affecting economic intercourse; the latter involves the building of multinational institutions (corporations, banks, etc.). Whereas the Treaty of Paris establishing ECSC emphasized structural integration,[16] the Treaty of Rome creating EEC provided essentially for *policy harmonization*. Consequently, the "European Common Market" has been successful mainly in providing a framework for policy harmonization without achieving large-scale structural interpenetration. In other words, the EEC accomplished a great deal in terms of coordinating agricultural policies and creating a customs union (resulting in economic growth and trade expansion) without, however, making real progress toward structural integration in either industry or agriculture. However, recent efforts in this direction consisted of two major initiatives on the part of the European Commission: the proposal for a "European company statute," and the plan for a basic reform of the agricultural sector ("Agriculture 1980"). Given the potential impact of these two projects in terms of the "Europeanization" of the whole economic sector, "structural reform" was selected as the "catalyst of integration" in this field.

By the end of the transition period, major cross-national industrial mergers had taken place only in a few instances.[17] Instead, "domestic" merger agreements (e.g., Rhone-Poulenc in France, and AKZO in the Netherlands) proliferated within the six states of the community—a sign of economic nationalism. This "defensive" type of arrangement among companies took place primarily in response to the perceived threat of outside domination by global international corporations. This phenomenon has been referred to by a perceptive European writer as the "American challenge"—a type of economic imperialism by gigantic US-controlled multinational corporations investing, producing, and marketing in Western Europe.[18]

This development is partly due to the built-in dilemma of the EEC Treaty which on the one hand calls for economies of scale through common economic policies in general and the free movement of factors (including capital) in particular (arts. 2 and 3), while on the other hand it prohibits restrictive business practices and monopolies (arts. 85 and 86). Although these antitrust regulations assure free competition, they place serious restrictions on potential industrial merger arrangements. Thus existing "state monopolies"—by definition incompatible with a common market—were legally obliged to adjust their business practices in the interest of achieving fair competition by January 1, 1970.[19] However, the treaty authorizes merger agreements, provided their overall effects are likely to be beneficial in terms of increased production, better distribution, and technological progress, but place only limited restraint on free competition and trade.

The Rome Treaty stipulates that the member states should coordinate national legislation regarding industrial concentrations, without advocating the creation of supranational European corporations. The concept of a European company, based upon a community statute, was only introduced in 1966 when the commission submitted a memorandum to the council proposing the creation of a "European incorporated company."[20] The rationale for the urgent need for widespread transnational amalgamations of industries can be summarized as follows: most firms in Europe are obsolete in terms of structure and business practices. Many have been established as small or medium-sized companies in previous centuries and continue to operate according to outmoded principles of production, distribution, and management. Consequently, they are unable to cope with the challenge of a common market in the 1970s since they cannot compete with the few European and numerous American industrial giants which are capable of investing enormous amounts of capital and manpower to assure successful operations with the use of modern technology. Logically, there are two possible approaches to transnational amalgamation: the absorption of one company by another (acquisition), or the merger of two or more companies into a new organization (consolidation). Three alternative types of operations are involved between companies with headquarters in different member states: industrial mergers, formation of holding companies, or establishment of joint subsidiaries (under European law). Each of these operations would in effect reflect the principles of freedom of establishment and services (arts. 52 and 59 of the EEC Treaty).

In view of the decisions taken in 1969/70 on the creation of an economic and monetary union (which necessarily involves Europe-wide industrial policies and structures), the commission submitted a draft of a "European company statute" to the council which, if adopted, would enable corporations engaged in industrial, commercial, and banking activities in the six countries to function on the basis of a unified European company law and be subject to the single jurisdiction of the Court of Justice of the community.[21] However, this proposed European company statute would not replace national rules regarding industrial mergers but would supplement, complement, and harmonize them, thus facilitating cross-national cooperation between firms with headquarters in different member states. In other words, the new charter would coexist with national laws and fill gaps that cannot be filled by "approximation" of national statutes on industrial mergers. The newly created European companies would have a minimum capital of $500,000 and would be entered in a European company register. For tax purposes, they would be considered to have their headquarters (if they have more than one) at the place from which they are actually managed. The European company would have a board of management (decision-maker), a supervisory board, and a general meeting of shareholders. Moreover, the workers would have a right of participation in management decisions; there would be a European works council and workers would be represented on the supervisory board. The consent of the works council would be needed for decisions by the board of management on hiring, firing, seniority, vocational training, industrial health and safety, creation and management of social facilities, wages, working hours, and vacations. Workers would be entitled to one representative on the supervisory board for every two representatives appointed at the general stockholders' meeting. Working conditions would be fixed by collective agreement between the company and the labor unions represented in its establishment; arrangements would also be made for the possible conclusion of European collective wage agreements.

In addition to this ambitious project initiated by the commission,[22] national company laws were "approximated" pursuant to art. 220 of the Rome Treaty, which calls on the member states to conclude conventions covering mutual recognition of companies, international mergers, and the transfer of company headquarters. The six governments signed a convention on the mutual recognition of companies of February 29, 1968, followed by a directive of the Council of March 9, 1968, coordinating the rules for the disclosure of important documents, the validity of commitments made for a company, and the nullity of limited-liability companies. On June 16, 1970, the Commission sent to the Council another proposal aimed at harmonizing company law; it requires states to adopt merger regulations and inform all interested parties of new merger agreements.[23]

The "European company" approach boldly suggests that the Nine define a new, identical set of rules permitting the creation of supranational corporations. The new statute would coexist with existing national corporate laws and would assure that a "European company" (with autonomous structures or as a subsidiary of a national company) would be treated like a domestic company in all member states. Having one statutory type of European company would also have an important psychological advantage. Given the reluctance of firms to change their "nationality" in cross-national mergers, participation in a supranational corporation would remove this obstacle to transnational company formation.

Representatives of the industries in the community reacted positively to this proposal by the commission.[24] Their favorable reaction was to be expected since business and industry have benefited most from the successful operations of the Common Market ("L' Europe des affaires").[25] Businessmen and industrialists have not only accepted the Common Market as a *fait accompli* but consider its future as a going concern. This has been demonstrated both by their attitudes to European integration, and by actions taken in response to the challenge of the EEC. According to an opinion survey conducted in 1968, "it was found once more that businessmen and their administrative personnel led the public in holding views favorable to integration. . . . Their response has been massive and sustained."[26] This favorable attitude is reinforced by concrete measures undertaken to assure optimum benefits from the existence of the Common Market. First, large enterprises appointed specialists on European integration problems to serve as expert advisors on questions relating to the evolution of the European Community as it affects the particular enterprise. They are "hard-bitten partisans of Europe" and promote transnational business cooperation in a pragmatic way rather than through glowing rhetoric.[27] Thus "a rising trend of transnational business collaboration within the EEC has become manifest during the last decade," evidenced by a substantial increase of transnational mergers between small and medium-size firms.[28]

In the light of these developments it is therefore not surprising that the business community became conscious of the need for a legal basis for the creation of Europe-wide corporations. This supranational design also has the support of the "Union des industries de la communauté européenne" (UNI-CE),[29] a European pressure group created in 1959, and composed of representatives from the various national business associations, such as the BDI (Bundesverband der Deutschen Industrie) in Germany, the CNPF (Conseil National du Patronat Français) in France, and the CONFIDUSTRIA (Confederazione Generale dell' Industria Italiana) in Italy.[30] The significance of European interest groups such as the UNICE increased as they became regular participants in the decision-making process of the European Community at all levels—in the Economic and Social Committee, the European Commission, and the European Parliament. Moreover, their importance is enhanced by the fact that the commission does not in principle maintain official contacts with national pressure groups.[31] It is therefore only natural that the commission responded to the proclaimed need for a European company statute—as advocated by the UNICE—with its proposal for establishing the legal framework for European corporations. However, the commission did not deal with this crucial project in isolation but linked the legal aspects of adopting a European company statute to the promotion of a European industrial policy, which in turn involves progress on a European patent accord, a common capital market, fiscal harmonization, a European research and technology policy, a common energy and transport policy, as well as the restructuring of agriculture and the problem of regionalization.

At the summit meeting in the Hague, Netherlands (December 1969), the Six agreed to establish an "economic and monetary union" by 1980, an ambitious objective involving the harmonization of general economic policies and the creation of a common currency. If progress towards this goal is to take place against the background of balanced growth, the following interdependent measures would have to be undertaken subsequently to, or simultaneously with, the adoption of a European company statute:

1. Harmonization of industrial policies involving a European patent law, a common fiscal policy, financial support for the adaptation and modernization of industries, and a common commercial policy
2. Approximation of research and development policies designed to achieve a European technological community

3. Coordination of energy policies necessary to assure maximum independence from outside sources (oil, natural gas, coal, nuclear energy) (See Table 5-2.)
4. Promotion of a common transport infrastructure permitting the free flow of products within a common market
5. Adoption of a common regional policy to assure the harmonious development of underdeveloped areas and the successful transformation of rural regions into urban, industrialized communities.

Table 5-2
European Energy Needs

European Energy Consumption (in millions of tce*)

	1950	1960	1970	1971
Coal	210	243	189	177
Lignite	23	32	33	32
Oil	35	138	500	521
Natural Gas	1	12	73	93
Primary Electricity	31	39	49	48
Total	300	464	844	871

*metric tons coal equivalent
Source: *European Community*, no. 158 (August-September 1972).

European Energy Needs (projected for 1985)

	Million Tons of Coal Equivalent (t.c.e.)	%
Oil	1,100	60
Natural gas	280	15.5
Solid fuels	207	11.5
Nuclear energy	175	10
Miscellaneous	48	3
	1,810	100

Source: *European Communities* (London, Feb. 7, 1972).

Main Oil Suppliers of the European Community (in millions of metric tons)

	1970	1971
Mideast	194.6	234.8
North Africa	157.4	115.8
Equatorial Africa	24.3	35.8
Western Hemisphere	12.5	10.3

Source: *European Community*, no. 158 (August-September 1972).

Regional development has become one of the most pressing problems facing the Six because nearly half of the community's territory is comprised of agricultural regions with a population density of 80 people per square kilometer. In contrast, industrial regions occupy one-fifth of the community's territory and average 390 inhabitants per square kilometer; semiindustrial areas cover one-third of the land mass and have an average density of 160 persons per square kilometer.[32] This proportion between agricultural and industrial regions is typical for underdeveloped countries where the percentage of farmers in the total working population is extremely high. For modern industrialized countries the percentage is usually less than 10 percent. For instance, in the United States the number of farmers in 1969 was only 3,606,000 out of a total labor force of about 80 million, whereas in Italy farmers totalled 4,023,000 out of a labor force of 19,336,000.[33] However, the percentage of the total working population in the community engaged in agriculture declined from a high of 28 percent in 1950 to 20.7 percent in 1960 to 14 percent in 1970 as farmers migrated to urban areas. By 1980—the target date for the reform of agricultural structures— the percentage should fall to about 7 percent (comparable to the US figure). Because migration from rural to urban regions takes place largely on a voluntary basis, the commission suggested that it intervene actively in the process and assure that the total agricultural labor force in the community would not exceed 5 million workers.[34] It has been estimated that between 1960 and 1970, 4.7 million people left the agricultural work force, and more than 5 million are expected to leave farming between 1970 and 1980. Of these 5 million, about 2.5 million will retire because of age and the other half will try to get jobs in industries.[35] In order to accomplish this transformation, the commission proposed to encourage farmers to leave agriculture through retraining and resettlement, to reduce the acreage of farmland in the community, and to increase the efficiency of the remaining farms through consolidation and phasing out of noncompetitive small farms.[36]

However, in order to avoid congestion of urban areas through massive migration from rural regions, it will be necessary to provide incentives to the young generation to remain in the region in which their farmer-parents reside by providing job opportunities for them in industrial plants. At the present time, industries are concentrated in certain parts of the community, such as the Ruhr Valley; most of the rest of the territory is used for agricultural or semiindustrial purposes. In an effort to decentralize the industrial sector of the economy and provide an incentive for industry to move into underdeveloped regions or establish subsidiaries in them, the commission recommended spurring on industrialization of these areas through common financing of investment projects. The most effective way of assuring a balanced regional development through industrial decentralization is the creation of supranational European corporations. Their large-scale operations in depressed areas of the community, coordinated effectively from Brussels, would enable the Six to restructure their economic sectors and adapt it to the requirements of the twentieth century (see Table 5-3).

Table 5-3
European Regions

Regions	Farm Workers in Labor Force	Inhabitants/ 2.6 Square Miles	Percentage of Community	
			Area	Population
Industrialized	0-10%	over 250	9	30
	10-20%	over 200	7	11
Semiindustrialized	0-15%	over 150	9	12.5
	over 15%	under 150	21	19
Agricultural	20-30%	under 100	12	6
	over 30%	under 100	42	21.5

Source: *European Community*, February 1970, no. 131.

In the light of the preceding considerations it can be argued that the ongoing structural reforms in the industrial and agricultural fields, constitute the most potent "catalyst of integration" in the economic sector of the European Community.

The Social Sector: Social Mobility

Transnational community formation is an essential ingredient of any ongoing process of integration at the international level. A large variety of indicators for gauging the intensity and trends of people-to-people contacts between nations can be identified; these indicators include both personal and professional factors. Among the personal factors are human rights, freedom of intermarriage, migration, tourism, and study abroad. Among the professional factors are freedom of establishment for professions and business, freedom of movement for workers, and equal social security benefits.

Given the salience of sociological factors for the success or failure of an integration movement on the one hand, and the potential of "Europeanization" in this area on the other, "social mobility" has been selected as the "*catalyst* of integration" in the social sector.

Europeans had experienced partial community formation across national borders in previous centuries when aristocracies formed a supranational elite, or when workers attempted to organize class solidarity across national lines. However, only during the last decades has progress been made in large-scale Europeanization involving the people per se. This development has been made possible and was stimulated by international organizations through the adoption of conventions and treaties permitting people to travel, reside, and work in other signatory countries. Pioneering in this field was the Council of Europe, which sponsored nearly fifty different conventions, agreements and protocols during the years 1950 to 1965, all designed to facilitate movement across national boundaries.[37] The first and most important of them was the "European Convention for the Protection of Human Rights and Fundamental Freedoms," concluded in Rome on November 4, 1950.[38] It entered into force in 1953 and is binding on most member states of the Council of Europe, which requires all of its members "to accept the principles of the rules of law and the enjoyment by all persons within its jurisdiction of human rights and fundamental freedoms."[39] The specific rights and freedoms guaranteed by the convention are the right to live; freedom from torture and inhuman treatment; freedom from slavery, servitude, and compulsory labor; the right to liberty and security of persons; the right to a fair trial; protection against retroactivity of the law; the right to respect for family life, home, and correspondence; the right to freedom of thought, conscience, and religion; the right to freedom of expression; the right of peaceful assembly and to freedom of association; the right to marry and found a family; and the right to an effective remedy when any violation occurs.[40] These rights and freedoms are also written into the "Universal *Declaration* of Human Rights" adopted by the United Nations General Assembly in 1948. However, whereas the UN document is merely a resolution (a political declaration of intent), the European Convention is a treaty according to international law and is binding on the signatory states. Moreover, the convention provides for two organs—the European Commission and the Court of Human Rights—to investigate violations of the charter in response to complaints lodged by individuals (a significant innovation in international law). Furthermore, the convention requires the contracting parties to grant these rights and freedoms to all persons within their jurisdiction (not only to their own nationals), another original feature of this progressive document.[41] In addition to the convention on human rights, the Council of Europe sponsored the following conventions of a social character: "Agreements on Social Security," the "Convention on Social and Medical Assistance," and the "European Social Charter," all designed to ensure that signatory states would, in applying their social legislation, treat foreign nationals on the basis of equality with their own citizens. Furthermore, the council was responsible for the conclusion of the "Convention on Establishment," which deals with the right of entry to, and residence in, member states, the exercise of gainful occupations, and the ownership of property in other countries; it further requires each member state to treat foreign nationals as equals.[42]

If the Council of Europe has been spearheading efforts to induce its member states to sign conventions equalizing social regulations, the European Community has succeeded in implementing several vital provisions designed to harmonize social legislation within the six member states. The Rome Treaty specifically calls for the "free movement of persons, services (and capital)" for workers and professionals.[43] It also created a "European Social Fund" to improve employment opportunities for workers in the Common Market[44] and made "social provisions" designed to improve the living conditions of labor.[45] The six states specifically agreed to cooperate in matters of employment, labor legislation, and working conditions, occupational and continuing training, social security, protection against occupational accidents and diseases, industrial hygiene, and collective bargaining procedures.[46] This original program was reiterated by the six heads of state at the Hague conference when they called for a closely concerted social policy and for a reform of the Social Fund.[47] Although this ambitious program had not been completely implemented by the end of the transition period in 1970, significant progress has been made in this field. For example, the community succeeded in achieving *freedom of establishment* and *freedom to supply services* for approximately 75 percent of self-employed activities in industry, commerce and the crafts upon entering its final state.[48] The *free movement of labor* within the community was formally achieved on July 29, 1968, when the Council of Ministers for Social Affairs adopted a regulation to this effect—eighteen months ahead of schedule (the EEC Treaty set the end of the transition period as the target date).[49] As a result of these agreements, no member state may discriminate against other member's citizens by giving priority in employment to workers of their own nationality; moreover, workers from other member states have prior claim over nationals from non-EEC countries. A community worker no longer needs a work permit, though he still needs a (renewable) residence permit for five years. Furthermore, community workers are to receive equality of treatment in every important field related to employment, including taxation, social insurance, the right to bring in family members who may also seek employment, the right to own and rent a house, and the right to be elected to organizations representing workers. Almost five million "guest workers" now live in the six community countries; many are immigrants, others are migrant workers who stay only a few years. This cross-national migration occurs mainly in a South-North direction—from relatively underdeveloped areas to the highly industrialized regions. For example, Germany was host to 1,023,747 foreign employees in 1967; 349,717 workers came from other community countries and the rest from Spain, Greece, Turkey, Portugal, and others. This foreign labor force constitutes 6 percent of Germany's working population; the comparative figure for France is 9.6 percent (1.8 million foreign workers).[50] Under the social security regulations of the community for migrant workers beneficiaries totalled approximately 2 million in 1968.[51] The reformed European Social Fund, with a projected annual budget of $250 million and charged with implementing a community-wide employment policy, will also assist all migrant workers in retraining and resettlement—a function that originally applied only to community citizens.

The interests of the working population in the European Community are represented at the supranational level by the "European Confederation of Free Trade Unions," created in the Hague on April 25, 1969, and chaired by Mr. Ludwig Rosenberg of Germany's powerful labor federation, DGB.[52] This new

European pressure group has a combined membership of 12 million workers from the six community countries. Its principal aims are the following: harmonization of social policies among the member states, resulting in a "European social policy"; community-wide procedures for collective bargaining between labor and management; introduction of a "European income and wealth policy"; a more effective representation of labor in the community institutions (European Social and Economic Council), and a reform of the European Social Fund. In addition to these demands in the social field, the new ECFTU Congress adopted a unanimous resolution on political issues of greatest importance. The 150 assembled delegates pledged to promote a democratic and supranational community of all European democracies, accompanied by a strengthening of all Community organs.[53]

An additional body concerned with problems of labor is the new Standing Committee on Employment of the EEC. Created by the Council of Ministers in June 1970, it gives trade unions and management a voice in the coordination of employment policy at the supranational level.[54] The commission also assists the committee by promoting cooperation between management and trade unions in the member states on subjects relating to employment, labor legislation and working conditions, social security, industrial health and safety, and trade and union rights. Furthermore, the Commission studies ways of integrating social goals (adaptation of workers to structural change, high level of employment, and improved living and working conditions) with common economic, agricultural, industrial, transport, and regional policies of the community.[55]

The efforts toward "upward harmonization" of social policies (primarily of living and working condition) undertaken by the European Community have been complemented and reinforced by the progressive establishment of partnerships between cities in the six member states. These *jumelages* are arrangements between local communities for the purpose of "Europeanizing" social intercourse at the grassroots level by means of exchanging workers, municipal officials, teachers, students, etc. These partnerships (or pairings or twinnings) have proliferated all over Europe; however, they developed most rapidly and numerously within the European Community, and particularly between France and Germany (there were more than 350 pairings by 1968).

Successful partnerships expand to include additional communities, thus serving as multipliers of grassroots "Europeanism." For example, in the case of Nancy and Karlsruhe, the original partnership was extended to include Berlin and Trier, sparking a potentially vast network of pairings in many countries.[56] These *jumelages* are actively supported by the "Council of European Municipalities," a cooperative association of mayors and municipal councillors established in Geneva in January 1951. Initially eight countries were represented in its assembly by their local officials (Belgium, Denmark, France, Germany, Italy, Luxembourg, Netherlands, and Switzerland), who stated that communal self-government is the bulwark of personal freedom. They also declared that the central governments of their states interfered with local autonomy and individual freedom and that only a European federation would permit the expression of these vital democratic privileges. "They insisted that the mayors and elected representatives of the local communities . . . are in direct contact with political reality and the people, through their functions as administrators facing problems which transcend all frontiers, [and] are co-workers in the building of a free and united Europe."[57]

The concern of the "Council of European Municipalities" for the informal, social rapprochement between the local citizenry of the municipalities involved in *jumelages* is best expressed in its motto: "For the Europe of Peoples" (rather than "of states"), the emphasis being on the development of human contacts and relationships rather than on public manifestations of political unity. However, given the cultural and social differences that initially exist between cities to be paired, "intelligent management [of public demonstrations and festivities] must accompany the felt desire to fraternize . . . since *jumelages* are more likely to promote . . . a sense of community among the people involved if there is little talk about the political aspects."[58] Because of the sometimes profound differences between local communities, social tensions and cultural shock are inevitable during the initiation of pairings. Yet "from the standpoint of inquiry into the formation of European community sentiment—a European consensus—it is noteworthy that the objections and resistance to a partnership are most pronounced at the time it is entered upon . . . [but gradually they] decline."[59]

If partnerships between local communities serve as initial agents of transnational community formation, they are accompanied by, and further stimulate, cross-national contacts between individuals in the form of intermarriage and tourism. Although tourism usually provides only for relatively superficial human interaction, it is nevertheless considered as one indicator of international integration.[60] The figures for mass "holiday migrations" for 1966 show that German tourists travelled mainly to Italy (5,507,100) and France (1,746,000) whereas French tourists preferred Spain (7,745,928) to Italy (4,689,700) and Germany (65,610).[61]

The importance of tourism was recognized by the European Commission in the spring of 1972, when it proposed large-scale community action in this field. Among the recommendations made to the council were the creation of a common body responsible for the promotion of tourism in the European Community. Specifically, this coordinating agency would assure the harmonization of national policies in this field on the basis of a new "European Charter" for travel agencies, which would provide for flexible border controls, standardization of training for employees in tourist services, and protection for tourists.[62]

The significance of tourism for the transformation of political cultures and individual attitudes towards "foreigners" has been illustrated by an experience of two young Germans and two Frenchmen, one of whom summarized his tourist venture as follows: "En montant la voiture, nous étions deux Français et deux Allemands; en'descendant, il n'y avait plus que quatre amis."[63]

Of much greater significance in terms of community formation is the social factor of intermarriage. Indeed, "impressionistic similarities between the institution of marriage, the evolution of nationalities, and the hypothetical emergency of supranationalities are not coincidental: marriage, nationalism, and international community formation are all community formation processes. Each starts with at least two separate human units (individuals or groups); each produces a state of affairs in which the initially separate units achieve mutual identification; each becomes subject, under conceptually similar conditions, to strains, deterioration, and divorce. Most important for purposes here, whether it binds two people in wedlock, two tribes in a nation, or two nations in an international community, community formation is reflected in characteristic transaction flow patterns."[64] In other words, in terms of the "index of relative acceptance" between two peoples, intermarriage ranks among the most important indicators of community formation. It is therefore significant to note that the number of marriages between Frenchmen and Germans (undoubtedly the key nations in European social integration) has increased from 966 in 1962 to 1,527 in 1966.[65] Such reduction of social distance and mutual suspicion between two former enemy nations through "intensive social intercourse" is most certainly a valid indicator of transnational community formation in Western Europe. This development is naturally accompanied by a significant increase in mutual trust, predictability of behavior, mutual identification, cross-nation migration, and transactions.[66]

Since transnational interaction on a large scale is one of the vital formative elements of an incipient political community, social mobility has been selected as the most effective "catalyst of integration" in the social sector.

The Cultural Sector: Education
(Euro-Socialization)

The cultural sector had long been virtually ignored as a salient dimension of the process of European integration. The reason for this neglect was twofold: in the first place, Europeans have been traditionally proud of their diverse cultural heritage and emphasized the uniqueness of their respective languages, customs and traditions, including their national political cultures. They tended to regard cultural diversity as a major claim to fame that contrasted favorably with the allegedly oppressive conformity prevailing in other advanced societies. The second reason for neglecting culture as an important political variable was the initial focus of the "Europeans" on the economic dimension of integration as the most promising take-off base for political unification.

It was not until the Summit Meeting in the Hague in 1969 that the leaders of the European Community officially acknowledged the need for promoting cultural integration. As the first step in this direction they urged the creation of a European University which was to become a means of associating the young generation with the European enterprise. The significance attached to the greater involvement of young people in the work of the European Community was underlined by a subsequent proposal of the commission which recommended the creation of two youth committees: first, a "Committee for Youth Questions" in charge of coordinating the actions of the member states with regard to associating young people with the construction of the community; and second, a "Consultative Committee on Youth" as an instrument through which the young could express their opinions on projects relating to the application of the Rome Treaties.[67]

Efforts to develop a genuine "European consciousness" have been hampered by the diversity of educational systems and the conflicting views of the teachers on the role of their nation-states in European politics. The first attempts to promote a "European political culture" and educate a generation of "Europeans" were made by international organizations.

The most far-reaching attempts to harmonize European education has been undertaken by the Council of Europe through its Council for Cultural Cooperation. Established in 1949, the Council of Europe is an intergovernmental organization purporting to promote European unity mainly through cultural, as well as social and legal cooperation. In 1959 the council's Committee of Ministers instituted the European Cultural Fund to finance its cultural activities, which are directed by the Council for Cultural Cooperation (created in 1962). With an annual budget of approximately 2 million Francs, the Council for Cultural Cooperation is made up of national representatives, three members of the Consultative Assembly, and the chairmen of the Council of Europe's three standing committees: Higher Education and Research; General and Technical Education; and Extracurricular Education. The council's program covers the humanities and the social and natural sciences; "it also concerns itself with developing a European civic education, that is to say, the problems involved in creating a European loyalty."[68]

In an effort to achieve this long-term goal, the Council for Cultural Cooperation sponsored research and publication of European (rather than national) textbooks, especially in history, geography and civics. The rationale was the following: "Since the rise of nationalism in Europe, the emphasis in textbooks has understandably been on national resources, national heroes, national needs and desires ... [whereas the new "European" texts show] how the idea of Europe can be central in a history text without either belittling any one nation—thus undermining patriotism—or denigrating the rest of the world."[69] In geography, the problem consists not so much in the distortion of facts as in the omission of crucial material in national textbooks and atlases.

Traditionally, geography textbooks stressed national boundaries, resources, industrial capacity, economic structures, etc., without taking the European dimensions into consideration. Therefore, the Council for Cultural Cooperation demonstrated that a regional approach to describing natural resources and international boundaries is more realistic since it takes the elements of inter-dependence into consideration, permitting the student to see his country in the European perspective.[70]

In response to a resolution of the Committee of Ministers of the Council of Europe of October 6, 1964, which stated that in secondary education there is an "imperative duty . . . to inculcate an awareness of European facts and problems," the Council for Cultural Cooperation published a "European" text for civics courses. This text demonstrated that support for the European cause is perfectly compatible with the existence of patriotism and suggested that students think in terms of concentric circles to describe their allegiance: "In mounting progression from municipality to county or province, and then to country, the scope of syllabi and textbooks should also extend to Europe and the world which form, as it were, the fourth and fifth concentric circles."[71] This attempt to transcend nationalism at the crucial secondary school level in favor of the concept of multiple loyalties is perhaps the most significant and potentially decisive method of Euro-socialization.

Apart from its involvement in "Europeanizing" education at the secondary school level, the Council for Cultural Cooperation developed a Documentation Center for Education in Europe and has been instrumental in implementing the Cultural Convention, which consists of three important agreements: on the equivalence of diplomas, the equivalence of periods of university study, and the recognition of university qualifications.[72] Although these conventions are only binding on the signatory countries (rather than on all member states of the Council of Europe), their significance for the achievement of genuine freedom of establishment—one of the principal goals of the European Community—is paramount.

Other international organizations concerned with cultural-educational affairs are UNESCO (on a worldwide basis), OECD (for the Atlantic area) and the European Community (through its Press and Information Service), as well as the Franco-German Youth Office (mainly concerned with student exchanges). The Press and Information Service of the European Community underwrites research on European problems undertaken in many of the European study centers by encouraging young scholars (through stipends) to investigate the legal, economic, social, and political aspects of European integration. The Service also publishes documents pertaining to the activities of the community institutions, disseminates statistics, distributes statements by European officials, and publishes communiqués.[73] Furthermore the Service makes systematic use of opinion surveys and arranges for frequent visits by educators and students to Brussels for the purpose of providing them with the opportunity to meet with community officials in round table discussions.[74] These meetings are arranged either in cooperation with individual academic institutions or study centers, or jointly with the European Association of Teachers, a ten-member organization of undergraduate and graduate faculty founded in 1956. This potentially influential "European pressure group" stated its mission as follows; "(a) to create among teachers an awareness of European problems and to disseminate information which has a bearing on the realization of European federation; (b) to work by all available means towards a deeper understanding of those essential qualities which are characteristic of European civilization and to ensure their preservation, notably by increasing the number of international contacts at the personal level; (c) to develop a similar understanding among the pupils and in all other fields where the teacher may exert an influence; (d) to support all activity directed to this end and to collaborate with other organizations which have similar international objectives."[75]

In addition to supporting this genuine "multiplier" of the federal cause, the Press and Information Service works closely with the Association of European Journalists. Created in 1963 in Brussels by eighty journalists representing leading newspapers, news agencies, journals, and television and broadcasting stations from the six community countries, the association's statute calls for the building of a democratic, federal Europe. It also provides for the supranational character of the association, which pursues the following objectives: "to participate actively in the formation of a European consciousness; to deepen the knowledge of European problems and to enlighten public opinion about the activities of the European institutions."[76]

The Press and Information Service of the European Community is also a strong supporter of the European Schools, located in Luxembourg; Brussels and Mol, Belgium; Karlsruhe, Germany; Varese, Italy; and Bergen, Norway. These truly international institutions with an enrollment of 8000 pupils in 1971, provide secondary education mainly for the children of European officials, using multilingual instruction and an international faculty. The twin objectives of the six European Schools are: to promote a European consciousness without eroding patriotism. Graduates are prepared to enter all universities in Western Europe and in the United States; they speak at least two languages (French, German, Dutch, or Italian).

Another agency closely associated with the Press and Information Service is the European Community Institute for University Studies founded in 1958 in Brussels. Under its chairman, Max Kohnstamm (who is also vice-president of Monnet's Action Committee for the United States of Europe), the institute sponsors research and conducts seminars on European integration; it also publishes an annual compendium of studies on European subjects called "University Research and Studies on European Integration."

Educational Centers. In addition to the European Community Institute for University Studies, there are many independent postgraduate study centers concerned with teaching and research on problems of international relations in general, and European integration in particular. Most of them are members of the Association of Institutes of European Studies (AIEE), an umbrella organization in charge of coordinating activities among them. The following study centers have been organized for the purpose of providing higher education at the European level, with some of them approaching the ideal type of supranational education—a goal to be achieved mainly through the new European University in Florence, Italy.

The College of Europe. A direct outgrowth of the European Movement, the college, founded in 1949 and located in Bruges, Belgium, is a postgraduate institution for specialized study in the problems of European unification. One of its founders was Henri Brugmans, the first Rektor of the College and a well-known writer on European topics.[77]

The European Institute for Advanced International Studies. The IEHEI is sponsored by the Centre International de Formation Européenne, a Paris-based federalist organization presided over by Jean Rey (former commission president), which published the *Federalist Charter* in 1963.[78] The European Institute was founded in 1965 in Nice under its Director Alexandre Marc, a prominent European federalist.[79] The institute is associated with the University of Nice and organizes annual study sessions on problems of European integration and international affairs. Students are drawn from all of Europe, Africa, and the Americas, and live in a pluricultural environment during an entire academic year. Among the faculty members are professors from major European and American universities who also serve as lecturers during the summer sessions of the affiliated University College for Federalist Studies in Aosta, Italy. This European Institute for Advanced International Studies is destined to evolve into a genuine international university with a multinational faculty and student body, a complete academic program of higher education; it is to be administered by an international board of directors.[80]

Among the other European study centers are the Graduate Institute of International Studies and the Centre Européen de la Culture (directed by the federalist Denis de Rougemont) in Geneva, Switzerland; the Institut Européen d'Administration des Affaires in Fontainebleau, France; the Instituto di Studi Europei in Rome, Italy; the Forschungsinstitut der Deutschen Gesellschaft Für Auswärtige Politik in Bonn, Germany; the Kennedy Institute in Tilburg, the Netherlands; the Institute for European Studies in Vienna, Austria, and many others. Among the centers directly associated with major universities are the School of Advanced International Studies in Bologna, Italy; the Centre Universitaire des Hautes Etudes Européennes in Strasburg, France; the Europa Institute in Leyden, the Netherlands; and the European study centers of the following British universities: London School of Economics, Sussex, Exeter, Lancaster, Leicester, and Manchester.

The Project of the "European University." The European academic community has always been highly pluralistic, both in structure and programs. This widespread fragmentation of scientific endeavors in the field of higher education has thus far prevented the establishment of an "intellectual common market" in Western Europe. Each European university has its own tradition and insists on its institutional autonomy as well as the academic freedoms of its faculty. The first development in the direction of organized cooperation between institutions of higher learning took place in 1955, when the quinquennial "Conference of European Rectors and Vice-Chancellors" met in Cambridge, U.K., to discuss common problems. In this European-wide organization, universities are represented by their top administrators, with the Common Market countries having the majority out of the 200-odd seats. Due to the size of this assembly and its infrequent meetings, it has been largely ineffective in advancing the cause of a European academic community, although it has served as a useful instrument in forging university partnerships.[81] These *jumelages* are most frequent in the six nations of the European Community, and particularly between French and German universities—a beneficial result of the application of the "Treaty of Friendship and Cooperation" concluded between France and Germany in January 1963. Such mutually beneficial partnerships enable universities to routinize contacts between their respective faculty and students, thus gradually institutionalizing patterns of academic cooperation and promoting friendship between the intelligentsia of the nations involved.

In November 1970, some 160 university officials from a dozen European countries met at a symposium in Grenoble, France, to lay the foundations of a system of effective cooperation between European universities. The summary report of the Grenoble Colloquium emphasized the need for a mobilization of the existing university potential for the purpose of creating a European university community and declared, "Today, cooperation is still the exception rather than the rule. . . . From now on we must go beyond this phase of cooperation [by extending the *jumelage* idea to] several hundreds of institutions of higher education, to thousands of teachers, and hundred thousands of students . . . [since] the creation of an Educational European Community will be as decisive for the future of Europe as the creation, twenty years ago, of the first European Community."[82] In order to achieve this objective, the members of the symposium recommended the creation of an "Association of European Universities," through multilateral agreements between institutions of higher education, allowing for the free movement of faculty and students and the recognition of diplomas and periods of study at another university. The association should next establish a "University Committee" to represent it before the Council of Europe and the Commission of the European Community. Furthermore, this committee should take part in the organization of a "European Center for Research on Innovation in Higher Education" and of a "European Office for University Information." The financing of these operations (including the granting of "European scholarships") should be ensured by assigning 1 percent of the national budgets devoted to higher education to the new "Association of European Universities."[83]

The first concrete steps toward the building of a European "cultural community" were taken in the fall of 1971 when the Council of Education Ministers of the Six met in Brussels to discuss the project of a European academic institution. At this first encounter of the six national officials responsible for cultural affairs, it was decided to create a "European University Institute" in Florence, Italy, jointly financed and administered.[84] This supranational postgraduate institute is to be a multilingual center for study and research in four areas: history and civilization, political and social science, economics, and law. The five official languages of the Institute are French, German, Italian, Dutch, and English; it is administered by a governing body ("upper council") composed of representatives from the member states and from the community. The institute is to award "doctorates" to its students, following its official opening in the academic year 1972/73.[85] However, the European University Institute falls short of the ambitious design of a genuine "European university" with seven departments (law, economics, political science and sociology, history, mathematics, physics, comparative languages, literature, and art history) proposed by the Italian government in 1961.[86]

In addition, the six ministers of education accepted, in principle, the French proposal for the establishment of a "European Center for the Development of Education" with the final objective of "defining a model for European culture in correlation with the integration of Europe."[87]

Cultural Exchanges. Systematic exchanges of students and faculty are organized regularly by the Franco-German Youth Office according to the provisions of the Friendship Treaty between France and Germany of 1963. The *leitmotiv* of the Office Franco-Allemand pour la Jeunesse is, "To appreciate one another, one must know one another; to know one another, one must meet." To that end, over a million young Frenchmen and Germans have visited each other's countries under the auspices of the office since its founding in 1963.[88] The efforts of the Franco-German Youth Office to encourage mutual visits between the younger members of the two traditionally hostile nations are reinforced and complemented by the activities of educational institutions such as the Alliance Française and the Goethe Institut (especially through language training and comparative literature studies).

Recent studies on the effects of exchange programs on the mutual images of French and German youth demonstrated that old prejudices have not been completely eradicated, even if they have been watered down: "Germans still considered the French likeable but lazy, vivacious but superficial; and the French still thought the Germans were hard-working but aggressive, courageous but cold."[89] Exchange visits, it was found, could even be a two-edged weapon.

"After visiting France and meeting young French people, young Germans tended to like the French more than before—but they also became more aware of what they regarded as their unattractive characteristics."[90] One of the authors of these studies[91] underlined the important role of the family and the school in reducing the most blatant prejudices. Furthermore, he stressed that the objective teaching of history is of crucial significance in eliminating clichés, since most of the deepest, least conscious and most dangerous prejudices result from chauvinistic stories pervading textbooks in primary and secondary schools.[92]

Despite the inconclusive results of the Franco-German exchange program, there is no doubt that intensive cultural exchanges help eliminate misunderstandings, promote knowledge and reduce prejudices—the basic proposition of the original Fulbright concept. Although it would be incorrect to attribute the spectacular rapprochement between the French and German people during the last decades to cultural activities alone, nobody would deny that they played a vital role in it. In fact, "the process of 'learning to like one another' becomes yet another barometer of international community formation. Indeed, it becomes an impressive one when . . . it shows shifts from deep enmity to widespread amity . . . [as in the case of] Frenchmen and West Germans [who] interacted with, trusted, and liked each other a great deal more in 1965 than in 1954 . . . [and] Franco-German integration at the societal or 'people-to-people' level made impressive progress. . . . [Particularly] when viewed in the light of a long history of deep mutual hostility and preferred mutual isolation, the reductions in international social distance between Frenchmen and West Germans during the 1950s and early 1960s are almost phenomenal."[93]

Mutual trust or predictability of behavior (to use Deutsch's term) between French and Germans was, and continues to be, the *sine qua non* for any progress toward European unity. Once this mutual amity had been firmly established among the two key people, transnational community formation took place without great difficulties among the other people involved in the European unity movement. However, there were marked differences between the degree of "Europeanness" of the adults on the one hand, and the youth on the other, in all West European countries.

This cleavage or attitudinal generation gap was first discovered by Ronald Inglehart in an opinion study of young Europeans in 1966.[94] Basing his findings on a sample survey of a representative group of students in France, the Netherlands, West Germany and Britain, he found that "the youngest generation in each of these countries is significantly more favorable to European integration than the group fifty-five and over—the age group which now holds most top-level positions of political power in these countries."[95] These conclusions were reinforced by a study conducted by a group of European public opinion research institutes in the spring of 1970 in the European Community and Great Britain. The breakdown of the results by age showed that "young voters are decidedly more enthusiastic about the unification of Europe than older voters in every country and for almost every question."[96] By age the following percentages of replies were in favor of European political unification:[97]

	G	B	N	L	F	I	GB
18 or 21-34	74	58	65	72.5	65	60.5	36
35-64	64	59	58	63	60	53	29
65 and over	52	39	51.5	59	49	34	19

The following table shows the percentage breakdown by country and age group concerning four proposals for European unification in 1970:[98]

1) For the "United States of Europe":

Age Group:	Germany	Netherlands	France	Belgium	Italy	Britain
Youth (21-34)	75	69	71	67	66	33
Adults (50-64)	64	65	71	61	57	30

2) For a European Parliament:

Age Group:	Germany	Netherlands	France	Belgium	Italy	Britain
Youth (21-34)	73	64	64	54	60	30
Adults (50-64)	62	61	63	57	51	23

3) For a European government, responsible for foreign affairs, defense, economy:

Age Group:	Germany	Netherlands	France	Belgium	Italy	Britain
Youth (21-34)	66	54	53	52	57	28
Adults (50-64)	53	51	51	51	49	21

4) Would vote for a president of a US of Europe from another country:

Age Group:	Germany	Netherlands	France	Belgium	Italy	Britain
Youth (21-34)	81	73	73	58	59	54
Adults (50-64)	61	57	59	51	40	34

The age groups selected in this table are made up of "potential leaders" (age 21-34) and the "establishment," ruling class or power holders (age 50-64)—the two groups that are most salient in this intergenerational, cross-temporal comparison of "pro-European" attitudes. The results clearly demonstrate that the new generation consistently gives higher levels of support for supranational European integration. In order to obtain optimum reliability of data on the attitudinal gap between parents and children on questions of European unification, the European Community Information Service carried out a survey in 1969 in which a number of parent-child pairs were asked three identical questions on European integration. The interviews, conducted in the same households respectively in France, Germany and Britain, yielded the following results:[99]

1. In response to a question about the concept of a United States of Europe:

	Germany		France		Britain	
	Parents	Youth	Parents	Youth	Parents	Youth
For	71%	92%	65%	83%	31%	76%
neutral	21%	5%	26%	15%	22%	10%
against	8%	3%	9%	2%	48%	15%

2. In response to a question about a unified European army:

	Germany		France		Britain	
	Parents	Youth	Parents	Youth	Parents	Youth
For	54%	72%	47%	57%	32%	47%
neutral	26%	16%	35%	25%	18%	11%
against	20%	11%	18%	18%	50%	42%

3. In response to a question on a supranational European government:

	Germany		France		Britain	
	Parents	Youth	Parents	Youth	Parents	Youth
For	37%	50%	46%	48%	21%	45%
neutral	31%	20%	31%	17%	12%	7%
against	31%	30%	24%	35%	67%	48%

In the words of Inglehart: "A rather striking set of intergenerational differences appears: in every case the youth give a higher level of positive response than their parents—sometimes by 30 percentage points or more."[100]

Using the concepts of political socialization, it can be argued convincingly that there are valid causes for this "opinion gap" between the adult population (raised prior to World War II) and the young generation (brought up after WW II): there is a tendency to develop a sense of national identity early in life and to maintain it thereafter relatively unchanged. Applying this argument to the cleavage described above, it stands to reason that adults who were socialized in an era of conflicting nationalisms would retain their nationalist outlook and would be reluctant to accept the concept of supranational integration, whereas young people who grew up in a political climate of "Eurosphere" in which European institutions successfully perform many functions that "sovereign" nation-states can no longer fulfill effectively (both in the realms of defense and welfare), would favor supranational integration, the *Weltanschauung* of the 1970s.

This line of reasoning, based upon recent intergenerational survey data, is supported by a perceptive analyst of the European political scene when he writes that "the difference of generations in the West stands out in their view of Europe; men in their thirties and men in their early twenties, talking about the continent, seem to have different maps. The young generation in the West accept all the inheritance from the 'Europeans'—the open frontiers, the reconciliation, the prosperity, the free trade. Ignoring boundaries, popping between France and Germany, speaking three languages, assuming a common European consciousness, they might be a living advertisement for the achievement of the earlier generation, and particularly for the Franco-German exchange."[101]

In summary, it can now be stated that within the cultural sector, education is the long-range catalyst of European political unity. This conclusion is based upon the following rationale: The present power elites in Europe were brought up in an era of nationalism and experienced the emotional and physical involvement in World War II, an experience that usually left psychological scars (and often bodily ones) upon the participants. The result was a natural animosity toward former enemy nations and scepticism toward the new allies.[102] After all, the older generation had been indoctrinated in school to look at their country in exaggerated images of glory and power while at the same time being encouraged to downgrade the virtues of other nations and maximize their shortcomings. As a result they developed distorted images of other people and perpetuated obsolete clichés which were detrimental to their human and political relationships. In contrast, their children were raised in a setting of internationalism and were socialized to become "good Europeans" by teachers who made an effort to enlighten them about the destructive nature of nationalism and the virtues of peaceful cooperation across national borders. This Euro-socialization has been facilitated by the fact that the young generation has no memory of the war and is therefore not predisposed to xenophobic or paranoic behavior vis-à-vis their peers in other countries. On the contrary, young Europeans disregard national boundaries and consider each other's countries as part of their natural habitat for purposes of study, travel, and political activities. In short they are the potential builders of the united Europe.

Catalysts of Disintegration

There are essentially two kinds of centrifugal forces or systemic barriers to political integration. One transcends national and regional borders and places "global systemic constraints" on the European Community; the other is the direct result or indirect by-product of the operations of the Common Market, or "regional systemic effects." These "catalysts of disintegration"[103] are largely autonomous in that they have different origins and causes. Moreover, some are subject to correction and modification, while others are deterministic and develop or disappear in response to factors beyond the control of regional or national authorities: they increase or diminish "par la force des choses" and serve as symbols of a heterogeneous sociopolitical reality. An effort will be made to identify the objective, pragmatic catalysts of disintegration, rather than to detect some "Machiavellian conspiracies" on the part of the opponents of European unity.

In this context it should be recalled that we regard the integration-disintegration syndrome as being "neutral" in the sense that integration (or disintegration) may be considered advantageous by one group of nations and unfortunate by another. Thus advocates of a global or intercontinental approach to international harmony may welcome (or not oppose) disintegration in a region such as Western Europe.

Global Systemic Constraints

Europe has been the "big prize" in the continuing game of power politics played by the two superpowers since the end of World War II. The principal object of attention and the central political problem are both Germany and its future role in Europe. Although the cold war has been gradually replaced by a cautious rapprochement between the two ideological camps, the essentially bipolar strategic-military balance between the Warsaw Pact and NATO is largely unaltered. This détente diplomacy is sanctioned by all major actors in the European political arena: the Soviets call it "peaceful coexistence"; the Americans and British talk about "bridge-building"; the French refer to it as *détente, entente et coopération*; and the Germans label it *Ostpolitik*. The purpose of this new diplomacy is perceived as the ratification of the *status quo* by the Soviet Union, and as a method of liberalizing Eastern Europe and promoting German reunification by the Western allies. The Germans have the greatest stake in the success of this new policy, which is designed to overcome the *immobilisme* and frustrations of the era of confrontation and eventually lead to German unity. Undoubtedly, the division of Germany is both the cause and effect of Europe's partition, which, in turn, mortgages international peace. Furthermore, a consolidation of the European Community also requires some kind of final solution of the German issue in order to permit the creation of an equilibrium in Western Europe—a goal that cannot be achieved as long as West Germany has a justified claim on a political settlement of the German question.

According to Chancellor Willy Brandt, the German Federal Republic is merely an "economic giant but a political dwarf." But this condition would change with the reunification of the two Germanies since it would result in the creation of a sovereign superstate—the second strongest power on the European Continent. However, the potential rise of a new rival to the Soviet Union on the European Continent seems unacceptable to Moscow, and the preponderant role of a united Germany in Western Europe is also anathema to Paris and London. Indeed, "the perpetuation of the division of Germany is the lynchpin of the Soviet efforts to promote both Soviet security and (West) European disunity—and the two goals are seen by Moscow as interrelated.[104] This open opposition to German reunification by the Soviet Union (except, of course, on Soviet terms) is shared, although not stated publicly, by many Western leaders who "love Germany so much that they would always like to have at least two of them."

Therefore, it appears as if the Germans—but not all of them—are the only ones who are serious about accepting the expected results of the *Ostpolitik*. The existence of the Berlin Wall is a symbol of the artificial and inhuman separation of a people into two states: Germans cannot be blamed for trying to find a solution to this intolerable relict of the last war. However, Germany faces a fundamental dilemma: she can pursue a policy of *status quo*, remaining a staunch ally of the US in exchange for an American security guarantee; or she can take the calculated risk of making a direct deal with the Russian bear in the hope that a *modus vivendi* on the German issue can be found. The latter maneuver is fraught with enormous dangers: West Germany would be an unequal partner in such bilateral negotiations, and their outcome may already be determined before they begin. But a continuing division of Germany is an unnatural and explosive time bomb which should be defused as soon as possible. To find a solution to this dilemma is the responsibility of the German government, but it is also a vital concern of the other members of the European Community since its destiny is inextricably linked to the future of Germany.

Hence it can be argued that the German question per se is a destabilizing factor in the European Community. All alternative strategies open to the Bonn government are subject to systemic constraints, thus constituting a "catalyst of disintegration": the first option—solidarity with the U.S. in return for military protection—may prevent a "European defense community" from materializing. The second option, a possible sell-out to the Soviet Union, may result in the collapse of the European Community. A third possible alternative—the German *Verzicht* of East Germany and total integration into a West European confederation with an independent defense force—would entail drastic changes in the legal provisions of the WEU Treaty, which imposes severe limits on German nuclear rearmament and may precipitate a Soviet cancellation of the non-aggression treaty with West Germany.

It should also be noted that the *Ostpolitik*, which is conditioned on West Germany's position of strength as a NATO member, may paradoxically lend support to the argument for withdrawing US troops from Europe in that it supposedly aims at a reduction of tensions, which in turn would eliminate the need for maintaining American forces in Europe. The result of such a development could well be the "Finlandization" of the entire Continent through de facto control (rather than military occupation) by the USSR.

Transcommunal Interdependencies

Since integration is a global phenomenon, its manifestation within a region may have a disintegrative effect on other areas of the world. Conversely, regional integration may be impeded by forces that transcend the boundaries of the particular region. Thus the European Community is also subject to the workings of centrifugal forces that may, in turn, promote integration at a higher level.

Among the most obvious examples for global interdependence are the problems of peace, development aid, and the environment. Examples of transcontinental ("Atlantic") problems are strategy and defense in the nuclear age, the reform of the international monetary system, and the question of trade liberalization. Global interdependence in the economic field is best symbolized by the proliferation of multinational companies which spread their tentacles octopus-like from their headquarters across national boundaries on various continents. This development seems to foreshadow not only the eclipse of national sovereignty but might also give rise to questions about the adequate scope of regional groupings, such as the European Community. Thus a European observer points at the "dysfunctional character of a European federation" and argues that the agenda of the 1970s "is crowded with issues all of which are beyond the grasp of the Community."[105] Among these issues are arms control and security, trade, aid to developing nations, technological cooperation, planning, urbanization, education, cultural cooperation, crisis prevention and crisis management. Consequently, the Dutch writer proposes that different functional organizations should be in charge of different tasks, each one fulfilling its respective responsibility at a different level.

Transcommunal Loyalties

People in pluralistic societies always have multiple loyalties to different authorities at various levels of the social and political systems. Thus a citizen of a nation is usually loyal to authorities at the local, state or provincial, and national level. However, he may also develop transnational loyalties to regional, continental, transcontinental or global authorities. A good example is the notorious solidarity over an extended period of time on the part of most Germans with the United States. In response to the question, "with which of the following countries will Germany continue to share common interests for a long period," a large majority of the Germans invariably choose the United States over any other country.[106] This German-American solidarity could be explained in terms of a dependence syndrome on the part of the Germans, given the perceived need for American protection. However, this does not explain the surprising attitudes of the French, who responded to same question by naming the members of the European community and the United States as almost equally important.[107] It is also common knowledge that many Dutch and British feel much closer to the United States than to any other European country. A tangible evidence of this strong trans-Atlantic solidarity in the economic sector (and based upon the profit motive) is the fact that many national companies in Europe "given the choice between joining an American company and another European company, nearly always choose the first."[108]

The increasing importance of multiple loyalties has been underlined by another analyst, who concluded his opinion survey of West European students with the following statement:

Our data strongly suggests that Europeanness tends to go with a broader internationalism: the predominant tendency is for those who support European integration to also support measures favorable to Atlantic ties or even global political integration. This tendency applies to all of our national samples including the French. The strength of the connection between Europeanness and internationalism varies from country to country but consistently points in the same direction. Those of our students who were pro-European tended to adhere to the Monnet conception of an outward-looking Europe and did not seem to view European unification as a means of resisting domination from outside. They were more likely to favor closer ties with the United States than were the less European-minded students and seemed relatively favorable toward broader forms of internationalism.[109]

One possible reason for this cosmopolitan outlook among many European students could be the fact that there are significantly more exchanges of academic personnel between European and American universities than between universities within the European Community.[110]

In the light of these findings, it may well be that "Euro-America is coming into being at the same time as the Common Market, and in some respects even more rapidly."[111]

Regional Systemic Effects:
The Resilience of the Nation-State

In the aftermath of World War II, European states were exhausted and dependent on outside assistance for both military security and economic welfare. The impotence of all nation-states in Western Europe was gradually overcome through generous American support in terms of providing a protective nuclear umbrella and restoring the economies of both victors and vanquished. The principal European instrument for economic recovery became the Common Market, a joint undertaking of six nations that turned out to be a spectacular success as it produced the highest growth rates and living standards in the history of Europe.

Therefore, it seems illogical and even paradoxical to consider the possibility that its success in the economic realm could have negative repercussions in the political sphere. And yet the possibility that the European Community's very achievements may have been partially counterproductive cannot be rejected out of hand. Indeed, "the irony is that the success of integration can be . . . used against the architects of that success. [It] . . . strengthened the hand of the most consistent opponent of that system and weakened that of its supporters."[112] There is no doubt that national governments indirectly benefitted from the success of the European Community in so far as they could claim responsibility for it, and were in fact given credit for it, by the people who were unable to assess the real effect of the Common Market's operations. Thus President de Gaulle frequently masqueraded in the role of the "good European" who was allegedly intent upon promoting the European cause but in reality used the European Community to reinforce French national power and prestige. Such involuntary service in the national interest, performed by the community over the last twenty years, resulted in a reassertion of national strength and resurgence of nationalism—effects that were never intended by the "Eurocrats."

Economic recovery permitted nation-states such as France not only to assure its people an unprecedented standard of living but also to build nuclear weapons arsenals to serve as status symbols of national sovereignty.[113] Although these small *forces de frappe* are dysfunctional because their cost far outweighs their potential usefulness, they maintained their prestige through the lack of opportunity for testing them. In fact, it is the very absence of the threat of war that eliminates the incentive for further integrative steps and masks the totally unviable and unrealistic concept of "national defense" in the nuclear era as a chimera of governments.

The improvement of the "national situation"[114] in the Western European states also removed the inclination toward "national self-abdication" on the part of national bureaucracies: they could again justify their *raison d'être* as relatively self-sufficient and autonomous agents of the nation-state, capable of providing for the essential needs of their people by means far less drastic than hara-kiri.

The instinct for self-preservation is, of course, a natural characteristic of all bureaucracies as long as they are composed of human beings with a vested interest in the *status quo*. Undoubtedly, "few organizations disband willingly, as neither executives nor members are eager to end the activity that rewards them."[115] Moreover, there is the "natural proclivity of any organization's members to keep the organization alive to function successfully even when the bureau really 'ought' to die."[116] Applied to the European context, this proposition means that no French, German, Italian or British civil servant is naturally predisposed voluntarily to delegate his powers to a Eurocrat since such an idealistic gesture of generosity would almost necessarily result in his own demise or at least in a diminution of autonomy and prestige (unless he is among the minority to be promoted to a position at the European level). This propensity on the part of national bureaucrats to cling to their functions in the service of their respective state has been underlined by empirical data derived from interviews with a number of national officials in the higher ranks of various ministries of the six EEC member states. Although almost all of them expressed support for European political unification, a majority opposed any contraction of functions.[117] The discrepancy between ideal and practice is obvious, and "apprehension about the contraction of functions cannot but militate against support for political integration which by necessity entails a transfer of functions to a higher level and may well reduce the power and importance possessed by national officials."[118]

Apart from the incidental political effect of the European Community on the structure of the nation states in the sense of indirectly invigorating them and thus justifying their continued existence, it had an unwarranted social effect as well. The community was originally designed to benefit all member nations and to assure a balanced growth of all regions within the system. Although this original concern has remained official community policy (e.g., "regional policy"), the actual benefits of the Common Market were not always evenly distributed. Despite the fact that the vast majority of Europeans derived tangible benefits from the achievements of the Common Market, there remained a minority of underprivileged in each country. Convinced that the Common Market left them "out in the cold," these groups formed pockets of resistance to community policies. Frustrated, they tend to form what has been called a "nationalist coalition"[119] composed of small businessmen, various labor unions, many small farmers and, of course, directly threatened bureaucratic officials such as national customs officers.

Notwithstanding conscious efforts on the part of the European Commission to equalize benefits and gain the loyalty of all social groups, the requirements of modernization and planning for the enlarged European Community necessarily produces unintended inequities. For instance, the large-scale restructuring of the agricultural sector entails massive, revolutionary social changes which are still not clearly visible in terms of their exact meaning for the farm population—except that they will gradually be "urbanized." Although the "Mansholt Plan" is still little known in Europe, the agricultural Common Market is widely regarded as detrimental to the farmers of some members of the European Community.[120]

Opposition to the European Community also comes from diverse youth groups that can be called the "New Left," composed of alienated students and other elite groups concerned with the social aspects of economic integration in Western Europe. They attack the community on two grounds: as a capitalist enterprise under American hegemony that cares little about the welfare of the common man; and as an impersonal bureaucratic monster that performs functions beyond democratic control and permits no popular participation in its organization. Furthermore, they argue that "affluence is no longer its own justification. Affluence perhaps—but for what, for whom, and at what cost."[121] On the occasion of a meeting with the commission, a youth committee on "European Policy Towards Society" attacked the technocratic and capitalist orientation of the community and urged it to "serve man instead of capitalist interests."[122] In other words, they challenge the traditional slogan, "you never had it so good—therefore support the Common Market," as capitalist utilitarianism that should be modified to meet the needs of all people.

In this chapter we tried to demonstrate the complexity and ambivalence of the integration-disintegration syndrome in the European context. Whereas Chapters 3 and 4 dealt with the various *actors* identified in the "Gestalt model," Chapter 5 focused on the prevailing centripetal and centrifugal *forces* at work in the contemporary European setting. It can be concluded that most of the propositions about the "integration-disintegration" phenomenon advanced in Chapter 2 have been tested and found valid (although this initial, limited—rather than systematic—attempt to apply the "Gestalt model" clearly requires methodological improvements and refinement).

In terms of the findings of this chapter, it can be stated that there seems to be a "stand-off" between the potential catalysts of integration and disintegration in the European Community at the present time. This unsatisfactory but realistic finding therefore prevents us from making a categorical judgment as to the short-term prospects for European political unification. However, the long-range prospects for European unity appear to be favorable given the increasing momentum of "Euro-socialization" involving the younger cohorts and future leaders of the New Europe. In other words, once the post-war elites will have assumed positions of authority in the 1980s, they can be expected to provide the impetus necessary to unite Europe.

Part III:
Prospects for the New Europe
and External Relations

6

The Enlargement of the Common Market and Its Implications

Enlargement of Membership

The negotiations on the creation of a Free Trade Area, sponsored by the British government broke down in 1958. Consequently the United Kingdom tried to find a reasonable alternative to this defunct project. Faced with a *fait accompli*—the inauguration of the EEC—the British government first proceeded to organize EFTA (1960), a free trade zone which was considered as a rival bloc of the EEC and/or as a bridge between the "Outer Seven" and the "Inner Six." However, the dynamic nature of the Common Market and the interdependent trade relations between the members of the two blocs led to their *de facto* rapprochement during the 1960s, culminating in the British application for membership in the Common Market. Unable to resist the centripetal force of the European Community in both the economic and political fields, Her Majesty's government had come to the conclusion that the only realistic course for Britain consisted in seeking accession to the EEC as soon as feasible. Therefore, Prime Minister Macmillan in a speech in the House of Commons requested the opening of negotiations with the Common Market in order to determine whether satisfactory arrangements could be made permitting the United Kingdom to join the European Community (July 31, 1961). The formal British request was submitted to the Council of Ministers in Brussels on August 10, together with a similar proposal by Denmark; Ireland had already applied for membership in the EEC on August 1, 1961. The three neutral members of EFTA—Austria, Sweden, and Switzerland—followed the British lead when they applied for association with the Common Market on December 15 of that year. When Norway applied for EEC entry on April 30, 1962, EFTA appeared to be condemned to disintegration.[1] However, the "bridge-building" strategy adopted by the Six and the Seven failed to take into consideration an "independent variable" of greatest importance—General de Gaulle. Convinced that the "albion perfide" could only have oblique motives if it suddenly adopted a *volte face*—from an unsuccessful attempt to sabotage the community to the decision to join it—the French President was determined to block British entry. However, he did not act immediately but awaited a crisis phase in the ongoing negotiations between the British delegation (chaired by Edward Heath) and the commission in Brussels late in 1962, after a year of intensive discussions on detailed issues. Speaking at a press conference in Paris on January 14, 1963, de Gaulle pronounced the verdict on the British candidature for admission to the EEC: he called Britain "insular,"

163

"maritime" and "profoundly different" from the continental nations and concluded that the best solution consisted in discontinuing the negotiations until Britain becomes "more European" sometimes in the future.[2] This Gaullist veto resulted in the formal suspension *sine die* of the first "Brussels Round" on January 29, 1963, despite the fact that substantial progress had been made between the two negotiating teams on several important items of the agenda. Following the breakdown of the negotiations between Britain and the EEC, the other EFTA countries[3] withdrew their requests for affiliation with the Six, and EFTA continued to function quite successfully until 1967, when the British Labour government decided to make another attempt to join the Common Market.

This second initiative on the part of Her Majesty's government differed from the first on four counts: first, it was undertaken by Prime Minister Harold Wilson, a member of the traditionally antimarket Labour party and a reluctant "convert" to the European cause. Second, whereas the Macmillan government had only requested "negotiations to see if any satisfactory arrangements could be made to meet the special interests of the United Kingdom" before deciding to make an application, the Wilson government "decided to make an application under Article 237 of the Treaty of Rome for membership" in the EEC, as well as in ECSC and Euratom.[4] Thirdly, the Labour government no longer insisted on the "five conditions" for British entry which the Macmillan government considered as *préalables* for accession to the Rome Treaty: safeguards for British sovereignty in foreign policy and economic planning, protection of agriculture, and satisfactory arrangements for all the EFTA countries and the Commonwealth. Instead, Mr. Wilson submitted the formal application of May 10, 1967, for British entry without conditions, although he identified certain "special problems" which could arise from membership in the European Community, especially with regard to Britain's adjustment and contribution to the common agricultural policy. Fourthly, in contrast to its negative position in 1961, the majority of the Labour party (now in power) agreed on the political objective of joining the Common Market in 1967; the Conservatives—now in the opposition— continued to favor entry, as they did in 1961.[5]

This "change of heart" on the part of the Labour party and Prime Minister Wilson's conversion, however, failed to impress General de Gaulle. Refusing to reopen the negotiations on British entry into the Common Market, the French president, speaking at a press conference on November 27, 1967, in effect vetoed the plan for the second time.[6] Despite continuing French opposition to British membership in the European Community, Her Majesty's government refused to withdraw its application. The situation remained unchanged until General de Gaulle resigned on April 28, 1969, and was succeeded by President Pompidou. The new French government, in cooperation with the new German Chancellor Willy Brandt (elected on October 21, 1969), organized the summit conference at the Hague at which the six heads of state called for the enlargement of the community.[7] With the Gaullist obstacle removed, formal negotiations between the Common Market and the United Kingdom, Denmark, Ireland, and Norway began on June 30, 1970. The British delegation was headed by Mr. Geoffrey Rippon, who represented the new Prime Minister Edward Heath, who had succeeded Mr. Wilson on June 19, 1970. Contrary to the first "Brussels Round" in 1962, the six members of the European Community provided the commission with the negotiating mandate (rather than participating in an intergovernmental conference between the Six and the Four). This new concept of a "single negotiator" was proposed by the French, who wanted to prevent the British from playing one government off against another, and in the process, perhaps, isolating the French. Consequently the community's negotiating team was led by the foreign minister of the country that presided over the council during the six-month period, but the commission was charged with the detailed negotiating.[8] Naturally, the negotiations focused on the British case because it posed the greatest problems and because the other applicants wanted to await the outcome of these negotiations before making their decision. After almost one year of hard bargaining, the first breakthrough came on May 13, 1971, when the two chief negotiators, French Foreign Minister Maurice Schuman and Mr. Geoffrey Rippon of Britain, announced that a major turning point had been reached. In fact, full agreement had been achieved on Britain's transitional arrangements for aligning its farm prices with those of the Six as well as on a basic formula for calculating Britain's contributions to the Community's autonomous budget.[9] This initial success in the negotiations created a favorable climate for the summit meeting between President Pompidou and Prime Minister Heath in Paris on May 21, 1971. In a joint communiqué, the two leaders expressed their satisfaction with the progress made in Brussels and "considered that it was desirable and possible to reach early agreement on the main outstanding issues. . . ."[10] The Franco-British accord provided the final impetus for the successful conclusion of the negotiations on June 23, when complete consensus was reached on a "package" agreement between the community and the United Kingdom.[11] Although some minor technical details were left for follow-up negotiations, all basic political problems were settled and the foundations for British entry were established.

The final "package" contained the following five principal elements of agreement: the new institutional framework, a transition period for British membership in the three communities, British contributions to the common budget, arrangements for Commonwealth countries, and an interim period (1971-73).

The Transition Periods for British Accession to the Three Organizations

Whereas Britain needed virtually no transition period for joining the ECSC and only one year to enter Euratom, the United Kingdom was granted a five-year transition period (1973-78) for both industry and agriculture. Consequently, a customs union for industrial products will come into existence by July 1, 1977, and internal tariffs will be cut in five stages between April 1, 1973, and July 1, 1977, with reductions of 20 percent at each stage. At the same time, the new members will align their tariffs vis-à-vis the rest of the world with the community's common external tariff (CET) in four steps: a 40 percent reduction on July 1, 1974, and three other cuts of 20 percent each on January 1, 1975, January 1, 1976, and July 1, 1977.[12] As far as agriculture was concerned, Britain accepted the common agricultural policy (CAP) of the community and agreed to align its food prices with those of the Six during the transition period in six steps, beginning 1973. Special arrangements were made for fisheries, hill-farming and horticulture.

The British Contribution to the Community Budget

With the end of the transition period, the United Kingdom will fully participate in the autonomous system of financing the community (effective 1978). During the first year of membership (1973), Britain's maximum contribution to the common budget was to be 8.64 percent of the total. This figure was estimated to be equivalent to a gross British contribution of $288 million in 1973, based upon the assumption that the community's budget of that year will be about $3.3 billion. Subsequently, the British contributions will rise during the transition period to the following maximum percentages: in 1974, 10.85 percent; in 1975, 13.34 percent; in 1976, 16.02 percent; and 18.92 percent in 1977, corresponding to the UK share of the gross community product. In order to avoid any sudden increase in Britain's contribution between the end of the transition period and 1978, the United Kingdom was given two additional years during which its share will be limited. However, beginning 1980, Britain, like any other member country, will hand over to the community all revenue from customs duties and farm import levies, as well as a percentage of revenue in the United Kingdom on January 1, 1973.

Commonwealth Relations

It was agreed that the enlarged community will offer association arrangements to most Commonwealth countries and dependent territories, as well as Hong Kong. Moreover, an accord was reached safeguarding sugar imports from certain Commonwealth countries. Only New Zealand constituted a special problem because of its intimate economic relationship with the United Kingdom. The compromise formula decided upon guarantees this country exports to the community for 71 percent of its dairy products traditionally sent to the British; by 1977 the guarantee for cheese will be abolished and the situation with regard to butter will be reexamined in 1975.

Interim Arrangements

The target date for signing the treaties of accession between the community and the four applicant countries was set for January 1, 1972, so as to permit their entry into force on January 1, 1973, following the ratification of the treaties by the ten states concerned. In an effort to involve the four applicants in community operations during this intermim period, it was decided to adopt common procedures to ensure that decisions taken by the Six would take due account of the interests of the candidate countries as future members. Specifically, the Six and the Four agreed to consult with one another on all important issues prior to adopting a decision. This consultation machinery became operational on July 5, 1971, when the commission decided to institute contact procedures with the applicant countries without awaiting the signature of the treaties.[13] The consultation machinery for the "preinterim period" was first used during the monetary crisis of September, 1971, when the six finance ministers consulted with their British counterpart on common measures to be taken in response to the American initiative of August 15.

In order to underline its "Europeanness" the British government also assured the Six that it will gradually phase out the pound sterling as a reserve currency. Furthermore, all four applicant countries agreed to consult with the Six on any projected bilateral trade agreement with third nations in view of formulating the community's common commercial policy as of 1973.

The Role of the Commission

In this context it should be noted that the successful outcome of the enlargement negotiations was largely due to the efficient preparatory work by the European Commission, which had supported the principle of enlargement ever since 1961 and had provided specific recommendations for compromise solutions prior to each new round of talks between the community and the candidates for membership. The commission first expressed its full support for the initial British attempt to negotiate an agreement for adhesion to the EEC in a press communiqué issued on August 1, 1961.[14] Following President de Gaulle's veto of British entry of January 14, 1963, Commission President Hallstein presented an objective summary report of the actual state of negotiations as of January 29 to the European Parliament on February 5, 1963. On this occasion Mr. Hallstein said that there was no reason for discontinuing the ongoing negotiations in Brussels and stressed that the commission wanted to succeed; he added that the commission considered British accession to the EEC as merely postponed and promised to keep the door open and try to find an early solution.[15] This favorable attitude on the part of the commission was again expressed following Britain's second application in May 1967. Subsequently, the commission submitted four "opinions" on this matter to the council in

September 1967, April 1968, October 1969, and December 1970. The "Communication to the Council concerning the transitional mechanisms for the enlargement of the Community," submitted on December 4, 1970, contained the most detailed and up-to-date analysis of the salient issues involved in the problem of enlargement of the community.

Prior to considering the substantive elements of this important document, a brief comparative analysis of the principles identified in the preceding "opinions" will permit us to gauge the evolution of the commission's thinking over a period of time. Originally, the commission had placed emphasis on the more technical aspects involved in the enlargement of the community, such as the harmonization of agricultural and commercial policies (the former mainly concerning Britain, the latter involving the Commonwealth nations), whereas the legal, financial, institutional issues and relations with EFTA were hardly touched upon during the Brussels negotiations in 1962.[16] By 1967 the commission had changed its priorities, focussing on agriculture and monetary problems. In 1969 the commission devoted considerable attention to the negotiating procedures and the need for strengthening them. Other key points of this October 2 "opinion" were that simultaneous entry of all four applicants should be the goal of negotiations; that the candidates should accept the principles of the common farm policy; and that all should express their readiness to participate fully in the creation of a politically and economically united Europe.[17] The purpose of the commission's "communication" of December 1970 was to provide an overall view of the most important problems involved in the organization of the transition period for the four applicants. The following five issue areas were identified: (1) transitional arrangements for adaptation to the common agricultural policy; (2) stages for the elimination of internal tariffs and for the introduction of the CET to the outside world; (3) the financing of Community policies and the progressive extension of the system of Community resources to the applicant countries; (4) special cases (involving Commonwealth imports); and (5) institutional questions.[18] Together with the previous recommendations, these proposals constituted the framework within which negotiations between the Community and the four applicant countries began on June 30, 1970. In his opening statement, Mr. Jean Rey, the commission's president, expressed his satisfaction with the reopening of the negotiations and promised that the commission would do all it could to bring them to a successful conclusion. However, Mr. Rey emphasized that enlargement should not jeopardize progress toward the creation of the economic, monetary and political union: "It is essential . . . that this development should be neither arrested nor slowed down by the negotiations on enlargement."[19] He also stressed that the

strengthening of the Community is not merely a question of the pursuit of internal policies; the institutional machinery is also concerned . . . [and] the adaptation which is indispensible . . . must be accomplished in such a way as to maintain the efficiency of the system and to compensate for the effect which enlargement might have on the institutional machinery. . . . [Therefore] it is of fundamental importance that the conditions necessary in order to maintain the cohesion and dynamism indispensible to an enlarged Community should be satisfied.[20]

Following the successful outcome of the second "Brussels Round," the Commission of the European Community issued an official statement on June 24, which read as follows:

The Commission of the European Communities considers that the negotiations with Great Britain on its application for membership in the European Economic Community have now been completed at a political level. It is convinced that the outstanding problems will be settled rapidly and that the negotiations with the other three candidate countries are bound to enjoy the same success.

For the enlargement of the Community, the Commission has mobilized all its energy and determination. The event is one of world importance, for expansion of the Community will strengthen its already considerable influence in international trade and spur a new start towards economic and monetary union.

The enlarged and reinforced Community is called upon to shoulder special responsibility in relations between the industrialized countries and the developing countries and to make a decisive contribution to the process of détente in Europe and the world. To achieve this aim, the Commission is determined to pursue a forward course of action in conformity with the Community Treaties and the spirit of The Hague summit conference.[21]

The United Kingdom at Historical Crossroads

Once the foundations for British membership in the European Community were laid as the result of the agreement on the political principle arrived at between the Six and the United Kingdom, it was up to Parliament to decide whether the terms of entry negotiated in Brussels were acceptable. In an effort to provide the members of both Houses of Parliament as well as the British people with a concrete basis for making this crucial decision in the fall of 1971, the Heath government published a "white paper" which was presented to the House of Commons on July 7, 1971. In this document, the government formally reaffirmed its intention of joining the Common Market on the basis of the "just and reasonable" terms negotiated with the community in June. In the introduction, the government firmly rejected any alternative policy and stated that a negative decision would constitute a "rejection of an historic opportunity and a reversal of the whole direction of British policy under successive governments during the last decade." Instead, the government recommended an affirmative vote, because:

the choice for Britain is clear. Either we choose to enter the Community and join in building a strong Europe on the Foundation which the Six have laid, or we choose to stand aside from this great enterprise and seek to maintain our interests from the narrow—and narrowing—base we have known in recent years.

The rationale given was the following: "Individually, no European country can ensure that its voice is heeded; collectively . . . the voice of the Community cannot be ignored." In an astute move, the government associated the former prime minister with its proMarket policy by quoting Mr. Wilson's statement of May 1967 that "together we can ensure that Europe plays in world affairs the part which the Europe of today is not at present playing."[2 2]

In another important section, the white paper dealt with the issue of national sovereignty and stressed that the United Kingdom would be able to make its voice heard in the Council of Ministers, which reflects the reality of sovereign governments. Furthermore, national identities would not be blurred in the community, and its members would retain their monarchs, courts, and local administration.

On the economic aspects of Common Market membership, the white paper pointed at the advantages for Britain: she would benefit from the spectacular achievements and the dynamic growth of the community. Entry would also lead to improved efficiency and productivity, a higher rate of investment, and a faster growth of real wages. The government argued that these advantages would largely compensate for the short-term costs of membership, particularly the temporary increase in food prices for the British consumer as a result of the impact of the CAP and the discontinuation of duty-free food imports from the Commonwealth. Finally, the document commented on the future British contribution to the community budget, which would amount to 100 million pounds in 1973 and double by the end of 1977. In sum the white paper underlined the extremely favorable and equitable terms agreed upon in Brussels and urged Parliament to accept them in the interest of the nation.

The debate on the basis of the white paper began immediately and increased in intensity as the date of the historic vote approached. The atmosphere in the House of Commons was characterized by a "now or never" mood of many MPs and stimulated by such pro-Europeans as Mr. Bruce-Gardyne, a Conservative, who held that "the road to independence leads via Europe," and by anti-marketeers such as Mr. Peter Shore (Labour), who feared that "the supranational dynamic would lead to the dismantling of the State."[2 3] Lord George Brown, former Labour Foreign Minister and an ardent European, called on his party to support the government's plan on the ground that "we would become victims of events instead of being their architects" should Britain remain outside the community. Yet, despite these admonitions and his previously pro-European policy, Mr. Wilson, now opposition leader, first hesitated to commit himself and eventually became critical of the policy pursued by the Conservative government. In a detailed reply to the white paper, the Labour party published a document entitled "No entry on the Terms Obtained by the Tories," which stressed that the leadership of the party was (and still is) against the entry terms only, not against the principle of entry. After referring to the negotiations of Brussels as a total failure, the Opposition asserted that "we are not anti-Common Market, still less are we anti-Europe. Our attitude to membership has always depended on the terms for entry."[24] In its drive to rally public opinion behind its position, the Labour party continuously pointed at the economic costs of Common Market membership and finally adopted a formal resolution at its Annual Conference in which it rejected British entry under the terms negotiated by the Conservatives and asked for general elections on the question of entry.[25]

With public opinion polls still showing a majority of the people opposed to Britain joining the European Community, the government launched an all-out propaganda effort to create a political atmosphere favorable to its project by the time of the crucial vote in Parliament. The Tories' commitment to the European cause was subsequently underlined when the Conservative Party Conference enthusiastically approved Britain's accession to the Community under the terms negotiated in June.[26]

The historic decision came on October 28, when Parliament voted on the following Government resolution: "This House [of Commons] approves her Majesty's Government's decision in principle to join the European Communities on the basis of arrangements which have been negotiated."[27] Prior to the vote, Prime Minister Heath had made a dramatic appeal to Parliament when he declared that "never in times of peace has a British Prime Minister asked to take a decision of such capital importance as this evening. Today the world is looking toward Westminster. Our decision will be of vital importance for the balance of forces in the world for many years to come."[28] Mr. Heath's final statement was followed by the vote. The result was announced by the Speaker and welcomed with a tremendous ovation; the government's resolution was adopted by a majority of 112 votes, or 356 to 244.[29] The majority in the House of Lords was even more impressive.[30]

Immediately after the vote, Mr. Heath said, "We stand ready to take our first step into a new world full of new opportunities. Our historic decision has been made: the British people accept the challenge. Let us show ourselves to that new world as we would wish it to see us—confident, proud and strong."[31]

The Opposition was split between the pro-European "rebels" who had voted for the government resolution (about one-fourth of the Labour vote) and the antimarketeers (who had been joined by 39 Tories); the "Europeans" were led by Roy Jenkins, the deputy leader of the Labour party, while Mr. Harold Wilson led the majority of his party against British entry into the European Community. The Opposition leader was appalled by the size of the Labour defection and pledged to fight the government on each individual bill of the enabling legislation which had to pass Parliament before Britain could formally enter the Common Market.

Abroad, Parliament's decision was hailed by both European and American leaders. In Brussels, the president of the European Commission, Mr. Malfatti, declared that "this historic decision marks the success of the building of Europe, and above all, provides it with the necessary dimension and status. An enlarged Community of ten members, by the very virtue of cohesion and democratic stability, will be in a position to take up increasing world responsibility."[32]

The British vote in favor of "Europe" was also welcomed in all West European capitals, particularly in Bonn, where Chancellor Brandt and the leaders of the opposition party hailed Parliament's decision.

The Accession Treaty

The formal, legal act of enlargement took place in Brussels on January 22, 1972, when the four applicant states and the six members of the European Community signed the Accession Treaty which was to become effective as of January 1, 1973, following ratification by the ten parliaments involved. The constitutive act of accession was based upon the provisions for enlargement outlined in the Rome Treaties—articles 237 (EEC) and 205 (Euratom)—and in the Treaty of Paris (article 98). The entry into force of the Accession Treaty was subject to ratification in accordance with the various procedures of the ten states concerned. In Britain Parliament had to pass enabling legislation in order to give the provisions of the Accession Treaty the force of domestic law; once Parliament authorizes a treaty, the Queen customarily ratifies it. On February 18, 1972, the British House of Commons adopted the second reading of the European Communities Bill by 309 votes to 301. The majority was composed of 304 Conservatives and 5 Liberals. 286 Labourites voted against it and 6 abstained; also 15 Tories opposed the bill and 6 abstained.[33]

In Ireland the Lower House of Parliament decided on membership in the European Community through a constitutional amendment. However, prior to this act, a national referendum had to be held. Although only a simple majority was necessary, 83.1 percent of the Irish people voted in favor of Ireland's joining the European Community.[34]

In the Norwegian Parliament, a three-fourths majority was required for a decision on a constitutional issue such as joining the European Community. Prior to it a referendum had to be held in which the Norwegians rejected membership in the European Community by a narrow margin of votes—54 percent were against and 46 percent for accession.[35]

The Danish Constitution provided for a simple parliamentary majority backed by the positive result of a national referendum in which 63.5 percent of the Danes voted in favor and 36.5 percent against Common Market membership.[36]

On the occasion of the signature of the Accession Treaty in Brussels on January 22, 1972, the presidents of the Council of Ministers and of the Commission of the European Community, as well as the representatives of the four applicant states made the following statements:[37]

Franco Maria Malfatti, *Commission President*

The Community of Six had fanned the spark of European unity into a flame. It was now up to the Community of Ten to transform it into the great flame of united Europe, Mr. Malfatti said.

Enlargement would create the necessary dimensions and the conditions for the Community to develop and complete the political design behind the Paris and Rome Treaties. In the immediate postwar period, the idea of a united Europe had stemmed mainly from the agonizing contemplation of two civil wars in Europe. Today, the idea of European unity drew its strength from the feeling that it was the answer to the worries of the present.

Mr. Malfatti said the Community was revolutionary when compared with earlier historic experiments, for the unifying process set in motion was a joint venture undertaken by every member state, linked within the Community by complete equality of rights and duties. It was original because it was characterized by an institutional structure for which no equivalent could be found in earlier models.

"This structure rests on a European Parliament, consisting of representatives of the peoples of the Community . . . on a Council consisting of the representatives of the member states and endowed with a power of decision; on a Commission with powers of its own, whose duty it is to propose and watch over Community rules and to share in shaping the acts of the Council; and, finally, a Court of Justice which ensures that Community law is observed. These are the essential features of the edifice which we must defend and strengthen in a democratic framework, since it is they which confer on the budding Community its particular character."

The Commission President said that the new Community was not, and did not seek to be, a new bloc but a wide Community of free and peaceful states and peoples. It was a Community of ten democratic countries that were among the most highly developed in the world, and it was determined to make the process of unification irreversible in order to consolidate its friendships, contribute decisively, on a footing of equality, to the development of the less favored nations, and to develop, as a new element of equilibrium in a better international order, new cooperative relationships with all the peoples of the earth.

"Never before has one generation had so many opportunities to contribute in a concrete manner to the unity of Europe, the task to which so many eminent statesmen have in the past devoted their efforts and their thought. This is the stirring challenge of our day, a challenge that we can, we must take up," Mr. Malfatti concluded.

Gaston Thorn, *Luxembourg Foreign Minister and Current President of the Council of Ministers*

In joining the Community, the new members "renounce neither their history, nor the virtues and traditions peculiar to each of these nations, any more than the states of the Community, as hitherto existing, have lost their own identities by pooling their economies and by embarking upon the course of political unification."

Mr. Thorn said that the enlarged Community responds above all to the aspirations of a new generation, for whom our quarrels of yesteryear pale into insignificance before the prospects of a future Europe no longer controlled by sectarian interests, but conscious of the potentials of this great enterprise and demanding their immediate realization.

Edward Heath, *British Prime Minister*

The ceremony marked the conclusion of more than a decade of arduous negotiations and another step towards the removal of divisions in Europe, Mr. Heath said. Success had not been preordained, and there would be nothing inevitable about the next stages in the construction of Europe. Imagination would be needed to develop institutions which both honored the member states' traditions and their individuality and had the strength to guide the enlarged Community's future course.

Mr. Heath concluded: "What design should we seek for the New Europe? It must be a Europe which is strong and confident within itself. A Europe in which we shall be working for the progressive relaxation and elimination of east-west tensions. A Europe conscious of the interests of its friends and partners. A Europe alive to its great responsibilities in the common struggle of humanity for a better life.

"Thus this ceremony marks an end and a beginning. An end to divisions which have stricken Europe for centuries. A beginning of another stake in the construction of a new and greater united Europe. This is the task for our generation in Europe."

John Lynch, *Irish Premier*

Despite its location on the periphery of the Continent, Ireland is an integral part of Europe, bound to it by centuries of shared civilization, traditions, and ideals, Mr. Lynch said. The Irish Government sees in the Community the best hope and the true basis for the creation of a united and peaceful Europe, a belief which his Government thinks the Irish parliament and the Irish people share.

Of the European Parliament's role in the enlarged Community, Mr. Lynch commented: "All recognize a government's obligation to involve the people of the nations as closely as possible in the processes of government. There will equally be an obligation on us jointly to bring the peoples of the enlarged Community into closer contact and involvement with the decisions, policies and workings of the Community.... The Irish Government considers it of the highest importance that the part to be played by the Parliament in the enlarged Community should be the subject of the closest study by our governments acting together."

Jens Otto Krag, *Danish Premier*

The Community should pursue its internal policies in a progressive spirit of social consciousness, Mr. Krag said. "We have learned how to achieve economic growth. But we still have to learn how to administer it in a way that will not only bring more material wealth to us all but also correct social imbalances for the benefit of the least privileged. At the same time, the problems of preservation and improvement of the human environment as a whole in the industrial society becomes ever more acute. We can solve these problems by common action. Each country itself will hardly be able to," Mr. Krag said.

He hoped that the external policies of the Community would be open and outward-looking, especially towards other members of the European Free Trade Association (EFTA) which had taken part in European cooperation since the last war.

Trygve Bratelli, *Norwegian Premier*

The Community, extending from Sicily to Finmark [Northern Norway], must find varied and flexible means of action to solve its problems, Mr. Bratelli said.

Norway considers the Common Market Treaty goal of promoting harmonious and balanced development of every region in the Community an extremely important goal.

Economic integration would enable the enlarged Community to solve economic problems more easily and to ensure full employeignt. A common industrial policy would enable it to master the problems created by large multinational corporations. Only by common action could the Ten effectively protect the environment, he concluded.

An official White House Statement of January 22, 1972 read as follows:

The President welcomes the signing today in Brussels of the treaty enlarging the European Community to include the United Kingdom, Ireland, Denmark and Norway.

The United States has always supported the strengthening and enlargement of the European Community. Upon the occasion of this historic act, the President wishes to emphasize that this support is as strong as ever. The development of European unity will enable the peoples of Europe more effectively to contribute to the enhancement of world peace, security and prosperity.

The President reaffirms that close cooperation between the United States and the emerging Europe is a cornerstone of our foreign policy.

Implications of Accession to the European Community

The United Kingdom

Parliament's vote in favor of "Europe" and Her Majesty's government's signing of the Accession Treaty to the European Community signaled the beginning of a new era in British domestic and foreign policy. To be sure, the Conservative government had prepared the British people for this historic moment in gradual steps, starting with the introduction of decimal coinage in 1970, the subsequent phasing in of the metric system, and culminating in the (still pending) conversion of British motorists to drive on the "right" side of the road. All these apparently technical measures were part of a psychological process of adjustment to a new sociopolitical necessity: the sharing of Britain's destiny with that of the Continental nations of Western Europe. Therefore, Parliament's vote did not come as a real surprise to the British people. Indeed the latest polls showed that they were "resigned" to Britain joining the Common Market (although a majority of them did not "favor" this course). Nevertheless, the government's decision to seek membership in the European Community marked a significant turning point and a momentous change in traditional British policy from a nostalgic, tenacious attachment to national independence to the pragmatic realization that the pooling (rather than the abolition) of sovereignty with other European nations is Britain's only option. After all, the United Kingdom had "lost an empire and not found a new role" (to quote the late Dean Acheson) and close association with the European Community had become the only realistic alternative to clinging to a disintegrating Commonwealth or playing the unpleasant role of dependent junior partner in a "special relationship" with the United States.

Yet the conversion of the British government to the European cause took place rather slowly and amid scepticism and reluctance on the part of both officials and the public. Although Winston Churchill had championed the ideal of a united Europe as early as 1946, he had also maintained that Britain was "with, but not of," Europe. This aloofness from European politics, a remnant of the previous policy of "splendid isolation," did not change until the success of the European Community was a *fait accompli*. As Jean Monnet had predicted, the notoriously pragmatic British joined the Common Market as soon as the ambitious experiment in transnational community formation had become a political reality. Indeed, the centripetal force of the European Community eventually affected perfidious Albion, whose mood changed from initial scepticism to "reserved enthusiasm" (the maximum type of emotional involvement acceptable to an English gentleman). The great reluctance of many Britishers to face the challenge of a united Europe resulted from a *folie de grandeur à la Française*. The apparent justification for this nationalistic attitude lay in the fact that Britain (like France) had emerged as a formal victor in World War II, whereas the other European states were either occupied and/or defeated. This unrealistic British view did not, of course, take into consideration another fact, namely that the United States and the USSR had won the war and Britain was *de facto* (although not *de jure*) among the defeated powers of the last war. However, both Mr. Wilson and Mr. Heath recognized the fallacy of continued attachment to national sovereignty and opted for joining the European enterprise convinced that Britain's new role has to be *within* the new power center which constitutes the nucleus of any future united Europe.

To be sure, Britain's entry into the Common Market involves painful measures of adjustment for the British people, especially the consumers. For centuries, English housewives benefitted from the low food prices made possible by duty-free imports of agricultural products from the Commonwealth countries ("Imperial preferances"). Britain's joining of the Common Market (a customs union with a common external tariff) meant that Commonwealth preferences had to be eliminated and food prices were bound to rise to the higher level of the Common Agricultural Policy of the "Six." British farmers, in turn, no longer receive "deficiency payments" from the government in compensation for keeping the price of their food products at a low level. However, they do receive higher prices for their agricultural produce because the CAP is largely protectionist in the sense that it fixes "market prices" and assures a decent minimum income for all farmers in the Community, thus shielding inefficient enterprises against foreign competition. Moreover, British farmers will find it easier to adjust to the CAP not only because the size of their farms favors mechanization but also because the proportion of the labor force engaged in agriculture is relatively small (4 percent, as compared to France's 18 percent) and because British farmers have always been very efficient.

Industrial producers will find it quite easy to participate in the common market for manufactured goods. They will have access to new markets for their products and will benefit from increased investment as well as from the general dynamism of the European Economic Community.

In short, the British government decided that the long term political benefits would outweigh the short-term economic costs of joining the European Community.

Ireland

Given Ireland's traditional dependence on trade with the United Kingdom, negotiations for entry into the European Community proceeded parallel with those between Britain and the Six. Once the obstacles to British membership in the Common Market had been removed, Irish accession to the community was virtually assured. Despite its political neutrality and nonadhesion to EFTA—two unique features of this applicant state since the other three were members of NATO and EFTA—Ireland did not raise any difficult issues that delayed negotiations for entry into the EEC. As a small, largely rural country on the periphery of the European Community, Ireland's economy clearly depends on adhesion to this dynamic market and its potential for modernizing the socio-economic structures of the country. Politically, the Irish government has demonstrated great fervor for the European cause, an attitude that may in part be based upon the expectation that the problem of Northern Ireland may be solved in a larger European context.

Denmark

Like Ireland and Norway, Denmark made its membership in the European Community conditional on British entry. As a fellow-member in EFTA, the United Kingdom had absorbed almost 50 percent of Danish farm exports; accession to the EEC simultaneously with Britain was supposed to ensure continued access to this traditional, vital market for Danish food products. The only major political issue concerned the possible impact of Common Market membership on the Nordic Union of Scandinavian nations, but it was soon resolved in favor of "Europe."

Norway

Although the Norwegian Parliament—the Storting—had approved the government's application for membership in the European Community by an overwhelming majority in 1970, the subsequent negotiations with the commission and the council in Brussels turned out to be more difficult than with any other applicant state, except Britain. The reason for the protracted debates between the Norwegian delegation and the representatives of the European Community was the unique and sensitive issue of fisheries. The Rome Treaty provides for free access to the fisheries of all community countries by fishermen from the member states. Applied to Norway, this policy was expected to conflict with the elaborate legislation adopted by the Storting to protect the small Norwegian fishing companies from powerful foreign enterprises. Negotiations over the relative merits of "open fisheries" versus "territorial waters reserved for national fishing companies" had almost failed when a last-minute compromise permitted the Norwegian government to sign the Accession Treaty.

In anticipation of the forthcoming ratification of the treaty by the Storting (parliament), Norwegian government representatives joined their colleagues from the Six and the other three applicant states in deliberations on common issues. It came as a real shock to the Government and the members of the Storting (most of whom were in favor of accession) when the Norwegian people rejected membership in the European Community in a referendum on September 26, 1972. Although this referendum was merely "consultative," the Storting respected the will of the people and the Norwegian government resigned since it had made its tenure dependent on a positive outcome of the popular referendum. Its negative result was not only deplored by the vast majority of Norwegian officials but also by the leaders of all other Common Market nations who regarded it as a disappointing set-back for the European cause.

Among the principal reasons for the negative outcome of the Norwegian referendum were the following: concern on the part of a large number of nationalists over the possible loss of sovereignty, and fear by the large majority of fishermen about economic competition from British and German fishing fleets.

As an alternative to full membership in the European Community, Norway is expected to seek a free trade arrangement patterned after the accord concluded between the Common Market and the other REFTA nations in July 1972. The chances for such an agreement appear favorable (after all, Norway exports more than half of its products to the EEC) and it would not foreclose Norway's joining the European Community in the future.

Six Plus Three: Progress or Regression?

The Effect of Enlargement on the European Community

Logically, the enlargement of the Common Market can produce either positive or negative results depending on the "input" of the new members and their evolving relationship with the "old" members. For instance, a new member state may try to establish its "European" credentials by initiating innovative proposals designed to promote political unity, or it may force the other members to proceed on the basis of the lowest common denominator by insisting on traditional sovereign prerogatives. Moreover, a new member may be tempted to play out one partner against another, or to serve as a conciliatory agent in an effort to overcome political conflicts. Finally, the numerical increase in membership may complicate decision-making, or it could facilitate it by placing the issue in a larger context and thus making it amenable to compromise.

Undoubtedly, the evolution of the enlarged European Community will be largely influenced by the attitude of the United Kingdom which will, in turn, greatly affect the policies of the other new member states. It may well depend on Britain's leadership whether the community regresses toward a glorified customs union or moves on toward the United States of Europe.

As far as her future role *within* the European Community is concerned, Britain should be given the benefit of the doubt and regarded as a potential contributor to, rather than a spoiler of, the European cause. In any case, Prime Minister Heath is committed and devoted to the concept of a united Europe as the only realistic foreign policy approach available to the United Kingdom. After all, it is in the interest of all parties involved:

Britain needs Europe and Europe needs Britain. Most responsible Europeans now hope that the coming of the new members will stimulate the Communities, give them the opportunity of remedying many defects, and provide a fresh drive towards political union For Britain, no less, the prospects of a greater market and of political influence through Europe are highly welcome after the years of withdrawal and retreat.[38]

To be sure, there are risks involved in the enlargement of the community, since according to an expert, "the Community institutions are already cumbersome and slow-moving, and simply adding new members, however 'European-minded' they may be, will add to the difficulties."[39] This pessimistic view is opposed by another observer, who argued that "Britain's arrival could serve, paradoxically, to consolidate this identity [of the EEC]. For it is highly likely that the British will enter Europe with all the ardor of the converted. A nation does not consciously turn its back on centuries of history to board a sinking ship."[40] In any case, Britain is entitled to a "period of adjustment" which may last several years. However, given the fact that the new members have already had an extended "waiting period" since their initial application, the official transition period of five years should suffice to acclimatize their representatives to the complex consensus-formation procedures in Brussels and involve them gradually in the *engrenage* syndrome of the European Community.

The Impact of Enlargement on the Free World

The expansion of the European Community from six to nine members is bound to have political-economic repercussions on outsiders, both in Europe and in North America. (See Table 6-1.) The crucial issue can be summarized as follows:

Table 6-1
Trade Between the European Community and the World (1970) (in Millions of Dollars)

	Exports	Imports
EEC	88,499[a]	88,422[c]
Enlarged EEC	114,631[b]	119,795[c]
Austria	2,857	3,549
Finland	2,306	2,637
Iceland	147	157
Portugal	946	1,556
Sweden	6,782	7,005
Switzerland	5,711	6,467
EEC + EFTA	133,380	141,166
USA	43,226	39,963
USSR	12,800	11,739
Japan	19,318	18,881
World	309,400[c]	

[a]Including intracommunity trade of the six = $43,301 million.
[b]Including intracommunity trade of the ten = $59,302 million.
[c]Including intracommunity trade.
Source: Statistical Office of the European Communities

will the New Europe become an introspective club of the rich, or an outward-looking group of nations aware of its responsibilities toward the other industrialized nations and the Third World? The future orientation of the European Community will be decisively influenced by the policies of the United Kingdom as the second (Germany being the first) most important "outward-looking" member of the Common Market. Indeed, given her traditional position on free trade, Britain can be expected to join Germany in further efforts to liberalize trade relations between the Nine and the rest of the world, although Britain will have to adhere to the protectionist guidelines of the CAP. Nevertheless, "with Britain in the Community, the common agricultural policy is more likely to be modified in ways favorable to US exports. Britain should reinforce Germany's negative view of the CAP in a long-time dispute with France within Community institutions."[41] Moreover, British entry is expected to bring enormous expertise in monetary affairs into the community which is important since "Continental countries have a more limited and parochial view (of the world monetary system) but the United States and Britain have a global view. [Hence] British membership in the Common Market ought to improve trans-Atlantic understanding and cooperation in this field."[42]

The argument that the enlargement of the European Community by the entry of Britain (and two other "free-trade"-minded newcomers) is likely to have a liberalizing effect on the external policies of the Common Market and thus benefit the United States and other outsiders has been corroborated by the former head of the US Mission to the European Community in the following terms:

An enlarged Community, including Great Britain, will bring new problems—but also new opportunities. I see no reason why we should not do at least as well with an enlarged Community as we have with the present Community. Fundamentally, such a large and prosperous area with fairly open economic policies should benefit American trade and investment substantially. The enlarged Community should also be in an even better position to contribute to the problem of the underdeveloped world. In saying this, I am naturally assuming that both the Europeans and we will continue to follow sensible and constructive policies on international economic issues. I do not want to gloss over the problem areas. Agriculture will remain particularly difficult for some time to come, and enlargement is not likely to make things any easier in the short run. My hope is twofold: First, that we and the Europeans can settle certain pressing specific issues now and, secondly, that over a longer period of time we can come to grips jointly with the underlying problems on both sides of the Atlantic.

Beyond this it seems to me a matter of fundamental self-interest that the Community and the United States accept one another; more or less as we are. We must approach one another with a degree of maturity. This implies a recognition that any such large, democratic and evolving societies as the Community and the United States are bound to generate problems and that our relations will be marked by imperfections. Reasonable men should not lose their sense of proportion that these day-to-day problems obscure completely the broad political and economic benefits both sides of the Atlantic derive from this relationship.[43]

Ambassador Schaetzel's views were subsequently reinforced by both President Nixon and Secretary of State Rogers in official policy declarations. For instance, Mr. Nixon welcomed British entry into the European Community in both Foreign Policy Reports to Congress,[44] while Mr. Rogers did so in his annual report in which he welcomed the signature of the Accession Treaty by the four prospective members and expressed his conviction that the enlargement of the European Community is in the interest of both Europe and the United States.[45]

Association Agreements

Since the provisions for full membership (according to article 237, EEC Treaty) in the community apply only to European states willing to accept the political principles and all socioeconomic obligations laid down in the Rome Treaty, the signatory states made allowance for an arrangement that falls short of full membership and is not limited to European countries. These agreements of association, according to article 238, can be concluded between any third country or international organization on the one hand and the community on the other, creating reciprocal rights and obligations, as well as joint actions and procedures. Both European and African countries have concluded such association agreements with the community, although their respective reasons for seeking links with the EEC differed in each case.

Relations with African Nations

The first group of nations to be associated with the EEC were the former French colonies when, in 1957, the Six signed a joint Association Agreement with Overseas Countries and Territories.[46] As these African dependencies achieved independence in the early 1960s, they concluded the so-called Yaoundé Convention with the community (1963) for a five-year period (renewed 1969 through 1975).[47] The convention provides for an institutional mechanism, in charge of the eventual formation of a free-trade area between the community and each of the Eighteen while permitting the association states to export most products to the community on a duty-free basis. These preferential privileges are one-sided in as much as the African nations are permitted to impose or maintain duties on goods imported from the community in order to protect their infant industries. The community's import from the Eighteen rose from $913 million in 1958 to $1,889 million in 1970; exports to the Eighteen rose from $713 million to $1,249 million.[48] The organism in charge of channelling development aid, the European Development Fund, provided grants of $80 million under the Yaoundé Convention for the first five-year period.[49] Other African countries which are not former colonies of the Six, signed association agreements under the Arusha Convention of 1968, renewed in 1969 and operational until 1975.[50] Tunisia and Morocco became partially associated with the community in 1969; Malta in 1971.[51]

Transitional Association Agreements

A different type of association agreement links Greece and Turkey to the European Community. Both countries consider their association as temporary in the sense that they aspire toward full membership as soon as their economic development has reached a stage when they can compete with the Nine. Thus they differ from the African associates in that both Greece and Turkey, being eligible under article 237, accept the long-term political implications of membership in the community. Greece signed the association agreement on July 9, 1961, and Turkey became an associate on September 12, 1963. Both agreements provided for substantial investment aid by the community and envisaged the eventual creation of an economic union in the 1980s.[52]

Relations between the Community and the
Rest of EFTA (REFTA)

Apart from the four countries that applied for full membership in the community according to article 237, there are a number of European nations that are seeking an informal affiliation with the EEC. (See Table 6-2.) Most of them are nonaligned countries interested in trade links with the community but either unwilling or unable to become full members. Although their relationships

Table 6-2
Vital Statistics on the Six Nonmember Countries

Austria	
Population	7,398,000
Gross National Product	$14,352 million
GNP per Capita	$ 1,940
GNP by Sector	
Agriculture	7.0%
Industry	46.8%
Other Sectors	46.2%
GNP Average Annual Growth Rate (1965-1970)	5.1%
External Trade	
Imports	$4,151 million
From the Enlarged Community	65.2%
From the Enlarged EC and EFTA states	76.0%
Exports	$3,138 million
To the Enlarged Community	50.5%
To the Enlarged EC and EFTA states	66.1%
Exports as a Percentage of GNP	28.8%
Finland	
Population	4,603,000
Gross National Product	$10,035 million
GNP per Capita	$2,180
GNP by Sector	
Agriculture	14.7%
Industry	41.3%
Other Sectors	44.0%
GNP Average Annual Growth Rate (1965-1970)	4.8%
External Trade	
Imports	$2,796 million
From the Enlarged Community	46.6%

Table 6-2 (cont.)

Finland (cont.)	
From the Enlarged EC and EFTA States	66.2%
Exports	$2,357 million
To the Enlarged Community	49.5%
To the Enlarged EC and EFTA States	65.3%
Exports as a Percentage of GNP	26.6%

Iceland	
Population	205,100
Gross National Product	$469,700,000
GNP per Capita	$2,290
GNP Average Annual Growth Rate (1965-1970)	2.1%
External Trade	
Imports	$180 million
From the Enlarged Community	56.1%
From the Enlarged EC and EFTA States	52.3%
From the Enlarged EC and EFTA States	
Exports	$180 million
To the Enlarged Community	38.3%
To the Enlarged EC and EFTA States	52.3%
Exports as a Percentage of GNP	47.2%

Portugal	
Population	9,588,000
Gross National Product	$6,328 million
GNP per Capita	$660
GNP by Sector	
Agriculture	17.7%
Industry	42.8%
Other Sectors	39.7%
GNP Average Annual Growth Rate (1965-1970)	6.2%
External Trade	
Imports	$1,772 million
From the Enlarged Community	50.2%
From the Enlarged EC and EFTA States	58.4%
Exports	$1,033 million
To the Enlarged Community	43.1%
To the Enlarged EC and EFTA States	53.8%
Exports as a Percentage of GNP	24.4%

Table 6-2 (cont.)

Sweden	
Population	8,083,000
Gross National Product	$30,877 million
GNP per Capita	$3,820
GNP by Sector	
Agriculture	5.9%
Industry	45.2%
Other Sectors	48.9%
GNP Average Annual Growth Rate (1965-1970)	3.9%
External Trade	
Imports	$7,059 million
From the Enlarged Community	61.6%
From the Enlarged EC and EFTA States	71.5%
Exports	$7,440 million
To the Enlarged Community	61.1%
To the Enlarged EC and EFTA States	71.2%
Exports as a Percentage of GNP	23.1%

Switzerland	
Population	6,202,000
Gross National Product	$20,218 million
GNP per Capita	$3,260
GNP by Sector	
Agriculture	6.4%
Industry	49.6%
Other Sectors	44.0%
GNP Average Annual Growth Rate (1965-1970)	3.7%
External Trade	
Imports	$7,227 million
From the Enlarged Community	68.1%
From the Enlarged EC and EFTA States	76.2%
Exports	$5,763 million
To the Enlarged Community	47.7%
To the Enlarged EC and EFTA States	58.1%
Exports as a Percentage of GNP	37.8%

Note: External trade figures refer to 1971 apart from the geographical distribution percentages which are based on 1969 trade.

Sources: Organization for Economic Cooperation and Development, Statistical Office of the European Communities, and the European Free Trade Association.

with the Common Market were not formally dependent on the outcome of the negotiations between the Six and the four applicant countries, a *de facto* interdependence was created by the EFTA membership of the European neutrals. Consequently, Austria, Sweden, and Switzerland applied for a sociation with the EEC on December 15, 1961, following the first request of the British government to negotiate membership in the Common Market. Whereas the problem of the other EFTA countries–Denmark, Norway, Iceland, and Portugal, all members of NATO–was essentially one of accomodation in the economic realm, the issue for the four European neutrals (Austria, Sweden, Switzerland, and Finland) had political-legal dimensions. Because of their neutral status, these four countries merely desire an economic association with no obligation to accept the political aims or the institutional framework of the European Community. Moreover, Portugal and Iceland present particular problems because of their underdeveloped economies, which are unable to compete in the Common Market. In these two instances, the association agreements with Greece and Turkey provided a model for a transitional arrangement until full membership is possible. The nature of Portugal's regime was a major political issue.

Negotiations between the European nonmember countries and the European Community opened in 1970 when the Council of Ministers met with the representatives of the countries concerned for the purpose of finding mutually acceptable formulae for affiliation with the EEC. On November 10, the council met with Austria, Sweden, and Switzerland, and on November 24, with Portugal, Finland and Iceland.[53] The economic problems were simplified by the fact that these six small nations had free-trade arrangements for industrial products with the four applicant countries (Britain, Denmark, Ireland, and Norway). Naturally, the REFTA countries were reluctant to reintroduce trade barriers vis-à-vis the four applicant states after tariffs on manufactured goods had been eliminated as a result of the Stockholm Convention of 1960 creating EFTA. The political problems of Sweden and Switzerland are basically self-imposed in the sense that there are no compelling legal reasons preventing them from adjusting their neutral status to the requirements of the Rome Treaty.[54] In other words, Sweden and Switzerland have a free choice between making concessions to European political unity in return for economic benefits as members of the EEC, whereas Austria and Finland have limited options in view of the intransigent attitude of the Soviet government on this question (making an association agreement between these two neutrals and the EEC the only realistic maximum solution).

In fact, the Soviet Union intervened officially in the exploratory talks held between the Common Market and the European neutrals when *Pravda* warned Austria, Switzerland, and Sweden on January 6, 1971, that membership in the European Community would jeopardize their sovereignty and neutrality because they would be forced to follow NATO's policies. The paper commented that "this is precisely what the most aggressively minded Western circles want, aiming to tie Austria, Switzerland, and Sweden to the NATO military-political bloc by the establishment of close political ties with the Common Market."[55] These accusations are clearly designed to put diplomatic pressure on the European neutrals and thus create political obstacles to any kind of agreement between them and the Common Market. This Soviet criticism was all the more irrelevant as neither of the three neutral nations were seeking full membership—the only type of affiliation that could conceivably be constructed as a *de facto* involvement with NATO.

Another political obstacle to the rapid conclusion of preferential trade agreements between the European Community and the nonapplicant EFTA countries was strong opposition of the United States, which based its case upon a legal argument involving article XXIV of GATT. This article authorizes only the formation of customs unions and free-trade areas, if restrictions are removed on "virtually all trade,"[56] or if a preferential trade agreement is designed as a step toward a free-trade area.

However, the United States recognized that the problem of REFTA countries was a complex one since nobody desired the erection of new trade barriers that were previously abolished. Therefore, the United States—while disapproving of preferential agreements in principle—hopes that the association agreements with REFTA countries would not have prejudicial repercussions on the American economy.[57]

The Individual Problems of REFTA Countries

Austria. Austria is indeed a special case because her economic destiny is almost totally linked to that of the European Community;[58] in political-legal terms Austria is committed to "permanent neutrality." Although this principle of international law had not been written into the Austrian State Treaty of May 15, 1955 (by which Austria regained sovereignty following ten years of Allied occupation), the Austrian Parliament adopted a constitutional law on October 26 of that year in which it voluntarily opted for permanent neutrality according to the Swiss model.[59] Faced with the dilemma of the economic necessity of close affiliation with the EEC and the legal obstacle to full membership, the Austrian government tried to negotiate "an arrangement sui generis." This became necessary since the Soviet Union was opposed even to Austria's association with the EEC under article 238 and applied diplomatic pressure to prevent any "close link" between Austria and the Common Market.[60] The Soviet argument was based upon the contention that such an association would be incompatible with Austrian neutrality and would constitute a *de facto* *Anschluss* with West Germany—an act declared illegal by the postwar agreements between Austria and the Allies. These political arguments of the Soviet government have been refuted on the grounds that associate membership would be based upon a multilateral treaty with all member states of the European Community and not just with the Federal Republic.

Because of her delicate position of dual dependence on the EEC for economic survival, and on the USSR for political approval, Austria was the only EFTA country not to withdraw its request for a "special arrangement" with the Six following the breakdown of the first round of negotiations with Britain in 1963. However, talks held between 1965 and 1967 were blocked by Italy because of the dispute over South Tyrol. Once this conflict had been resolved, negotiations between Austria and the European Community resumed on November 25, 1970, and resulted in an "interim agreement" in 1971, providing for a 30 percent cut in tariffs on industrial goods pending the final conclusion of a settlement between the Six and the nonapplicant EFTA states.[61] This interim-accord became operational soon after Austria signed the free trade agreement of July 22, 1972, with the European Community.

Finland. Finland's position is similar to, and as delicate as, that of Austria in the sense that it is also a neutral country and under Soviet pressure to maintain this legal status. Finland's dilemma is aggravated by a geopolitical factor—common borders with the USSR—which exposes it to direct Soviet control. Because of Moscow's diplomatic pressure, Finland could only become an associate member of EFTA and had to grant similar treatment to Soviet exports.[62] Consequently, Finland was merely seeking a free-trade arrangement with the European Community and Helsinki felt that even this formula might be vetoed by the Soviet Union on the ground that Finland would be indirectly affiliated with NATO since all Common Market nations belong to it. But in view of the fact that sixty-seven percent of Finland's foreign trade flows to the combined Six and Seven, some kind of commercial agreement between the Six and Finland was imperative.[63] It materialized when Finland signed the free trade accord of July 1972, with the Community.

Switzerland. The Swiss type of neutrality can best be characterized as "traditional" and based upon international custom as well as a national attitude. Thus Switzerland does not even belong to the United Nations, since membership in this international organization might prejudice Swiss neutrality.[64] This hypersensitivity about its sovereignty and neutrality prevented Switzerland from seeking full membership in the European Community although economically such an agreement would be beneficial to the Swiss. Instead, Switzerland was seeking "the most comprehensive solutions possible," an arrangement even short of associate membership.[65] Within this context, Switzerland favored the abolition of trade barriers with the Common Market, proposed to cooperate in the economic and monetary field, and agreed to collaborate in the technological sector. However, the Swiss insisted on full national control over commercial policy and have reservations about the customs union and the CAP.[66] Switzerland also proposed the formation of a joint committee with the community which should open a way to "formative cooperation."[67] Finally, in July 1972 Switzerland signed the free trade accord with the Common Market.

Sweden. Sweden's brand of neutrality is most amenable to modification because it is of a political rather than legal nature. In other words, the Swedish government has total flexibility in defining the meaning of "neutrality" at any time according to the national interest. However, in view of the fact that Sweden has benefitted from its political neutrality in the past, the government is reluctant to change it. Therefore, Sweden insisted that her neutrality must be safe-guarded in any arrangement with the European Community, a demand that ruled out full membership but permitted an association agreement. Specifically, the Swedish government wanted not only to maintain its freedom of action in foreign and commercial policies, but also had serious reservations about the projected evolution of the Common Market. Thus Sweden told the Six that "limits are also set to her possibilities of accepting a transfer of the right of decision-making from national to international institutions within the framework of an economic and monetary union."[68] On the other hand, Sweden regarded full participation in the customs union and in the CAP as an essential part of any arrangement negotiated with the community and would therefore adopt the common external tariff on industrial and agricultural products of the Six vis-à-vis the outside world, subject only to transitional measures.[69]

In the long run, however, it can be expected that Sweden will seek full membership in the European Community, thus overcoming political reservations for tangible economic benefits. Meanwhile, Sweden decided to sign the free trade agreement with the Common Market in July 1972.

Portugal. The case of Portugal is complicated by several political issues and its relatively underdeveloped economy. The principal obstacle seems to be the very nature of the Portuguese political system, an authoritarian regime that differs fundamentally in its structure and ideology from those of the member states of the European Community. Moreover, Portugal still has colonies in Africa (Angola and Mozambique) that are euphemistically referred to as "non-European provinces." Because of its low level of economic development, Portugal initially applied for "as close a relationship as possible" with the Six, which in practical terms meant an association according to article 238. However, the Portuguese government stressed that its ultimate goal is full membership in the European Community, given Portugal's European heritage and Western traditions.[70]

The Portuguese clearly expected that the Six would be willing to apply the evolutionary association formula used in the case of Greece and Turkey, two underdeveloped nations aspiring to eventual full membership in the European

Community. However, the recent decision to "freeze" the association with Greece (which is under the control of a military dictatorship), and the reluctance of the Six to establish closer links with authoritarian Spain, diminished the chances for Portugal in the near future. Nevertheless Portugal succeeded in joining the new European free trade area in July 1972.

Iceland. The problem of Iceland, EFTA's latest member, was purely economic. The basis of Iceland's economy being her fishing industry, she was unwilling to contemplate full membership in the Common Market, which would force her to give up fishing rights over territorial waters as required by the common fisheries policy of the community. Consequently, Iceland was seeking an arrangement similar to that governing her relations with EFTA—a free-trade agreement that would assure maximum control over its territorial fishing waters. In July 1972 Iceland succeeded in this effort when it became a member of the newly created European free trade area, composed of the nine Common Market nations and the other REFTA countries (except Norway).

Free Trade Zones

The "European Free Trade Area"

The design of a free trade zone for Western Europe, originally conceived in 1957 by the British Government as an alternative to the EEC, was accepted fifteen years later as a viable objective by fifteen nations and will become reality in 1977. Meeting in Brussels on July 22, 1972, the leaders of the European Community and of the REFTA countries signed a series of agreements providing for the gradual formation of an industrial free trade area covering virtually all of free Europe—the largest single commercial bloc in history.

It was the same powerful magnetism of the European Community that attracted the United Kingdom, Denmark, Norway and Ireland to seek full membership in the Common Market, that subsequently prompted Austria, Iceland, Portugal, Sweden, Switzerland (plus Liechtenstein), and Finland to come to terms with the "Six." Effective January 1, 1973, these agreements provided for the successive establishment of a free trade area in industrial products over a period of five years.[71] Tailored to the individual needs of the six countries involved, the agreements—except for that with Finland—include an "evolutionary clause," permitting the extension and deepening of cooperation with the New Europe in the future. In other words, the free trade agreements are generally considered as a first step in the direction of greater cohesion among the participating nations and do not foreclose later agreements on full or associate membership status for the REFTA countries (including Norway which had signed the treaty in July as a prospective member of the enlarged Community).

The "Mediterrean Free Trade Area"

Over the last decade the European Community has negotiated a number of trade agreements with countries of the Mediterranean region. Instead of proliferating such bilateral, commercial arrangements in a mosaic fashion, proposals were made by various Community officials to define a common trade policy for this important region on the periphery of the European Community. Among the potential members of this "Mediterranean free trade area" would be the Maghreb nations (Algeria, Morocco, and Tunisia), Egypt, the Lebanon, Israel, and Spain, as well as Greece and Turkey.[72]

The "North Atlantic Free Trade Area"

Originally proposed by US Senator Javits as an alternative to the enlargement of the European Community, following President de Gaulle's refusal to admit Britain to the Common Market in 1963, this revived NAFTA might include the new European Free Trade Area, plus the United States and Canada, as well as Japan and Australia (plus New Zealand). Eventually, NAFTA could be extended to include the South Atlantic sub-regional groupings of the Central American Common Market and the Latin American Free Trade Association (LAFTA).

Trade Agreements with Third Countries (Art. 113)

The community has negotiated trade agreements with many countries involving mutual tariff reductions on industrial and agricultural products. A five-year preferential agreement with Israel came into force in October 1970. At the same time the community concluded such an agreement with Spain. Yugoslavia became the first Communist state to benefit from a three-year nonpreferential trade agreement which came into force on May 30, 1970.[73] The first nonpreferential trade agreement with a Latin American nation, Argentina, was signed on November 8, 1971.[74] The community also played an important role in developing the UNCTAD scheme for generalized tariff preferences for semi-finished and manufactured exports from developing nations. Acting upon a decision of March 1971, the community put into effect its plan for generalized preferences on July, 1971, to ninety-one developing countries, primarily from the Asian and Latin American areas.[75]

The proliferation of preferential trade agreements between the community and third countries raises the question whether they are not in conflict with the fundamental GATT rules of nondiscrimination in international trade. The argument is complicated by the fact that the developing nations involved actually benefit substantially from these agreements. However, at the same time the agreements result in *de facto* discrimination against outsiders, including the United States.

Relations with International Organizations

The European Community is considered as independent entity by both states and international organizations. A valid indication of the autonomous status of the European Community in certain areas of international relations is the fact that more than eighty diplomatic representatives are accredited to it at its headquarters in Brussels. In turn the community has gradually upgraded its own representation abroad. During the first ten years of its existence, the community established information offices in several Western countries. Its information service in the United States, created in 1954, became a "liaison office" in 1967. On October 20, 1971, a "permanent delegation," headed by Signor Aldo Maria Mazio (Italy) was established in Washington, D.C.

The European Community also has official delegations to the OECD in Paris, and to the United Nations agencies in Geneva. In both instances, there are frequent contacts between the community and these international organizations on problems of common interest, but there is no institutionalized cooperation.

In this chapter we focused on the European Community as a magnetic nucleus whose internal dynamics attracted skeptical outsiders to join it in support of a common cause. We depicted the centripetal effect of the European Community in terms of three concentric circles: the inner circle, consisting of the original six nations ("Little Europe") and the three new members; the intermediate circle, composed of the actual and potential associates (Greece, Turkey, REFTA countries, and African nations); and the outer circle, made up of numerous countries (mostly of the "Third World") that are linked to the Community through preferential trade arrangements. We also discussed the internal and external impact of enlargement, and the nature of relations between the European Community and various international organizations.

7

Alternative Political Structures for the New Europe

European Political Union: The Constitutional Dilemma

Ever since the inception of the European Community, political leaders, constitutional lawyers, and social scientists have been locked in a controversy over the ultimate structural design for a united Europe. This constitutional debate continues to center around the fundamental dichotomy—federation or confederation. The dispute involves essentially two groups of advocates, both of which claim to have the ideal blueprint for a European union: the federalists and the nationalists. The former are considered radicals and utopians by the latter, who look upon themselves as patriotic realists. The federalists, in turn, depict the proponents of confederalism as conservative chauvinists lacking both vision and courage. Although both have the same objective—the construction of a political union—they differ as to the means necessary to achieve it. This disagreement has its roots in the divergent interpretation of the notion of "realism." The federalists argue that realism consists in recognizing objective political needs and in taking the necessary action to meet them (i.e., the creation of a European federal government capable of acting on behalf of Europe). The nationalists interpret realism as the ability to face the facts of political life and proceed from this basis (i.e., building a confederation of existing nation-states through intergovernmental cooperation). The pragmatists hold a "middle of the road" position.

The following scheme identifies the major ideological groups in terms of their respective goals and means (see Table 7-1).

Out of this controversy over the polarized concepts for political union emerged several concrete proposals for a constitutional framework for the future United States of Europe.

The European Political Community

The first blueprint was drafted under the auspices of the so-called *ad hoc* Assembly of ECSC in 1953 by a group of European leaders including Paul-Henri Spaak and René Pleven. Therefore it had a distinctly federalist character. The draft for this "European Political Community" included provisions for a European authority in charge of foreign policy, defense, and trade.[1] Its declared aim was to set up a supranational, indissoluble union of peoples and states (art.

Table 7-1
Typology of European Political Groups

	Objective	Strategy	Tactic
Nationalists (Gaullists)	Preserve the nation-state structure and sovereign prerogatives	Claim realism while denouncing utopian federalist schemes	Organize inter- governmental cooperation along confederal lines
Pragmatists (Eurocrats)	Transcend the nation-state in favor of a United States of Europe	Encourage delegation of powers to supranational organs	Promote gradual integration of specific functions
Radicals (Federalists)	Replace the nation-states by novel political and social structures rather than pre- serve them in palliative models (Community, confeder.)	Signal the obsolescence of the nation- state and of the fiction of sovereignty	Advocate the direct election of a European Parliament and the creation of a European federal executive (by a federal pact or a constituant assembly)

1). The institutional structure was to be made up of a bicameral "Parliament" (with chamber and senate), a Janus-headed administration composed of a "European Executive Council" and a "Council of National Ministers," a judiciary called "Court of Justice," and an "Economic and Social Council" (Part II). These institutions were to operate as follows: the "Peoples' Chamber" was to be elected by direct universal suffrage and to represent the people at large, whereas the senate was to represent the states; this parliament was to initiate and enact legislation and exercise control over a common autonomous budget. The Council of Ministers was to exercise its powers specified in the statute with a view of harmonizing the actions of the European Executive Council with that of the governments of the members. The president of the Executive Council was to represent the Community, and the Court of Justice was to ensure the application of the rule of law and settle disputes between the community and the states. The Economic and Social Council was to assist the European Executive Council and Parliament in an advisory capacity.

This proposed European Political Community was to exercise the powers of ECSC and the European Defense Community. However, since the treaty establishing the latter was never ratified, the "Statute" remained on paper since it formed an integral part of the EDC Treaty.

The Fouchet Plan

In 1961 the French government sponsored and promoted a plan drafted by President de Gaulle. This "Fouchet Plan" for a union of states contained the following elements:

Article 1. There is established by the present treaty a *union of States* hereafter described by the term "the Union." The Union is based on respect for the personality of the peoples and member States, and for the equality of their rights and obligations. It is indissoluble.

Article 2. The Union has as its *aim*: To arrive at the adoption of a *common foreign policy* on questions in which the member States have common interests. To assure by close co-operation of member States in the fields of *science and culture* the further development of their common heritage and the safeguarding of the values which give their civilization its worth; to contribute thus within the member States to the defense of the rights of man, of fundamental liberties and democracy. To reinforce, in *co-operation with the other free nations,* the security of member States against any aggression by means of a *common defense policy.*

Articles 5 and 6. The *Council* meets every four months at the level of *Heads of State* or Government and in the intervening period at least once at the level of Foreign Ministers. . . . The Council discusses all questions whose inscription on its agenda has been requested by one or several member States. It adopts, by *unanimous vote*, the decisions required for the realization of the aims of the Union. The absence or abstention of one or of two members does not prevent the reaching of a decision. Decisions by the Council are binding for the member States which have taken part in their adoption.

Articles 7 and 8. The *European Parliamentary Assembly* . . . will *discuss* matters concerning the aims of the Union. It can address to the Council oral or written questions. It can present *recommendations* to the Council. . . . The Council will present each year to the EPA a report on its work.

Articles 9 and 10. The *European Political Commission* is comprised of senior *officials belonging to the foreign service of each member State.* It will have its meeting place in *Paris.* . . . The Commission will *assist* the Council. It will prepare and act upon the Council's deliberations. It *carries out the tasks* which the *Council entrusts* to it.

Article 16. Three years after the entry into force of the present treaty it will be submitted to a general revision which will have for its aim the examination of methods suitable to reinforce the Union, account having been taken of the progress already accomplished. This revision should have for its principal aims the achievement of a united foreign policy and the *progressive establishment* of an *organization centralizing,* in the framework of the Union, the *European Communities.* . . .

Article 17. The Union is open to the adhesion of member States of the Council of Europe which accept the aims fixed in Article 2 above and which have previously joined the European Communities. . . . The *admission* of a new State is decided by the Council by *unanimous* vote.[2] (Emphasis added.)

Ostensibly, this "Gaullist Manifesto" differed from the earlier "Federalist Statute" in its basic political philosophy. Thus the Fouchet Plan provided for confederal structures and preserved the sovereignty of national governments in all important areas. Due to this manifest lack of supranational elements, France's five partners in the European Community rejected the Fouchet Plan in 1962 (they were also motivated by de Gaulle's opposition to British membership in the Common Market).

The Davignon Formula

It was not until after General de Gaulle's departure from the political scene that new efforts were undertaken in the direction of European political union. The first step was taken by the six heads of state at the summit meeting of the Hague (1969). In their final communiqué, the six governmental leaders instructed their respective ministers of foreign affairs to study the problem of "political unification," within the context of enlargement and to make proposals before the end of July 1970. This deadline was met by the six foreign ministers when they convened in Brussels on July 20, 1970, to adopt a "Report on European Political Unification" prepared by the Davignon Committee, composed of the political directors of the six foreign ministries under a Belgian chairman, M. Davignon. This report was subsequently submitted to the six governments and the four applicant countries, debated at the October session of the European Parliament, and adopted in its definitive form on October 27, 1970, by the foreign ministers meeting in Luxembourg (see Appendix C). According to the privisions of this accord, the foreign ministers are to meet at least every six months "to consult on all important questions of foreign policy." These meetings are being held under the chairmanship of the foreign minister of the country providing the president *pro tempore* of the Council of the European Community (and in the country of the chairman). The ministerial meetings are prepared by the Political Committee composed of the six political directors, who meet at least four times a year. Although these intergovernmental sessions focus on foreign policy issues, member states are free to propose other subjects for political consultation which may involve the European Commission and the European Parliament in a consultative role.

The first meeting of the six foreign ministers took place in Munich, Germany on November 19, 1970, under the chairmanship of Mr. Walter Scheel, representing the German Federal Republic; the other participants were M. Schuman

(France), M. Pedrini (Italy), M. Luns (Netherlands), M. Harmel (Belgium), and M. Thorn (Luxembourg). They were accompanied by the six political directors who make up the important Political Committee; also invited was M. Malfatti, the president of the European Commission. This first "regular" meeting on political cooperation between the Six since the breakdown of the negotiations on the Fouchet Plan in 1962 was hailed by Chairman Scheel as "a new phase of political cooperation [and] a decisive step towards the political unification of Europe . . . [making] rapprochement of viewpoints possible—the ultimate goal being to enable Western Europe to speak with one voice."[3] This initial encounter was followed by meetings in Paris (May 1971), Rome (November 1971), and Luxembourg (May 1972). The four applicant countries were also represented at these biannual consultations which dealt primarily with the issues of a "European Security Conference." Beginning in 1973, the nine foreign ministers are meeting four times a year.

Purpose and Implications of the Davignon Report

Purpose. According to the report, political cooperation among the six governments was to have two objectives: "1) to ensure greater mutual understanding with respect to the major issues of international politics, by *exchanging information* and *consulting* regularly; and 2) to increase their solidarity by working for a *harmonization* of views, *concentration* of attitudes and joint action when it appears feasible and desirable." (Emphasis added).

Scope. Political consultation focusses on all major questions of *foreign policy*; however, the member states are free to propose any other subject for consultation.

Organization. In the absence of common decision-making institutions, there is an *intergovernmental conference* of the nine foreign ministers which convenes at least every three months (unless there is a serious crisis or special emergency, in the event of which an extraordinary meeting can be called); a political committee, composed of high level civil servants, that meets at least four times a year to lay the groundwork for the ministerial meetings; and an *ad hoc* permanent secretariat (without a physical location) consisting of "liaison officers" in the nine foreign ministries; plus *ad hoc* expert groups.

The similarities between the Davignon Report and the Fouchet Plan of 1961 are so striking that one must assume that the Davignon Report constitutes an *ersatz* for the preceding scheme for political cooperation. Although the Davignon Report places political consultation within the framework of the European Community and its enlargement (contrary to the Fouchet Plan), it "rediplomatizes" relations between the Nine (by regressing from the "community method" of the Rome Treaty), thus giving rise to the same criticism that led to the failure of the Fouchet Plan. Furthermore, it falls short of the "compulsory consultation clause" of the Franco-German Treaty of 1963. However, the Davignon Report goes beyond the practice in the WEU Council—where ministers merely inform each other of their government's views—and aims at harmonizing views, prior consultation and, if possible, common decisions and actions. Contrary to the Fouchet Plan (which covered the areas of foreign policy, defense, culture, and economics), the Davignon Report confines political consultation to major questions of foreign policy (although defense matters are intimately related). Finally, in contrast to the elaborate institutional framework proposed by the Fouchet Committee, the Davignon Report does not provide for any common decision-making organ with a permanent seat (in fact, it does not mention the word "institution"). Instead, it arranges for a conference of foreign ministers à la "Concert of Europe," an intergovernmental forum or symposium which meets in regular intervals to discuss foreign policy issues without an obligation to come to a decision on any one of them.

A sophisticated European analyst (writing from a federalist perspective) referred to the Davignon Report as a "diplomatic protocol . . . that does not constitute any progress towards the political unification of Europe."[4] He goes on to criticize the document on the following grounds: (1) it refuses to fix *long-term objectives* of a politically united Europe ("If we do not know where we are going, it is impossible to say that we will go there together"); (2) it does not provide for *institutions*—present or future—but merely for a "consultation machinery . . . of such limited scope [that] everybody can join without compromising themselves . . . a political free trade area"; (3) it *limits the field of action* to foreign policy ("Political unification cannot be limited to foreign policy"); (4) it is *undemocratic* since it neither provides for democratic controls, nor for the information of public opinion ("conversations behind closed doors are not a model of democratic information"). He concludes that the Davignon Report creates just "another European forum . . . but Europe needs something else" (presumably federal structures).[5]

In contrast, a German member of the European Commission[6] argued that the Davignon formula constitutes the most promising pathway toward European unity since it abandoned the supranational illusion of the "first Europe" in favor of a pragmatic approach to the intergovernmental reality. This "second Europe" would be more successful because its leaders are realists rather than utopians and proceed on the basis of intergovernmental cooperation and the use of unanimous voting.

The Political Secretariat

This proposal resulted from the experience of the Davignon Committee in charge of the coordination of foreign policies between the members of the enlarged

European Community. In the absence of a logistic infrastructure, the Political Committee felt the increasing need for a permanent secretariat. As an auxiliary diplomatic body, this political secretariat would serve the purpose of improving the preparation of the regular meetings of the nine foreign ministers and facilitate communication between them.[7]

The idea of a political secretariat was subsequently advocated by President Pompidou, who conceived of it as a "flexible and lightweight organism" hopefully located in Paris.[8] Although other European leaders favored the institutionalization of cooperation in foreign policy, they were opposed to Paris as headquarters of the Political Secretariat. This negative attitude was based upon their fear that the French government would thus be able to prevent a linkage between the operations of this body (in charge of political cooperation) and the institutions of the European Community in Brussels (responsible for economic integration). Most European leaders, however, prefer to associate political unification with economic integration and therefore favor Brussels as headquarters for any future Political Secretariat.

Proposals for a Confederation

On January 21, 1971, President Pompidou provided a new impetus to the "institutional debate" at a news conference in Paris when he declared, "One can only build starting with what is already there, a *confederation of States* (italics added), resolved to harmonize their policy and integrate their economies and if one looks at it in this way one sees that the quarrel over supranationality is a false one. If one day the European confederation becomes a reality there will have to be a government whose decisions are binding on all member States." However, he added, that for the present time, the "European confederation," represented by the Council of Ministers of the European Community, is operating on the basis of the unanimity rule: "Important decisions can only be taken if there is unanimity and that is a political fact far more than a legal rule. . . . " Having demonstrated his loyalty to the Gaullist creed of national sovereignty, Pompidou paid tribute to the "spirit of the Hague" and promised his support for the consolidation and enlargement of the community.[9]

The official character of President Pompidou's plan for a European confederation was underlined by one of his principal lieutenants on March 2, 1971. Speaking in Brussels, French Foreign Minister Maurice Schuman confirmed that "President Pompidou's doctrine is confederalist . . . [and] it is quite obvious that the nucleus of the European government he has in mind and which he refers to, i.e., a confederal European government, is the Council of Ministers . . . [and] the Minister representing his country in Brussels would become a Minister in the confederation. . . . " He added that France's European policy is twofold: "economic integration and political cooperation. . . . Since we are not considering the disappearance of States, it is better to take account of their existence, their independence and sovereignty, and organize cooperation between them which is perfectly compatible with economic integration."

Chancellor Willy Brandt's first substantial contribution to the debate on political structures came two days after President Pompidou's famous press conference. In an address to the Action Committee for the United States of Europe, meeting in Bonn on February 24, 1971, the German Chancellor rejected the "academic argument which federalists and confederalists have conducted in the past" and instead proposed a *European Government* equipped with the powers to make decisions in all fields of common policy and subject to parliamentary control."[11]

In an interview with the French journalist André Fontaine on July 4, 1971, Chancellor Brandt was asked whether he shares President Pompidou's hopes that an interstate organization will become the nucleus of a European confederation. In his reply, Herr Brandt first observed that "the step-by-step creation of political union for the future Western European Community is a process which has no precedent in history . . . comprising elements of a European government and forms of cooperation transcending the kind usually practiced between different states." Referring to the final phase of the future economic and monetary union "in which Community institutions will make the essential decisions quickly and efficiently, policy being controlled by a European parliament," the Chancellor concluded that "the best thing . . . would be to consolidate cooperation step by step and then, judiciously, to institutionalize it. In this ultimate goal I agree with the ideas outlined by the French President."[12]

The leader of the third of the "Big Three," Britain's Prime Minister Edward Heath, has always been a "good European"—in fact he represented the United Kingdom in the first "Brussels Round" in 1962 which was terminated by de Gaulle's famous veto. Immediately following his rise to highest political office in Britain in 1970, Prime Minister Heath began to establish diplomatic contacts with the political leaders of the six nations of the European Community in order to explore the chances for Britain's admission to the EEC. At the decisive meeting between President Pompidou and the British Prime Minister in Paris on May 21, 1971, Mr. Heath fully accepted the French plan for a confederation of European states when he stated that "I share your satisfaction with the outcome of these talks. You have said we have been able to consider the future of Europe, its nature, institutions, its place and its influence in the world, and we find ourselves in very close agreement in our views about these aspects of our own continent." As the prototype of the British pragmatist, Mr. Heath did not use any specific terminology regarding future political structures, except to affirm his belief in the principle of European unity: "Throughout my political life, I have believed in, and worked for, the ideal of a united Europe, of which I wanted my own country to be a part."[13] However, Mr. Heath, in an address in Zurich (commemorating Churchill's "European" speech of September 19,

1946), advocated a common foreign policy for the future enlarged community and added that "it seems inevitable that progress towards a common foreign policy should be accompanied by greater cooperation in the field of defense."[14]

A representative of the Italian government used the term "confederation" for the first time on July 26, 1971. In an address to the Italian parliament, Foreign Minister Aldo Moro said: "starting from the recognition of the realities existing in Europe today, . . . though not involving solely the frontiers created by the War but also the union of states which has been in the process of emerging in Western Europe for twenty years, and which is aiming at confederation, we should try to arrive at a balanced, confident, and humane order. . . ."[15]

With this declaration in support of the confederal concept by its foreign minister, Italy joined Germany and Britain in accepting the official French confederal design for a future united Europe.

Proposals for a Federation

One of the most powerful national political leaders within the European Community, Franz-Josef Strauss, has always been an ardent federalist. The head of the Christian Social Union (the Bavarian branch of the German Christian Democratic Union) believes that "only a genuinely federal structure can do justice, within a united Europe, to the true significance of nations. . . . It would be wrong to think that Europe can be created as a power in its own right through a voluntary coordination of foreign and defense policies by setting up a kind of confederation under France's leadership but without creating federal institutions."[16] Mr. Strauss also warns against the delusion that the Common Market will automatically evolve toward a European Federal State.[17]

European Ministers

In an effort to avoid the painful choice between the federal and confederal designs, French and German officials in 1971 launched the idea of "European Ministers" with high ranks in their respective national governments. These "superministers" would function as coordinators between the various departmental ministers in charge of community affairs (ministers of economics, trade, finance, agriculture, etc.). An alternative to the appointment of such all-powerful "European Ministers" in each of the nine member governments would be the appointment of secretaries or undersecretaries for European affairs who would work under the authority and supervision of the foreign minister in each country. Neither the European minister nor the secretaries or undersecretaries for European affairs would formally replace the Permanent Representatives as the traditional liaison committee between Brussels and the national capitals. However, they might well preempt *de facto* many responsibilities of the Permanent Representatives. The European ministers might also have to face the dilemma of having sweeping authority over many complex policy areas without being competent to deal with all of them effectively. Nevertheless, these European ministers could fulfill the vital function of harmonizing measures in the fields of economic integration and political cooperation insofar as they would monitor the activities of the Council of Ministers of the European Community and those of the foreign ministers of the member states. Last but not least, there is the problem of the balance of power within this quasi-government at the European level: would all nine ministers have one vote each or would the major powers have a proportionately greater influence through weighted votes? In sum, the appointment of "European Ministers" without superior authority would not necessarily result in greater political cohesion.

Extension of the "European Orbit"

Under the impact of the enlargement of the European Community from six to nine members and given the relatively limited sectors to which the community treaties apply, there seems to be a real need for revision. In fact, the treaties have been exhausted in the sense that most original goals have been achieved at least in principle and new objectives have been added without formal amendments (e.g., economic and monetary union).

Thus there seems to be an opportunity to link the consolidation of the three community organizations with the expansion of its competences beyond the existing sectors. Such a complementary protocol or revised treaty would permit the organic construction of the European edifice. In addition to adding new goals, such a treaty could also feature provisions for phased achievements in new policy areas patterned after the transition periods of the Treaty of Rome, which permitted successful economic integration through placing legal constraints and political pressure on the national officials to accept compromises in the common interest. It could also eliminate the controversy over the majority-unanimity voting principle by permitting governments opposed to the majority view to abstain from voting and thus avoid the blame of obstinacy à la de Gaulle.

The vehicle for such complementary protocols would be articles 235 and 236 of the EEC Treaty, which provide for the extension of the powers of the community institutions, as envisaged at the Paris Summit (see p. 283).

Among the major areas to which the constitutional powers of the European Community might be extended could be education, environment, aid to developing nations, science and technology, defense and procurement, and foreign policy.

All of these subjects are dealt with in other sections of this study, except for the problem of a European defense community. Despite the failure of the original project for a EDC in 1954, the issue will again become extremely relevant in the 1970s. However, its establishment would have to be preceded (or complemented simultaneously) by the creation of a European political authority (i.e., a supreme commander). Furthermore, security in the atomic age would involve a nuclear deterrent force with a modicum of credibility. This European deterrent could be based upon the existing British and French nuclear forces. Britain's membership in the European Community improves the prospects for such a force because Prime Minister Heath favors the creation of a "European defense system [which] might also include a nuclear force based on the existing British and French forces which could be held in trusteeship for Europe as a whole."[18] The framework of the Western European Union might serve as a useful structure for the launching of such a European nucleus within NATO, although for the participation of the German Federal Republic a special formula would have to be devised that is acceptable to all parties involved (as well as to the Soviet Union).[19] Nevertheless, a start could be made through the adoption of common arms procurement policies by a European Defense Support Organization, complemented by the formation of a European Nuclear Planning Group in NATO.[20]

Proposals by European Pressure Groups

Apart from the Action Committee for the United States of Europe, there are a number of private European organizations that serve as pressure groups for the cause of a united Europe. Most of them are affiliated with the European Movement, which was founded in Paris in 1947 to promote a sense of Europeanism and serve as an organizational superstructure for various pro-European groups and associations.[21] Paradoxically (or symbolically for the state of European affairs), the European Movement is structured along confederal lines although most of its member organizations are composed of militant federalists.

During 1971 the European Movement of the Netherlands and the Europa Union Deutschland adopted resolutions in which they advocated specific steps toward the creation of a European federation. Both groups proposed the following institutional framework (which corresponds largely to the statute of 1953): first, a federal executive (or European government) of a collegial nature, elected by the parliament, and representing the federation; second, a bicameral European parliament, composed of a chamber of representatives (directly elected by the people) and a senate (or chamber of states) whose members are appointed by national authorities (parliaments or governments) and represent the federal units. Third, a court of justice, elected by the parliament as supreme judicial organ. Fourth, an economic and social council with advisory capacity.[22]

This European federation would have competence in the following fields: foreign policy, defense, currency and public finance, external economic relations, economic policy, transport and communications, and energy supply.[23]

Whereas most other European pressure groups are in basic agreement on both the proposed institutions and competences of the future European federation, they disagree on the methods and *tactics* of implementing these objectives. Most importantly, they differ on the *timing* of the measures to be taken in the pursuit of their common goals. Thus the European Federalist Movement proclaims the need for immediate and radical measures to establish a European federation. According to its leader, it is necessary to "sensitize the peoples of Europe to demand a United States of Europe . . . [since] it would be an illusion to expect a confederation of states to herald in a new era" because the unanimity rule would render it ineffective.[24] In contrast, the honorary president of the European Center for Federalist Action stated that "it does not disturb me . . . that the road to European federation will probably have a confederal stage as an intermediate point [since historically] confederations nearly always lead to federations."[25] In the words of another militant federalist, the plan for a confederation is acceptable "on the condition that . . . the second and third stages [of political unification] were not relegated to a vague future but were subject to a formal commitment [to further renunciation of sovereign prerogatives] entered by the national Governments."[26]

The Pragmatic Approach to European Unity

The European Community has been constructed gradually and according to the strategy of pragmatism. The remarkable achievements of this organization *sui generis* are uncontested. They were the result of slow but persistent steps undertaken by patient and optimistic Europeans in the absence of a genuine "European consciousness" on the part of the people, and against the reluctance of national governments to renounce sovereign prerogatives to European authorities. In view of the fact that these conditions have not been substantially altered in the early 1970s, the most attractive strategy remains pragmatism. However, this approach would only yield tangible results if the original rules of the game were maintained. In other words, political unification could only progress on the basis of a phased plan with a fixed timetable outlining the immediate measures as well as the ultimate goals.[27] In the words of Jean Monnet: "Economic integration is not political unity; but it is the basis of the latter. It is gradually binding the member countries together by means of organized common interests. By these means, the governments . . . are acquiring the experience of common action, of its requirements and of its effectiveness."[28] This view has also been expressed by an American pragmatist who wrote, "there may be various roads to European cooperation. The one . . . calling for institutionalized meetings of foreign ministers and sub-cabinet officials . . . has the advantage of producing some immediate results without foreclosing the future."[29] Indeed, confederation can be a step toward federation.

European Public Opinion (Mass and Elite)

Among the principal indicators of trends toward political unity (or the lack of it) are public opinion sample surveys. Numerous attempts have been made by European and American scholars and pollsters to take the "temperature" of both European elites and the masses. Whereas most respondents favored the general idea of a united Europe, there were some disagreements as to the specifics and the strategies. In an effort to test the proposition that public support for the Common Market (economic integration) implies or generates attitudinal support for a European federation (political integration), Puchala concluded that "despite universally increasing approval of the Common Market and apparently widespread perceptions of rewards from EEC operations between 1957 and 1962, there was little evidence of increasing support for regional political federation."[30] He qualified this statement by adding that "it is most accurate and meaningful to say that within France, West Germany, and Italy there was considerable support for moving beyond economic integration toward political federation and there was also considerable support for limiting regional integration to the economic sector, so that the real centers of the debate about the appropriate scope of regional integration were within [these three nations]."[31] Thus Puchala attributes the lack of progress toward political unity to the lack of consensus *within* the major countries of Western Europe rather than to differences *between* the principal nations.

In 1967, a controversial study of elite attitudes on European integration contradicted the optimistic findings of previous opinion surveys with the conclusion that "the movement toward structural European unification since 1957 has been largely halted or very much slowed down [and] the next decade of European politics is likely to be dominated by the politics of nation-states, and not by any supranational European institutions."[32] The first scholar to disagree with this "stagnation diagnosis" was Ronald Inglehart, who argued that "European integration may have moved into full gear only *since* 1958,"[33] basing his conclusion on recent sample surveys conducted in Western Europe in 1966. The findings of the Deutsch study were also vigorously contested by another expert scholar in the field on the ground that once institutions have been created there is no need to continue creating them,[34] thus criticizing the very relevance of the Deutsch conclusion in principle. A complementary criticism has been levelled against this study by William E. Fisher, who questioned the validity of Deutsch's sociocausal paradigm and presented his findings concerning the development of the capacity of European institutions since their birth in 1952. Having used decisions, regulations, directives, and recommendations of the Council and Commission of the European Community as indicators, he computed a total output score showing a rise from 176 to 1487 during the period from 1953 to 1964. Summing up his argument, Fisher states that "since the overall trend of the total Communities' output scores which served as an indicator of institutional output performance growth in Western Europe can be characterized as increasing at a constant rate and since the output scores manifest more than a sevenfold increase between 1953 and 1964, we must conclude that supranational institutional decision-making and allocating authority in Western Europe is increasing."[35]

Deutsch' findings, based on elite surveys, also differ from conclusions derived from elite panel interviews conducted by Lerner and Gorden, who had asked French and German panels (during the Gaullist era in 1961) the following crucial question: "Which of the following two political concepts do you consider the more effective in the long run: a confederation of sovereign states (*Europe des patries*) or a United States of Europe (a common government and citizenship)?" Panelists in Germany expressed themselves in favor of federation (51 percent to 45 percent) and the French preferred a federal Europe to a confederation by 52 percent to 31 percent.[36] This "elitist" preference for federal structures has also been observed by a European expert in this field, who referred to a Gallup International Poll of 1962 which stated that "the most remarkable thing which emerges from the study of mass opinion in the six countries of the Community is the extent of public support for the idea of European unification" and points out that "it is noticeable that the percentage of those in favor of a 'European political federation' is distinctly higher among the upper classes."[37] Rabier also noted that the rank order of motives for support of European unity was as follows: security, prosperity, progress (spiritually), Europe as a world power, and the obsolescence of the nation-state.[38] Whether opting for federal or confederal structures, there is no doubt that both elites and the people in general are ahead of official governmental policies. Indeed, "European public opinion is much more favorable to the idea of continental integration than the governments, which are still attached to national prejudices, despite all their European declarations."[39]

Most students of European public opinion would agree that since the early 1950s majorities in France, Germany, Italy, and Britain were in favor of efforts toward European unity, with the Germans usually ranking as the most pro-European. In 1955 a two-thirds majority of the German public already favored building a "united States of Europe." This figure rose to a peak of 81 percent by 1961, declined to 78 percent in 1967, and was only slightly above its 1955 level (with 69 percent in favor) in the spring of 1970. Comparable data for France show that as of 1957 only 35 percent of the French public was in favor of a federation; this figure rose to 38 percent in 1962, 42 percent in 1964, and 55 percent in 1966, reaching its peak in 1970 (67 percent in favor of a United States of Europe). Indeed, "this emerging European consensus seems to support supranational political integration—it apparently is ready for a 'United States of Europe.'"[40] Furthermore, there is no doubt that "among the most important developments seems to be a convergence of opinion within the European Community in support of measures which would have

Table 7-2
European Public Opinion Survey (1970)

A public opinion poll, the first of its kind, was conducted in January and February 1970 in the six countries of the European Community and Great Britain by a group of information organizations.[a] It was made independently, but at the suggestion of the Press and Information Service of the European Communities Commission.

The 12,000-person sampling was representative of the voting-age population (21 in the Community, 18 in Great Britain) in each of the countries surveyed.

The questions and answers, expressed in percentages, were as follows:

Are you for or against the development of the Common Market into a United States of Europe?

	G	B	N	L	F	I	GB
For	69	60	64	75	67	60	30
Against	9	10	17	5	11	7	48
No response	22	30	19	20	22	33	22

Are you for or against Great Britain's entry into the Common Market?

	G	B	N	L	F	I	GB
For	69	63	79	70	66	51	19
Against	7	8	8	6	11	9	63
No response	24	29	13	24	23	40	18

Are you for or against the election of a European Parliament by direct universal suffrage, in other words, a parliament elected by citizens in every member country?

	G	B	N	L	F	I	GB
For	66	56	59	71	59	55	25
Against	9	11	21	10	15	6	55
No response	25	34	20	19	26	39	20

Would you accept, above your own government, a European government, responsible for a common policy in foreign, defense, and economic affairs?

	G	B	N	L	F	I	GB
Yes	57	51	50	47	49	51	22
No	19	19	32	35	28	10	60
No response	24	30	18	18	23	39	18

In the event of the election of a President of the United States of Europe by universal suffrage, would you vote for a candidate of a different nationality than your own if his personality and program fit your ideas better than the candidates' of your own nationality?

	G	B	N	L	F	I	GB
Yes	69	52	63	67	61	45	39
No	12	24	18	20	22	19	41
No response	19	24	19	13	17	36	20

[a]Het Laatste Nieuws, *covered Belgium and Luxembourg with the assistance of the International Research Associates* (INRA). Magazin *and* Zweites Deutsches Fernsehen, *covered Germany and West Berlin with the help of the Institut fur Demoskopie, d'Allensbach.* Paris-Match *covered France with the help of the Institut Français d'Opinion Publique.* Epoca *covered Italy with the help of the* DOXA *Institute.* De Telegraaf *covered the Netherlands, with the help of the Institut Weldkamp.* The Daily Express covered Great Britain with the help of the Louis Harris Research Institute.

Source: *European Community,* no. 134, May 1970, p. 15.

been considered unfeasible a decade or so ago, and the development of a European public within which nationality is a variable of secondary importance (ranking behind such variables as formal education, age, social class, and sex), . . . "[41] (See Table 7-2.)

In conclusion it could be argued that while there may not yet be a genuine European consciousness that replaces the traditional allegiance to the nation-state, there are indications that many people develop multiple loyalties. Thus a person residing in Munich would find it compatible to be at once a citizen of his city, of the Land of Bavaria, of Germany, and of the United States of Europe. However, the existence of a "permissive consensus" on the desirability of European political unity among the elites and the people at large does not suffice. What would be needed to "cross the Rubicon" would be an act of will on the part of the nine national governments involved to sign a constitutional pact providing for a European political authority capable of acting on behalf of the future "European Union."

8

Europe and the World

European Foreign Policies

Assuming that the member states of the New Europe will eventually succeed in establishing a European government capable of speaking with one voice in international diplomacy, the following theoretical options for its foreign policy would be available: first, a politically independent and militarily neutral posture based upon the assumption that Europe would be able to play the role of a third superpower, in addition to the United States and the Soviet Union; second, a *renversement des alliances* through the formation of an alliance with the Soviet Union as an alternative to the Atlantic Alliance. Third, a continuing trans-Atlantic partnership with the United States (and Canada). However, *Realpolitik* reduces the three theoretical options to one—the third. This argument is based upon the truism that the sociopolitical values of the people of Western Europe are shared by most Americans, creating a natural community of destiny in the Atlantic area. This solidarity precludes an entente with the USSR, without foreclosing a détente and cooperation with Eastern Europe.[1] The concept of a "third force," while not inconceivable at some future time, is nevertheless unlikely to materialize in the near future, although some French officials have long been in favor of severing Trans-Atlantic ties and building a "truly independent Europe" (as opposed to an "Atlanticized one").[2]

The most consistent and outspoken member of the European Community to advocate a close association with the United States has been the German Federal Republic. Ever since the Adenauer era, all three German political parties have been on record in support of Germany's membership in the Atlantic Alliance and of solidarity between the uniting Europe and North America. For instance, on February 25, 1972, the SPD/FDP, and the CDU/CSU passed a committee resolution in the Bundestag which called, in identical language, for a "permanent institutionalized dialogue with the United States."[3] A Christian Democrat, Dr. Franz-Josef Strauss, stated that "the Atlantic Partnership—a partnership between the nations which together make up the advanced civilization of the West, the nations linked to one another by the Atlantic—the Mediterranean of the modern age—is probably the most valuable concept to have emerged during this century. It is up to us to preserve this concept intact and to make it a living fact."[4] A Free Democrat, Foreign Minister Walter Scheel, speaking in Berlin on April 21, 1972, declared: "I am convinced that the nations of Europe and the United States are destined for partnership."[5] Chancellor Willy Brandt, representing the

209

Social Democrats, confirmed the pro-Atlantic orientation of the Federal Republic when he wrote that "as far as security is concerned, the United States and Western Europe will retain their close connection and remain dependent on each other ... [and] the joint responsibility of the United States and Europe for a global economy developing on the basis of a stable currency system, which will also help growth and stability in the third world, makes inevitable the establishment of an organized alliance between the US and the European Community in the not too distant future."[6]

Moreover, speaking at Harvard University on June 5, 1972, in commemoration of the 25th anniversary of the Marshall Plan, Chancellor Brandt formally declared that "American-European partnership is indispensable."[7]

This German position on the future of European-American relations is also shared by the British government. Thus Prime Minister Heath, referring to the Atlantic partnership concept, wrote that "the metaphor of the two pillars ... still serves its purpose."[8] A similar view was expressed by Mr. Aldo Moro, the Italian Foreign Minister when he declared that "there was no contradiction between participation in the Atlantic Alliance and the consolidation of the European Community.... [instead] European unity can consolidate the Atlantic Alliance while giving Europe a greater role."[9]

As far as Western Europe's relationships with Eastern Europe are concerned, the German Foreign Minister, Walter Scheel, set the record straight when he declared, "Anyone who thinks that the consolidation of Western Europe and the North Atlantic Alliance can be replaced by a rather vague pan-European development is wrong.... A conference on European security matters should create more East-West European cooperation; but in no case can such cooperation replace that which already exists in NATO between the states of Western Europe and the US and Canada in the area of security, no more than it can replace the increasing integration within the European Community."[10] To paraphrase Chancellor Willy Brandt, Germany's—and by extension Europe's—*Ostpolitik* is not a substitute for its *Westpolitik*, but the latter is an essential precondition for the success of the former.

Insofar as the future policy of the European Community vis-à-vis the rest of the world is concerned, its "outward" looking orientation seems to be assured. According to Chancellor Willy Brandt, "the Federal Republic of Germany ranks foremost among those who insist that the European Community must not encapsulate itself but should be turned outward to the world.... We must, therefore, strive for liberal world trade policies in order not to upset the entire international economy."[11] In the words of Foreign Minister Walter Scheel, "The European Community should be outward-looking. It should not be a club established by the wealthy to defend privileged positions in international trade. The policies and aims of the Community should also include better opportunities for the developing countries, peace between North and South, and stability for the entire world economy."[12] A similar viewpoint was expressed by Prime

Minister Heath when he wrote that Europe "must contribute to the ever rising standards of peoples all over the world" by assisting developing nations.[13] This strong German-British consensus on an "open-door policy" for the enlarged European Community is substantiated by its proportionately large aid program: For instance in 1970 the Common Market plus Britain and Denmark spent an average of 1.14 percent of their GNP (or a total of $6,172 billion) for development assistance—as compared to 0.64 percent (or a total of $6,254 billion) allocated by the United States (with a GNP almost twice as large).[14] In the light of these data and the combined liberal policy posture of Germany and Britain, the prospects for an "outward-looking" community are favorable.

Economic Relations Between the European Community and the United States

Following the successful implementation of the Marshall Plan in Western Europe, the United States decided to continue its "European policy" of support for political unification through economic integration. This strategy was rightly considered to be in the enlightened self-interest of the United States, although implicit in it was the risk of facilitating the emergence of an economic rival across the Atlantic. Notwithstanding these obvious risks inherent in its pro-European policy, the American government welcomed the creation of the Common Market and encouraged its development, thus consciously facilitating the consolidation of the European Community which inevitably emerged as a competitor in the economic realm. In recognition of its successful European policy, the United States proposed the concept of Atlantic Partnership as a framework for economic (and eventually political) cooperation between the uniting Europe and the United States. Alas, this "grand design" was rejected by General de Gaulle, who advocated a Europe independent from America. Since President de Gaulle claimed to speak in the name of Europe, American enthusiasm for the European cause progressively diminished in the 1960s. This disenchantment was reinforced by the widespread popular belief that the European Community was an "inward-looking" group of nations solely concerned with their material well-being and motivated by narrow commercial interests. Despite official governmental efforts to explain the situation in terms of temporary growing pains on the part of the Common Market, certain myths about its malevolent and introspective nature tended to persist. Indeed, "Americans often depict the Common Market as repaying US postwar assistance and leadership towards an open world economy with cynicism of economic nationalism—erecting a bristling wall of trade barriers to US products, fighting reform of the international monetary system, and of luring more and more nations inside and outside Europe into preferential economic arrangements which discriminate commercially against the US without any redeeming political virtue." Conversely, many Europeans "see the mirror image of the American picture. They tend to see the United States as a disingenuous giant trying to have its cake and eat it. It dominates the world and challenges outer space with its technology, exploits the primacy of the dollar to buy up European industries on credit, and at the same time scurries self-righteously to protect its older and less efficient industries from the first breath of foreign competition."[15]

As a result of these undercurrents in public opinion on both sides of the Atlantic, a mutually reinforcing mythology developed which tends to depict the other side as a protectionist and neoisolationist economic unit.

These unfortunate and largely unsubstantiated negative images are reinforced by the asymmetry of political power. Thus many Americans "perceive the European Community and its associates as a common bloc, capable of a common policy or a common initiative, [whereas] the perception in Europe is one of European weakness, of being in bed with the American elephant. . . ."[16]

Consequently this difference of perspective conjures up the notion of an adversary relationship in which Americans and Europeans "not only see themselves as weak and the other strong but also regard each other as malevolent as well. [Moreover,] a growing number of high officials on both sides of the Atlantic appear to be falling victim to illusions of injured innocence."[17]

Friction between the United States and the European Community reached a crisis on August 15, 1971, following President Nixon's announcement of a "New Economic Policy" which had direct repercussions on all American allies and trading partners around the world. The bold initiative of the American President was precipitated by a domestic problem which could not be separated from its international dimensions: the US balance of trade, for the first time in modern history, had shown a deficit of about $2 billion. In view of the fact that the US balance of payments also showed a record deficit of over 20 billion dollars, President Nixon had to act. In his own words, "We faced an emergency; I acted decisively to put our own house in order and to turn the crisis into an opportunity for the West to put the international monetary house in order as well. We brought home to our partners that we were serious."[18] Thus his unilateral declaration intended to serve a dual purpose: to reverse the US balance of payment deficit and to generate steps toward the reform of the international monetary system. The principal measures to achieve these goals consisted in the temporary suspension of the dollar's convertibility into gold; the imposition of a temporary surcharge of ten percent on all imports; temporary export subsidies for American corporations, referred to as "Domestic International Sales Corporation" (DISC); and a 10 percent reduction in foreign aid.

The shock therapy administered by the American president had the expected salutary effect: Europeans realized that the United States was serious about the urgent need for reforms of the international economic system. Naturally, Mr. Nixon was severely criticized for acting unilaterally and without prior consultation with anybody. However, the American President argued that his steps were necessary in view of the fact that the principal trading partners of the United States had been reluctant to enter into meaningful negotiations on the burning commercial and financial issues facing the Western world.[19]

Among the major American grievances were the allegedly protectionist CAP of the Common Market and the projected preferential trading agreements with certain EFTA members and a number of countries in the Mediterranean region. In the monetary field, the US President aimed at a simultaneous realignment of Western currencies through a *de facto* devaluation of the dollar accompanied by a revaluation of manifestly overvalued currencies, thus limiting imports and boosting exports.

European critics argued that the NEP was an ill-conceived attempt to unload a purely American problem on the shoulders of other nations and that this "beggar-my-neighbor" strategy would shift onto the free world the economic burden of readjustment that is the sole responsibility of the United States.[20]

Undoubtedly, European officials were correct in arguing that the American President had placed undue emphasis on the trade aspect when he implied that the Common Market's trading policies were detrimental to the US economy. After all, the United States had consistently had a surplus in its balance of trade with the European Community. According to the Secretary of State, "the record of our economic relations with the European Community has been good. The overall balance of our merchandise trade with the Community has been favorable through most of the decade, with surpluses averaging more than $1 billion a year."[21] This statement was complemented by a declaration of the head of the US Mission to the European Community, who noted:

We and the Community have been good for one another. Without laboring the facts I should like to summarize here the extent to which we have benefitted from the Community, more particularly from its impressive record of economic activity and growth. From 1958 to 1970 the gross national product of the EC increased from $159 billion to about $500 billion, while per capita gross national product rose from $963 to about $2,600. With this growth Community imports increased from $16 billion in 1958 to over $45 billion in 1970 and imports from the US rose from about $3 billion to $9 billion. The US share of Community imports increased from 17% to about 20% in the same period. In 1970, the US trade surplus with the EC was $1.7 billion. Indeed, the US has had a trade surplus of $1-2 billion a year since 1958. Since 1958, US investments in the EC have increased fivefold and now amount to some $10.2 billion. The annual return flow from this investment is about $750 million annually. The EC's economic growth enables it to contribute to the growth of the LDC's in terms of both trade and aid. Community imports from developing countries amounted to some $16 billion in 1970 compared to exports of $11.5 billion, leaving a trade deficit with the LDC's of some $4.5 billion. [Furthermore] the Community aid flow compares favorably with that of the US.[22] [For details see Tables 8-1, 2, 3, 4, 5]

Table 8-1
EC-US Trade Balance (1958-1971) (in Billions of 1971 Dollars)

	Exports to United States	Imports from United States	Community Deficit in Trade with United States
1958	1.664	2.808	−1.144
1959	2.371	2.651	−.280
1960	2.242	3.830	−1.588
1961	2.232	4.054	−1.822
1962	2.447	4.458	−2.011
1963	2.563	5.051	−2.488
1964	2.849	5.438	−2.589
1965	3.425	5.693	−2.268
1966	4.098	6.022	−1.924
1967	4.424	5.898	−1.474
1968	5.769	6.393	−.624
1969	5.958	7.335	−1.377
1970	6.634	9.040	−2.406
1971	7.694	8.976	−1.282

Source: Statistical Office of the European Communities.

Opposition to the allegedly unfair measures announced by the US president was formally expressed by the Common Market commissioner in charge of external trade on August 26, 1971. Speaking at GATT in Geneva, Mr. Ralf Dahrendorf denounced the NEP as protectionist and in violation of the GATT rules, resulting in a *de facto* cancellation of the Kennedy Round tariff cuts.[23] He maintained that the United States had always benefitted from the success of the Common Market. He added that American exports to the EEC have risen 341 percent since 1958 (while they increased only 269 percent towards the rest of the world). Furthermore, Mr. Dahrendorf pointed out that Common Market imports from the United States had risen from $6.3 billion in 1968 to $9 billion in 1970.[24]

The official position of the European Community was best characterized by the president of the commission, Mr. Malfatti, who declared that "it is clear that for the European countries, the prime objective is the removal, if possible before the end of the year [1971] and at the same time as a selective realignment of all currencies takes place, of the American measures which have a protectionist character. The continued existence of these measures, apart from causing a reduction in Community exports, would put all the trading partners in very difficult situations. Not only would we be under the serious threat of seeing mounting measures and counter-measures of a protectionist nature, but the psychological and political climate of the talks with the United States would be altered."[25]

Table 8-2
Direct US Investments in the Economic Community (1958-1970)—in Billions of 1971 Dollars

	1958	1959	1960	1961	1962	1963	1964	1965	1966	1967	1968	1969	1970
Germany	.666	.796	1.006	1.182	1.476	1.780	2.082	2.431	3.077	3.486	3.785	4.276	4.579
France	.546	.640	.741	.860	1.030	1.240	1.446	1.609	1.758	1.904	1.904	2.122	2.588
Italy	.280	.315	.384	.491	.554	.668	.850	.982	1.148	1.246	1.275	1.422	1.521
Netherlands	.207	.245	.283	.309	.376	.446	.593	.686	.859	.942	1.069	1.227	1.495
Belgium/Lux.	.208	.211	.231	.262	.286	.356	.455	.596	.742	.867	.981	1.214	1.510
EC	1.908	2.208	2.644	3.104	3.722	4.490	5.426	6.304	7.584	8.444	9.012	10.255	11.695

Source: *Survey of Current Business*, US Department of Commerce.

Table 8-3
Direct EC Investments in United States (1960-1970)—in Billions of 1971 Dollars

	1960	1961	1962	1963	1964	1965	1966	1967	1968	1969	1970
Germany	.103	.120	.152	.149	.156	.209	.247	.318	.387	.617	.675
France	.168	.175	.183	.182	.197	.200	.215	.265	.288	.319	.294
Italy	.071	.089	.100	.102	.082	.087	.087	.086	.092	.095	.100
Netherlands	.947	1.023	1.082	1.134	1.231	1.304	1.402	1.508	1.750	1.966	2.121
Belgium/Lux.	.157	.151	.158	.161	.175	.175	.193	.228	.273	.309	.338
EC	1.446	1.558	1.675	1.728	1.841	1.975	2.144	2.405	2.790	3.306	3.528

Source: *Survey of Current Business*, US Department of Commerce.

Table 8-4

Reserve Assets of Major Western Nations (in Billions of US Dollars and Units of Account (UC)[e] or Special Drawing Rights)[a]

	Total in UC or SDR	Total in New Dollars	Gold Value in New Dollars	% of Total	SDR Value in New Dollars	% of Total	IMF Reserve Position Value in New Dollars	% of Total	Foreign Exchange Value in New Dollars	% of Total
Belgium/Lux.	3.199	3.473	1.676	48.3	0.440	12.7	0.651	18.7	0.706	20.3
Germany	17.189	18.662	4.426	23.7	0.493	2.6	1.171	6.3	12.571	67.4
France[b]	6.905[df]	7.494[f]	3.523[f]	46.9	0.347[f]	4.6	0.421[f]	6.0	3.203[f]	42.6
Italy[c]	6.251	6.787	3.131	46.1	0.247	3.6	0.378	5.6	3.030	44.6
Netherlands	3.497	3.797	2.073	54.6	0.619	16.3	0.699	18.4	0.406	10.7
EC "6"	37.041	40.213	14.829	36.9	2.146	5.3	3.320	8.3	19.916	49.5
Denmark	0.664	0.721	0.069	9.6	0.049	6.8	0.057	7.9	0.547	75.9
United Kingdom	6.062	5.015[g]	0.778[g]	15.5	0.553[g]	11.0	–	–	3.684[g]	73.5
Ireland	0.917	0.996	0.017	1.7	0.029	2.9	0.038	3.8	0.911	91.5
Norway[h]	1.063	1.154	0.036	3.1	0.060	5.2	0.067	5.8	0.992	86.0
EC "10"	45.757	48.099	15.729	32.7	2.837	5.9	3.482	7.2	26.050	54.2
Canada	5.249	5.699	0.860	15.1	0.404	7.1	0.361	6.3	4.074	71.5
Switzerland	6.416	6.966	3.158	45.4	–	–	–	–	3.805	54.6
Japan	14.147	15.359	0.737	4.8	0.307	2.0	0.532	3.5	13.783	89.7
Sweden	1.022	1.110	0.217	19.5	0.079	7.1	0.091	8.2	0.723	65.1
United States	12.148	13.190	11.080	84.0	1.190	9.0	0.630	4.8	0.280	2.1

aSource: International Monetary Fund (International Financial Statistics), 1971
bBank of France
cBank of Italy
dApproximate figure
e1 UC = $1.08571
fFigure of November 1971
gFigure of September 1971
hNorway rejected membership in the EC in 1972

Table 8-5
Economic Data on Five Major Powers (1970)

	Six	Ten[b]	USA	USSR	Japan
Population (in thousands)	189,787	257,242	205,395	244,000	103,540
Gross National Product (in millions of dollars)	485,200	637,400	933,300	288,000	179,180
Imports (percentage of world total)[a]	18.3	25.8	17.2	5.1	8.1
Exports (percentage of world total)[a]	19.2	25.2	19.7	5.8	8.8
Total Production Cereals (Average 1968/70 in thousands of tons)	69,161	91,187	192,966	160,145	1,742
Total Meat Production (1969 in thousands of tons)	11,669	16,216	23,227	9,250	1,136
Milk Products (1969 in thousands of tons)	75,834	98,924	52,707	81,500	4,513
Primary Energy Production (in thousands of tons coal equivalent)	330,828	520,356	2,151,397	1,386,090	71,392
Primary Energy Internal Consumption (in millions of tons coal equivalent)	845.8	1,235.8	2,250.6	–	379.6
Petroleum Products Total Production (in thousands of tons)	391.661	504,208	565,488	–	159,689
Total Gross Production of Electrical Energy (in billions of kilowatt hours)	580,393	909,165	1,738,142	740,926	350,590
Steel Production (in thousands of tons)	109,191	138,943	122,120	116,000	93,322
Motor Vehicles Production (passenger cars & commercial vehicles)	8,029,000	9,670,000	6,550,000	348,000	3,179,000
Rail Transport Passenger/Kms (millions)	120,711	155,748	10,568	266,300	181,921
Merchant Shipping 1/7/70 (thousands of tons)	28,656	77,317	18,463	14,832	27,004

[a]All figures exclude intracommunity trade between the Six or the Ten. Figures for the United States, USSR, and Japan are percentages of world trade excluding intracommunity trade between the Ten.

[b]This table treats Norway as a member *in spe* of the EC.

Source: European Community Information Service.

However, the Common Market officials refrained from taking any retaliatory measures which could have led to a trade war; instead they reserved their right to take compensatory steps under art. 13 of GATT.

Whereas the imposition of the import surtax by the US government was contested as not being in conformity with GATT regulations, President Nixon's decision to suspend the convertibility of the dollar into gold was criticized as an inconsiderate step on the part of the most powerful member of the international monetary system vis-à-vis the other Western nations; it amounted to the withdrawal of the guarantee of the US Treasury to exchange gold for dollars at a fixed rate of $35 per ounce, thus endangering the very foundation of the international monetary system which is based upon the dollar as the principal reserve currency.

After President Nixon had severed the link between gold and the dollar on August 15, 1971, all floating European currencies were revalued. The German DM, which began floating in May, was revalued by approximately 8 percent; the French "financial Franc" about 3 percent; the Italian Lira about 2 percent; and the Benelux currencies by about 5 percent. Although the dollar had in effect been devalued on August 15, its official value remained unchanged until 1972.

In the light of this lack of American cooperation in the common effort to restore the US balance-of-payments equilibrium, the European Community officially proposed that the dollar be devalued. Speaking on behalf of the commission, Vice-President Raymond Barre, who was in charge of monetary affairs, declared that the United States is morally, politically, and economically obligated to devalue the dollar: First, because even the most poweful nation has a moral obligation to recognize the rules and responsibilities of membership in the international community. Second, citizens of other nations object to shouldering burdens which are not of their own creation and wonder why they should float their currencies upward without an accompanying devaluation of the dollar by the United States. Finally, a country whose balance of payments is in fundamental disequilibrium and whose currency is overvalued has an economic obligation to change its own parity. Mr. Barre concluded that "it would be unreasonable to think that the reordering of international monetary relations could be achieved without sacrifices from everyone, including the United States." He assured the American government that the community's position is in no way inspired by animosity toward the United States "for which Europe feels friendship and gratitude"; neither does the community wish to isolate the United States but hopes instead to find a common solution "which will be inspired by a spirit of international cooperation."[26]

Since both the United States and the European Community were in basic agreement on President Nixon's twin objective—to restore the US balance of payments equilibrium and to reform the international monetary system—negotiations began to find mutually acceptable means of achieving these desirable goals. The logical arenas within which these negotiations had to take place were the IMF (composed of 118 representatives from virtually all free nations) and the so-called Group of Ten, made up of the free world's richest nations: Belgium, Canada, France, Germany, Italy, Japan, the Netherlands, Sweden, the United Kingdom, and the United States, with Switzerland participating as an observer.

Whereas the Group of Ten constitutes the powerful (though informal) nucleus of the IMF, it is this specialized agency of the UN that is officially in charge of regulating the international monetary system. Created at Bretton Woods, N.H., on July 22, 1944, the International Monetary Fund is to promote international monetary cooperation, facilitate the expansion and balanced growth of international trade, promote exchange stability, eliminate foreign exchange restrictions, and shorten the duration and lessen the degree of disequilibrium in the international balances of payments. In discharging these responsibilities, the IMF became the guardian of the parities of currencies which were to be convertible, i.e., exchangeable or transferable at a fixed rate (or price) of exchange with other currencies. The principal "reserve currency," i.e., the currency which was universally considered to be equivalent to gold (at $35 per ounce), was the US dollar, which had been accepted as a reserve asset by all free nations (in addition to gold and the Special Drawing Rights).

During the immediate postwar era and until the 1960s, the dollar had rivaled gold as a reserve asset. However, with the emergence of the European Community and its major economic power, Germany (as well as Japan), the quasi-monopoly of the dollar was challenged by the German DM, the French Franc, the Italian Lira, the Dutch Guilder (and the Japanese Yen), as well as—paradoxically—the so-called Euro-dollar (US dollars deposited in major European banks, and mainly used by multinational corporations, and beyond the control of the US Treasury—or any other authority, for that matter).

As inflationary pressures eroded the value of the dollar, the currencies of the other free nations were also affected since they were pegged to the US dollar (which, in turn, was pegged to gold). Any change in the dollar's real value, as reflected in the foreign exchange market, was automatically transmitted to other currencies under the IMF system of fixed exchange rates, which only allowed variations up to 1 percent from par value. Therefore demands for greater flexibility of exchange rates (a "wider band") were made by many experts, who proposed that moderate, more realistic widening of currency fluctuation margins be set at 2 or 3 percent of either side of the official parity.[27] This formula was designed to eliminate rigid, unrealistic exchange rates and to achieve maximum stability of the monetary system. Indeed, the introduction of minimum flexibility of exchange rates between currencies would facilitate their revaluation or devaluation without leading to anarchy in the international monetary system.

This realignment of currency exchange rates involved primarily the major currencies: the US dollar in terms of devaluation; the D-Mark and other European currencies (as well as the Yen) in terms of revaluation. However, governments had been traditionally reluctant to modify fixed parities, or to permit currencies to "float" uncontrolled in the market place until they find their true value because they associated devaluation with a loss of national prestige, and revaluation with a reduction in the volume of exports due to the resulting rise in the price of each product.

In an effort to prevent an escalation of lawlessness and a world money war following the *de facto* devaluation of the dollar (resulting from President Nixon's decision to sever the link with gold and permit the dollar to float rather than remain at fixed parity with the other currencies), the IMF's Board of Governors, meeting in Washington on October 1, 1971, requested all member states "to collaborate and, as promptly as possible, establish a satisfactory structure of exchange rates, maintained within appropriate margins, for the currencies of members, together with the reduction of restrictive trade and exchange practices."[28] Not surprisingly, attention focused on the restricted and informal Group of Ten which met frequently during the latter part of 1971. Finally at its December session in Rome, the nine finance ministers presented the following package proposal to US Secretary Connally: A 5 percent devaluation of the US Dollar combined with a 6 percent revaluation of the German Mark, a 3 percent revaluation of the Belgian Franc and the Dutch Guilder, and no change for the French Franc, the Italian Lira, and the British Pound.[29]

During these passionate and delicate debates over the magnitude of the currency realignment needed to cope with the world monetary crisis, Secretary Connally for the first time showed a willingness to compromise when he raised a "hypothetical question": what would the other nine nations do if the US devalued the dollar by 10 percent.[30]

Once the "unmentionable" term—devaluation—had been used by an American government official, the ban was broken. The formal acceptance of the inevitable (devaluation of the US dollar) followed shortly afterwards at a historic meeting between Presidents Nixon and Pompidou in the Azores on December 14. Their summit conference climaxed in an agreement on the principle of the dollar's devaluation and the reform of the international monetary system. In their joint statement to the press, the two presidents specifically "agreed to work towards a prompt realignment of exchange rates through the devaluation of the dollar and revaluation of some other currencies. This realignment could, in their view, under present circumstances be accompanied by broader permissible margins of fluctuation around the newly established exchange rates."[31]

The broad agreement on the principles of reform of the international monetary system constituted the basis for the subsequent consensus on the technical details of the first significant revision of the Bretton Woods accord. It came at a meeting of the Big Ten finance ministers in Washington on December 18, 1971. On this occasion, the top monetary officials of the ten wealthiest non-Communist nations reached agreement on a new system of currency exchange rates built around a dollar devaluation of 8.57 percent. President Nixon hailed the event as "the most significant monetary agreement in the history of the world" and added that nobody had lost but "the free world as a whole has won."[32]

According to the official communiqué, the ministers and Central Bank governors of the Big Ten agreed on the following items: (1) "an interrelated set of measures designed to restore stability to international monetary arrangements and to provide for expanding international trade"; (2) "a pattern of exchange rate relationships among their currencies"; the new exchange rates were fixed as follows:

Currency:	Exchange rate against $	Revaluation in terms of gold
Belgian Franc	44.81	+ 2.76%
Deutsche Mark	3.223	+ 4.61%
French Franc	5.116	−
Italian Lira	581.50	− 1.0%
Dutch Guilder	3.245	+ 2.76%
Swiss Franc	3.85	+ 4.61%
British Pound	2.605 (dollars to Pound)	−
Swedish Crown	4.813	− 1.0%
Japanese Yen	308.0	+ 7.66%

(3) "that provision will be made for 2 1/4 percent margins of exchange rate fluctuation above and below the new exchange rates"; (4) "the United States agreed to propose to Congress a suitable means for devaluing the dollar in terms of gold to 38.00 dollars per ounce," and on the suppression of the 10 percent import surcharge and relating provisions; and (5) discussions in the framework of the IMF should promptly begin on the long-term reform of the international monetary system.[33]

To be sure, this "grand accord" of Washington on the currency realignment constituted only the beginning of a long, difficult road toward the restructuring of the international monetary system that formally collapsed when the United States cut the link between the dollar and gold on August 15, 1971; but it was the crucial first step.

In accordance with the "grand accord," President Nixon officially announced the removal of the American surtax on imports in a proclamation preceding his summit meeting with Prime Minister Heath in Bermuda.[34]

With this principal bone of contention removed from the diplomatic agenda, the trade negotiations between the US and the EEC (agreed upon at the summit meeting between Presidents Nixon and Pompidou, and reaffirmed in the "grand accord" of the Big Ten) started in Brussels on December 21.[35] The negotiations were expected to involve several phases (1972, 1973) and various issues, including the question of burden-sharing in defense matters and general trade negotiations within GATT, aiming at further liberalization measures à la Kennedy Round. However, the immediate issue for 1972 was a "small trade package" consisting of the following elements: better American access to community markets for citrus fruit, grain, cereals, and tobacco; US concessions on imports of dairy products and on various restrictive practices, such as the "American selling price" for chemicals and others. After two months of intensive negotiations between the commission and President Nixon's Special Representative for Trade Negotiations, an accord was reached on February 4, 1972, in Brussels. The trade package was subsequently approved by the Council of Ministers and by the American President. It contained a series of short-term trade adjustments consisting mainly of concessions by the Common Market on increased US exports of oranges, grapefruit, and wheat.[36] The American part of the bargain was the Administration's promise to submit the so-called "gold bill" to Congress for rapid approval of the dollar's devaluation.[37] The agreement between the United States and the European Community also provided for the principle of mutual advantage and reciprocity as the basis for the solution of pending trade issues during future negotiations in the framework of GATT:

The United States and the Community recognize that it is necessary to undertake *a complete re-examination of the whole of international economic relations*, with a view to negotiating improvements in connection with the structural changes which have occurred in the last few years. This re-examination will cover, among other things, all aspects of trade including measures hindering or distorting the pattern of trade in agricultural products, raw materials and industrial products. Special attention will be given to the problems of the developing countries.

The United States and the Community undertake to initiate and actively support *wide-ranging multilateral talks in the framework of the GATT*, to commence in 1973 (subject to any internal authorization which may be required to this end) with the aim of expanding and liberalizing world trade as much as possible and of raising the living standards of the peoples, aims which can be attained by, among other things, the gradual removal of obstacles to trade and the improving of the international framework governing world trade. The Community states that in appropriate cases, the concluding of *international agreements on individual products* is also one of the ways in which these aims can be attained. The United States declares that such agreements are not a useful approach for the attainment of these aims.

These multilateral talks will be held on the basis of *mutual advantage and a mutual commitment involving overall reciprocity*, and will cover both agricultural and industrial trade. The talks should involve *the active participation of the largest number of countries possible*.

The United States and the Community have agreed to initiate and support in 1972 an analysis and evaluation, in the framework of the GATT, of various techniques and modalities for multilateral negotiations on long-term problems affecting all aspects of world trade.

The United States and the Community will try *to make use of every opportunity within the GATT to settle specific trade problems, the elimination of which is likely to attenuate present frictions*, and will seek to make further progress in matters which are being discussed by the committee for trade in industrial goods and the committee for agriculture of the GATT. They recognize that progress within the GATT towards the solution of specific problems in 1972 could make it easier to take new major initiatives within the GATT aimed at dealing with longer term trade problems.[38]

Formal, large-scale negotiations on international trade were expected to begin later in 1973, following the enlargement of the European Community and the authorization by the US Congress to permit the administration to participate in a new round of talks ("Nixon Round").

The rationale for further trade liberalization was given by President Nixon in his Report to Congress of February 9, 1972, when he said:

Trade, like monetary issues, is a multilateral problem which must be addressed in a spirit of multilateral cooperation. Today the European Community, Japan, the United States and other nations maintain trade barriers which adversely affect each other's exports. ... In 1971 we took actions to remove restrictions against our exports and to encourage renewed international efforts to remove trade barriers. A broad international assault on such barriers is necessary. The only sustainable system for the future must be one seen to be of mutual advantage for all. A retreat by any nations or group of nations into protectionism, or attempts to gain advantage over others by means of neo-mercantilist policies, will deal a severe blow to the international cooperation which underlies the strength and prosperity of all nations. ... In 1971 we set the stage for fundamental and long-term reforms in the international economic system. . . . Our [future] goals will be to: reform the international monetary system [and] to set the stage for major international negotiations leading to mutual reduction in trade barriers.[39]

Officials of the European Community also confirmed that the fundamental decision in favor of negotiations on the reform of the international monetary and trading systems, beginning in 1973, had been made in Brussels.[40]

"Burden-sharing" in the Atlantic Alliance

Ever since the end of World War II the United States has carried a disproportionately large share of the costs for the defense of the Western world. Although the percentage of US contributions to NATO defense expenditures is gradually being scaled down under the impact of the "Nixon Doctrine" and Congressional pressures for the withdrawal of American troops in Western Europe, the United States still carries the brunt of the financial burden for Atlantic defense. (See Table 8-6.) For instance, in 1969 the total US defense expenditures amounted to $79,774 billion, whereas the European members of NATO contributed only $23,167 billion.[41] In percentage terms of GNP, this means that the United States spent 8.6 percent whereas the average percentage of European nations was only 3.9.[42] Furthermore, in terms of annual per capita defense expenditures, the American taxpayer devoted $373, his German counterpart $127, a Frenchman $122, and a Britisher $106.[43]

To be sure, the United States, a superpower with global interests, has to maintain a proportionately higher defense budget than its regionally-oriented European allies. However, NATO's principal goal has always been the defense of

Table 8-6
Defense Expenditures of NATO Countries (1949-1971)

Country (0)	Currency Unit (1)	1949 (2)	1954 (3)	1962 (4)	1963 (5)	Actual 1964 (6)	1965 (7)	1966 (8)	1967 (9)	1968 (10)	1969 (11)	1970 (12)	Forecast 1971 (13)
Belgium	Million Belgian Francs	7,653	19,925	21,111	22,230	24,853	25,036	26,313	28,432	30,110	31,488	34,866	37,431
Canada	Million Canadian $	372	1,771	1,810	1,712	1,813	1,659	1,766	1,965	1,927	1,899	2,061	2,061
Denmark	Million Danish Kroner	360	885	1,551	1,651	1,764	1,974	2,080	2,249	2,591	2,640	2,757	3,039
France	Million Francs	4,787	11,710	22,184	22,849	24,280	25,300	26,732	28,912	30,200	31,700	33,200	35,000
Fed. Rep. of Germany[a]	Million DM	–	6,287	17,233	19,924	19,553	19,915	20,254	21,408	19,310	21,577	22,573	25,713
Greece	Million Drachmae	1,630	3,428	5,102	5,385	5,647	6,290	7,168	9,390	11,003	12,762	14,208	16,062
Italy	Milliard Lire	301	543	861	1,031	1,118	1,212	1,342	1,359	1,403	1,412	1,562	1,637
Luxembourg	Million Luxembourg Francs	112	566	355	348	462	477	497	413	374	391	416	456
Netherlands	Million Guilders	680	1,583	2,186	2,307	2,661	2,714	2,790	3,200	3,280	3,682	3,968	4,346
Norway	Million Norwegian Kroner	370	1,141	1,371	1,465	1,570	1,897	1,947	2,097	2,399	2,502	2,774	3,001
Portugal	Million Escudos	1,419	2,100	5,744	5,724	6,451	6,680	7,393	9,575	10,692	10,779	12,501	12,773
Turkey	Million Liras	556	936	2,940	3,157	3,443	3,281	3,996	4,596	5,159	5,395	6,237	8,111
United Kingdom	Million £s Sterling	779	1,569	1,814	1,870	2,000	2,091	2,153	2,276	2,332	2,303	2,444	2,697
United States	Million US $	13,503	42,786	52,381	52,295	51,213	51,827	63,572	75,448	80,732	81,443	77,827	77,791
Area													
Total Europe[b]	Million US $[c]	4,825	11,741	17,408	18,756								
Total North America	Million US $[c]	13,875	44,557	54,096	53,879								
Notal NATO[b]	Million US $[c]	18,700	56,298	71,504	72,635								

Table 8-6 (cont.)

19,706	20,574	21,475	22,994	22,296	23,251	24,553	26,723
52,890	53,362	65,205	77,265	82,515	83,199	79,733	79,697
72,596	73,936	86,680	100,259	104,811	106,450	104,286	106,420

aBefore it acceded to the North Atlantic Treaty Organization (May 1955), the Federal Republic of Germany contributed to the defense budgets of certain NATO countries by the payment of occupation costs; moreover, it bore certain other costs which also fall within the NATO definition of defense expenditures. In addition to defense expenditures (NATO definition), the German authorities are obliged to incur large annual expenditures for Berlin owing to the exceptional situation of this city and the need, in the interests of defense of the free world, to ensure its viability. These expenditures, which are not included in the figures given above since they do not come within the NATO definition, are forecast to be 3,876 million DM in 1971.

bThe totals for Europe and for NATO do not include defense expenditures of the Federal Republic of Germany for 1949 and for this reason they are not directly comparable to the totals for the following years. Moreover, as these totals have been established on the basis of the official exchange rates in force, comparisons made between two successive years could be slightly distorted if one or more countries modified their exchange rates during the course of one of these years.

cSince August 1971 a certain number of countries have floated their currencies and their exchange rates are consequently subject to fluctuation. For purposes of comparison, it has been judged preferable to continue to use the official exchange rates for 1970 in converting 1971 data into US dollars.

Note: The figures given in here represent payments actually made or to be made during the course of the calendar year. They are based on the NATO definition of defense expenditures. In view of the differences between this and national definitions, the figures shown may diverge considerably from those which are quoted by national authorities or given in the national budgets.

The figures relating to the United States and Canada include expenditures for military aid programmes. The figures shown for European NATO countries do not include the value of end-items received under military aid programmes from the United States and Canada.

Source: *NATO Review* (January/February 1972); revised.

Western Europe and thus is the foremost responsibility of European governments, although the United States has undoubtedly a vital interest in the security of the whole North Atlantic area and hence remains committed to the Atlantic Alliance. Therefore, the United States has approximately 300,000 troops stationed on European soil at an annual cost of about $14 billion.[44] However, a large part of these expenditures—mainly the costs for supporting 200,000-odd US troops stationed in West Germany—is compensated for by an offset agreement with the Federal Republic which reimburses the American government for about $2 billion a year.[45] Moreover, the United States economy benefits significantly from the continuing return flow of capital from American investments in Western Europe, which amounts to about $750 million annually.[46]

In the 1970s the New Europe will face mounting pressures to assume greater responsibility for European defense in terms of additional contributions in manpower and finances. After all, the combined population of the enlarged European Community as well as its reserve assets surpass that of both superpowers, although its collective GNP and its per capita income remain significantly smaller than that of the United States.[47]

The preceding analysis of the three major economic issues confronting the United States and Western Europe demonstrates the complex and interdependent nature of the problems of Atlantic commerce, finance, and defense expenditures. This argument has been supported by the head of the US Mission to the European Community, who explained that the financial crisis precipitated by the deficit of the US balance of payments has forced the administration to insist "that the inter-connection among finance, trade and burden sharing cannot be ignored. In reality this insistence is merely a recognition of the fact of life"[48] —the reality of political interdependence.

Security Aspects of Atlantic Relationships

Security is essentially a function of geopolitics. To paraphrase Napoleon's famous dictum, the foreign policy of Western Europe is determined by its geography. In other words, as long as the people of Western Europe cherish the values of democracy, their governments are likely to maintain an alliance with the United States. The rationale for this argument is based upon the asymmetry of forces existing between the Soviet Union (and its East European satellites) on the one hand, and Western Europe on the other. This imbalance of forces is compounded by the strategic advantages of the Soviet Union in the nuclear age which enable it to exercise hegemonial control over the European peninsula. It was against the background of these considerations that the leaders of Western Europe joined the United States in forging the Atlantic Alliance following the end of World War II.

Although the basic rationale for NATO still exists, given the imbalance of forces between Eastern and Western Europe, the perception of the Soviet threat to free Europe has changed from one of "clear and present" danger to one of *détente* and relaxation of tensions. This evolution from "cold war" to "cold peace" on the European Continent is reinforced by the emergence of the European Community as an economic giant and by the simultaneous trend toward a gradual retraction from political-military involvement in international affairs on the part of the United States.

However, the "Nixon Doctrine" does not usher in an era of neoisolationism but merely urges American allies to contribute their fair share to the common defense efforts in all parts of the world. Applied to Europe, the new American policy consists in adjusting the Atlantic Alliance to the realities of the 1970s: while maintaining the US strategic nuclear forces as both an "umbrella" for

European defense and as a "sword" for a possible retaliatory counterattack against an aggressor, the American government favors the progressive enlargement of the European role in providing for an effective "shield" through the build-up of modern conventional forces in accordance with the strategic doctrine of "flexible response," which permits options instead of necessitating immediate recourse to nuclear weapons in a *casus belli*.

In the words of the Secretary of State, "The unique US military contribution is, of course, our nuclear deterrent capability, but our forces assigned to NATO also provide an indispensable element of NATO's conventional deterrent capability, as well as a tangible link to the US nuclear deterrent. It is also important to note that these US forces, while contributing to the defense of our allies, represent our own first line of defense."[49]

It is precisely because of NATO's vital role for American national security that President Nixon has consistently opposed any unilateral withdrawal of US troops from Europe; thus he stated in his Foreign Policy Report of 1972, "It is the policy of this Government to maintain and improve our forces in Europe and not to reduce them except through reciprocal reductions negotiated with the Warsaw Pact. With such mutual reduction now on the agenda of East-West diplomacy, this is precisely the moment *not* to make unilateral cuts in our strength."[50]

In fact, the condition *sine qua non* for any successful agreement on mutual and balanced force reductions in Central Europe is an approximate parity in the relative strength of NATO and the Warsaw Pact. In other words, in order to enable Western diplomats in future MBFR negotiations to strike an equitable bargain with the Soviets—to get a *quid pro quo*—any prior unilateral withdrawal of US troops would eliminate the incentive on the part of Moscow to reduce their own forces. Hence the US insists on linking the ESC to MBFR.

In the light of the persistent deficit of the US balance of payments, Congressional pressures for a numerical reduction of American troops stationed in Europe are likely to intensify. "Thus, the question is not whether, but when and how, such a reduction will take place."[51] However, such withdrawals would have to be offset by additional European ground forces earmarked for NATO. After all, there is no magic number of US troops to be stationed on European soil, although "American forces should not be reduced to the role of a hostage, triggering the automatic use of nuclear weapons (as the only alternative to capitulation)."[52]

In this context it should be stressed that the very *raison d'être* of NATO continues to exist as the era of negotiations replaces that of confrontations. After all, the potential threat from the East has two dimensions: Communist intentions and Soviet capabilities. Even if the political dimension of this threat is eroded by the "spirit of detente," the military weapons arsenal at the disposal of the Warsaw Pact nations is still formidable.[53] In fact, the build-up of Soviet naval power is the most tangible evidence for Moscow's continued emphasis on improving its military posture vis-à-vis the West. In short, the deterrence function of NATO has not been invalidated by the rapprochement between East and West and it is risky to regard NATO as an "alliance in search of an enemy." However, the necessary (deterrence) should be complemented by the desirable (détente).

In the absence of a mutually acceptable settlement of the twin problem of European partition and the division of Germany, NATO is likely to remain a necessary factor of political-military stability in the complex strategic equation. A genuine solution to the European problem could result from two interconnected developments: a successful European Security Conference (i.e., involving *mutual* concessions) and the emergence of a united Western Europe.

Sociocultural Dimensions of the "Atlantic Community"

Ever since the discovery of the New World by Europeans, its destiny was inextricably linked to that of the Old World. Indeed, the Atlantic community has always been a cultural entity with common traditions and values that transcended temporary conflicts in the political or economic realms. The core of "Western civilization" has always been made up of Europeans in the wide sense of the term (including ancient Greeks, Romans, and Americans). However, the nature of their bonds and the intensity of their interactions varied in accordance with the changing power relationship between the members of this Atlantic community of nations.

In modern times, Europe and America have not always been partners in some formal association, but the leaders of both the Old and the New Worlds recognized their responsibilities vis-à-vis one another as demonstrated by the common efforts to preserve the ideals of freedom and democracy against totalitarian aggression. In the light of these persistent transoceanic ties, it has been argued that "the Atlantic Ocean is not the frontier between Europe and the Americas. It is the island sea of a community of nations allied with one another by geography, history, and vital necessity."[54] In other words, the Atlantic has become to the West what the Mediterranean had been to the ancient world. For the same reason, Western civilization has been referred to as a "civilisation de dialogue," a term that denotes the creative dialectical relationship between Europeans and Americans.

It was only recently that the fundamental principles of this North Atlantic civilization were defined specifically and grouped in a conceptual framework which included the following six headings:

(1) Firstly, respect for the intrinsic value of the human person as such, a value transcending all idolatrous and absolute conceptions of the State.
(2) Secondly, the inseparability of freedom from the moral responsibility of the individual, which presupposes reference to a higher law, however, the latter may be designated.

(3) Thirdly, the inseparability of freedom from human solidarity and the duty to promote progressively the material and spiritual welfare of all mankind.

(4) Fourthly, the Atlantic Community is a 'civilization of dialogue': this implies toleration and free discussion of opinions, but a toleration kept within bounds ensuring the maintenance of the institutions which make such free discussion possible.

(5) Fifthly, it is essential that the members of the Atlantic Community realize that these principles are not their exclusive property but are shared by other civilizations.

(6) Finally, the Atlantic Community is aware of the need to re-examine itself continually, and aware also of the internal and external dangers jeopardizing the survival of these principles. It therefore stresses the continual and urgent need to demonstrate these principles to successive generations and to incorporate them in its institutions. [55]

While this statement of general principles concerning the West can be considered as the "Credo of the Atlantic Community," the Atlantic Congress of 1959 added the "Bill of Rights of Free Men." Both declarations together constitute what might be called the "Magna Charta Atlantica."

The existence of the Atlantic community as a sociocultural entity has been solidified by the creation of an institutional infrastructure composed of NATO and OECD, symbolizing respectively solidarity in defense and economic interdependence between Western Europe and America (including the United States and Canada). Numerous scholars on both sides of the Atlantic have examined the properties of this Atlantic community in terms of its sociocultural, economic, and political dimensions in an effort to identify the persistent versus the ephemeral aspects of this complex trans-Atlantic relationship. [56]

Sociocultural links between Western Europe and the United States have been identified by several political analysts. Karl Deutsch and his associates discovered a pattern of intensive trans-Atlantic communications consisting of transaction flows (trade, travel, mail) [57] as well as complementary attitudes. This mutual responsiveness between Europeans and Americans has been particularly strong on the part of elites on both sides of the Atlantic. In the United States (especially on the East Coast) there has always been a large and influential group of "Atlanticists" who maintained close relations with their counterparts in Western Europe. This transnational elite network is supported by a majority of people in Western Europe who consistently express greater trust toward Americans than toward any other single European nation. [58]

These findings concerning popular attitudes on the part of West Europeans with regard to the United States were corroborated by two other analysts, who also detected a distinctly pro-American orientation in Germany, Britain, Italy, and France, expressed in terms of "net good feelings and trust" toward the United States. [59] This "Americanophilia," however, is not inconsistent with the fact that the majority of Europeans also support the objective of European unity. On the contrary, pro-European sentiments and an Atlantic orientation on the part of young Europeans tend to overlap and are part of a general internationalist outlook.[60]

The compatibility of the goals of European integration and Atlantic partnership among European elites has been amply documented by Lerner and Gorden, who concluded their elite opinion survey as follows: "The differences among them as to Europe and Atlantica are minor as compared with their deep commitment to the Euramerican system of relations and its eventual institutionalization in some Euratlantic pattern. . . . Euratlantica—at least as a confederated set of nations bound by a common world policy—is very likely to grow and prosper . . . [and] the Euratlantic system is already beyond the point of no return."[61]

In short, there seems to be sufficient evidence to support the contention that the sociocultural dimension of the Atlantic community is a living reality and constitutes a vital factor in European-American relations.

The Political Dynamics of European-American Relations: From Tutelage to Equality

Undoubtedly the most serious problem facing the governments of Western Europe and the United States is how to handle "the transition from tutelage to equality—a process to which no nation has ever adjusted easily."[62] This effort requires wisdom and patience on both sides of the Atlantic for two reasons: In the United States there exists a certain ambivalence between affirmations of the desirability of European unity and a reluctance to see it consummated out of fear that it might pursue policies independent from, and possibly inimical to, the United States. The danger for Europeans consists in the temptation "to unite against" the United States. Indeed, "in a period of declining concern with the Soviet threat, Europe has too often been defined negatively in terms of counterpoise to, and independence from, American hegemony."[63]

The situation is complicated by the fact that, although European and American leaders are officially in favor of European unity, progress is slow because "tutelage is a comfortable relationship for the senior partner; but it is demoralizing in the long run. It breeds illusions of omniscience on one side and attitudes of impotent irresponsibility on the other."[64] Thus Europeans tend to take American protection for granted and show reluctance to shoulder a greater burden for their defense while remaining free to criticize the hegemonial power in the Atlantic Alliance.

Whereas these strains in NATO are mainly due to the asymmetry of power between a giant and a group of dwarfs, the tensions in OECD are caused by the rise of the European Community as an economic rival. They were reinforced by a tendency toward neoisolationism on both sides of the Atlantic. The European

Community often appeared to be "inward-looking," showing little concern for the outside world, while the United States witnessed a rising tide of protectionism, accompanied by a "growing sentiment for isolationism. [Although] everyone deplores isolationism . . . everyone seems to practice it when it serves his political interest. [But] expediency is habit-forming, and part-time isolationism is no exception."[65]

Notwithstanding the fact that neither partner intends to practice neoisolationism given its manifestly counterproductive effects, the negative mutual perceptions suffice to create a myth that frequently transcends realities. In short, "domestic" preoccupations tend to obscure the fundamentally common interests of Western Europe and the United States.

Against the background of these tensions in the complex, multidimensional Atlantic relationships, the need for an institutionalized Atlantic partnership becomes evident.

An Atlantic Partnership for the 1970s

In the late 1960s it appeared as if the grand design of an Atlantic partnership between the uniting Europe and the United States had evaporated under the impact of President de Gaulle's anti-American policies. However, following his departure from the political scene in 1969, the prospects for its revival began to improve significantly; instead of having suffered a mortal blow, the grand design was merely "frozen" and ready to be "reactivated" in the 1970s.

This argument will be substantiated following a summary presentation of the original concept of Atlantic partnership.

The fundamental assumptions underlying the grand design were the following: (1) European unity is a desirable political objective since it contributes to greater cohesion of the West, (2) the supranational Monnet approach to achieve this goal was preferable to intergovernmental cooperation because economic integration was expected to lead inexorably to political unification; (3) Britain would become part of a united Europe and ensure its pro-Atlantic orientation; (4) only a united Europe with federal-type institutions would constitute a viable, equal partner capable of sharing the burdens of Atlantic defense and fulfilling the joint responsibilities of the industrialized nations of the West toward the developing countries of the Third World.

To be sure, "the grand design was not a devious scheme to promote American dominance, but a framework at once pragmatic and idealistic, capable of modification to meet the vital interests of Europeans."[66] According to a European analyst, "partnership implies trust in . . . the advantages of working together . . . [and] mutual persuasion demands a genuinely reciprocal relationship in which each partner feels his position is an honorable one. The Europeans cannot be drawn into a permanent association with the United States (and vice versa) unless Europe's autonomy is accepted. Otherwise the suspicion that partnership is a cloak for supremacy will recur again and again. . . . Only those who feel free to make their own choices can choose not to assert their freedom. . . . [Hence] paradoxical though it sounds, recognition of the potential bipolarity of the West is essential to its cohesion."[6][7]

Although this grand design of an Atlantic partnership involved primarily the United States and the European Community, it was not conceived as an exclusive club of the rich, industrialized nations of the Atlantic Alliance but as an open-ended arrangement permitting access by all other members of the free world. In the words of an American analyst, "its essence [of the grand design] is creative harmony between the United States and Europe for economic, military, and political purpose. It would bring together in a working Atlantic partnership two separate but equal entities. On the one hand would be this country with its special ties to Canada, Latin America, and the Pacific, notably Japan. On the other would be Western Europe with its special ties in Africa, and the Dominions of the Commonwealth. . . . By cooperative arrangement, the two partners would first adjust mutual differences; and then, while combining forces to hold Communist aggression in check, apply their manifold strengths to the harmonious development of the Southern Continents."[6][8]

The grand design of an Atlantic Partnership disintegrated when General de Gaulle challenged its fundamental assumptions by the following "counter-policies": first, the French President defined "Europe" as extending from the "Atlantic to the Urals," thus excluding the United States; second, he opposed the supranational method and instead advocated intergovernmental cooperation among European states; third, he vetoed British entry into the Common Market, primarily on the grounds that the United Kingdom would play the undesirable role of a "Trojan horse" for the United States within the European Community; fourth, General de Gaulle's vision of Europe's future role was that of an independent "third force" juxtaposed to the two superpowers rather than linked to the United States within an Atlantic framework.

However, with the beginning of the post-Gaullist era, the politics of statism was replaced by the politics of movement—both in Europe and in the Atlantic area. This development enhanced the chances for an eventual implementation of the grand design considerably. The argument is based upon the following considerations: first, notwithstanding continued efforts to promote an East-West détente, the notion of a pan-Europe from the Atlantic to the Urals has been rejected as a chimera by all realistic leaders in Western Europe (including de Gaulle's successor). Second, although the notion of a confederal "Europe of States" is still regarded as a useful approach to European unity, it is widely considered as a means toward the creation of a federal United States of Europe (rather than as a goal in itself). Third, British membership in the Common Market is likely to assure its outward orientation in terms of recognizing its world responsibilities and maintaining its pro-American posture. Fourth, as the

European Community moves toward an economic and monetary union, it can be expected to emerge as a viable entity capable of assuming the role of a genuine, equal partner of the United States.

Ultimately, the rationale for an Atlantic partnership is not based on idealistic architectonics but on the realistic concept of enlightened self-interest for both the United States and the uniting Europe, especially because there seems to be no reasonable alternative to this grand design for the West.

In his Foreign Policy Report of 1972, President Nixon entitled one of the chapters "European Unity and Atlantic Partnership" and reiterated his support for this twin-concept.[69] Henry Kissinger also advocated an "Atlantic Partnership" and urged the simultaneous pursuit of increased European cohesion.[70] On the other side of the Atlantic Jean Monnet stated that "the unification of Europe and the establishment of an equal partnership between the uniting Europe and the United States are the first steps towards the organization of a lasting peace between West and East and progressive disarmament."[71]

Institutions for the Atlantic Dialogue

Once the United States had committed itself to the support of the European unity movement in general and to the construction of a supranational European Community in particular, the psychological basis for an Atlantic dialogue had been established. Naturally, such a dialogue necessitated the identification of a spokesman for each of the two partners involved. If the logical representative of the United States was the American president, the Europeans faced a serious issue: "Who speaks for Europe?" Although President Kennedy, who had first asked this question in public, generously conferred the title of "Mr. Europe" on M. Jean Monnet (who deserved it more than anybody else), General de Gaulle appointed himself as the first *de facto* spokesman for Europe in the diplomatic arena. This unwarranted and widely contested "self-appointment by fiat" led to a virtual communication breakdown (*dialogue de sours*) between the United States and Western Europe. The resulting impasse lasted for almost a decade and the negative reverberations are still troubling diplomatic Atlantic waters in the 1970s. Since this trans-Atlantic communication gap was neither in the interest of the United States nor of the European Community, attempts were made to restore the interrupted Atlantic dialogue as soon as the Gaullist obstacle was removed from the scene.

Given the key position held by the German Federal Republic in Atlantic relationships, it was only natural that Chancellor Brandt took the initiative in proposing an "organized dialogue" between Europe and the United States in early 1970.[72] The first result of this German initiative was an informal agreement between Washington and Brussels to hold regular meetings between representatives from the community and the United States. In October 1970, the so-called Samuels-Dahrendorf Committee met for the first time: the American delegation, composed of representatives from the Departments of State, Agriculture and Treasury, was headed by Deputy Undersecretary of State Nathaniel Samuels. Leading the European delegation was Dr. Ralf Dahrendorf, the European Commissioner in charge of external trade affairs. Although these biannual talks have not produced any spectacular agreements, they nevertheless led to a useful exchange of views between the two groups by permitting the airing of controversial positions.

The relative importance of this limited Atlantic dialogue was underlined by the fact that President Nixon referred to it in his second "State of the World" message in which he stressed that Europe and the United States have a "heavy responsibility" and that "informal regular consultation . . . began in 1970 between the Commission of the European Community and the United States."[73] He added that "there have been suggestions for expanding our consultation, including the possibility of higher-level Community representation in Washington. We would welcome the implementation of any such suggestion the Community might propose because of the importance of close consultation."[74]

Only six months later, the European Community decided to upgrade its representation in Washington through the creation of a quasi-embassy, called a "liaison office," headed by a European official with ambassadorial rank. Shortly afterwards, the European Commission proposed to "institutionalize" the regular consultations held between the European Community and the United States.[75]

The institutionalization of the Atlantic dialogue is indeed imperative if European-American relations are to be improved. However, the complexities of the problem are enormous for the following reasons: first, there exists a natural and logical interdependence between questions of trade, finance, and defense burden-sharing among the Western nations. Although these issues are functionally connected, they are being dealt with by different international organizations—the so-called Group of Ten (or Big Ten) within the International Monetary Fund serves as the forum for the discussion of monetary problems.[76] On trade matters the European Community negotiates with the United States within the framework of GATT. Finally, the question of equitable burden-sharing in defense is handled by NATO, where the Europeans are represented by the so-called Eurogroup composed of ten different members.[77] This triple-layered Atlantic dialogue epitomizes the problem of overlapping and conflicting jurisdictions.

The functional problem is aggravated by another—political—difficulty rooted in the "dualism" of both American and European governmental structures: the tandem Congress-Executive in the United States, and its European corollary, the interlocking community system composed of the legislature (Council of Ministers) and administration (European Commission). This dualism inevitably leads to both unintended and fabricated delays: the former are the product of complicated consensus-formation procedures; the latter are often due to the understandable desire of one side to procrastinate by blaming the tandem partner for inaction. To be sure, the frequent, unabashed use of such delaying tactics is necessarily counterproductive as it benefits nobody in the long run.[78] One solution to this problem of intrasystemic maneuvers might consist in a formal grant of negotiating authority from Congress to the Executive in the United States, and in a clear mandate for the Commission of the European Community, enabling both to negotiate with authority. The alternative procedure would consist in the creation of formal machinery for the regular conduct of the Atlantic dialogue.

The concept of an institutionalized Atlantic partnership was first formulated by a group of distinguished European and American leaders in a "Program for Transatlantic Action." The group was composed of such statesmen as Will Clayton, Gabriel Hauge, Lord Franks, and René Mayer, with Pierre Uri as their spokesman. They declared that "in a partnership of two equals there is no alternative to agreement by both if any effective action is to be taken," and proposed the creation of Atlantic institutional machinery:

It should bring together on an equal footing the United States on the one hand and an enlarged European Community on the other in a Council that would meet at a ministerial level. On the United States side, this would mean the heads of government, department or federal agencies. On the European side, representation would not have to be rigidly laid down. It would comprise, depending on circumstances, members of the Common Market Commission, ministers of national governments, or both at the same time. (Nor should we exclude Europe's representation, at some future date, by members of an eventual federal government.)[79]

In view of the nature of a partnership—sovereignty would remain with each of the two partners—Uri considered it "advisable to set up, on a permanent basis, a group of three or four 'Wise Men'—outstanding public figures distinguished for their impartiality, imagination and experience, whose moral influence would make up for what they lacked in delegated authority.... The Wise Men's responsibility would be to give continuous attention to the most pressing problems of the moment, and to make proposals concerning them which would be automatically placed in the agenda of the Council...." Furthermore, Uri believed that "the likelihood of effective action would be increased by the further creation of a joint Parliamentary Assembly... [which] could stimulate the Council to action, discover its errors and compel discussion of its work.[80]

A similar idea was launched five years later by the Monnet Committee. Following the successful outcome of the Kennedy Round in 1967, in which the European Community negotiated as an equal of the United States for the first time, the *Action Committee for the United States of Europe* adopted a resolution in which it urged the establishment of a "Committee of Entente" composed of representatives of the American government and the European Community. Its task would consist in presenting and debating the American and

European viewpoints before taking decisions on major questions of common concern, such as the international monetary system, the balance of payments, American investments in Europe, technological exchanges, and aid to developing countries.[81]

The Action Committee reiterated its proposal in another resolution adopted four years later, in which it called for the establishment of a "permanent organ for reciprocal consultation" in which the European Community and the United States would be represented at a high level on the basis of equality, and which would serve as a forum for regular discussions on questions of common interest.[82]

In view of the increasingly complex and interdependent problems facing the United States and the European Community in the 1970s, there seems to be no alternative to such an organized trans-Atlantic dialogue which would serve the interests of both partners involved.

Although the above-mentioned proposals were originally made in the 1960s, "there is no reason whatsoever to retract these recommendations. Quite the contrary: developments in the sixties and the manifold changes in the first two years of the seventies have made them even more valid than they were ten years ago. It can well be argued that, had they been followed, the Atlantic world would hardly find itself in the disarray that it does now. . . . "[83]

For lack of an overall framework, trans-Atlantic negotiations have been conducted on an *ad hoc* basis within numerous functional bodies that proliferated over the last decades. As a result, unnecessary tensions and conflicts arose during such multilateral negotiations which aggravated rather than alleviated the malaise among Western nations. Therefore, "summit meetings of heads of governments from major European countries, the United States and Canada should become a regular institution of Atlantic relations. Preferably, they should take place about once a year [and] prepared by a standing Atlantic committee of experts."[84]

An alternative to this minimalist approach to Atlantic consensus formation would be a maximalist solution—the institutionalization of the Atlantic Community.[85]

In this chapter we portrayed the foreign policy options of the New Europe—toward Eastern Europe, the "Third World," and vis-à-vis the United States. Emphasis was placed on the analysis of the various dimensions and complexities of contemporary trans-Atlantic relationships.

The European Community in
Perspective

Methodological Reflections

This study focuses on the European Community as an experiment in regional integration. The first two chapters dealt with the principal concepts and theories of international integration and culminated in an attempt to explore new frontiers in integration theory. This admittedly risky venture in conceptual synthesizing resulted in the construction of an original paradigm for political unification. The "Gestalt model" was used as the conceptual framework for the following chapters. Given the ambitious nature of the research design, this effort was at best partially successful since not all variables contained in the comprehensive taxonomy were systematically and adequately dealt with. Nevertheless, the major elements of the conceptual framework were considered in the analysis and most propositions were (at least in part) tested in Part II of the book. Given the complex and constantly evolving nature of the European Community, an analysis of this elusive political animal is essentially a "time and motion study." Consequently, most findings are tentative and lack homogeneity, consistency, and finality.

Notwithstanding the validity of these caveats, there appeared to be a positive correlation between the original propositions of the "Gestalt model" about the integration-disintegration syndrome and the actual performance of the European Community.

Instead of reexamining the relative significance of each variable and every proposition of the "Gestalt model" in the light of the findings of Part II, a summary evaluation may serve a more useful purpose. Hence we will organize the findings in legal, developmental, and political-normative terms.

The European Community as a Political System

Ever since its creation in the 1950s, the European Community has developed according to a pattern of ebb and flow, rather than in linear progression. Its story has been, and is likely to remain, one of intermittent successes and failures in formulating common policies, and one of growth and decline of its institutional capacity—in short, a case study of "integration-disintegration." These two rival processes have been simultaneously at work from the very beginning, symbolizing the continuing struggle between the forces of nationalism and regionalism. The persistent ambiguity about the state of the European Community at any given point in time is demonstrated by the prevailing uncertainty, both in official and academic circles, over the "nature of the beast" and its integrative potential. Political analysts who follow the developments on the European scene closely often arrive at contradictory conclusions in their assessment of certain events, depending on whether they focus on the political, economic, or social aspects of the integration process. However, there appears to be a consensus that while economic integration has been fairly successful, political unification has not progressed at the same pace over the last two decades. In other words, task expansion has accelerated much faster than supranational power, following a pattern of emerging regional entities in which the development of collective performances precedes the creation of collective control mechanisms.[1]

The most authoritative scholar on the European Community, Ernst Haas, originally considered both the ECSC and the EEC as having federal characteristics. Thus he referred to the High Authority as federal "executive," and he believed that "the EEC Treaty is one of the rare *federative agreements* which leaves its own central organs a tremendous degree of discretionary power."[2] At that time (the 1950s) Haas projected that "even though supranationality in practice has developed into a hybrid in which neither the federal nor the intergovernmental tendency has clearly triumphed, these relationships have sufficed to create expectations and shape attitudes which will undoubtedly work themselves out in the direction of more integration, . . . [the] consequences [of supranationality being] plainly *federating* in quality.[3] In the 1960s, he still believed that the EEC's "chances of automatic politicization [were] *good*" compared to those for other regional organizations.[4] This early concept of "automatic spillover" from the economic to the political sectors was subsequently revised under the impact of President de Gaulle's "dramatic-political" actions in 1966.[5] Haas's most recent reference to the European Community has been in terms of an "asymmetrically overlapping" configuration with authority being asymmetrically divided among several centers of power, having as its corollary multiple loyalties.[6]

According to Haas, European integration has to be measured in terms of "authority-legitimacy transfer" to common institutions; the process of integration is called "apprentissage institutionnel" (Michel Crozier's term), similar to the notion of "actor socialization" and "Europeanization."[7]

Two other eminent students of European integration, looking at the European Community as an incipient political system, dealt with the problem of institutional growth and capacity at great length and found that significant progress had been made in terms of expansion of the scope of supranational powers. Rejecting the notion that the European Community is a mere economic entity without political functions, these authors define politics not by *substance*, but by *process* and argue accordingly that "the sure sign of political integration is a system which can make authoritative decisions for the entire community, regardless of whether these are military, economic, or social welfare decisions."[8]

Treating the European Community as a political system, they divided the scope of its functions into four principal categories, namely external relations, political-constitutional, social-cultural, and economic functions, totaling twenty-two systems functions. Subsequently, they established a scale of the locus of decision-making within this system, ranging from low to high integration. The result of their tabulation over a period of approximately twenty years (with the years 1950, 1957, 1968 and 1970 as landmarks) showed the following changes in the overall distribution of decision-area scores: purely national decisions decreased from twenty-two in 1950 to five in 1970; beginning community decisions increased from zero to five over the same period; cooperative decisions with national predominance increased from zero in 1950 to eight in 1970; cooperative *decisions* with community predominance rose from zero to four during the same time span (no "all community" decisions were taken).[9]

Lawyers on both sides of the Atlantic have frequently referred to the European Community as "limited (or partial) federation,"[10] and as "federation in the making" or "prefederal" (quasi-federal) configuration, following Robert Schuman's reference to the community.[11] A sophisticated Euro American scholar, Carl Friedrich, recently referred to the European Community as an "emergent nation" involved in a "federalizing process [which] will continue as long as the Europeans who are engaged in specific efforts . . . are determined to solve concrete problems which require European solutions."[12] Other students of the European Community phenomenon have referred to it respectively as a "regional subsystem" and "partial international system";[13] a "would-be polity" or nascent "political system";[14] as a "sector integrated supranational system";[15] as a "regional conglomerate"[16] and as a "concordance system."[17]

The diverse nomenclature used by students of the community seems to underline the fact that "the Community system defies ready categorization. It is neither federal nor confederal, intergovernmental or supranational, sovereign or dependent, but it shares some of the characteristics of all."[18]

Probably the most accurate and balanced description of the European Community system has been offered by Miriam Camps, who referred to it as "a mixed system, a construction that is *sui generis*, which cannot be equated with either a federal state or an international organization in the conventional sense, although it has some of the attributes of each. It promises to remain a mixed system for a long time, with the members acting collectively for some purposes, individually for others, with the amount of coordination of policy and of common action depending on the extent to which the interests of the member countries coincide and with the advantages to be gained from common action."[19]

In short, the European Community is a pluralistic system in evolution from nationalism to regionalism using economic integration as a means of promoting political unity.

The Developmental Perspective

The European Community has been referred to as an "economic giant but a political dwarf" since it succeeded in becoming the most powerful commercial unit in history without giving itself commensurate political structures. In other words, economic integration has often been regarded as a substitute for political unification. There has been an excessive preoccupation with the content and process (e.g., approximation of policies) rather than a serious concern for the building of institutions. Furthermore, it can be argued that while "negative integration" (i.e., the removal of obstacles to free trade) has been largely achieved, "positive integration" (i.e., the formulation of common external policies) has been lagging behind. In the words of two British analysts: "The present members [of the Common Market] have failed to solve the political problem of effective integration. The institutions they have set up . . . are much too weak. The national governments have locked their economies together but have failed to take bold enough steps to develop a common posture on political issues, such as defense and foreign policies. The creation of a United States of Europe would require a conscious policy of pooling sovereignty and building up strong and democratic institutions at the European level."[20] This criticism seems to be justified since a political platform and ambitious designs are no substitute for the creation of a European government capable of implementing them. All along there has been a persistent tendency toward equivocation on the question of means and a lack of precision on how to make Europe a single actor in world affairs.

Most national leaders preferred pro-European declarations to formal commitments leading to the creation of a European political authority. In other words, governmental bureaucrats are afraid of their own logic: if Europe is to emerge as an independent world power, it must be capable of speaking with one voice in the international system. Such a European strategy necessarily involves the delegation of sovereign powers to a European president and, conversely, the abdication of national governments. Given the compelling logic of this equation, it is not surprising that the *amour-propre* of many national leaders prevents them from embracing Cartesianism all the way.

In the light of these ambivalent and reluctant attitudes of the member states, it has been argued that the European Community has "entered a phase of 'communal polycentrism.' Europe's center of gravity is shifting away from communal institutions because the national governments are continually reinforcing their decision-making powers. It is not unfair to say that the European Community is falling apart."[21] This Cassandra cry by a prominent French

"European" politician was corroborated by a British antimarketeer who stated that "the pace set in the Treaties of Paris and Rome has been too fast for what was then wanted and too slow for what is now needed. The whole history of the Communities, the methods by which their successes were achieved and their still long list of unachieved objectives show how well based were the fears of those who saw the difficulties facing every other federation and doubted whether the roots of European nationalisms could be pulled up by the rationalistic processes of the Spaaks, the Monnets, and the Hallsteins.... [Hence the European Community is] both premature and outdated, realistic in some of its limitations but unrealistic in its dreams."[22]

This negative verdict has been opposed by another Britisher who flatly predicted the creation of a federal political authority in Western Europe within five to ten years.[23] His projections were reinforced by an American authority who wrote that "Western Europe is only about halfway toward integration now.... With luck it might achieve integration in the 1980s or 1990s, but it will not be a quick or easy matter."[24]

Undoubtedly, progress toward European unity is a function of the intensity of nationalism and the extensiveness of renascent state sovereignty. While it is true that "Europe must unite in some form if it is to play a major role in the long run,"[25] it might well take another generation of Europeans to complete this objective. In the words of Jean Rey, a former commission president: "Building Europe is like building a gothic cathedral. The first generation knows that it will never see the work completed, but they go on working."[26] Yet, considering the actual, if limited, achievements of the European Community and its "demonstration effect" on other regions of the world, it seems appropriate to place it in historical perspective as follows: "One of the most significant developments in the West since the end of World War II has been the growth of European integration. Since the days of Charlemagne there have been numerous plans and various attempts (some by force) to unify Europe, but prior to 1945 none of these succeeded.... Within fifteen years after the close of WW II, it was evident that the competitive nation-state system was changing in Europe.... The full impact of the European integration movement remains unmeasured, yet within a relatively short time-span it has already produced certain revolutionary changes."[27]

The European Community as a Regional Organization

Although the treaties establishing the European Community contain no reference to art. 51 of the UN Charter, the community can be regarded as a regional organization in accordance with the principles of the United Nations. This judgment is based upon the following two criteria: the intent of the "founding fathers" of the European Community and its performance since its inception.

From the outset, European leaders emphasized that "the creation of a United Europe must be regarded as an essential step towards the creation of a United World."[28] This universal perspective was explained by a prominent European federalist as follows: "Europe is not a goal in itself; it is but a means. The means to solve the tangible, real and serious problems facing humanity in the twentieth century."[29] Indeed, many European federalists are "federalists" first and "Europeans" second: they consider a European Federation to be, not an ultimate goal, but a building block—a means of achieving a world federation.

This awareness of Europe's global responsibilities was subsequently expressed by the signatories of the Rome Treaty: they confirmed their solidarity with overseas countries and promised to assist them in their development "in accordance with the principles of the Charter of the United Nations."[30]

If the Rome Treaty underlined the community's concern for the promotion of the UN goal of economic development, the Treaty of Paris stressed the importance of peaceful relations between nations, the overriding principle of the UN Charter. In this document, the governments of the six countries recorded their determination "to substitute for historic rivalries a fusion of their essential interests . . . and to lay the bases of institutions capable of giving direction to their future common destiny."[31]

The peaceful revolution that accompanied the *ridimensionamento* in Western Europe following the end of World War II was evaluated by an early observer in the following terms: "Except for the creation of the United Nations, the efforts European leaders have been making to provide viable supranational or transnational institutions constitute virtually the sole example of a serious attempt to meet the integrative need of our century. It is certainly the only contemporary example of a *deliberate, uncoerced, popular effort to modify the traditional nation state pattern*, establish political jurisdictions broad enough to satisfy the political and economic needs of our time, and thus successfully counter the curiously unhistorical centrifugal organizational trends."[32] (Emphasis added.)

In the following section we will briefly look at the performance of the European Community as a regional IGO during the last twenty years. In the area of international security, the European Community has undoubtedly contributed to the preservation of peace in Western Europe by creating a "security community" between the former arch-enemies, Germany and France. The ECSC literally served as an instrument of pacification by making war between these two nations physically and politically impossible. In view of the fact that both world wars resulted primarily from a Franco-German confrontation, it is incontestable that the European Community has indirectly contributed to world peace through regional peace-keeping efforts as encouraged by the UN Charter.

As far as the promotion of welfare at the international level is concerned, the European Community has also performed creditably. Not only did the six members initially agree to assist—financially and technically—their former colonies in Africa, but they also negotiated generous preferential trade agreements with other countries of the Third World during the last decades. In 1971 the European Community became the first industrialized group of nations to grant generalized tariff preferences to ninety-one nations under a scheme sponsored by UNCTAD.

The preceding analysis of the original intent and subsequent performance of the European Community seems to indicate that this regional organization is operating within the parameters of United Nations principles. The evidence of complementarity between these two IGOs is of utmost importance in view of the fact that "only two have emerged as significant international actors in their own right: the United Nations and the European Economic Community. They can and do exert influence on a similar scale to that of many medium-sized powers and are certainly more influential internationally than most newly independent, small underdeveloped states."[33] This categorical statement has *prima facie* validity and could be supported by such quantitative data as newspaper editorials, headlines, and dissertations in the social sciences. It does not, however, take into consideration one significant difference, which consists in the respective purpose and membership of these two IGOs. The UN is a universal organization concerned with international security and welfare; the European Community is a regional grouping focussing essentially on the promotion of the socioeconomic welfare of its member nations. The common denominator of these two IGOs is that they were originally established by treaties or charters, formulated and signed by sovereign states.

Inevitably, the question arises as to the relative success and comparative impact of these two important actors in the international arena. This comparative analysis can be conducted through the application of three mutually interdependent tests designed to determine the organization's capacity to act more or less independently in international affairs. The first is the degree of autonomous decision-making power given to the organs of the IGO; the second is the extent to which it performs significant and continuing functions with an impact on interstate relations; and the third is the degree to which national governments take the IGO into consideration in their foreign policies. Judged against these (admittedly tentative and approximate) criteria, the European Community "has had a more precise impact on contemporary international relations than the U.N."[34] If this judgment is correct, the differential impact of these two IGOs may result from a structural divergence: whereas the UN is structured "horizontally" (with universal membership and safeguards for domestic jurisdiction), the European Community has "vertical" structures (limited membership with elements of transnational and supranational powers vested in common organs), although it is not devoid of horizontal elements. In fact, the UN Charter sanctions the traditional nation-state system and the sovereign rights of governments by recognizing such principles as "territorial integrity, domestic jurisdiction and sovereign equality."

Specifically, traditional IGOs operate within the following framework of conventions and procedures: (1) member states may join and withdraw from an IGO (for instance, the Treaty of Washington contains explicit provisions for withdrawal from NATO); (2) each member government remains free to interpret unilaterally the rules to which it has consented by joining the IGO (e.g., the "optional clause" in art. 36 of the Statute of the International Court of Justice permits states to ignore the compulsory jurisdiction of this tribunal although all UN members are *ipso facto* parties to the statute); (3) executive organs of IGOs have little influence over policy formulation and virtually no coercive powers (e.g., international monetary policy is made and executed in the IMF by the so-called Big Ten industrialized nations); (4) administrative bodies of IGOs have no direct rapport with private citizens of the member states; (5) decisions in IGOs are normally arrived at by unanimous vote, although the unanimity principle is occasionally modified (e.g., in the UN General Assembly a simple majority suffices in procedural matters); (6) except for the members of the UN Secretariat who may not receive instructions from any external authority, most officials of IGOs are subject to control by their respective national governments.[35]

In contrast to these constraining features of traditional IGOs, the treaties establishing the European Community enable it to function more effectively since it operates at four levels: at the supranational, international, infranational, and transnational levels.[36]

The term *supranational* refers to those features which involve the lodging of authority and competence in organs standing and operating *above* that of national sovereignty; the term *international* refers to relations *at* the level of national sovereignty between the community organs and member governments; the term *infranational* denotes the ability of community organs to reach down *below* national governments and deal directly with individuals and corporate units within the member states; and the term *transnational* directs attention to the horizontal interrelationships that cut across national boundaries and involve interactions between societal elements.

Although the community officials were given unprecedented formal powers, they remained largely free of supranational pretensions and illusions. Therefore, it has to be recognized that "impressive achievements of the community of the Six are attributable less to the formal capacity of its institutions to function without the cooperation of governments than to their success in stimulating that cooperation. The effectiveness of these institutions has rested not upon the elimination of the veto in theory but upon the achievement of unanimity in practice."[37]

The unprecedented nature of the institutions, powers, and operations of the European Community seems to justify the label *sui generis*. Therefore it seems appropriate to argue that "the European Community stands as the most striking confirmation of the thesis that organizational creativity may flourish at the regional level."[38] This judgment has been corroborated by another prominent student of comparative regionalism who found that, compared with other regional movements, "the EEC is by far the most successful union."[39] Moreover, an expert-scholar discovered that the European Community deserves a high mark in terms of its superior ability to cope with the ever-increasing burdens of interdependence—in contrast to the declining capability of other regional, intergovernmental organizations.[40]

In sum it can be argued that to the extent that the European Community has aimed at, and contributed to, the preservation of peace in an important region of the globe, has demonstrated an awareness of its responsibility vis-à-vis the Third World, and has pioneered supranationalism, it can be regarded as a successful experiment in regionalism.

If it has been established that the European Community has been a force of peace and a supporter of developing nations ever since its inception, a larger issue transcends these findings: Given the increasingly important phenomenon of global interdependence, what is the optimal size of an ideal political unit in the twenty-first century? Which organizational system can best and most effectively provide for maximum security and human welfare for the people concerned? Is it the nation-state? the regional federation? the continental confederation? the trans-Continental Alliance? or the universal configuration?

Undoubtedly, "the whole thrust of the technological development of our times pushes beyond the war and beyond the economic fences of nation-states . . . toward pluralistic security communities [and] regional federations."[41] Assuming that the demise or nation-states is inevitable (which may or may not be the case), is a federation the best alternative form of organization? According to a European authority, the answer is negative because the "changing world society constantly raises new problems of arms control, technological coopera-tion, development cooperation, etc., which can no longer be solved merely by forming a petty European federation for welfare, defense, and foreign policy. The issues engaging the European federalists will no longer be the crucial issues of the Seventies."[42] Another European scholar argued that "the only long-range perspective seems to be a free world confederacy, based on regional, continental federations."[43]

It could well be that the problem should be presented in terms of national independence *within* the context of global interdependence rather than in a polarized zero-sum game fashion (independence *or* interdependence). The either-or proposition appears to be a fallacy in view of the fact that govern-mental leaders make pragmatic choices in order to achieve desired objectives most effectively. Consequently, state authorities tend to adapt to a specific challenge in different ways: they could either handle it themselves, or volun-tarily delegate the function to a higher problem-solving authority such as a regional or global organization. This flexible disposition to "pass the buck" to supranational organs whenever it seems appropriate to the national officials has been referred to as "adaptive capacity" of the modern nation-state. The "adaptation model acknowledges the growing interdependence of world affairs, allows for the emergence of new, supranational political entities to process the problems created by interdependence, and at the same time assumes that the nation-state system, with all its accompanying conflicts and procedures, will persist undiminished. If the model is valid, the new world politics of the future will supplement, but not replace, the world politics that has prevailed for centuries."[44]

In such an asymmetrical, interdependent world the independent nation-state would, therefore, not face an eclipse but accept a certain amount of informal or direct interpenetration without loosing control over its destiny. In short, national governments would coexist with supranational organizations and each one would perform those functions that they are best equipped to handle most effectively.[45]

10 Summary and Conclusions

Summary

Following the establishment of the political rationale for the study in the preface, and of its scholarly purpose in the introduction, the first chapter was devoted to the examination of the properties of the contemporary international system. It also contained a conceptual framework for the study of international organization.

The second chapter surveyed and evaluated in a comparative fashion the major approaches to regional integration and included an original, comprehensive model for the study of political unification.

Chapter 3 dealt with the external and internal, as well as the direct and indirect, forces that codetermined the evolution of the European Community ever since its inception according to the "challenge-response" pattern: the Soviet Union (the hostile external federator), the United States (the benevolent external federator), the European Commission (the official internal federator), the Action Committee for the United States of Europe (the unofficial internal federator), and the negative impact of Gaullism (inhibitor).

The fourth chapter contained an up-to-date performance evaluation (including a detailed matrix) of the Common Market. It concluded that while economic integration (or policy harmonization) has progressed successfully over the last two decades, institutional amalgamation has not yet occurred because no genuine European authority with supranational powers has been created so far.

Chapter 5 first identified four "catalysts of integration" within the various societal sectors: (1) In the political sector, it was the European Parliament, endowed with limited budgetary control and eventually elected by direct, universal suffrage; (2) in the economic sector, it was the expected adoption of a "European company statute" that would permit the establishment of economies of scale in Western Europe and thus facilitate transnational teamwork among industry and labor; (3) in the social sector, it was the growing amount of "social mobility" within the borders of the European Community for workers, students, and professionals, permitting more intensive cross-national communication and leading to greater mutual understanding and rapport; (4) in the cultural sector, it was the ongoing process of "Euro-socialization" which aims at the education of a new generation of genuine Europeans. The major "catalysts of *dis*integration" identified were: global systemic constraints blocking European unification, transcommunal interdependencies with the United States, and the resilience of the nation-state.

The sixth chapter attempted to depict the external relations of the European Community in terms of three concentric circles: the inner circle, composed of its full members (the original Six plus the three newcomers); the intermediate circle, consisting of the various (actual and potential) associates; and the outer circle, made up of a number of nations that are linked to the European Community through some kind of trade agreement. It also analyzes the internal effects and external repercussions of the Community's enlargement from six to nine member states.

Chapter 7 dealt with the conflicting designs for the future political structure of the New Europe, including the proposals for a confederation, for a federation, and for a pragmatic development of the European Community from a common market to a political union, as advocated by political leaders and interest groups.

Chapter 8 focused on the role of the New Europe in the world, especially its relations with the United States. It analyzed the current political-economic issues of interest to the two partners and stressed the need for an institutionalized dialogue between the United States and the European Community.

The ninth chapter contained a summary evaluation of the European Community in perspective: methodological reflections preceded the examination of the European Community as a political system; it was followed by a balanced appraisal of the organization's political potential; and culminated in a critical evaluation of the European Community as a regional entity within the global context of international organization.

The following *conclusions* will project political trends and thus provide an outlook into the future.

Conclusions

This is a study of the European Community in perspective. Given the structural complexity and political dynamism of this mixed system in transition, it stands to reason that no single conclusion would serve the purpose. Instead, an effort will be made to identify the major unifying factors that tend to consolidate the European Community without ignoring the serious constraints placed upon its development by both internal and external forces.

The original motives for the European unity movement and the pro-European attitudes of the people were—in that order, but interrelated—security from an outside attack and internal stability, economic recovery and prosperity, social progress, prestige (Europe as a world power), and the recognition of the obsolescence of the nation-state as a viable entity to assure independence and welfare. The paradox of the situation consisted in the fact that the European nation-states were at once too small to be sovereign and autarkic in an age of *grand ensembles*, and too large and entrenched to be subordinated to a European federal government.

However, the growing interdependence between the nation-states made European unification imperative. Thus the creation of the European Community became an historical necessity. Crisis management was endemic and constant change came to symbolize constructive progress toward regional unity.

At this point in time, the European Community stands at historical cross-roads as three new nations join the original six member states in an effort to make the New Europe a major world power. The means by which this overall objective is to be achieved consist in the consolidation and strengthening of the European Community through the extension of its competences in the economic and monetary fields and the progressive coordination of foreign and defense policies among the member governments.

Although the community of the Six has not achieved all the goals outlined in its "constitution," it has nevertheless already become a prominent part of the global political landscape and the relatively most successful experiment in regional integration. Among its principal achievements are the establishment of a (pluralistic) security community in Western Europe through the pacification of a notoriously conflict-ridden area; the institutionalization of a dialogue between the national governments and the supranational organs of the community through the creation of a diarchy (i.e., a government with two sets of authority); the achievement of an unprecedented level of economic prosperity from which both Europeans (through higher standards of living) and outsiders (through expanded exports to the community) derive tangible material benefits; and finally, the gradual transformation of the attitudes of the people from exclusive allegiance to individual nation-states toward multiple loyalties and identification with regional, supranational goals and organs.

However, despite its enormous successes in the socioeconomic field, the European Community has not yet emerged as a political power in the international system. Thus the "economic giant"—the largest commercial entity in the world—paradoxically remains a "political dwarf" lacking the capacity to act authoritatively on behalf of the New Europe. This dichotomy between economic potential and political power is due to the still prevailing existence of national sovereignties and the lacking will on the part of the governments to renounce their prerogatives in favor of a supranational European organ in charge of diplomacy and security.

If European unity has not yet become a *fait accompli* it has nevertheless emerged as an *idée force* since most enlightened Europeans have come to recognize that the nation-state is no longer capable of coping with the transnational challenges of interdependence in the domains of defense, technology, ecology, trade and monetary affairs. However, notwithstanding their prevailing pro-European attitudes, a sizeable number of people in the community have so far failed to acquire a genuine "European consciousness" that would permit them to shift their allegiance and loyalty from the nation-state to a European federation. In other words, the majority of Frenchmen, Germans, and Italians still consider themselves national citizens first and "Europeans" second. At the same time, they desire that the uniting Europe play a greater role in world politics without realizing that the achievement of this goal would require the creation of a single European authority capable of speaki ng for all West Europeans.

Thus it appears as if the "ideal world" for most Europeans would look as follows: The New Europe should emerge as a world power endowed with common institutions capable of assuring economic prosperity and military security (while leaving the nation-state intact), without alienating the United States (which is needed as the ultimate protector or "security blanket"), or antagonizing the Soviet Union (which holds the key to any final pan-European settlement). Alas, the understandable desire to have the best of all worlds by having the cake and eat it, is based upon a number of irreconcilable assumptions that prevent the implementation of this ideal model. The three fallacies are the following: first, the essential requirement for Europe's capacity to act as a major power is the creation of a common political authority in charge of representing it in international diplomacy; however, this goal cannot be achieved short of a merger of national sovereignties—something that no government has yet consented to since it would ultimately imply its own demise. Second, the United States is reluctant to accept the notion of a Europe that is economically prosperous and competitive but unwilling and unable to effectively assume political and financial coresponsibilities for Western defense and development assistance. Third, the Soviet Union remains opposed to the idea of a united Western Europe since it would be incompatible with the principle of divide and rule which assures *de facto* Soviet hegemony on the European Continent. In short, the dream of a united Europe is still blocked by the vicissitudes of political reality—unless and until there emerges a common will to establish a United States of Europe.

Alternative Contours for the New Europe

In terms of the structural patterns, the New Europe of the 1970s could realistically assume the following three contours.

1. *The United States of Europe.* This optimal solution to the problem of European unification would involve the adoption of a federal constitution providing for a territorial region-state with a federal government in charge of foreign policy and defense, fiscal and monetary affairs, and international trade and finance on the one hand, and a number of regional authorities with residual powers in all other fields. Although an exclusive political system, it would be organized according to the principle "as much decentralization as possible—as much centralization

as necessary" in order to preserve the cultural heritage of its diverse ethnic and national groups.

2. *The Association of European States.* A pluralistic community with multiple centers of decision-making according to functional requirements, this "fragmented Europe" would be the minimal solution. Following the model of "federalism à la carte," this mixed system of overlapping competences and competing authorities would be open-ended and pragmatic, according to the principle of efficiency: the organ most competent for performing a given function at the lowest cost would assume responsibility for it. In this multilateral association of states, policies would be coordinated according to cost-effectiveness criteria without regard to any ideological or architectonic design.

To illustrate this decentralized system of functional decision-making, the following organizational framework for a rational "division of labor" could be sketched:

(a) European Community—economic and monetary affairs of Nine
(b) Western European Union (expanded to nine)—foreign and defense policy and weapons procurement
(c) Council of Europe (caucus of Nine)—social and cultural questions
(d) European Nuclear Energy Agency (EURATOM of Nine)—science and technology
(e) NATO (Eurogroup, in cooperation with Canada and the United States)—Atlantic nuclear strategy, East-West security, MBFR negotiations
(f) OECD (European caucus)—development assistance, and free trade in the Western world
(g) IMF (European caucus)—reform and management of the international monetary system
(h) UN Agency for Environmental Protection (European caucus)—ecology
(i) UN Security Council (European caucus)—international peace and security

While the first two models are within the realm of the possible, the third one is the most probable scenario for Europe in the 1970s:

3. *European Confederation.* This coalition of nation-states would be governed by a European government to which national authorities delegate powers that are subject to withdrawal as soon as a member state feels that its vital interests are jeopardized. Whereas majority voting would be possible as long as all members agree to this procedure, the unanimity rule would prevail in most instances. Conceivably, both voting principles might be applied in two parallel areas: the supranational

formula would be used in the European Community which would be responsible for economic and monetary policies, as well as science, technology, and education; the intergovernmental form of political cooperation would be used in the field of foreign and defense policies (Grosspolitik). In this dual-system, the "first Europe" of Monnet and Hallstein would be complemented by the "second Europe" of Fouchet and Davignon. It would constitute the prototype of a flexible, pragmatic compromise arrangement that would correspond to the prevailing views of the Big Three—France, Britain, and the German Federal Republic. Although untidy and unsatisfactory to the federalist, this model has the advantage (as does the second) to be flexible and not to foreclose future maximalist solutions. In view of the fact that the leaders of the governments in Paris, London, and Bonn presently favor the intergovernmental approach, especially in foreign and defense policies, the confederal model is likely to be the predominant one in the 1970s.

Europe's Role in the World

In the introduction a number of normative questions were raised concerning the desirability of European unity from the objective viewpoint of an outsider. In these conclusions an effort will be made to present some answers to these queries.

A preliminary statement seems to be appropriate with regard to the legal concept and political strategy of "international integration": noncoercive, *de jure* unification is preferable to the alternative form of regional integration—imperialism (a *de facto* merger by superior force). With this value judgment in mind, it has to be added that integration by definition entails discrimination vis-à-vis outsiders, even if the members of the exclusive club have no such intent and leave the door open for new participants who are willing and able to play by the original rules of the game.

The following criteria could be applied to evaluate the actual and potential performance and policy attitudes of the European Community as an actor in the international system:

1. *War and peace.* Intraregionally, the European Community has facilitated the pacification by democratic means of the core area of internecine warfare during modern history. Interregionally, it has been nonprovocative in its policies and peaceful in its actions.
2. *International trade.* Intraregionally, the European Community has managed to increase the trade volume by about 500 percent during the last two decades. Interregionally, it has had a trade-creating (rather than trade-diverting) effect by providing large markets for imports from the rest of the world.

3. *Development assistance.* Although far from having fulfilled the desirable quota of 1 percent of the combined European GNP established by UNCTAD, the European Community has performed on the average slightly better than most other industrialized countries or regions.

4. *Burden-sharing in defense.* Given their limited regional interest in assuring security on the European Continent, most members of the European Community have contributed their fair share to Western defense in the field of conventional weapons.

5. *Attitudes of the people.* Many Europeans, but especially the elites and young cohorts, have developed multiple loyalties which permit them to reconcile allegiance to their nation, to Europe, and to the world, thus demonstrating that patriotism, Europeanism, and internationalism are compatible ideologies.

6. *Orientation toward the United States.* All members of the European Community belong to the Atlantic Alliance (although France is not a formal member of NATO) and to OECD. Neither de Gaulle nor his successors have opted for an open break between France and the United States and all other members of the European Community consider Atlantic solidarity as the maxim of their foreign policy. Nevertheless, there are a large number of Europeans (mostly but not exclusively French) who advocate the establishment of an "independent Europe" which would not necessarily be antagonistic to the United States but pursue its own, possibly neutral, foreign policy vis-à-vis the Communist world and the developing nations. However, it can be anticipated that this plan for a "Europe Third Force" is not likely to materialize as long as Germany, Britain, Italy, and the Benelux countries remain strongly attached to the grand design of an Atlantic partnership with the United States, which is, after all, the most realistic and mutually beneficial option for the nations of the free world.

In sum, the New Europe will be distinct from, but not opposed to, the United States.

The conclusions were reinforced by the Paris Summit Conference of October 1972 (see Appendix D). On that occasion the leaders of the nine members of the enlarged European Community charted the course of the New Europe for the next decade and set 1980 as the target date for the creation of a "European Union" with its own personality and mission in international relations. Aware of its responsibilities toward the Third World, this incipient European confederation is determined to continue a policy of détente with Eastern Europe, and to pursue a constructive dialogue with the United States on all issues of concern to the Western world.

Appendices

Appendix A: Communique of the Meeting of the Heads of State or Government at the Hague on December 1 and 2, 1969

1. On the initiative of the Government of the French Republic and at the invitation of the Netherlands Government, the heads of state or government and the ministers for foreign affairs of the member states of the European Communities met at the Hague on December 1 and 2, 1969. The Commission of the European Communities was invited to participate in the work of the conference on the second day.

2. Now that the Common Market is about to enter upon its final stage, they considered that it was the duty of those who bear the highest political responsibility in each of the member states to draw up a balance sheet of the work already accomplished, to show their determination to continue it, and to define the broad lines for the future.

3. Looking back on the road that has been traversed, and finding that never before have independent states pushed their cooperation further, they were unanimous in their opinion that by reason of the progress made the Community has now arrived at a turning point in its history. Over and above the technical and legal sides of the problems involved, the expiry of the transitional period at the end of the year has therefore acquired major political significance. Entry upon the final stage of the Common Market not only means confirming the irreversible nature of the work accomplished by the Communities, but also means paving the way for a united Europe capable of assuming its responsibilities in the world of tomorrow and of making a contribution commensurate with its traditions and its mission.

4. The heads of state or government therefore wish to reaffirm their belief in the political objectives which give the Community its meaning and purport, their determination to carry their undertaking through to the end, and their confidence in the final success of their efforts. Indeed, they have a common conviction that a Europe composed of states which, in spite of their different national characteristics, are united in their essential interests, assured of its internal cohesion, true to its friendly relations with outside countries, conscious of the role it has to play in promoting the relaxation of international tension and the rapprochement among all peoples, and first and foremost among those of the entire European Continent, is indispensable if a mainspring of development, progress and culture, world equilibrium and peace is to be preserved.

The European Communities remain the original nucleus from which European unity has been developed and intensified. The entry of other countries of this Continent to the Community—in accordance with the provisions of the Treaties of Rome—would undoubtedly help the Communities to grow to dimensions more in conformity with the present state of world economy and technology.

The creation of a special relationship with other European states which have expressed a desire to that effect would also contribute to this end. A development such as this would enable Europe to remain faithful to its traditions of being open to the world and increase its efforts in behalf of developing countries.

5. As regards the completion of the Communities, the heads of state or government reaffirmed the will of their governments to pass from the transitional period to the final stage of the European Community and accordingly to lay down a definitive financial arrangement for the common agricultural policy by the end of 1969.

They agreed progressively to replace, within the framework of this financial arrangement, the contributions of member countries by their own resources, taking into account all the interests concerned, with the object of achieving in due course the integral financing of the Communities' budgets in accordance with the procedure provided for in Article 201 of the Treaty establishing the E.E.C. and of strengthening of the budgetary powers of the European Parliament. The problem of the method of direct elections is still being studied by the Council of Ministers.

6. They asked the governments to continue without delay within the Council the efforts already made to ensure a better control of the market by a policy of agricultural production, making it possible to limit budgetary charges.

7. The acceptance of a financial arrangement for the final stage does not exclude its adaptation by unanimous vote, in particular in the light of an enlarged Community and on condition that the principles of this arrangement are not infringed.

8. They reaffirmed their readiness to further the more rapid progress of the later development needed to strengthen the Community and promote its development into an economic union. They are of the opinion that the integration process should result in a community of stability and growth. To this end, they agreed that within the Council, on the basis of the memorandum presented by the Commission on February 12, 1969, and in close collaboration with the latter, a plan in stages should be worked out during 1970 with a view to the creation of an economic and monetary union. The development of monetary cooperation should depend on the harmonization of economic policies.

They agreed to arrange for the investigation of the possibility of setting up a European reserve fund in which a joint economic and monetary policy would have to result.

9. As regards the technological activity of the Community, they reaffirmed

their readiness to continue more intensively the activities of the Community with a view to coordinating and promoting industrial research and development in the principal sectors concerned, in particular by means of common programs, and to supply the financial means for the purpose.

10. They further agreed on the necessity of making fresh efforts to work out in the near future a research program for the European Atomic Energy Community designed in accordance with the exigencies of modern industrial management, and making it possible to ensure the most effective use of the common research center.

11. They reaffirmed their interest in the establishment of a European university.

12. The heads of state or government acknowledged the desirability of reforming the Social Fund, within the framework of a closely concerted social policy.

13. They reaffirmed their agreement on the principle of the enlargement of the Community, as provided by Article 237 of the Treaty of Rome. Insofar as the applicant states accept the Treaties and their political finality, the decisions taken since the entry into force of the Treaties and the options made in the sphere of development, the heads of state or government have indicated their agreement to the opening of negotiations between the Community on the one hand and the applicant states on the other.

They agreed that the essential preparatory work could be undertaken as soon as practically and conveniently possible, by common consent—the preparations would take place in a most positive spirit.

14. As soon as negotiations with the applicant countries have been opened, discussions will be started with such other EFTA members as may request them on their position in relation to the E.E.C.

15. They agreed to instruct the ministers for foreign affairs to study the best way of achieving progress in the matter of political unification, within the context of enlargement. The ministers would be expected to report before the end of July 1970.

16. All the creative activities and the actions conducive to European growth decided upon here will be assured of a better future if the younger generation is closely associated with them, the governments are resolved to endorse this and the Communities will make provision for it.

Source: European Community Information Service

Appendix B: Resolution of the
Council and of the
Representatives of the
Governments of the Member
States on Economic and
Monetary Union, adopted in
Brussels on February 9, 1971

THE COUNCIL OF THE EUROPEAN COMMUNITIES AND THE REPRE-
SENTATIVES OF THE GOVERNMENTS OF THE MEMBER STATES,

HAVING REGARD to the Final Communique of the Conference of Heads of
State or Government held on December 1 and 2 at The Hague, and in particular
to point 8 which expressed their wish to see the Community develop into an
economic and monetary union through the implementation of a phased plan,

HAVING REGARD to the joint conclusions of the interim report of the
Committee set up by a Council Decision of March 6, 1970 and placed under the
chairmanship of Mr. Pierre WERNER, President and Minister of Finance of the
Luxembourg Government, which were adopted by the Council at its 116th
meeting on June 8-9, 1970,

NAMELY that:

(1) the ultimate objective, as laid down by the Conference of Heads of State or
Government, appears to be attainable within the present decade, provided
that it receives permanent political support from the Governments;

(2) economic and monetary union implies that the main economic policy
decisions will be taken at Community level, and therefore that the necessary
powers will be transferred from the national to Community level. This could
eventually lead to the adoption of a single currency which will guarantee the
irreversibility of the undertaking;

(3) between the point of departure and the point of arrival, action will have to
be taken simultaneously and progressively on a number of fronts. Some of
these measures will necessitate amending the Treaty of Rome, and the
preparatory work for this purpose ought to be successfully concluded right
from the first stage. However, the present provisions already permit substantial progress to be made;

(4) the first stage should begin on January 1, 1971 and be completed within a
specific period; from the technical point of view, a period of three years
appears appropriate. This stage is intended to render Community instruments more and more effective and to mark the beginning of the Community's identity within the international monetary system;

261

(5) the first stage cannot be considered as an aim in itself; it cannot be dissociated from the overall process of economic and monetary integration. It should therefore be embarked upon with the determination to attain the final objective;

(6) this first stage should include a strengthening of consultation procedures, by methods yet to be determined; the budgetary policy of the Member States should be conducted in the light of Community objectives; some degree of fiscal harmonization must be introduced; monetary and credit policies should be closely coordinated and the integration of financial market intensified;

(7) the Community should progressively adopt common standpoints in regard to monetary relations with third countries and international organizations; in particular, it should not in exchange dealings between Member States, avail itself of any provisions that might render the international exchange system more flexible.

HAVING REGARD to the suggestions drawn up by that Committee in its final report and sharing the views expressed on the factors essential for the existence of an economic and monetary union and on the economic policy consequences implied by such a union,

AWARE of the profound political significance of the achievement of the economic and monetary union for the Community and for the Member States which comprise it,

DESIROUS of affirming the irreversible nature of the measures which the Heads of State or Government have decided to undertake with a view to establishing an economic and monetary union,

HAVING REGARD to the draft prepared by the Commission,

HAVING REGARD to the Opinion of the European Parliament,

HAVE ADOPTED THE FOLLOWING RESOLUTION:

I. In order to bring about a satisfactory growth-rate, full employment and stability within the Community, to correct structural and regional imbalances therein and to strengthen the contribution of the latter to international economic and monetary cooperation, thereby achieving a Community of stability and growth, the Council and the Representatives of the Governments of the Member States express their political will to introduce, in the course of the next ten years, an economic and monetary union, in accordance with a phased plan commencing on January 1, 1971.

The measures to be carried out must be such that at the end of this process the Community shall:

1. constitute a zone within which persons, goods, services and capital will move freely and without distortion of competition, without, however, giving rise to structural or regional imbalances, and in conditions which will allow persons exercising economic activity to operate on a Community scale;
2. form an individual monetary unit within the international system, characterized by the total and irreversible convertibility of currencies, the elimination of fluctuation margins of rates of exchange and the irrevocable fixing of parity rates—all of which are indispensable conditions for the creation of a single currency—and including a Community organization of the Central Banks;
3. hold the powers and responsiblities in the economic and monetary field enabling its Institutions to organize the administration of the union. To this end, the required economic policy decisions shall be taken at Community level and the necessary powers shall be given to the Institutions of the Community.

Powers and responsibilities shall be distributed between the Institutions of the Communities, on the one hand, and the Member States, on the other hand, in accordance with the requirements for the cohesion of the union and the efficiency of Community action.

The Institutions of the Community shall be enabled to exercise their responsibilities with regard to economic and monetary matters with efficiency and speed.

The Community policies implemented within the framework of the economic and monetary union shall be subject to discussion and control by the European Parliament.

The Community organization of the Central Banks shall assist, within the context of its own responsibilities, in achieving the objectives of stability and growth in the Community.

The principles laid down above shall be applied to the following subjects:

(1) the internal monetary and credit policy of the union;
(2) monetary policy vis-à-vis the external world;
(3) policy in respect of the unified capital market and movements of capital to and from third countries;

(4) budgetary and fiscal policy as it affects the policy of stability and growth; as regards budgetary policy proper, the margins within which the main items of all the public budgets must be situated shall be determined at Community level, with particular reference to the variation in their sizes, the extent of the balances and the methods of financing and using the latter;

(5) the structural and regional measures called for in the context of a Community policy possessing appropriate means, so that these, too, may contribute to the balanced development of the Community, in particular with a view to solving the most important problems.

II. As progress is made towards the final objective, Community instruments shall be created whenever they appear necessary in order to take over from, or supplement, the operation of national instruments.

In all fields, the measures to be undertaken shall be interdependent and complementary; in particular, the development of monetary unification should be based on parallel progress in harmonizing and subsequently unifying economic policies.

III. In order to achieve these objectives, the Council and the Representatives of the Member States have agreed to initiate, as from January 1, 1971, a number of measures to be carried out in the course of a first phase lasting three years.

1. The Council shall lay down, on a proposal from the Commission, provisions on the reinforcement of the coordination of short-term economic policies in such a way as to make this coordination genuinely effective, in particular by means of intensifying and generalizing cocompulsory prior consultations. This coordination of short-term economic policies shall take into account the guidelines of the medium-term economic policy programs.

    To this end, the Council has agreed to adopt, either on a proposal from the Commission, which will have first consulted both sides of industry within the Economic and Social Committee, or by some other means, the broad outlines of economic policy at Community level and quantitative guidelines for the essential items of the public budgets.

    In order to facilitate the coordination of economic policies, the Council, on a proposal of the Commission and the light of opinions from the Committees concerned, has agreed to take the measures required for progressive harmonization of the instruments of economic policy, and, in particular, to align the timetables of national budgetary procedure.

2. In order to accelerate the effective liberalization of movements of persons, goods, services and capital and the interpenetration of the economies, the Council, on a proposal of the Commission, shall, giving due weight to each, decide on measures concerning:

(i) the Community rules laying down the uniform base for the TVA (tax on the value-added) within the terms of the Council Decisions of April 21, 1970;

(ii) the harmonization of the scope and base of and procedures for levying excise duties, in particular those having an appreciable effect on trade;

(iii) the harmonization of certain types of tax which might have a direct effect on capital movements within the Community, and in particular the harmonization of the tax system applicable to interest on fixed interest transferable securities and on dividends;

(iv) further harmonization of the structure of company taxation;

(v) the progressive extension of tax exemptions granted to private persons on crossing intra-Community frontiers.

Before the end of the first phase, the Council shall examine the studies undertaken and any proposals from the Commission regarding the alignment of TVA and excise duty rates.

3. In order to promote the free movement of capital, the Council, on a proposal of the Commission, shall:

(i) adopt a directive laying down procedures for progressive liberalization which will allow the issue of transferable securities on the financial market without any discrimination, and abolishing any differential treatment as regards placing transferable securities issued by residents of other Member States on the stock market;

(ii) lay down a procedure providing for progressive coordination of the policies of the Member States with regard to financial markets.

4. In order to reduce, by taking action in the regional and structural sphere, any tensions which might jeopardize the timely achievement of economic and monetary union, the Council shall decide, on a proposal of the Commission, on the measures required to provide an initial solution to the most urgent problems, due account being taken of the guidelines laid down by the third medium-term economic policy program, in particular by making available to the Community the appropriate means under the Treaties currently in force.

5. In order to strengthen coordination in the field of the monetary and credit policy, of the Member States, the Council has agreed that:

   (i) compulsory prior consultations shall be intensified within the Monetary Committee and the Committee of Governors of Central Banks;

   (ii) to the extent that their powers and their own responsibilities permit, the Central Banks are invited to coordinate their policies within the Committee of Governors of Central Banks, in conformity with the general economic policy guidelines to be defined by the Council;

   (iii) the Monetary Committee and the Committee of Governors of Central Banks, acting in close collaboration, shall continue to work on the harmonization of the instruments of monetary policy.

6. The Council has agreed that the Community should progressively adopt common standpoints in regard to monetary relations with third countries and international organizations; in particular, it should not, in exchange dealings between Member States, avail itself of any provisions that might render the international exchange system more flexible.

7. The Council and the Member States invite the Central Banks of the Member States, from the beginning of the phase and by way of experiment, to keep fluctuations in the rates between Community currencies within margins narrower than those resulting from the application of the margins in force for the U.S. dollar, by means of concerted action vis-à-vis the dollar.

   The Council has agreed that further measures may be taken as circumstances and the results of the harmonization of economic policies require. Such measures shall consist in the transition from a *de facto* system to a *de jure* system, in interventions in Community currencies and in a repeated narrowing of the fluctuation margins between Community currencies. The Committee of Governors of Central Banks shall report twice a year to the Council and to the Commission on the operation of the concerted action by the Central Banks on the exchange markets and on the advisability of adopting new measures in this sphere.

8. The Council invites the Monetary Committee and the Committee of Governors of Central Banks to draw up, in close collaboration and by June 30, 1972, at the latest, a report on the organization, functions and statute of a European Monetary Cooperation Fund, to be integrated at a later stage into the Community organization of Central Banks provided

for under paragraph I, 2 above, in order to allow the Fund, in the light of the experience gained with respect to the reduction of margins and the convergence of economic policies, possibly to be set up during the first phase. They shall submit this report to the Council and to the Commission.

9. In order to promote the harmonious execution of the plan for economic and monetary union, and above all in order to provide the required parallelism between economic measures and monetary measures, the term of validity of the monetary provisions, i.e., III. 7 and 8, and the term of application of the machinery for medium-term financial aid shall each be of five years as from the beginning of the first phase. The provisions referred to above shall remain in force, once it has been agreed to move on to the second phase.

IV. The Council notes that the Commission is prepared to submit to it before May 1, 1973:

(i) an assessment of the progress made during the first phase, due account being taken of the parallelism which must be observed between the coordination of economic policies and progress in the monetary field within the Community;

(ii) a report drawn up in cooperation with the relevant Consultative Committees on the distribution of powers and responsibilities between the Community Institutions and the Member States as required for the smooth running of an economic and monetary union, particularly in the fields of short-term economic policy, currency and credit policy and budgetary policy.

The Council and, where necessary, the Representatives of the Governments of the Member States shall, on a proposal of the Commission and before the end of the first three-year phase, adopt the measures leading to the complete achievement of economic and monetary union after transition to the second phase: (i) on the basis of the existing provisions of the Treaty; or (ii) on the basis of Article 235; or (iii) on the basis of Article 236 of the Treaty.

Source: European Community Information Service

Appendix C: Report by the Foreign Ministers of the Member States on the Problems of Political Unification (Davignon Report), Adopted in Luxembourg on October 27, 1970

Part One

1. The Foreign Ministers of the Member States of the European Communities were instructed by the Heads of State or Government meeting at The Hague on 1 and 2 December 1969 "to study the best way of achieving progress in the matter of political unification, within the context of enlargement" of the European Communities.

2. In carrying out these instructions, the Ministers have been anxious to remain faithful to the spirit in which the Hague communiqué was written. The Heads of State or Government said in particular in the communiqué that the construction of Europe had reached "a turning point in its history" with entry upon the final stage of the Common Market. They stated that "the European Communities remain the original nucleus from which European unity has been developed and intensified." And they expressed their determination to pave "the way for a united Europe capable of assuming its responsibilities in the world of tomorrow and of making a contribution commensurate with its traditions and its mission."

3. The Heads of State or Government affirmed their "common conviction that a Europe composed of States which, in spite of their different national characteristics, are united in their essential interests, assured of its internal cohesion, true to its friendly relations with outside countries, conscious of the role it has to play in promoting the relaxation of international tension and the *rapprochement* among all peoples, and first and foremost among those of the entire European continent, is indispensable if a mainspring of development, progress and culture, world equilibrium and peace is to be preserved."

4. United Europe, conscious of the responsibilities incumbent on it by reason of its economic development, industrial power and standard of living, intends to step up its endeavours on behalf of the developing countries with a view to setting international relations on a basis of trust.

5. A united Europe should be based on a common heritage of respect for the liberty and rights of man and bring together democratic States with freely

elected parliaments. This united Europe remains the fundamental aim, to be attained as soon as possible, thanks to the political will of the peoples and the decisions of their Governments.

6. The Ministers therefore considered that their proposals should be based on three facts, in order to ensure consistency with the continuity and political purpose of the European design which were emphasized so forcefully by the Hague Conference.

7. The first fact is that, in line with the spirit of the Preambles to the Treaties of Paris and Rome, tangible form should be given to the will for a political union which has always been a force for the progress of the European Communities.

8. The second fact is that implementation of the common policies being introduced or already in force requires corresponding developments in the specifically political sphere, so as to bring nearer the day when Europe can speak with one voice. Hence the importance of Europe being built by successive stages and the gradual development of the method and instruments best calculated to allow a common political course of action.

9. The third and final fact is that Europe must prepare itself to discharge the imperative world duties entailed by its greater cohesion and increasing role.

10. Current developments in the European Communities make it necessary for the Member States to step up their political cooperation and, in the initial stage, to provide themselves with ways and means of harmonizing their views in the field of international politics.

The Ministers therefore felt that foreign policy concertation should be the object of the first practical endeavours to demonstrate to all that Europe has a political vocation. The Ministers are, in fact, convinced that progress here would be calculated to promote the development of the Communities and give Europeans a keener awareness of their common responsibility.

Part Two

The Ministers propose that:

Being concerned to achieve progress towards political unification, the Governments should decide to cooperate in the field of foreign policy.

I. Objectives

This cooperation has two objectives:

(*a*) To insure greater mutual understanding with respect to the major issues of international politics, by exchanging information and consulting regularly;

(*b*) To increase their solidarity by working for a harmonization of views, concertation of attitudes and joint action when it appears feasible and desirable.

II. Ministerial meetings

1. (*a*) The Foreign Ministers will meet at least once every six months, at the initiative of the President-in-office.

(*b*) A conference of Heads of State or Government may be held instead if the Foreign Ministers consider that the situation is serious enough or the subjects to be discussed are sufficiently important to warrant this.

(*c*) In the event of a serious crisis or special urgency, an extraordinary consultation will be arranged between the Governments of the Member States. The President-in-office will get in touch with his colleagues to determine how such consultation can best be arranged.

2. The meetings shall be chaired by the Foreign Minister of the country providing the President of the Council of the European Communities.

3. The ministerial meetings shall be prepared by a committee of the heads of political departments.

III. Political Committee

1. This Committee, comprising the heads of the political departments, will meet at least four times a year to do the groundwork for the ministerial meetings and to carry out any tasks entrusted to it by the Ministers.

In exceptional circumstances the President-in-office may, after consulting his colleagues, convene this Committee at his own initiative or at the request of one of the members.

2. The chairmanship of the Committee will be governed by the rules laid down for the ministerial meetings.

3. The Committee may set up working parties for special tasks.

It may instruct a panel of experts to assemble data relating to a specific problem and to submit the possible solution.

4. Any other form of consultation may be envisaged if the need arises.

IV. Matters within the scope of the consultations

The Governments will consult each other on all major questions of foreign policy.

The Member States will be free to propose any subjects they wish for political consultation.

V. Commission of the European Communities

The Commission will be consulted if the activities of the European Communities are affected by the work of the Ministers.

VI. European Parliament

Public opinion and its spokesmen must be associated with the construction of the political union, so as to ensure that it is a democratic process.

The Ministers and the members of the Political Affairs Committee of the European Parliament will hold six-monthly meetings to discuss questions which are the subject of consultations in the framework of foreign policy cooperation. These meetings will be informal, to ensure that the parliamentarians and Ministers can express their views freely.

VII. General

1. The meetings will normally be held in the country of their chairman.

2. The host State will take all due steps to provide a secretarial service and for the practical organization of the meetings.

3. Each State will appoint one of its foreign affairs officials as the correspondent of his counterparts in the other countries.

Part Three

1. To ensure continuity in the task embarked on, the Ministers propose to pursue their work on the best way to achieve progress towards political unification and intend to submit a second report.

2. The work in question will also cover improvement of foreign policy cooperation and a search for new fields in which progress can be made. It will have to allow for any studies undertaken in the context of the European Communities, more particularly with a view to strengthening structures so as to ensure that they can, if necessary, cope satisfactorily with the extension and growth of their tasks.

3. To this end, the Ministers shall instruct the Political Committee to arrange its work in such a way that it can discharge this task and to report back at each of their half-yearly meetings.

4. Once a year, the President-in-office of the Council will provide the European Parliament with a progress report on the work in question.

5. Without prejudice to any interim report they may deem it opportune to submit, if the studies have progressed far enough, the Foreign Ministers will submit their second general report two years at the latest after the introduction of consultation on foreign policy. This report is to include an assessment of the results of the consultation in question.

Part Four

Proposals on associating the applicant countries with the work specified in Parts II and III of this report.

1. The Ministers stress the correlation between membership of the European Communities and participation in activities making for progress towards political unification.

2. The applicant States must be kept informed of the progress of the work of the Six, since they will have to be consulted on the objectives and machinery described in the present report and will have to adhere to them when they join the Communities.

3. Bearing in mind the various objectives, the following procedures are proposed for keeping the applicant States informed.

(a) Ministerial meetings

At each of their half-yearly meetings, the Ministers will fix the date of their next meeting.

Concurrently, they will decide on a date to be proposed for a ministerial meeting of the Ten, which should be held as near as possible to and normally after the meeting of the Six, with due allowance for the opportunities which some or all of the ten Ministers have already had to meet each other.

After the ministerial meeting of the Six, the President-in-office will inform the applicant countries of the items which the Ministers propose to put on the agenda of the ministerial meeting of the Ten and provide any other information calculated to make the discussion of the Ten as fruitful as possible.

As there will have to be some flexibility in this provision of information and these discussions, it is understood that they will become more detailed when the agreements by which the applicant countries accede to the European Communities have been signed.

(b) Meetings of the Political Committee

This Committee will provide the applicant countries with information which may be of interest to them. The information in question will be transmitted by the President-in-office, who will ascertain the reactions if any of the applicant countries, and notify them to the Political Committee.

Source: European Community Information Service

Appendix D: Communique of the Summit Conference of the Heads of State of the New Europe in Paris, October 19–20, 1972 and Excerpt from the Opening Address by President Pompidou

The heads of state or of government of the countries of the enlarged Community, meeting for the first time on October 19 and 20 in Paris, at the invitation of the President of the French Republic, solemnly declare:

— At the moment when enlargement, decided in accordance with the rules in the Treaties and with respect for what the six original member states have already achieved, is to become a reality and give a new dimension to the Community,
— At a time when world events are profoundly changing the international situation,
— Now that there is a general desire for détente and cooperation in response to the interest and wishes of all peoples,
— Now that serious monetary and trade problems require a search for lasting solutions that will favor growth with stability,
— Now that many developing countries see the gap widening between themselves and the industrial nations and claim with justification an increase in aid and a fairer use of wealth,
— Now that the tasks of the Community are growing, and fresh responsibilities are being laid upon it, the time has come for Europe to recognize clearly the unity of its interests, the extent of its capacities, and the magnitude of its duties, Europe must be able to make its voice heard in world affairs and to make an original contribution commensurate with its human, intellectual, and material resources. It must affirm its own views in international relations, as befits its mission to be open to the world and for progress, peace, and cooperation.

To this end:

I. The member states reaffirm their determination to base the development of their Community on democracy, freedom of opinion, the free movement of people and of ideas, and participation by their peoples through their freely elected representatives.
II. The member states are determined to strengthen the Community by establishing an economic and monetary union, the guarantee of stability

and growth, the foundation of their solidarity and the indispensible basis for social progress, and by ending disparities between the regions.

III. Economic expansion is not an end in itself. Its first aim should be to enable disparities in living conditions to be reduced. It must take place with the participation of all the social partners. It should result in an improvement in the quality of life as well as the standards of living. As befits the genius of Europe, particular attention will be given to intangible values and to protecting the environment, so that progress may really be put at the service of mankind.

IV. The Community is well aware of the problem presented by continuing underdevelopment in the world. It affirms its determination within the framework of a worldwide policy towards the developing countries, to increase its effort in aid and technical assistance to the least favored people. It will take particular account of the concerns of those countries towards which, through geography, history, and the commitments entered into by the Community, it has specific responsibilities.

V. The Community reaffirms its determination to encourage the development of international trade. This determination applies to all countries without exception.

The Community is ready to participate, as soon as possible, in the open-minded spirit that it has already shown, and according to the procedures laid down by the International Monetary Fund (IMF) and the General Agreement on Tariffs and Trade (GATT) in negotiations based on the principle of reciprocity. These should make it possible to establish, in the monetary and commercial fields, stable and balanced economic relations, in which the interests of the developing countries must be taken fully into account.

VI. The member states of the Community, in the interests of good neighborly relations which should exist among all European countries whatever their regime, affirm their determination to pursue their policy of detente and of peace with the countries of Eastern Europe, notably on the occasion of the Conference on Security and Cooperation in Europe, and the establishment on a sound basis of a wider economic and human cooperation.

VII. The construction of Europe will allow it, in conformity with its ultimate political objectives, to affirm its personality while remaining faithful to traditional friendships and to the alliances of the member states, and to establish its position in world affairs as a distinct entity determined to promote a better international equilibrium, respecting the principles of the charter of the United Nations. The member states of the Community, the driving force of European construction, affirm their intention to transform before the end of the present decade the whole complex of their relations into a European union.

Economic and Monetary Questions

1. The heads of state or of government reaffirm the determination of the member states of the enlarged European Communities irreversibly to achieve the economic and monetary union, confirming all the elements of the instruments adopted by the Council and by the representatives of member states on March 22, 1971, and March 21, 1972.

   The necessary decisions should be taken in the course of 1973 so as to allow the transition to the second stage of the economic and monetary union on January 1, 1974, and with a view to its completion not later than December 31, 1980.

   The heads of state or government reaffirmed the principle of parallel progress in the different fields of the economic and monetary union.

2. They declared that fixed but adjustable parities between their currencies constitute an essential basis for the achievement of the union and expressed their determination to set up within the Community mechanisms for defense and mutual support which would enable member states to ensure that they are respected.

   They decided to institute before April 1, 1973, by solemn instrument, based on the EEC Treaty, a European Monetary Cooperation Fund which will be administered by the Committee of Governors of Central Banks within the content of general guidelines on economic policy laid down by the Council of Ministers.

   In an initial phase the Fund will operate on the following bases:

— concerted action among the Central Banks for the purposes of narrowing the margins of fluctuation between their currencies
— the multilateralization of positions resulting from interventions in Community currencies and the multilateralization of intra-Community settlements
— the use for this purpose of a European monetary unit of account
— the administration of short-term monetary support among the Central Banks
— the very short-term financing of the agreement on the narrowing of margins and short-term monetary support will be regrouped in the Fund under renovated mechanism. To this end, short-term support will be adjusted on the technical plane without modifying the consultation procedures they involve.

The competent bodies of the Community shall submit reports:

— not later than September 30, on the adjustment of short-term support,
— not later than December 31, 1973, on the conditions for the progressive pooling of reserves.

3. The heads of state or of government stressed the need to coordinate more closely the economic policies of the Community and for this purpose to introduce more effective Community procedures.

Under existing economic conditions they consider that priority should be given to the fight against inflation and to a return to price stability. They instructed their competent ministers to adopt, on the occasion of the enlarged Council of October 30 and 31, 1972, precise measures in the various fields which lend themselves to effective and realistic short-term action toward these objectives and which take account of the respective situations of the countries of the enlarged Community.

4. The heads of state or of government express their determination that the member states of the enlarged Community should contribute by a common attitude to directing the reform of the international monetary system towards the introduction of an equitable and durable order.

They consider that this system should be based on the following principles:

— fixed but adjustable parities
— the general convertibility of currencies
— effective international regulation of the world supply of liquidities
— a reduction in the role of national currencies as reserve instruments
— the effective and equitable functioning of the adjustment process
— equal rights and duties for all participants in the system
— the need to lessen the unstabilizing effects of short-term capital movements,
— the taking into account of the interests of the developing countries.

Such a system would be fully compatible with the achievement of the economic and monetary union.

Regional Policy

The heads of state or of government agreed that a high priority should be given to the aim of correcting, in the Community, the structural and regional imbalances which might affect the realization of economic and monetary union.

The heads of state or of government invite the Commission to prepare without delay, a report analyzing the regional problems which arise in the enlarged Community and to put forward appropriated proposals.

From now on they undertake to coordinate their regional policies. Desirous of directing that effort towards finding a Community solution to regional problems, they invite the Community institutions to create a Regional Development Fund. This will be set up before December 31, 1973, and will be financed, from the beginning of the second phase of economic and monetary union, from the Community's own resources. Intervention by the Fund in coordination with national aids should permit, progressively with the realization of economic and monetary union, the correction of the main regional imbalances in the enlarged Community and particularly those resulting from the preponderance of agriculture and from industrial change and structural unemployment.

Social Policy

6. The heads of state or heads of government emphasized that they attached as much importance to vigorous action in the social field as to the achievement of the economic and monetary union. They thought it essential to ensure the increasing involvement of labor and management in the economic and social decisions of the Community. They invited the institutions, after consulting labor and management, to draw up, between now and January 1, 1974, a program of action providing for concrete measures and the corresponding resources particularly in the framework of the Social Fund, based on the suggestions made in the course of the conference by heads of state and heads of government and by the Commission.

   This program should aim, in particular, at carrying out a coordinated policy for employment and vocational training, at improving working conditions and conditions of life, at closely involving workers in the progress of firms, at facilitating on the basis of the situation in the different countries the conclusion of collective agreements at European level in appropriate fields, and at strengthening and coordinating measures of consumer protection.

Industrial, Scientific and Technological Policy

7. The heads of state or of government consider it necessary to seek to establish a single industrial base for the Community as a whole.

   This involves the elimination of technical barriers to trade as well as the elimination, particularly in the fiscal and legal fields, or barriers which hinder closer relations and mergers between firms, the rapid adoption of a European company statute, the progressive and effective opening up of public sector purchases, the promotion on a European scale of competitive firms in the field of high technology, the transformation and conversion of declining industries, under acceptable social conditions, the formulation of measures to ensure that mergers affecting firms established in the Community are in harmony with the economic and social aims of the Community, and the maintenance of fair competition as much within the Common Market as in external markets in conformity with the rules laid down by the Treaties.

Objectives will need to be defined and the development of a common policy in the field of science and technology ensured. This policy will require the coordination, within the institutions of the Community, of national policies and joint implementation of projects of interest to the Community.

To this end, a program of action together with a precise timetable and appropriate measures should be decided by the Community's institutions, before January 1, 1974.

Environment Policy

8. The heads of state or of government emphasized the importance of a Community environmental policy. To this end they invited the Community institutions to establish, before July 31, 1973, a program of action accompanied by a precise timetable.

Energy Policy

9. The heads of state and heads of government deem it necessary to invite the Community institutions to formulate as soon as possible an energy policy guaranteeing certain and lasting supplies under satisfactory economic conditions.

External Relations

10. The heads of state or of government affirm that their efforts to construct their Community attain their full meaning only in so far as member states succeed in acting together to cope with the growing world responsibilities incumbent on Europe.
11. The heads of state or of government are convinced that the Community must, without detracting from the advantages enjoyed by countries with which it has special relations, respond even more than in the past to the expectations of all the developing countries.

    With this in view, it attaches essential importance to the policy of association as confirmed in the Treaty of Accession and to the fulfillment of its commitments to the countries of the Mediterranean Basin with which agreements have been or will be concluded, agreements which should be the subject of an overall and balanced approach.

    In the same perspective, in the light of the results of the United Nations Conference on Trade and Development (UNCTAD) and in the context of the development strategy adopted by the United Nations, the institutions of the Community and member states are invited progressively to adopt an overall policy of development cooperation on a worldwide scale, comprising, in particular, the following elements:

- the promotion in appropriate cases of agreements concerning the primary products of the developing countries with a view to arriving at market stabilization and an increase in their exports
- the improvement of generalized preferences with the aim of achieving a steady increase in imports of manufactures from the developing countries.

In this connection the Community institutions will study from the beginning of 1973 the conditions which will permit

- the achievement of a substantial growth target
- an increase in the volume of official financial aid
- an improvement in the financial conditions of this aid, particularly in favor of the least developed countries, bearing in mind the recommendations of the Organization for Economic Cooperation and Development (OECD) Development Assistance Committee.

These questions will be the subject of studies and decisions in good time during 1973.

12. With regard to the industrial countries, the Community is determined, in order to ensure the harmonious development of world trade:

- to contribute, while respecting what has been achieved by the Community, to a progressive liberalization of international trade by measures based on reciprocity and relating to both tariffs and non-tariff barriers
- to maintain a constructive dialogue with the United States, Japan, Canada, and its other industrialized trade partners in a forthcoming spirit, using the most appropriate methods.

In this context the Community attaches major importance to the multilateral negotiations in the context of GATT, in which it will participate in accordance with its earlier statement. To this end, the Community institutions are invited to decide not later than July 1, 1973, on a global approach covering all aspects affecting trade.

The Community hopes that an effort on the part of all partners will allow these negotiations to be completed in 1975.

It confirms its desire for the full participation of the developing countries in the preparation and progress of these negotiations which should take due account of the interests of those countries.

Furthermore, having regard to the agreements concluded with the European Free Trade Association (EFTA) countries which are not members, the Community declared its readiness to seek with Norway a speedy solution to the trade problems facing that country in its relations with the enlarged Community.

13. In order to promote detente in Europe, the conference reaffirmed its determination to follow a common commercial policy towards the countries of Eastern Europe with effect from January 1, 1973; member states declared

their determination to promote a policy of cooperation, founded on reciprocity, with these countries.

This policy of cooperation is, at the present stage, closely linked with the preparation and progress of the Conference on Security and Cooperation in Europe to which the enlarged Community and its member states are called upon to make a concerted and constructive contribution.

14. The heads of state or of government agreed that political cooperation between the member states of the Community on foreign policy matters had begun well and should be still further improved. They agreed that consultations should be intensified at all levels and that the foreign ministers should in future meet four times a year instead of twice for this purpose. They considered that the aim of their cooperation was to deal with problems of current interest and, where possible, to formulate common medium and long-term positions, keeping in mind, inter alia, the international political implications for and effects of Community policies under construction. On matters which have a direct bearing on Community activities, close contract will be maintained with the institutions of the Community. They agreed that the foreign ministers should produce, not later than June 30, 1973, a second report on methods of improving political cooperation in accordance with the Luxembourg Report.

Reinforcement of Institutions

15. The heads of state or government recognized that the structures of the Community had proved themselves, although they felt that the decision-making procedures and the functioning of the institutions should be improved, in order to make them more effective.

The Community institutions and where appropriate, the representatives of the governments of member states are invited to decide before the end of the first stage in the achievement of the economic and monetary union, on the basis of the report which the Commission, pursuant to the resolution of March 22, 1971, is to submit before May 1, 1973, on the measures relating to the distribution of competences and responsibilities among the Community institutions and member states which are necessary to the proper functioning of an economic and monetary union.

They felt it desirable that the date on which meetings of national cabinets were normally held should be the same so that the Council of the Communities could organize itself with a more regular timetable.

Desiring to strengthen the powers of control of the European Parliamentary Assembly, independently of the date on which it will be elected by universal suffrage under Article 138 of the Treaty of Rome, and to make their contribution towards improving its working conditions, the heads of state or government, while confirming the decision of April 22, 1970, of the

Council of the Communities, invited the Council and the Commission to put into effect without delay the practical measures designed to achieve this reinforcement and to improve the relations both of the Council and of the Commission with the Assembly.

The Council will, before June 30, 1973, take practical steps to improve its decision-making procedures and the cohesion of Community action.

They invited the Community institutions to recognize the right of the Economic and Social Committee in future to advise on its own initiative on all questions affecting the Community.

They were agreed in thinking that, for the purpose in particular of carrying out the tasks laid down in the different programs of action, it was desirable to make the widest possible use of all the dispositions of the Treaties, including Article 235 of the EEC Treaty.

European Union

16. The heads of state or government, having set themselves the major objective of transforming, before the end of the present decade and with the fullest respect for the Treaties already signed, the whole complex of the relations of member states into a European union, request the institutions of the Community to draw up a report on the subject before the end of 1975 for submission to a Summit conference.

Source: European Community Information Service

Excerpt from the opening address by President Georges Pompidou at the European Summit Conference of Paris on October 19, 1972:

"Our (European) links with this great country (the United States), the world's foremost economic power, with which eight of our countries are united within the Atlantic Alliance, are so close that it would be absurd to conceive of a Europe constructed in opposition to it. But the very closeness of these links requires that Europe affirm its individual personality with regard to the United States. Western Europe . . . must not and cannot sever its links with the United States."

Source: *The Washington Post*, October 20, 1972.

Appendix E: Chronology of
European Affairs (1946-1975)

1946

19 September   Speech by Sir Winston Churchill proposing the creation of the "United States of Europe" in Zurich, Switzerland.

1947

4 March   Signing of the Treaty of Alliance and Mutual Assistance between France and Britain at Dunkirk.

5 June   Speech at Harvard University by General George C. Marshall, United States Secretary of State, proposing the European Recovery Program.

29 October   Formation of the Benelux Economic Union.

1948

17 March   Signing of the treaty of military assistance between France, the United Kingdom, Belgium, the Netherlands, and Luxembourg in Brussels.

16 April   Signing of the OEEC Convention in Paris.

7-10 May   Meeting of the European Congress at The Hague.

1949

4 April   Signing of the North Atlantic Treaty in Washington.

5 May   Signing of the Statute of the Council of Europe.

1950

9 May   Statement by Mr. Robert Schuman, French Minister for Foreign Affairs, proposing to place Franco-German coal and steel production under a joint authority.

1951

18 April   *Signing of the Treaty instituting the ECSC in Paris.

1952

27 May   Signing of the EDC Treaty by the representatives of the Six in Paris.

23 July   Entry into force of the ECSC Treaty with Jean Monnet as President of the High Authority.

NOTE: The asterisk (*) denotes internal developments of the European Community.
     Projections are based on the Final Communiqué of the Paris Summit Meeting of 1972.

1953
6-11 March   The *Ad hoc* Assembly adopts the plan for a European Political Community.

1954
30 August   The French National Assembly rejects the EDC Treaty.
23 October   Signing of the treaty establishing the Western European Union in Paris.

1955
1-3 June   Messina Conference of the Six.

1956
18 January   Creation of the Action Committee for the United States of Europe under the presidency of Jean Monnet.

1957
25 March   *Signing of the Rome Treaties setting up the European Economic Community and Euratom.

1958
1 January   *Entry into force of the Treaties of Rome.
3 February   Benelux Treaty of Economic Union signed in The Hague.

1959
1 January   *First Tariff reductions in EEC.
14 May   The ECSC Council rejects the High Authority's plan to deal with the coal crisis.

1960
4 January   Signing of the Stockholm Convention instituting EFTA.
12 May   *EEC accelerates the timetable for implementing the Common Market.
14 December   OEEC becomes OECD.

1961
9 July   Greece and EEC sign association agreement with EEC.
18 July   "Bonn Declaration" of the Six aiming at political union.
1 August   Ireland applies for membership in EEC.
10 August   Britain and Denmark request negotiations for EEC membership.
18 November   Negotiations on British entry into EEC open in Brussels.
15 December   Austria, Sweden, and Switzerland apply for association with EEC.

1962

14 January	*EEC decides on basic principles for a common agricultural policy (CAP).
18 January	Second Fouchet Plan and "Draft Treaty for a European Union."
9 February	Spain applies for association with EEC.
17 April	Interruption of the negotiations on Political Union.
30 April	Norway applies for EEC membership.
15 May	*Second acceleration decision to speed up the timetable of EEC.
4 July	President Kennedy proposes an "Atlantic partnership."
16 July	Conclusion of 1960-62 negotiations for worldwide tariff cuts in GATT; Community substantially reduces common external tariff.
30 July	First regulations under the CAP of EEC take effect.

1963

14 January	Press Conference by President de Gaulle: France opposes British accession to the EEC.
22 January	Signing of the Franco-German Treaty in Paris.
29 January	The negotiations for British accession to the European Economic Community are broken off.
20 July	Signing of Yaoundé Convention between EEC and eighteen African States.
12 September	Turkey and EEC sign association agreement.

1964

| 4 May | Opening of the GATT negotiations (Kennedy Round) in Geneva. |

1965

31 March	*EEC Commission proposes a common budget and increased powers of the European Parliament.
8 April	*Signing of the treaty merging the three "executives" of the European Communities.
30 June	*Meeting of the EEC Council of Ministers on agricultural questions end in complete discord and results in a "constitutional" crisis; France boycotts the EEC meetings.
1 July	*EEC Council fails to meet the deadline on financing the CAP.

1966

| 17 January | *Meeting of the Six in Luxembourg; France ends boycott and normal operations resume. |

29 January	*Meeting of the Six in Luxembourg, resulting in an "agreement to disagree" on Rome Treaty rules regarding majority voting. ("Luxembourg Protocol").
10 March	France withdraws from NATO.
11 May	*EEC Council agrees to complete the customs union by July 1, 1968–18 months ahead of schedule.
24 July	*Common prices for beef, milk, sugar, rice, oilseeds, and olive oil agreed by Council, enabling free trade in agricultural products by July 1, 1968.

1967

8 February	*Adoption of first "medium term economic program" by EEC.
10 May	*Britain, Ireland, and Denmark submit applications for EEC membership.
15 May	Kennedy Round negotiations end in agreement to make major cuts in industrial tariffs.
30 May	Summit meeting of the Six in Rome.
1 July	*The "Merger Treaty" of April 1965 becomes effective, creating a single council and single commission (headed by Jean Rey).
13 November	British Prime Minister Wilson proposes a European Technological Community.
27 November	President de Gaulle vetoes British entry into EEC for the second time.
19 December	Council reaches deadlock on UK and other membership applications.

1968

20 January	Dr. Walter Hallstein, former President of the EEC Commission, is elected President of the European Movement in Rome.
1 July	*Customs Union of the Six becomes effective; creation of a common external tariff.
18-19 July	*Six adopt basic regulations for common transport policy.
20 July	*Community applies article 108 (mutual aid) of the Rome Treaty for the first time. The community authorizes France to impose some quotas to overcome her balance-of-payments difficulties.
26 July	Signature of an association agreement between the EEC Tranzania, Uganda, and Kenya at Arusha.
29 July	*EEC Council decides on the free movement of workers in the Community.
9 December	*Six adopt common foreign-trade policy for large section of community's imports.

10 December   *Launching of "Agriculture 1980"—a ten-year reform plan.

1969

12 February   *Commission submits memorandum to the council on economic and monetary cooperation in EEC.

25 March   Association agreement between EEC and Tunisia and Morocco approved by council.

23 April   Creation of the European Trade Union Confederation in The Hague.

28 April   President de Gaulle resigns.

4 May   *Commission renews its proposal for a community budget and control by European Parliament.

12 May   *"Work Program" for the community adopted by the council.

16 July   *Commission proposes that community activities be financed from its own resources by 1974, and that the Six increase the European Parliament's budgetary powers.

17 July   *Six agree to the principle of a short-term mutual-aid system and decide to hold prior consultations on proposed major short-term economic policy measures.

29 July   Renewal of the Yaoundé Convention.

1 September   Community's partial association agreements with Morocco and Tunisia become effective.

24 September   Kenya, Uganda and Tanzania renew association agreements with EEC.

2 October   *Commission transmits its revised opinion on the enlargement of the community to the council.

21 October   Willy Brandt becomes German Chancellor.

1-2 December   *Summit Meeting of the Six heads of state of government at The Hague.

22 December   *Council agrees on the principle of providing the community with its own resources.

31 December   *Completion of transitional twelve-year period by the EEC; beginning of "final stage."

1970

7 February   *EEC Council agrees on final regulation for the financing of the CAP, on giving the community its own resources, and on the budgetary powers of the European Parliament.

9 February   *Community central banks activate $2 billion short-term mutual-aid system.

22 April   *The Six sign a treaty in Luxembourg to strengthen the powers of the European Parliament and ensure the financial autonomy of the community.

11 May   *The council of the six foreign ministers agrees that negoti-

ations with the four applicant countries should start on June 30; it also reduces the membership of the commission from fourteen to nine (according to the Merger Treaty of 1965).

28 May	Portugal applies for an association with the EEC.
9 June	*Six set 1980 as target-date for monetary and economic union.
29 June	Signature of preferential trade agreement between the European Community, Israel, and Spain.
30 June	Formal negotiations between the council and the four applicant countries on accession to the EEC begin in Luxembourg.
1 July	Commission reduced from fourteen to nine members; Franco-Maria Malfatti succeeds Jean Rey as president.
27 July	*Six agree to give European Social Fund more powers to retrain and resettle workers.
31 July	*Foreign Ministers of the Six submit "Davignon Report" to heads of government advocating twice-yearly ministerial meetings on political cooperation.
27 October	*Formal adoption of the "Davignon Report" by the six foreign ministers in Luxembourg.
19 November	*The six foreign ministers hold their first regular meeting on political cooperation in Munich.
2 December	First meeting between the six foreign ministers and the four applicant countries in Brussels.
5 December	Association agreement between the EEC and Malta is signed.
17 December	*The council adopts a resolution on the reorganization of the Joint Nuclear Research Center.

1971

1 January	Second Yaoundé and Arusha Conventions come into force.
	*Community's "own-revenue" system comes into operation.
21 January	President Pompidou proposes a European Confederation at a news conference in Paris.
28 January	Chancellor Brandt, in his "Report on the State of the Nation," confirms Germany's commitment to European and Atlantic cooperation.
9 February	*The EEC Council agrees to proceed with plans for achieving economic and monetary union before 1980.
25 March	*The council adopts new guidelines for agricultural prices and structural reform.
23 June	*EEC Council agrees on the admission of Britain, Ireland, Denmark, and Norway to the Common Market.
1 July	The European Community grants generalized tariff preferences to ninety-one developing nations belonging to the "Group of 77" within UNCTAD.

7 July	The British government publishes a white paper and accepts the terms of entry into the Common Market as "just and reasonable."
15 August	President Nixon announces the "New Economic Policy."
20 October	The European Community establishes a "permanent delegation" to the United States in Washington, D.C., headed by Signor A.M. Mazio.
22 October	First round of regular talks between the United States and the European Commission (the so-called Dahrendorf-Samuels talks on economic affairs).
28 October	The British House of Commons approves in principle the terms for entry into the European Community.
5 November	Third meeting between the six foreign ministers (Davignon Committee) in Rome to discuss political cooperation and the European security conference.
18 December	The finance ministers of the Big Ten arrive at a "grand accord" on the realignment of free-world currencies, including the devaluation of the US dollar.
21 December	President Nixon announces the abolition of the 10 percent surtax imposed on foreign goods since August 15.

1972

1 January	EEC implements the last tariff cut agreed upon in the Kennedy Round.
22 January	*The Six and Britain, Denmark, Ireland, and Norway sign the Treaty of Accession to the European Community.
3 February	Successful conclusion of an interim trade agreement between the United States and the European Community.
17 February	The British Parliament approved legislation enabling the United Kingdom to join the European Community.
3 March	Franco-Maria Malfatti resigns as commission president.
18 March	Meeting between President Pompidou and Prime Minister Heath in the United Kingdom.
21 March	Sicco L. Mansholt becomes president of the commission.
21 March	*The Council of Ministers approves the narrowing of fluctuation margins between member currencies and closer coordination of economic policies.
3 April	President Nixon signs legislation to devalue the dollar by raising the price of gold to $38 an ounce.
13 April	Carlo Scarascia-Mugnozza becomes commissioner in charge of agriculture.
20 April	Meeting between Chancellor Brandt and Prime Minister Heath in London.
23 April	A majority of Frenchmen approves the enlargement of the European Community in a referendum.

27 April	Second round of "Dahrendorf-Samuels" talks in Brussels.
26 May	The ten foreign ministers (Davignon Committee) meet in Luxembourg to prepare the agenda for the next Summit Conference.
5 June	Chancellor Willy Brandt commemorates the twenty-fifth anniversary of the Marshall Plan in a speech at Harvard University and announces the establishment of a $45 million "German Marshall Fund of the United States."
19 July	The ten foreign ministers meet in Brussels to prepare the summit.
22 July	Agreement on the creation in 1973 of a free trade area between the European Community and the REFTA countries.
26 September	In a referendum Norway rejects Common Market membership.
3 October	In a referendum Denmark votes for entry into the EC.
30 October	Summit Conference of the nine members of the EC in Paris.

1973

1 January	The enlargement of the European Community to nine members, and the free trade accord with the REFTA countries become effective. The Community adopts a common commercial policy toward Eastern Europe.
February	Tentative date for the European Security Conference and for negotiations on mutual, balanced force reductions between NATO and the Warsaw Pact.
1 April	Creation of the "European Monetary Cooperation Fund." First tariff reductions between the EC and REFTA.
1 May	Commission reports on Stage II of the Economic and Monetary Union and on the strengthening of institutions.
30 June	The nine foreign ministers report on political cooperation.
31 July	Adoption of a common approach of the EC in GATT.
October	Negotiations on reform of the international monetary system.
31 December	Creation of the "Regional Development Fund." Completion of the study on harmonizing EC policies toward developing nations.

1974

1 January	Transition to Stage II of the Economic-Monetary Union.
31 December	Development of a common industrial and social policy.

1975

December	Report by the EC institutions to the next Summit Conference on measures to arrive at a "European Union" by 1980.

Notes

Notes:

Notes

Foreword

1. Gordon, Kermit, ed. AGENDA FOR THE NATION (Washington, D.C.: Brookings Institution, 1969), p. 599.
2. US FOREIGN POLICY 1969-1970: A REPORT OF THE SECRETARY OF STATE (Washington, D.C.: GPO, 1971), p. 9.
3. FACTS ABOUT NATO (Paris: NATO Information Service, 1962), p. 260.

Introduction

1. Morton A. Kaplan and Nicholas de B. Katzenbach. THE POLITICAL FOUNDATIONS OF INTERNATIONAL LAW (New York: Wiley, 1961), p. vi.
2. John W. Sloan and Harry R. Targ, "Beyond the European Nation-State," POLITY 3, no. 4 (Summer 1971): 520.
3. It is conceivable that the foremost American students of integration (Deutsch, Haas, and Friedrich) who were born in war-torn Europe were naturally predisposed to regarding the European integration movement as a possible remedy to interstate conflicts—a constructive bias that is shared by most European students of the subject. This author also believes in the virtues of regional integration as a means of pacification.

Chapter 1
Universalism, Regionalism, and Transnationalism:
Actors and Forces in the International System

1. Inis L. Claude, EUROPEAN ORGANIZATION IN THE GLOBAL CONTEXT (Brussels) Université Libre de Bruxelles, Institut d'Etudes Européennes, (1965), p. 24.
2. The phrase was coined by the late Hans Kohn.
3. PAIX ET GUERRE (Paris: Calmann-Levy, 1962), p. 300.
4. David Mitrany, "The Functional Approach in Historical Perspective," INTERNATIONAL AFFAIRS 42, no. 3 (London, July 1971): 543.
5. Stanley Hoffmann, "International Organizations and the International System," INTERNATIONAL ORGANIZATION 24, no. 3 (Summer 1970): 404.
6. —————, "Obstinate or Obsolete? The Fate of the Nation-State and the Case of Western Europe," in Joseph S. Nye, ed, INTERNATIONAL REGIONALISM (Boston: Little, Brown & Co., 1968), p. 178.

7. Edward H. Carr. THE TWENTY YEARS' CRISIS: 1919-1939 (New York: Harper & Row, 1964), p. viii.

8. See John H. Herz. "The Rise and Demise of the Territorial State," WORLD POLITICS 9, no. 4 (July 1957): 473-93 and "The Territorial State Revisited: Reflections on the Future of the Nation-State," POLITY 1, no. 1 (1968): 12-34.

9. Daniel Lerner and Morton Gorden. EURATLANTICA: CHANGING PERSPECTIVES OF THE EUROPEAN ELITES (Cambridge, Mass.: M.I.T. Press, 1969), p. 197.

10. Ibid., pp. 256 and 98.

11. Amitai Etzioni, "The Dialectics of Supranational Unification," AMERICAN POLITICAL SCIENCE REVIEW 56, no. 4 (December 1962): 147.

12. Karl W. Deutsch. NATIONALISM AND ITS ALTERNATIVES (New York: Knopf, 1969), p. 171. He jokingly refers to a nation as "a group of persons united by a common error about their ancestry and a common dislike of their neighbors" (p. 3). He also notes that nation-states are paradoxies since they administer a broadening scope of services but "cannot defend the lives of their people." (p. 172). For an authoritative treatment of nationalism see Hans Kohn. THE IDEA OF NATIONALISM. (New York: Macmillan, 1961).

13. "Constructive" from the vantage point of the leaders of the unity movements but not necessarily from the standpoint of an internationalist.

14. Nationalism differs from patriotism in that the former is an ideological movement whereas the latter is a feeling of solidarity among fellow citizens of a polity, usually accompanied by a need to identify with one's "In-group" which, in turn, produces the "we-they" syndrome in international relations.

15. According to Robert Strausz-Hupé, "national interest" means nowadays interest of the state dressed up democratically so as to simulate the interest of the people as a whole." See his POWER AND COMMUNITY (New York: Praeger, 1956), p. 56.

16. Alexis de Tocqueville already recognized that what are called necessary institutions are often only those which one is accustomed to. See also Anthony Downs. INSIDE BUREAUCRACY (Boston: Little-Brown & Co., 1967).

17. The only alternative, namely "Euro-socialization through education and generational change" is discussed in Part II.

18. John Pinder. EUROPE AGAINST DE GAULLE (London: Pall Mall Press, 1963), p. 156.

19. For an elaboration of this point see Sprout and Sprout. TOWARD A POLITICS OF THE PLANET EARTH (New York: Van Nostrand, 1971).

20. See Ernst B. Haas. TANGLE OF HOPES: AMERICAN COMMITMENTS AND WORLD ORDER (Englewood Cliffs: Prentice-Hall, 1969).

21. Ibid., p. 11.

22. See James N. Rosenau, ed. LINKAGE POLITICS (New York: Free Press, 1969); DOMESTIC SOURCES OF FOREIGN POLICY (New York: Free Press,

1967); INTERNATIONAL POLITICS AND FOREIGN POLICY (New York: Free Press, 1969). Also, Wolfram F. Hanrieder, ed. COMPARATIVE FOREIGN POLICY (New York: David McKay, 1971).

23. See Ernst B. Haas. BEYOND THE NATION-STATE. (Stanford: Stanford University Press, 1964).

24. Rosenau, LINKAGE POLITICS, p. 2.

25. "Interdependencies in World Politics," INTERNATIONAL JOURNAL (Canada) 24, no. 4 (Autumn 1969): 739.

26. "The Future of World Politics," THE POLITICAL QUARTERLY 37, no. 1 (January-March 1966): 21.

27. Edward L. Morse, "The Politics of Interdependence," INTERNATIONAL ORGANIZATION 23, no. 2 (Spring 1969): 314. See also his "Transnational Economic Processes," INTERNATIONAL ORGANIZATION, 25, no. 3 (Summer 1971): 373 ff.

28. Bruce M. Russett, "Interdependence and Capabilities for European Cooperation," JOURNAL OF COMMON MARKET STUDIES 9, no. 2 (December 1970): 143.

29. Robert O. Keohane and Joseph S. Nye, Jr., eds., "Transnational Relations and World Politics." INTERNATIONAL ORGANIZATION 25, no. 3 (Summer 1971): 332.

30. Ibid.

31. Ibid., p. 344.

32. Ibid., p. 730.

33. Ibid.

34. Ibid., p. 731-32.

35. Karl Kaiser, "Transnational Relations as a Threat to the Democratic Process," INTERNATIONAL ORGANIZATION 25, no. 3 (Summer 1971): 708.

36. Ibid., p. 708-10. See also his "Transnational Politics: Toward a Theory of Multinational Politics," INTERNATIONAL ORGANIZATION 25, no. 4 (Autumn 1971).

37. Keohane and Nye, "Transnational Relations," p. 743.

38. Ibid., p. 744.

39. YEARBOOK OF INTERNATIONAL ORGANIZATIONS, 13th ed., 1970/71, p. 1007. This yearbook is published in Brussels by the Union of International Associations—itself a typical NGO.

40. Werner J. Feld, "Nongovernmental Entities and the International System: A Preliminary Quantitative Overview," ORBIS, 15, no. 3 (Fall 1971): 885. Feld adds a third type, namely transnational political parties in the European Parliament, as nongovernmental entities (p. 881).

41. Ibid., p. 889.

42. Kjell Skjelsbaek, "The Growth of International Nongovernmental Organization in the Twentieth Century," INTERNATIONAL ORGANIZATION 25, no. 3 (Summer 1971): 431.

43. Feld, "Nongovernmental Entities," p. 887.

44. See Peter D. Bell, "The Ford Foundation as a Transnational Actor," INTERNATIONAL ORGANIZATION 25, no. 3 (Summer 1971) 465 ff.

45. Skjelsbaek, "International Nongovernmental Organization" p. 423.

46. Ibid., p. 434.

47. Feld, "Nongovernmental Entities" p. 896.

48. See Dusan Sidjanski, "Pressure Groups and the European Community," GOVERNMENT AND OPPOSITION 2, no. 3 (April-July 1967): 397 ff and Werner J. Feld, "National Economic Interest Groups and Policy Formation in the EEC," POLITICAL SCIENCE QUARTERLY 81 (1966): 392 ff.

49. See Louis T. Wells, Jr. "The Multinational Business Enterprise: What Kind of International Organization?" INTERNATIONAL ORGANIZATION 25, no. 3 (Summer 1971): 449.

50. "Economic Sovereignty at Bay," FOREIGN AFFAIRS 47, no. 1 (October 1968): 114.

51. Feld, "Nongovernmental Entities," p. 897.

52. This scheme has originally been proposed by Howard Perlmutter: see Anthony Sampson, ANATOMY OF EUROPE (New York: Harper & Row, 1968), p. 86.

53. Andrew Shonfield quoted in ibid.

54. George Ball quoted in ibid.

55. Vernon, "Economic Sovereignty," p. 116.

56. Thomas G. Watson quoted in ibid., p. 112.

57. See Jean-Jacques Sérvan-Schreiber. THE AMERICAN CHALLENGE (New York: Atheneum, 1968). He points out, for instance, that US-sponsored MNCs (such as IBM and GE) control over 70 percent of the European computer market (p. 56). Furthermore, between 1950 and 1969 the value of investments by US-sponsored MNCs in Western Europe rose from $1,733 million to $21,554 million; see Christopher Tugendhat, "Transnational Enterprise: Tying down Gulliver," THE ATLANTIC COMMUNITY QUARTERLY 9, no. 4 (Winter 1971-72): 505.

58. Vernon, "Economic Sovereignty," p. 117.

59. Feld, "Nongovernmental Entities," p. 900 and 904.

60. Ibid., p. 918. See also his TRANSNATIONAL BUSINESS COLLABORATION AMONG COMMON MARKET COUNTRIES: ITS IMPLICATIONS FOR POLITICAL INTEGRATION (New York: Praeger, 1970).

61. There are fifteen "specialized agencies" and six "special UN programs."

62. The spectrum of UN activities covers all important areas: political-security, economic-social, legal-humanitarian, and scientific-technological.

63. For a balanced appraisal of the performance and potential of the United Nations see for instance: Franz Gross, ed. THE UNITED STATES AND THE UNITED NATIONS (Norman: University of Oklahoma, 1964).

64. This dysfunctional attitude of the Security Council has been criticized as

follows: "While the Indian continent burns the United Nations fiddles" (THE GERMAN TRIBUNE, no. 506, Dec. 23, 1971).

65. Chadwick F. Alger, "Non-Resolution Consequences of the United Nations and Their Effect on International Conflict" in William D. Coplin and Charles W. Kegley, eds. A MULTI-METHOD INTRODUCTION TO INTERNATIONAL POLITICS (Chicago: Markham Publ. Co., 1971), p. 217.

66. The share of the United States, a traditional supporter of the UN, is less than 30 percent of the UN budget or about $60 million (only a fraction of 1 percent of the US defense budget), despite the fact that the amount spent by the UN on American territory for rent, supply, food, etc., vastly exceeds the US contribution to the UN budget.

67. Inis L. Claude, Jr. SWORDS INTO PLOWSHARES (New York: Random House, 1964), pp. 14 and 403. In the words of a practitioner: "The UN is being made the scapegoat of the member governments with whom the responsibility for failure actually lies. . . . What the UN needs most . . . is a clear recognition by the member governments that it is in their interest to make it work." (Charles W. Yost, "UN's Identity Crisis," VISTA 7, no. 4 (February 1972): 44.)

68. Immanuel Kant's idealism, expressed in his work ZUM EWIGEN FRIEDEN, differs substantially from the realistic concept of Thucydides who believed that the surest bond between states and individuals is the identity of interest.

69. Another example for the failure of the UN charter to define crucial terms is "aggression."

70. Joseph S. Nye. PEACE IN PARTS (Boston: Little, Brown & Co., 1971, p. 4. For the constitutional foundations of regional organizations see Ruth C. Lawson, ed. INTERNATIONAL REGIONAL ORGANIZATIONS (New York: Praeger, 1962).

71. This classification follows that of Nye, PEACE IN PARTS, p. 5. An example for the military type would be WEU or NATO; for the political type the OAS or OAU; and for the economic type the EEC or LAFTA.

72. See his INTERNATIONAL REGIONALISM, p. vii.

73. Claude, EUROPEAN ORGANIZATION, p. 5-6. On this occasion Professor Claude, a well-known student of the United Nations, added that "nobody supposes that a medical scientist who concentrates on cancer research must be in favor of cancer, but for some reason a UN specialist is widely assumed to be, by definition, a UN partisan." (Ibid.)

74. John G. Stoessinger. THE MIGHT OF NATIONS (New York: Random House, 1969), p. 401.

75. Ronald J. Yalem. REGIONALISM AND WORLD ORDER (Washington, D.C.: Public Affairs Press, 1965), p. 149.

76. Philip E. Jacob. "Organizing Nations in the 1970s," ORBIS 15, no. 1 (Spring 1971): 46.

77. Ibid., p. 49.

78. Karl W. Deutsch. NATIONALISM AND SOCIAL COMMUNICATION (Cambridge, Mass.: M.I.T. Press, 1953), p. 167.

79. Inis Claude, "The OAS, the UN, and the US" in Nye, ed. INTERNATIONAL REGIONALISM, p. 3.

80. REPORT TO CONGRESS on "US Foreign Policy for the 1970s," February 25, 1971 (Washington, D.C.: GPO, 1971), p. 29.

81. Claude, EUROPEAN ORGANIZATION, p. 13-14.

82. The convention entered into force on September 3, 1953, having been ratified by the necessary number of signatory states and is now binding on 15 members of the Council of Europe. See Part II. See also: A.H. Robertson, EUROPEAN INSTITUTIONS (New York: Praeger, 1966).

83. Herman Kahn and Norbert Wiener, THE YEAR 2000 (New York: Macmillan, 1967), p. 395.

84. Skjelsbaek, "International Nongovernmental Organization," p. 439.

85. Ernst B. Haas, "The Study of Regional Integration," INTERNATIONAL ORGANIZATION 24, no. 4 (Autumn): 645.

86. Nye, PEACE IN PARTS, p. 182-3.

87. Ibid., pp. 198-99.

Chapter 2
Approaches to the Study of Regional Integration

1. Ernst B. Haas, "The Study of Regional Integration: Reflections on the Joy and Anguish of Pretheorizing," INTERNATIONAL ORGANIZATION 24, no. 4 (Autumn 1970): 645.

2. Kenneth C. Wheare, FEDERAL GOVERNMENT (London: Oxford University Press, 1953) p. 11.

3. Carl J. Friedrich, "International Federalism in Theory and Practice" in SYSTEMS OF INTEGRATING THE INTERNATIONAL COMMUNITY, Elmer Plischke, (Princeton, New Jersey; D. Can Nostrand, 1964) p. 126-27.

4. See ed. Carl C. Friedrich's exposition of this point in EUROPE: AN EMERGENT NATION? (New York: Harper & Row, 1969), Chapter 2.

5. See Alexandre Marc, EUROPE: TERRE DÉCISIVE (Paris: La Colombe, 1959) See also: Henri Brugmans, and Pierre Duclos, LE FÉDÉRALISME CONTEMPORAIN. (Leyde: Sijthoff, 1963).

6. Denis de Rougemont, "Toward a New Definition of Federalism," THE ATLANTIC COMMUNITY QUARTERLY 8, no. 2 (Summer 1970): 224.

7. This argument is based upon Monnet's dictum that "Institutions unite people." For an elaboration of the juridical and sociological aspects of integral federalism see: Guy Héraud, LES PRINCIPES DU FÉDÉRALISME ET DE LA FÉDÉRATION EUROPÉENNE and L'EUROPE DES ETHNIES (Paris: Presse d'Europe, 1967).

8. Anthony Sampson, ANATOMY OF EUROPE (New York: Harper & Row, 1968), p. 430.

9. David Mitrany, A WORKING PEACE SYSTEM (London: Royal Institute of International Affairs, 1946), p. 14.

10. Ernst B. Haas, BEYOND THE NATION STATE (Stanford: Stanford University Press, 1964), p. 6.

11. Inis L. Claude, SWORDS INTO PLOWSHARES (New York: Random House, 1964), p. 354.

12. Karl W. Deutsch, THE ANALYSIS OF INTERNATIONAL RELATIONS (Englewood Cliffs, N.J.: Prentice Hall, 1968), p. 198.

13. Ernst B. Haas and Philippe C. Schmitter, "Economics and Differential Patterns of Political Integration" in INTERNATIONAL POLITICAL COMMUNITIES (Garden City, New York: Anchor Books, 1966), p. 261.

14. Ernst B. Haas, "The Uniting of Europe and the Uniting of Latin America," JOURNAL OF COMMON MARKET STUDIES 5, no. 4 (June 1967) 327.

15. Ernst B. Haas, "International Integration: The European and the Universal Process," INTERNATIONAL POLITICAL COMMUNITIES, p. 94.

16. Haas-Schmitter, "Political Integration," p. 262.

17. Haas, "The Uniting of Europe," p. 327.

18. Ibid., p. 329.

19. Haas, "International Integration," p. 98.

20. Ernst B. Haas, "The Study of Regional Integration," p. 638.

21. Ibid., p. 635.

22. "Political Integration," p. 278.

23. "The Operationalization of Some Variables Related to Regional Integration: A Research Note," INTERNATIONAL ORGANIZATION 23, no. 1 (Winter 1969): 153.

24. "A Revised Theory of Regional Integration," INTERNATIONAL ORGANIZATION 24, no. 4 (Autumn 1970): 705-737.

25. Ibid.

26. Philippe C. Schmitter, "Three Neo-Functional Hypotheses about International Integration," INTERNATIONAL ORGANIZATION 23, no. 1 (Winter 1969): 161-66.

27. "The European Community as a Political System: Notes Toward the Construction of a Model," JOURNAL OF COMMON MARKET STUDIES 5, no. 4 (June 1967): 359.

28. EUROPE'S WOULD-BE POLICY: PATTERNS OF CHANGE IN THE EUROPEAN COMMUNITY (Englewood Cliffs, New Jersey: Prentice Hall, 1970) pp. 67, 71.

29. Ibid., p. 69.

30. Ibid., p. 283-84.

31. "Political Integration as a Multidimensional Phenomenon Requiring

Multivariate Measurement," INTERNATIONAL ORGANIZATION 24, no. 4 (Autumn 1970): 683.

32. Ibid.

33. Among the principal critics or commentators of the neofunctionalist school are: Stanley Hoffmann, "Obstinate or Obsolete: The Fate of the Nation-State and the Case of Western Europe" in INTERNATIONAL REGIONALISM, p. 177-230. Paul Taylor, "The Concept of Community and the European Integration Process," JOURNAL OF COMMON MARKET STUDIES 7, no. 2 (December 1968): 83-101; Roger D. Hanson, "Regional Integration: Reflections on a Decade of Theoretical Efforts," WORLD POLITICS 21, no. 2 (January 1969): 242-71. Dahlberg, Kenneth A. "Regional Integration: The Neo-functional versus a Configurative Approach," INTERNATIONAL ORGANIZATION 24, no. 1 (Winter 1970): 122-28; Kaiser, Karl. "The Interaction of Regional Subsystems: Some Preliminary Notes on Recurrent Patterns and the Roles of the Superpowers," WORLD POLITICS 21, no. 1 (October 1968): 86-101. Nye, Joseph S. "Patterns and Catalysts in Regional Integration," INTERNATIONAL ORGANIZATION 19, no. 4 (Autumn 1965): 333-49; idem, "Comparative Regional Integration: Concept and Measurement," INTERNATIONAL ORGANIZATION 22, no. 4 (Autumn 1968): 855-80; idem, "Comparing Common Markets: A Revised Neofunctionalist Model." INTERNATIONAL ORGANIZATION 24, no. 4 (Autumn 1970): 796-835; Etzioni, Amitai. "The Epigenesis of Political Communities at the International Level" in James N. Rosenau, ed. INTERNATIONAL POLITICS AND FOREIGN POLICY, (New York: Free Press, 1969), pp. 346-58.

34. William H. Riker, FEDERALISM: ORIGIN, OPERATION, SIGNIFICANCE (Boston: Little, Brown & Company) 1964, p. 16.

35. Deutsch, "Political Community and the North Atlantic Area," in INTERNATIONAL POLITICAL COMMUNITIES, p. 37.

36. Ibid., p. 38.

37. Ibid., p. 2.

38. WORLD HANDBOOK OF POLITICAL AND SOCIAL INDICATORS (New Haven: Yale University Press, 1964).

39. INTERNATIONAL REGIONS AND THE INTERNATIONAL SYSTEM: A STUDY IN POLITICAL ECOLOGY (Chicago: Rand McNally, 1967) p. 11.

40. "Transactions, Community, and International Political Integration," JOURNAL OF COMMON MARKET STUDIES 9, no. 3 (March 1971): 228.

41. Ibid., p. 227.

42. Ibid., p. 230.

43. Russett, INTERNATIONAL REGIONS AND THE INTERNATIONAL SYSTEM, p. 208.

44. Ibid., p. 212.

45. Russett, "Transactions, Community, and International Political Integration," p. 233.

46. See: Oran R. Young, "Professor Russett: Industrious Taylor to a Naked Emperor," WORLD POLITICS 21, no. 3 p. 487.

47. "Integration and Disintegration in Franco-German Relations, 1954-1965," INTERNATIONAL ORGANIZATION 24, no. 2 (Spring 1970): 184.

48. Ibid., p. 185.

49. Ibid., p. 198-99.

50. "International Transactions and Regional Integration," INTERNATIONAL ORGANIZATION 24, no. 4 (Autumn 1970): 742-3.

51. Ibid., p. 762.

52. "Integration and Disintegration in Franco-German Relations, 1954-1965," p. 199-200.

53. See Philip E. Jacob and James V. Toscano, eds. THE INTEGRATION OF POLITICAL COMMUNITIES (Philadelphia: Lippincott, 1964).

54. "The Influence of Values in Political Integration," in ibid, p. 209-46.

55. Ibid., p. 212.

56. Ibid., p. 220.

57. Ibid., p. 236.

58. Ibid., p. 246.

59. Henry Teune, "The Learning of Integrative Habits," in ibid, p. 247-82.

60. "The Integrative Process. Guidelines for Analysis of the Bases of Political Community," in THE INTEGRATION OF POLITICAL COMMUNITIES, p. 1-45.

61. Ibid., p. 3.

62. Ibid., p. 10.

63. Ibid., p. 11-12.

64. Ibid., p. 13-14.

65. See for instance Robert A. Bernstein, INTERNATIONAL INTEGRATION (Ithaca, New York: Cornell University Press, 1971).

66. New York: Holt, Rinehart and Winston, 1965. The only previous comparative study involving an intercontinental perspective was essentially historical in nature (see: Deutsch et. al., POLITICAL COMMUNITY).

67. Ibid., p. 4.

68. Ibid., p. 15.

69. Ibid., p. 92.

70. "The Interaction of Regional Subsystems: Some Preliminary Notes on Recurrent Patterns and the Role of Superpowers," WORLD POLITICS 21, no. 1 (October 1968): 86.

71. Ibid., p. 92.

72. Ibid., p. 94.

73. Ibid., p. 94-95.

74. "Comparative Regional Integration: Concept and Measurement," p. 858.

75. Ibid., p. 859.

76. Ibid., p. 855.

77. See his argumentation in "Patterns and Catalysts in Regional Integration." For a similar criticism see: Stanley Hoffmann, "Discord in Community: The North Atlantic Area as a Partial Political System," in THE ATLANTIC COMMUNITY: PROGRESS AND PROSPECTS, F.O. Wilcox, and F.H. Haviland, eds. (New York: Praeger, 1963), pp. 3-31.

78. "Comparing Common Markets: A Revised Neo-Functionalist Model," p. 806.

79. Ibid., p. 821.

80. Nye, PEACE IN PARTS, pp. 87-93, 76.

81. "International Regions: A Comparative Approach to Five Subordinate Systems," INTERNATIONAL STUDIES QUARTERLY 13, no. 4 (December 1969): 361-380.

82. INTERNATIONAL INTEGRATION (Ithaca, N.Y: Cornell University Press, 1971).

Chapter 3
Federators and Inhibitors

1. Many students of comparative integration have recognized the saliency of this external factor, especially the representatives of the "configurative approach" (see Part I, Chapter 2).

2. Paul-Henri Spaak often referred to Stalin as the "father" and "cupid" of both the European and Atlantic unity movements.

3. Gerhard Mally, BRITAIN AND EUROPEAN UNITY (London: Hansard Society for Parliamentary Government, 1966), p. 7.

4. Timothy W. Stanley, NATO IN TRANSITION: THE FUTURE OF THE ATLANTIC ALLIANCE (New York: Praeger, 1965), p. 37.

5. Ibid.

6. A.H. Robertson, EUROPEAN INSTITUTIONS (New York: Praeger, 1966), p. 9.

7. The departure of Stalin from the political scene and the end of the Korean War resulted in a distinct slackening of the European unity movement (namely, failure of the EDC)—a reverse demonstration of the saliency of the Communist threat as a hostile external federator.

8. The Breshnev doctrine of 26 September 1968 states that "the sovereignty of each socialist country cannot be opposed to the interests of the socialist world." Quoted in Robert S. Jordan, ed. EUROPE AND THE SUPERPOWERS (Boston: Allyn and Bacon, 1971), p. 69.

9. See the 1971 data on the strategic balance published by the Institute of Strategic Studies (London).

10. Agence EUROPE, March 30, 1971, no. 777.

11. Agence EUROPE, May 10, 1971, no. 804.

12. EUROPEAN COMMUNITY, November-December, 1970, no. 140, p. 9.

13. Ibid.

14. Agence EUROPE, January 25, 1972, no. 970, p. 3.

15. Max Kohnstamm. THE EUROPEAN COMMUNITY AND ITS ROLE IN THE WORLD (Columbia: University of Missouri Press, 1964), p. 38.

16. Henry Kissinger in his foreward to Ernst H. van der Beugel. FROM MARSHALL AID TO ATLANTIC PARTNERSHIP (Amsterdam: Elsevier Publishing Co., 1966). p. ix.

17. George W. Ball, THE DISCIPLINE OF POWER (Boston: Little, Brown & Co., 1968), p. 59.

18. "Denazification" was the exception but can be explained as an application of the new principles of international law and morality to individual war criminals; apart from the Nuremberg trials this process did not yield any significant results.

19. It could also be regarded as the decisive buildingstone for the Atlantic Community since it established solidarity between the United States and all West European nations.

20. The book FREEDOM FRONTIER—ATLANTIC UNION NOW (Washington, D.C. Freedom and Union Press, 1961) was first published in 1940 and recommended the creation of a federal union of Western democracies.

21. Beugel, FROM MARSHALL AID, pp. 51-52.

22. Robertson, "European Institutions," p. 7.

23. Ibid., p. 12.

24. President Truman called the Schuman Plan "an act of constructive statesmanship." Beugel, FROM MARSHALL AID, p. 244. It should be added that American opposition to it might have been fatal (p. 238).

25. Ibid., p. 278.

26. Ibid., p. 293.

27. The treaty was rejected by a small minority of 55; the vote was 319 to 264. (Robertson, "European Institutions," p. 21).

28. Beugel, FROM MARSHALL AID, p. 297.

29. WEU enhanced European unity through the incorporation of West Germany; it subsequently facilitated a dialogue between the Six and the United Kingdom and may yet become the nucleus of a future politically unified Western Europe, particularly following Britain's accession to the European Community in 1973.

30. Beugel, FROM MARSHALL AID, p. 318.

31. Ibid.

32. Ibid., p. 319.

33. DEPARTMENT OF STATE BULLETIN (July 23, 1962), p. 132.

34. Ibid.

35. Ibid.

36. Ibid.

37. WESTERN EUROPEAN UNION: 1962 (Paris, March 1963) p. 51.

38. EUROPEAN COMMUNITY, no. 55 (August 1962), p. 2.

39. EUROPEAN COMMUNITY, no. 64 (July-August 1963), p. 2.

40. Pierre Uri. PARTNERSHIP FOR PROGRESS (New York: Harper & Row), p. 3.

41. Ibid., p. 4.

42. Ben T. Moore, NATO AND THE FUTURE OF EUROPE (New York: Harper & Row, 1958), p. 253.

43. George Ball quoted in Max Beloff, THE UNITED STATES AND THE UNITY OF EUROPE (Washington, D.C.: Brookings, 1963), p. 114.

44. Paul Henri Spaak, "Hold Fast," FOREIGN AFFAIRS (July 1963), p. 620.

45. DEPARTMENT OF STATE BULLETIN (January 6, 1964), p. 29.

46. THE NEW YORK TIMES, April 5, 1964.

47. Beugel, FROM MARSHALL AID, p. 381.

48. Henry A. Kissinger. AMERICAN FOREIGN POLICY: THREE ESSAYS (New York: Norton, 1969), p. 74.

49. Henry A. Kissinger, THE TROUBLED PARTNERSHIP (New York: McGraw-Hill, 1965), p. 243.

50. Harold B. Malmgren quoted in THE US AND THE EUROPEAN COMMUNITY: THEIR COMMON INTEREST (New York: Manhattan Publishing Co., 1971), p. 11.

51. US FOREIGN POLICY FOR THE 1970s. Report to Congress, February 18, 1970 (Washington, D.C.: GPO, 1970), p. 32.

52. US FOREIGN POLICY FOR THE 1970s: BUILDING FOR PEACE (Washington, D.C.: GPO, 1971), pp. 24, 25, 29.

53. Ibid., pp. 27, 29.

54. US FOREIGN POLICY FOR THE 1970s: THE EMERGING STRUC-TURE OF PEACE (Washington, D.C.: US Government Printing Office, 1972), p. 40.

55. UNITED STATES FOREIGN POLICY: 1969-1970. A REPORT OF THE SECRETARY OF STATE (Washington, D.C.: GPO, 1971), p. v.

56. Ibid., p. 8.

57. Ibid., p. v.

58. UNITED STATES FOREIGN POLICY, 1971: A REPORT OF THE SECRETARY OF STATE (Washington, D.C.: US Government Printing Office, 1972), p. viii.

59. Jean Monnet, speaking on the occasion of the presentation of the Annual Freedom Award to him on January 23, 1963, in New York. FREEDOM AND UNION, 18, no. 2 (February 1963): 20.

60. Ibid.

61. Alexandre Marc, editorial, "Les Etats-Unis et L'Europe," L'EUROPE EN FORMATION no. 81, (December 1966) p. 4.

62. For example, President Nixon, in his State of the World Message of February 25, 1971, invariably referred to "Western Europe," rather than to individual states.

63. Waldemar Besson, in Robert S. Jordan, ed. EUROPE AND THE SUPERPOWERS, (Boston: Allyn S. Bacon), p. 1.

64. This view is supported by an expert who stated that "the Kennedy Round helped shape the Common Market." See William Diebold, Jr., THE UNITED STATES AND THE INDUSTRIAL WORLD: FOREIGN ECONOMIC POLICY FOR THE 1970s (New York: Praeger, 1972), Chapter 9.

65. The current issues (trade, finance, and burden-sharing) will be discussed in Chapter 8.

66. For the "anatomy" of the commission and the other institutions of the European Community, see Chapter 4. In this context it is necessary to recall that the Council of Ministers makes decisions on the basis of proposals submitted by the commission which is the only official "idea machine" in the European Community.

67. Amitai Etzioni, EUROPEAN UNIFICATION, p. 42. For a complete listing of the treaty provisions governing the powers of the commission see Leon Lindberg. THE POLITICAL DYNAMICS OF EUROPEAN ECONOMIC INTEGRATION (Stanford: Stanford University Press, 1964), p. 307 ff.

68. Art. 155, Treaty establishing EEC. Similar powers had been given to the High Authority (art. 14, Treaty establishing ECSC) and the Euratom Commission (Treaty of Rome, Art. 124). Since the consolidation of the executives in 1967, a single Commission exercises the powers given to the three organs in the Treaties of Paris and Rome.

69. W. Hartley Clark, THE POLITICS OF THE COMMON MARKET (Englewood Cliffs: Prentice Hall, 1967), p. 77.

70. Art. 40, Treaty of Rome (EEC).

71. Lindberg-Scheingold, EUROPE'S WOULD-BE POLITY, pp. 144-145.

72. Ibid., p. 148.

73. Ibid., pp. 151, 173.

74. The estimated sum was $4 billion.

75. Press Conference of September 9, 1965 quoted in Leon N. Lindberg, "Integration as a Source of Stress on the European Community System," in Nye, ed., INTERNATIONAL REGIONALISM, p. 237.

76. Ibid., p. 250. See also Stuart A. Scheingold, "De Gaulle vs. Hallstein: Europe Picks Up the Pieces," THE AMERICAN SCHOLAR (Summer 1966).

77. See Chapter 4.

78. See Appendix A.

79. Eric Stein and Peter Hay, LAW AND INSTITUTIONS IN THE ATLANTIC AREA (Indianapolis: Bobbs-Merrill, 1967), p. 988.

80. Ibid., p. 900.

81. Ibid., p. 901.

308

82. Supplement to the BULLETIN of the European Communities, no. 3, 1969, p. 3.

83. "Introduction," TENTH ANNUAL REPORT ON THE ACTIVITIES OF THE COMMUNITIES (Brussels: Commission, 1967), p. 20.

84. Council decision of February 9, 1971 (AGENCE EUROPE, no. 614, February 10, 1971).

85. Supplement to the BULLETIN, no. 3, 1969 p. 9.

86. DOCUMENT of the European Commission published by the European Community Information Service, 1969.

87. Supplement to the BULLETIN, no. 7, 1970, annex 1, p. 19.

88. See Appendix A.

89. Supplement to the BULLETIN, no 7, 1970, annex 1.

90. Agence EUROPE, February 10, 1971, no. 614.

91. Agence EUROPE, March 9, 1972, no. 1002 (the "formal" act took place on March 22, 1972).

92. Ibid., p. 5.

93. Agence EUROPE, March 24, 1972, no. 1013. Other examples for initiatives by the commission are the following proposals: for a "European Committee for Research and Development" (June 2, 1972); for a "Joint European Development Strategy" (July 27, 1971); and for the "Strengthening of the Institutions" (May 31, 1972).

94. W. Randolph Burgess and James Robert Huntley, EUROPE AND AMERICA: THE NEXT TEN YEARS (New York: Walker and Company, 1970), p. 208.

95. Quoted in George W. Ball, DISCIPLINE OF POWER, p. 41. For further insight into the personality and working methods of Jean Monnet see: Richard Mayne, "The Role of Jean Monnet," GOVERNMENT AND OPPOSITION 2, no. 3 (April-July 1967), and Merry and Serge Bromberger, LES COULISSES DE L'EUROPE (Paris: Presses de la Cité, 1968).

96. Jean Monnet, LES ETATS-UNIS D'EUROPE ONT COMMENCÉ (Paris: Laffort, 1955), p. 102.

97. Walter Yondorf, "Monnet and the Action Committee: The Formative Period of the European Communities," INTERNATIONAL ORGANIZATION 19, no. 4 (Autumn 1965), p. 889. See also: Francois Duchêne, "The European Action Committee," INTERPLAY (December 1966).

98. Philip E. Jacob in Jacob-Toscano, THE INTEGRATION, p. 246.

99. Ball, DISCIPLINE OF POWER, p. 42.

100.   Members of the Action Committee in 1971

Socialist Parties

Messrs.
Willy Brandt   President of the German Social Democrat Party
                      (S.P.D.)

Herbert Wehner	Vice-President of the German Social Democrat Party.
Helmut Schmidt	Vice-President of the German Social Democrat Party.
Roy Jenkins	Deputy Leader of the British Labour Party.
Denis Healey	British Labour Party.
Walter Padley	British Labour Party.
Edmond Leburton	President of the Belgian Socialist Party.
Jos Van der Eynde	President of the Belgian Socialist Party.
J.M. Den Uyl	President of the Dutch Parliamentary Labour Party.
Guy Mollet	French Socialist Party.
Mauro Ferri	Secretary-General of the Italian Social Democrat Party (P.S.D.I.).
Antonio Cariglia	Deputy Secretary-General of the Italian Democrat Party (P.S.D.I.).
Pietro Nenni	Italian Socialist Party (P.S.I.).
Francesco De Martino	Secretary-General of the Italian Socialist Party (P.S.I.).
Antoine Wehenkel	President of the Luxembourg Socialist Party.

Christian Democrat Parties

Messrs.

Kurt Kiesinger	President of the German Christian Democrat Party (C.D.U.).
Rainer Barzel	President of the German Christian Democrat Parliamentary Group (C.D.U.).
Kurt Birrenbach	German Christian Democrat Parliamentary Group.
B. Biesheuvel	President of the Dutch Protestant Party.
V. Giscard d'Estaing	President of the French National Federation of Independent Republicans.
Joseph Herr	Vice-President of the Luxembourg Christian Social Party.
Robert Houben	President of the Belgian Christian Social Party.
Leo Tindemans	Belgian Christian Social Party.
J.T. Mellema	President of the Dutch Historical Christian Union Parliamentary Group.
Mariano Rumor	Italian Christian Democrat Party.
Arnaldo Forlani	Secretary-General of the Italian Christian Democrat Party.
Angelo Bernassola	Italian Christian Democrat Party.
Carlo Russo	Italian Christian Democrat Party.
Mario Scelba	Italian Christian Democrat Party.
Norbert Schmelzer	President of the Dutch Catholic Parliamentary Group.

Conservative Party

Messrs.

Sir Alec Douglas-Home British Conservative Party.

Geoffrey Rippon	British Conservative Party.
Sir Tufton Beamish	British Conservative Party.

Other Parties

Emile-Edg. Jeunehomme

Member of the Steering Committee of the Belgian Party for Liberty and Progress.

Giovanni Malagodi	Secretary-General of the Italian Liberal Party.
Walter Scheel	President of the German Liberal Party.
Eugene Claudius-Petit	President of the French Party for Progress and Modern Democracy (P.D.M.).
René Pleven	French Party for Progress and Modern Democracy (P.D.M.).
Maurice Faure	President of the French Radical Socialist Party.
Ugo La Malfa	Italian Republican Party.
Antoine Pinay	Former President of the French Social Action Group of Peasants and Independents.
Jeremy Thorpe	Leader of the British Liberal Party.

Trade Unions

Messrs.

Jacq Alders	Vice-President of the Dutch Confederation of Catholic Trade Unions.
André Bergeron	Secretary-General of the French Socialist Trade Unions (C.G.T.F.O.).
Auguste Cool	President of the European Confederation of Christian Trade Unions (C.I.S.C.-C.M.T.).
Enzo Dalla Chiesa	Italian Workers' Union.
Georges Debunne	Secretary General of the Belgian General Federation of Trade Unions.
Eugene Descamps	Secretary General of the French Confederation of Democratic Trade Unions.
Gerrit Gerritsen	Dutch Christian Trade Unions.
Mathias Hinterscheid	Secretary-General of the Luxembourg General Confederation of Labour.
Jozef Houthuys	President of the Belgian Confederation of Christian Trade Unions.
H. ter Heide	President of the Dutch Trade Union Federation.
Ludwig Rosenberg	Former President of the German Trade Union Federation (D.G.B.).
Heinz O. Vetter	President of the German Trade Union Federation (D.G.B.).
Walter Arendt	Former President of the German Miners' Federation.

Otto Brenner	President of the German Metalworkers' Federation.
Bernhard Tacke	Vice-President of the German Trade Union Federation.
Bruno Storti	Deputy Secretary-General of the Italian Confederation of Workers' Trade Unions.
Leon Wagner	Luxembourg Confederation of Christian Trade Unions.

President: Jean Monnet.

Vice-President: Max Kohnstamm.

Secretary-General: Jacques Van Helmont.

101. Yondorf, "Monnet and the Action Committee," p. 911. The German Socialists are a good example.

102. Note that the very title of this book is an example of a "self-fulfilling prophecy" (LES ETATS UNIS D'EUROPE ONT COMMENCÉ). Its logic is based upon the truism that "if things are defined as real, they are real in their consequences." (I.W. Thomas).

103. This view was supported by Lindberg and Scheingold, EUROPE'S WOULD-BE POLITY, pp. 241 and 243.

104. Yondorf, "Monnet and the Action Committee," p. 901.

105. Ibid., p. 902.

106. Ibid., p. 910.

107. Anthony Sampson, ANATOMY OF EUROPE, p. 10.

108. Etzioni, EUROPEAN UNIFICATION, p. 269.

109. Yondorf, "Monnet and the Action Committee," p. 907.

110. Ibid., p. 907.

111. Mally, BRITAIN AND EUROPEAN UNITY, p. 91.

112. Sampson, ANATOMY OF EUROPE, p. 11.

113. WESTERN EUROPEAN UNION: 1963 (Paris, March 1964), pp. 53-56.

114. Ibid., p. 54-55.

115. WEU: 1964 (Paris, March 1965), p. 45.

116. Mally, BRITAIN AND EUROPEAN UNITY, pp. 136 and 141.

117. WEU, MONTHLY NOTE NO. 3, (Paris: March 1967), p. 7.

118. WEU, MONTHLY NOTE NO. 5, (Paris: May 1967), p. 30.

119. EUROPEAN DOCUMENTATION, (October-December 1968), no. 4, p. 143.

120. EUROPEAN DOCUMENTATION, August 1969, no. 126, p. 4.

121. Ibid.

122. WEU: 1969, (Paris, May 1970), p. 111.

123. See Appendix A.

124. WEU: May 1970, p. 152.

125. Agence EUROPE, July 2, 1970, no. 584.

126. Agence EUROPE, February 23, 1971, no. 752 and February 24, 1971, no. 753.

127. Agence EUROPE, June 23, 1971, no. 834.

128. THE NEW YORK TIMES, October 29, 1971.

129. The concepts of the *staatsidee* and of the nation had been introduced by the German geopolitician Friedrich Ratzel and by the Italian statesman Giuseppe Mazzini respectively at the turn of the century.

130. THE WAR MEMOIRS OF CHARLES DE GAULLE (New York: Simon and Schuster, 1959), vol. 1, p. 3.

131. Ibid., vol. 3, p. 204.

132. MAJOR ADDRESSES, STATEMENTS, AND PRESS CONFERENCES OF GENERAL CHARLES DE GAULLE, 1958-64 (New York: French Embassy, Press and Information Service), p. 92. Press conference, December 5, 1960.

133. Ibid., p. 176. Press conference of May 15, 1962.

134. The five ministers—Bacon, Buron, Fontanet, Pflimlin, and Maurice Schuman (who later rejoined the Gaullist government)—were members of the MRP which strongly supported supranationalism. KEESING'S CONTEMPO-RARY ARCHIVES (London, 1961-62), vol. 13, p. 18828.

135. Quoted in Mally, BRITAIN AND EUROPEAN UNITY, p. 101.

136. "Hold Fast," FOREIGN AFFAIRS (July 1963), p. 614.

137. According to de Gaulle "There is a solidarity between Germany and France. . . . On this solidarity depend all hopes of uniting Europe. . . . In consequence the destiny of the whole of Europe, from the Atlantic to the Ural Mountains" (Press conference of May 15, 1962).

138. Press conference of July 29, 1963.

139. The PREAMBLE stipulated that Franco-German cooperation is to take place within the framework of the Atlantic Alliance and was intended to preserve a close partnership between Europe and the United States. Keesing's CONTEMPORARY ARCHIVES, vol. 24 (1963-64), p. 19507.

140. It should be noted that de Gaulle's own vision was inconsistent in that he aimed at the creation of a "third force" between the two superpowers on the one hand, and at the construction of a pan-European entity including the USSR on the other. Obviously, the attainment of the latter implies the demise of the first.

141. Elliot R. Goodman, "The World through de Gaulle's Looking Glass," ORBIS 11, no. 1 (Spring 1967): 92.

142. MAJOR ADDRESSES, p. 225. Address of April 19, 1963.

143. Harold van B. Cleveland, "The Common Market after de Gaulle," FOREIGN AFFAIRS 47, no. 4 (July 1969): 703.

144. Press Conferences of September 9, 1965 and July 29, 1963.

145. See Chapter 4.

146. Cleveland, "Common Market after de Gaulle," p. 697.

147. André Francois-Ponçet in LE FIGARO, November 27, 1961, p. 1.

313

148. Salvador de Madariaga. "de Gaulle versus Europe," SWISS REVIEW OF WORLD AFFAIRS 13, no. 1 (April 1963): 2.

149. Roy C. Macridis, ed., DE GAULLE: IMPLACABLE ALLY (New York: Harper & Row, 1966), p. xxxiv.

150. Roger Massip, DE GAULLE ET L'EUROPE (Paris: Flammarion, 1963), p. 28.

151. Stanley Hoffmann in Nye, ed., "International Regionalism," p. 213.

152. Cleveland, "Common Market after de Gaulle," p. 704.

153. Macridis, DE GAULLE, p. 29.

154. Louis Armand quoted in an address by Paul-Henri Spaak delivered in Memphis. THE ATLANTIC COMMUNITY QUARTERLY 7, no. 1 (Spring 1969): 47.

155. Goodman, "de Gaulle's Looking Glass," p. 89.

156. Ibid.

157. MAJOR ADDRESSES, p. 177. De Gaulle believed that such a federator did not exist in Europe; he apparently overlooked himself.

158. Contrary to the Treaty of Paris, the Rome Treaties did not provide for supranational organs; however, the principle of majority voting—a hallmark of the community—had been preserved.

159. "Nationalism is a habit, a conditioned reflex, that lies just below the surface of consciousness of modern men, ready to break out at any moment . . . [but] a strong leader can caputre and direct the conflicting forces [of nationalism] . . . I am not, therefore, much impressed when apologists argue that, because nationalism is a powerful force easy to arouse, it is the wave of the future." George W. Ball, DISCIPLINE OF POWER, p. 148.

160. "The Franco-German Treaty of 1963 never had much meaning . . . [and following Adenauer's death] de Gaulle concluded that the Franco-German gambit had outlived its usefulness." Ibid., p. 138.

161. Goodman, "de Gaulle's Looking Glass," p. 105.

162. Ibid.

163. For an examination of the problems of "European security" see Chapter 8.

Chapter 4
Policy Harmonization and Institutional Development

1. See Appendices A, B, and D.
2. Majority Voting Rules in Stage I (italics)
   a) For the rules of competition (article 87:1)
   b) For the prohibition of discrimination on the grounds of nationality (articles 7)

c) For the settlement of technical difficulties arising from the common external tariff (article 21:1)

d) For the granting, in certain cases, of tariff quotas to a member state (article 25:1)

e) For the granting of mutual assistance (article 108:2)

f) For the exclusion of certain activities from the right of establishment (article 55)

g) To oblige a member state to abolish certain measures restricting the free movement of capital (article 70)

h) With a view to the application of the principles prohibiting state aids (article 94)

i) To extend the right of establishment to the overseas countries and territories and to Algeria (implementing convention relating to the association with the community of the overseas countries and territories (articles 8 and 16), now superseded by the Yaoundé Convention

j) To revoke an authorization granted by the commission to a member state to take safeguard measures in the even of balance-of-payment difficulties (article 108:3)

k) To suspend safeguard measures taken directly by a state in the event of a sudden crisis in its balance of payments (article 109:3)

l) For the establishment of the community budget (article 203:3)

3. Majority Voting rules in Stage II (italics)

a) Elimination of distortions in the conditions of competition resulting from legislative measures taken by one of the member states (article 101)

b) Implementation of the General Program on freedom of establishment (article 54:2)

c) Implementation of the General Program on freedom to supply services (article 63:2)

d) Mutual recognition of diplomas to facilitate the exercise of nonwage-earning activities (article 57:1)

e) Coordination of administrative provisions concerning the exercise of nonwage-earning activities (article 57:2), with the exception of matters subject to legislative provisions and measures concerning the protection of savings, the allotment of credit, banking and medical, paramedical and pharmaceutical professions, which will still require a unanimous vote

f) The procedure for the gradual abolition of quotas (article 33.8)

4. Majority Voting Rules in Stage III (italics)

a) The putting into effect of a common agricultural policy (article 43:2)

b) The pricing of agricultural products (article 44:5)

c) Legislation regarding foreign nationals (article 56:2)

d) The free movement of capital (article 69)

e) International transport across a member state (article 75:1)

f) A common commercial policy (article 111)

g) The harmonization of export aids (article 112:1)

h) Trade negotiations with nonmember countries (article 113)

i) Powers to conduct trade negotiations (article 114)

5. WEU: 1966, Paris, March 1967, p. 76.

6. Ibid.

7. It is interesting to note that notwithstanding this disagreement between the members of the community, operations continued normally within the institutional framework, following the French boycott of the European Community during the crisis period from July to December 1965.

8. *Provisions of the "Luxembourg Protocol":*

1. It is desirable that the Commission, before adopting a proposal of particular importance, should, through the Permanent Representatives, make appropriate contacts with the governments of the member states, without this procedure affecting the right of initiative which the Commission derives from the Treaty.

2. Proposals and all other official acts which the Commission addresses to the Council and the member states shall only be made public after the latter have formally taken cognizance of them and have the texts in their possession. The 'Official Gazette' should be arranged so that legislative acts having a binding force are published distinctly as such.

3. The credentials of Heads of Mission of non-member states accredited to the Community shall be presented to the President of the Council and the President of the Commission, meeting together for this purpose.

4. The Council and the Commission will inform each other rapidly and fully of any approaches relating to fundamental questions made to either Institution by non-member states.

5. Within the scope of the application of Article 162, the Council and the Commission will consult together on the advisability of, the procedure for, and the nature of any links which the Commission might establish, under Article 229 of the Treaty, with international organizations.

6. Cooperation between the Council and the Commission on the Community's information policy, which was examined by the Council on September 24, 1963, will be strengthened so that the program of the Press and Information Service shall be drawn up and carried out jointly, in accordance with procedures to be defined later and which might include an ad hoc body.

7. Within the framework of the financial regulations for drawing up and putting into effect the Communities' budgets, the Council and the Commission will define methods of increasing the efficiency of control over the acceptance, authorization and execution of the Communities' expenditures.

9. Clark, POLITICS OF COMMON MARKET, p. 32.

10. The exact number of shelved proposals in 1972 was 350. (Agence EUROPE, March 16, 1972, no. 1007, p. 4).

11. The first president of the commission was Walter Hallstein (Germany) who served from 1958 to 1966; he was succeeded by Jean Rey (Belgium), who served until 1970; he was followed by Franco-Maria Malfatti (Italy) who resigned in 1972 and was replaced by Sicco Mansholt (Netherlands).

12. The 13 members of the new Commission of the enlarged European Communities are: President Francois-Xavier Ortoli, of France; Vice President Wilhelm Haferkamp, of Germany; Vice President Patrick J. Hillery, of Ireland; Vice President Carlo Scarascia-Mugnozza, of Italy; Vice President Christopher J. Soames, of Britain; Vice President Henri F. Simonet, of Belgium; Commissioner Albert Borschette, of Luxembourg; Commissioner Jean-Francois Deniau, of France; Commissioner Finn Olav Gunderlach, of Denmark; Commissioner Ralf Dahrendorf, of Germany; Commissioner Pierre J. Lardinois, of the Netherlands, and Commissioner George Thomson, of Britain.

13. See Chapter 3.

14. Paul Taylor, "The Concept of Community and the European Integration Process," JOURNAL OF COMMON MARKET STUDIES 7, no. 2 (December 1968): 91.

15. Lindberg-Scheingold, EUROPE'S WOULD-BE POLITY, pp. 93-94.

16. Clark, POLITICS OF COMMON MARKET, p. 77.

17. See his UNITED EUROPE: CHALLENGE AND OPPORTUNITY (Cambridge: Harvard Univ. Press. 1962), p. 11.

18. See his "Some of our 'faux problèmes' in the European Economic Community," THE WORLD TODAY 21, no. 1 (January 1965).

19. See Luxembourg Protocol, point 3.

20. EUROPEAN COMMUNITY (October 1967), no. 106, p. 5.

21. EUROPE DOCUMENTS, no. 594, September 24, 1970, p. 9.

22. WESTERN EUROPEAN UNION: 1964 (Paris: March 1965), p. 94.

23. Ibid.

24. EUROPEAN COMMUNITY, July 1968, no. 114, p. 3.

25. COMMISSION, Brussels, 1971, p. 21.

26. Agence EUROPE, July 29, 1971, no. 859, p. 3. The so-called Vedel Group was made up of Professors Georges Vedel (France), Jean Buchmann (Belgium), Leopoldo Elia (Italy), August Fleischer (Norway), Jochan Frohein (Germany), P.J. Kaptejn (Netherlands), Maurice Lagrange (France), John D. Mitchell (UK), Mary Robinson (Ireland), Ulrich Scheumer (Germany), Andrew Schonfield (UK), Max Sorenson (Denmark), Felix Welter (Luxembourg). (Agence EUROPE, October 14, 1971, no. 903).

27. For details see Chapter 5.

28. David Coombes, POLITICS AND BUREAUCRACY IN THE EUROPEAN COMMUNITY (Beverly Hills, Calif.: Sage Publications, 1970).

29. Ralf Dahrendorf (Germany) writing under the pseudonym of "Wieland

Europe" in DIE ZEIT. See Agence EUROPE, September 2, 1971, no. 873, p. 6.

30. Lawrence Scheinman, "Some Preliminary Notes on Bureaucratic Relationships in the EEC," INTERNATIONAL ORGANIZATION 20, no. 4 (Autumn 1966): 751.

31. Ibid.

32. Lawrence Scheinman, "Economic Regionalism and International Administration: The European Communities Experience," in Robert S. Jordan, ed. INTERNATIONAL ADMINISTRATION: ITS EVOLUTION AND CONTEMPORARY APPLICATIONS (New York: Oxford Univ. Press, 1971) pp. 195, 203.

33. See Chapter 7.

34. The Rome Treaty refers to this body as "Assembly," but it renamed itself twice in its history: to "European Parliamentary Assembly" (in 1958) to "European Parliament" (in 1962).

35. During the parliamentary year 1969/70, the delegates tabled a record number of 508 written questions, making this procedure one of the most significant means of exercising political control over the executives. EUROPEAN COMMUNITY, September 1970, no. 138, p. 15. For a detailed treatment of the European Parliament see: Kenneth Lindsay EUROPEAN ASSEMBLIES (London: Stevens, 1966).

36. The irreverent attitude of the Council vis-à-vis the Parliament is in part due to the fact that it serves as a forum where "converted European missionaries go to preach to other converted European missionaries" (THE ECONOMIST, June 1972).

37. European Parliament, POUR L'ELECTION DU PARLEMENT EURO-PÉEN AU SUFFRAGE UNIVERSEL DIRECT. Luxembourg, September 1969.

38. Agence EUROPE, November 9, 1971, no. 919, p. 2. See also Chapter 5.

39. Art. 164, 169, 173, 175, 176, 177 of the EEC Treaty.

40. Art. 170, 171, 182 of the EEC Treaty.

41. Art. 178, 179, 171 of the EEC Treaty.

42. Agence EUROPE, THE FACTS, p. 7. For a detailed analysis of the Court see Werner J. Feld, THE COURT OF THE EUROPEAN COMMUNITIES: A NEW DIMENSION IN INTERNATIONAL ADJUDICATION (The Hague: M. Nijhoff, 1964); and Stuart A. Scheingold. THE RULE OF LAW IN EUROPEAN INTEGRATION (New Haven: Yale University Press, 1965).

43. For an examination of the role of the ESC see Dusan Sidjanski, "Pressure Groups and the European Economic Community," GOVERNMENT AND OPPOSITION" 2, no. 3 (April-July, 1967).

44. Art. 108, EEC Treaty. This article has been invoked during the crisis caused by the devaluation of the Franc in August 1969.

45. See art. 15 of the Treaty establishing ECSC (1951).

46. See: Eric Stein and Peter Hay, DOCUMENTS FOR LAW AND INSTITUTIONS IN THE ATLANTIC AREA (Indianapolis: Bobbs-Merrill, 1967), pp. 194-207.

Chapter 5
Catalysts of Integration and Disintegration

1. See Appendix A. This decision marked the formal acceptance of the same (informal) proposal made by the commission under President Hallstein in March 1965 which subsequently led to the French boycott of the community and to the resignation of the first commission president.

2. EUROPEAN COMMUNITY, February 1971, no. 142, p. 8.

3. EUROPEAN COMMUNITY, February 1971.

4. The "Vedel Report," Agence EUROPE, April 15, 1972, no. 1027. See also Chapter 4.

5. Articles 43, 54, 56, 57, 75, 84, 87, 99, 100, 103, 113, 126, and 128 (EEC Treaty); article 31, 76, 85, and 90 (Euratom Treaty); and art. 24 (Merger Treaty).

6. Ibid.

7. Ibid.

8. Agence EUROPE, February 26, 1971, no. 755, p. 2.

9. EUROPEAN DOCUMENTATION, April-June 1970, p. 10.

10. Agence EUROPE, December 23, 1971, no. 950, p. 2. The British delegation to the European Parliament was sponsored by both a Conservative (Duncan Sandys, MP) and a Labour (Michael Stuart, MP) delegate.

11. Agence EUROPE, March 4, 1972, no. 999. p. 2.

12. Agence EUROPE, October 6, 1971, no. 897, p. 2. Of course, it could be argued that, given the recent decline of parliamentary powers in modern political systems, direct elections might not effectively enhance the influence of the European Parliament. Nevertheless it can be expected that an increase in the legitimacy of the Parliament will be accompanied by a relative increase of authority and vice versa.

13. This constituant assembly could emerge as early as 1978 and fulfill a function comparable to the Philadelphia Convention of 1787.

14. Robert L. Pfaltzgraff, "NATO and European Security," ORBIS 15, no. 1 (Spring 1971): 177. Note that the draft budget for the European Community in 1973 amounts to $5.5 billion. EUROPEAN COMMUNITY (October 1972), no. 159.

15. Karl Kaiser, "Transnational Relations as a Threat to the Democratic Process," INTERNATIONAL ORGANIZATION 25, no. 3 (Summer 1971): 715.

16. ESCS constitutes an example of limited structural integration among the six member states (coal and steel industries).

17. AFGA (Germany)–Gevaert (Belgium) in the photographic business (1965); Vereinigte Flugtechnische Werke (Germany)–Fokker (Netherlands) in the aircraft industry (1969); Dunlop (Britain) and Pirelli (Italy) in tire production (1970).

18. J.J. Sérvan-Schreiber, THE AMERICAN CHALLENGE (New York:

Atheneum, 1968). He warns that the third industrial power in the world, after the US and the USSR, will be American industry in Europe (not a united Europe) p. 3.

19. EUROPEAN COMMUNITY, February 1971, no. 142, p. 21.

20. INTRODUCTION TO THE TENTH GENERAL REPORT, Supplement to the Bulletin no. 7, Brussels, 1967, p. 25. The basis for this proposal was a draft statute for European companies prepared by the so-called Sanders Committee in 1966.

21. EUROPEAN COMMUNITY, August 1970, no. 137, p. 4. This draft of June 24, 1970, was based upon the commission's recommendations of 1966 and March 18, 1970; the latter were contained in the FOURTH GENERAL REPORT, 1970. Brussels, February 1971, p. 168.

22. It is subject to approval by the council after consultation with the Economic and Social Council and the European Parliament.

23. EUROPEAN COMMUNITY, August 1970, p. 6.

24. EUROPEAN COMMUNITY, September 1968, no. 116, p. 3.

25. Intracommunity trade increased by 530 percent (1958-1970); the community is the world's largest trader. THE FACTS, p. 2.

26. Friedrich, EUROPE: AN EMERGENT NATION? p. 49. Almost 90 percent were favorable to integration.

27. Ibid., p. 64.

28. Werner Feld, "Political Aspects of Transnational Business Collaboration in the Common Market," INTERNATIONAL ORGANIZATION, 24, no. 2 (Spring 1970): 209. Transnational mergers increased from 24 in 1959 to 565 in 1966 (p. 213).

29. Friedrich, EUROPE: AN EMERGENT NATION, p. 65.

30. Other European-wide interest groups for business and agriculture are the Conseil des Fédérations Commerciales d'Europe (CFCE) and the Comité des Organizations Professionelles Agricoles (COPA). The total number of European industrial associations increased from 88 in 1961 to 135 in 1965 (Friedrich, EUROPE, p. 75).

31. See Dusan Sidjanski, "Pressure Groups and the EEC," GOVERNMENT AND OPPOSITION, 2, no. 3 (April-July 1967): 407.

32. EUROPEAN COMMUNITY: PRESS RELEASE of June 22, 1971.

33. BASIC STATISTICS OF THE COMMUNITY, 1970, p. 20. The respective figures for France and Germany were: total labor force 20,494,000; in agriculture 3,011,000 and total labor force in Germany 26,516,000; agricultural workers 2,533,000.

34. AGRICULTURE 1980 (Brussels: Commission Document, 1968) p. 2.

35. Ibid.

36. Ibid. Another desirable by-product of this reform would be a substantial reduction of agricultural surplus products that have accumulated due to the numerous but inefficient agricultural production facilities.

37. Robertson, EUROPEAN INSTITUTIONS, p. 42 and 62. Although not all of these conventions were signed or ratified by all European states, the signatory nations derive mutual benefits from them.

38. Ibid., p. 43.

39. Art. 3 of the Statute of the Council of Europe.

40. Robertson, EUROPEAN INSTITUTIONS, p. 46-47.

41. Ibid.

42. Ibid., p. 43-44.

43. EEC Treaty, arts. 43-66.

44. EEC Treaty, arts. 123-128.

45. EEC Treaty, arts. 117-122.

46. EEC Treaty, arts. 118.

47. See Appendix A, item 12. The council decided on reform on Feb. 1, 1971.

48. FOURTH GENERAL REPORT, Brussels, February, 1971, p. 45.

49. EUROPEAN COMMUNITY, July 1969, no. 125, p. 14.

50. Ibid. The figure for Germany in 1970 rose to 3 million (GERMAN TRIBUNE, September 2, 1971).

51. FOURTH GENERAL REPORT, p. 115.

52. EUROPEAN COMMUNITY, May 1969, no. 123, p. 14.

53. EUROPEAN DOCUMENTATION, April-June 1969, p. 166.

54. THE FACTS, p. 19.

55. Ibid.

56. Friedrich, EUROPE: AN EMERGENT NATION? p. 159.

57. Ibid., p. 155.

58. Ibid., p. 164.

59. Ibid., p. 172.

60. See Puchala, "International Transactions and Regional Integration" INTERNATIONAL ORGANIZATION, 24, no. 3 (Autumn 1970), p. 748. The number of French and German tourists increased from 64,000 in 1929 to 1,207,400 in 1961.

61. OECD sources quoted in Sampson, ANATOMY OF EUROPE, inside cover.

62. Agence EUROPE, March 8, 1972, no. 1001, p. 6.

63. Quoted in Friedrich, EUROPE: AN EMERGENT NATION? p. 161.

64. Puchala, "International Transactions," p. 741.

65. Friedrich, EUROPE: AN EMERGENT NATION? p. 209.

66. Puchala, "International Transactions," p. 748. For example, the flow of mail between France and Germany increased from a total of 11.5 million letters in 1937 to 54.5 million letters in 1961.

67. Agence EUROPE, February 8, 1972, no. 980, p. 6.

68. Friedrich, EUROPE: AN EMERGENT NATION? p. 179.

69. Robert H. Beck et al, THE CHANGING STRUCTURE OF EUROPE:

ECONOMIC, SOCIAL, AND POLITICAL TRENDS (Minneapolis: University of Minnesota Press, 1970), p. 17. See also: A HISTORY OF EUROPE? (1960) and HISTORY TEACHING AND HISTORY TEXTBOOK REVISION (1967).

70. Ibid., p. 181. See: GEOGRAPHY TEACHING AND THE REVISION OF GEOGRAPHY TEXTBOOKS AND ATLASES (1963).

71. Ibid., p. 180. See: INTRODUCING EUROPE TO SENIOR PUPILS (1966). Note: Efforts are under way to organize a "European baccalauréat" under the auspices of the Council of Europe.

72. Robertson, EUROPEAN INSTITUTIONS, p. 62.

73. Periodic publications include: EUROPEAN COMMUNITY and EUROPEAN UNIVERSITY NEWS.

74. EUROPEAN COMMUNITY, February 1971, no. 142.

75. Beck, CHANGING STRUCTURE OF EUROPE, p. 176.

76. L'EUROPE EN FORMATION (Paris), November 1963, no. 44, p. 16.

77. PANORAMA OF FEDERALIST THOUGHT (Paris: La Colombe, 1956) and THE EUROPEAN IDEA: 1918-1965 (Bruges, 1965).

78. Paris: Presses d'Europe. The CIFE also publishes the monthly L'EUROPE EN FORMATION.

79. L'EUROPE DANS LE MONDE, (Paris: Payot, 1965), and LA RÉVOLUTION FÉDÉRALISTE (Paris: Presses d'Europe, 1970).

80. See Gerhard Mally, INTERNATIONAL UNIVERSITY NICE (Paris: CIFE, 1965).

81. For example between the following universities: Aix-Tübingen, Bordeaux-Hamburg, Grenoble-Freiburg, Lyon-Frankfurt, Montpellier-Heidelberg etc. See Friedrich's EUROPE: AN EMERGENT NATION? pp. 184, 188.

82. EUROPEAN UNIVERSITY NEWS (Paris) November 1970, p. 18.

83. Ibid., p. 21.

84. The initial financial support comes from the national budgets of the six member states: expenditures are apportioned as follows: 28 percent for France, Italy, and Germany; 7.9 percent for Belgium and the Netherlands and 0.2 percent for Luxembourg. Agence EUROPE, March 31, 1972, no. 1018, p. 4. The statute creating the EUI was officially signed on April 19, 1972.

85. Agence EUROPE, November 16, 1971, no. 923, p. 3.

86. Friedrich, EUROPE: AN EMERGENT NATION? p. 182.

87. Agence EUROPE, November 18, 1971, no. 925, p. 8. The Center would sponsor research on European educational problems such as harmonization of curricula; it would not be confined to the Six.

88. Beck, CHANGING STRUCTURE OF EUROPE, p. 175. Note that in addition to academic personnel, youth exchanges involve workers, artisans, and many other categories.

89. EUROPEAN COMMUNITY, June 1968, no. 113, p. 13.

90. Ibid. Asked what attributes they associated with France, 56 percent of the Germans said "elegance," 27 percent said "individuality," 15 percent said

"frivolity," 12 percent said "boasting," and 10 percent said "logic." The French responded as follows about the Germans: 76 percent said "discipline," 29 percent said "pride," 22 percent said "romanticism," 16 percent said "slowness of wit," and 12 percent said "aggressiveness."

91. Yvon Bourdet, whose Study PRÉJUGÉS FRANÇAIS ET PRÉJUGÉS ALLEMANDS was published by the Franco-German Youth Office in 1968.

92. EUROPEAN COMMUNITY, June 1968, p. 14.

93. Puchala, "Integration and Disintegration in Franco-German Relations," pp. 190-191.

94. "An End to European Integration?" APSR 61, no. 1 (March 1967).

95. Ibid., p. 93. The overall percentage for European unification was the following: France: Adults 72 percent, Youth 93 percent; Germany: Adults 81 percent, Youth 95 percent; Netherlands: Adults 87 percent, Youth 95 percent; Britain: Adults 65 percent, Youth 72 percent.

96. EUROPEAN COMMUNITY, May 1970, no. 134, p. 15. The five questions dealt with specific proposals for supranational integration.

97. Ibid.

98. Adapted from Ronald Inglehart, "Public Opinion and Regional Integration," INTERNATIONAL ORGANIZATION 24, no. 4 (Autumn 1970): 787.

99. Adapted from Ronald Inglehart, "Public Opinion and Regional Integration," INTERNATIONAL ORGANIZATION 24, no. 4 (Autumn 1970): 790.

100. Ibid.

101. Anthony Sampson, ANATOMY OF EUROPE (New York: Harper & Row, 1968), p. 420-1. Sampson's impressions on the rise of a "European generation" are shared by the author of this study who interviewed a large number of European postgraduates (potential leaders) as a faculty member of the Institut Européan des Hautes Etudes Internationales in Nice, France and of the Collège Universitaire d'Etudes Fédéralistes in Aosta, Italy (summer sessions 1963-1966). These impressions seem to confirm the truism that "nothing begets change like a change of generations."

102. For example, a Frenchman in his fifties who learned in school that the Germans are aggressive and ruthless, an image that was confirmed during the war when he was wounded or mistreated by German soldiers, will be reluctant to accept the "friendly neighbor" approach and supranational measures proposed by advocates of European unity.

103. This term does not contain or imply any value judgment; it merely describes the sociopolitical reality of conflicting trends in the European (and for that matter in any) regional setting.

104. Zbigniew Brzezinski, ALTERNATIVE TO PARTITION (New York: McGraw-Hill, 1965), pp. 85-86.

105. Frans Alting von Geusau, BEYOND THE EUROPEAN COMMUNITY (Leyden: Sijthoff, 1969), pp. 224, 230.

106. Karl W. Deutsch et al. FRANCE, GERMANY, AND THE WESTERN

ALLIANCE, p. 150. The percentage was 72 percent pro US; 35 percent EEC nations; 28 percent Britain (multiple responses were allowed; 1967).

107. In a survey conducted in November 1970, Germans still favored close cooperation with the following nations in that order: United States (86 percent), France (75 percent), Britain (62 percent) of multiple responses. EUROPEAN COMMUNITY, March 1971, no. 143, p. 18. Ibid., p. 71. The percentage was 88 percent pro EEC nations; 87 percent pro US; 52 percent pro Britain.

108. Sampson, ANATOMY OF EUROPE, p. 113.

109. Ronald Inglehart, "The New Europeans: Inward or Outward-Looking?" INTERNATIONAL ORGANIZATION 24, no. 1 (Winter 1970): 139.

110. EUROPEAN COMMUNITY (March 1972), no. 154, p. 18.

111. Merry and Serge Bromberger. JEAN MONNET AND THE UNITED STATES OF EUROPE (New York: Coward-McCann, 1969) p. 334.

112. Leon N. Lindberg, "Integration as a Source of Stress on the European Community System," in Nye, ed., INTERNATIONAL REGIONALISM, pp. 244-245.

113. Among other national symbols that resist "Europeanization" are: national news media (TV, radio, and the press) which is mainly "domestically" oriented and use their respective languages; airlines as national "flag-carriers" such as "Air France"; national school systems, and of course, national armed forces. Sometimes obnoxious tourists and radical exchange students may serve as divisive elements—a proof that communication is not necessarily a centripetal force.

114. See Stanley Hoffmann in Nye, ed. INTERNATIONAL REGIONALISM, p. 183.

115. Anthony Downs, INSIDE BUREAUCRACY, p. 8.

116. Ibid., p. 23.

117. Werner Feld, "The National Bureaucracies of the EEC Member States and Political Integration: A Preliminary Inquiry" in Jordan, ed., pp. 231, 234.

118. Ibid., p. 242. Feld explains this inconsistency in two possible ways: either they have not faced up to the implications of unification, or they may want to conceal consciously or subconsciously their understandable concern.

119. See André Gorz, STRATEGY FOR LABOR: A RADICAL PROPOSAL. (Boston: Beacon Press, 1969) p. 149. He contrasts this "nationalist coalition" with the "Atlantic Coalition" (neo-liberals, free-traders, bankers) and the "European Coalition" (Eurocrats and their allies).

120. For instance, 44 percent of the Germans and 34 percent of the Dutch stated in an opinion poll that the CAP is detrimental to farmers. (Agence EUROPE, February 16, 1972, no. 986, p. 9.)

121. Stuart J. Scheingold, "Domestic and International Consequences of Regional Integration," INTERNATIONAL ORGANIZATION 24, no. 4 (Autumn 1970): p. 992. See also Sampson, Anatomy of Europe, p. 421, and various issues of AGENOR. The lack of consumer representation at the European

Community level has also been deplored (THE GERMAN TRIBUNE, April 22, 1971).

122. EUROPEAN COMMUNITY (July 1970), no. 136, p. 18.

Chapter 6
The Enlargement of the Common Market and Its Implications

1. The only EFTA member to "hold out" until 1970 (when she applied for association with the EEC) was Portugal.

2. Mally, BRITAIN AND EUROPEAN UNITY, p. 20.

3. EUROPEAN COMMUNITY, February, 1971, no. 142. Only Austria did not withdraw her request.

4. EUROPEAN COMMUNITY, June, 1967, no. 103, p. 13. Articles 205 of the ECSC Treaty and 98 of the Euratom Treaty provide for the enlargement of these two organizations.

5. The vote in the House of Commons in 1967 was: 358 Labour MPs in favor, 36 against and 51 abstaining; 259 Conservatives in favor, 26 against and 29 abstaining; 12 Liberals for and one against British entry. Ibid., p. 14.

6. WEU: MONTHLY NOTE NO. 11, Paris, November, 1967, p. 6.

7. Appendix A, item 13.

8. EUROPEAN COMMUNITY, July, 1970, no. 136, p. 13.

9. EUROPEAN COMMUNITY, June 1971, no. 146, p. 17.

10. AMBASSADE DE FRANCE, Service de Press et d'Information, May 21, 1971.

11. EUROPEAN COMMUNITY, July-August, 1971, no. 147, p. 10.

12. Ibid. The same transition period was granted to the other three applicant countries and applies to most industrial and agricultural products. Most data in this section are based upon this issue of EUROPEAN COMMUNITY.

13. Agence EUROPE, July 5, 1971, no. 842, p. 3. In its edition of July 27, 1971, Agence EUROPE published the text of the commission's declaration on contact procedures during the interim period.

14. Mally, BRITAIN AND EUROPEAN UNITY, p. 53. It should be recalled that the United Kingdom had signed an "Agreement of Association" with the ECSC, on December 21, 1954 (without becoming a member).

15. Ibid., p. 23.

16. Ibid., p. 22. However, it should be noted that these questions would have been raised sooner or later if de Gaulle's veto had not intervened.

17. EUROPEAN COMMUNITY, November-December 1969, no. 129, p. 4.

18. EUROPE DOCUMENTS, no 608.

19. Ibid., pp. 5-6.

20. Ibid.

21. EUROPEAN COMMUNITY, no. 147.

22. Agence EUROPE, July 7, 1971, no. 844, p. 2. The following citations are also based on this issue.

23. BULLETIN of the European Communities, 4, no. 4, 1971, p. 153.

24. Agence EUROPE, September 6, 1971, p. 2.

25. Agence EUROPE, October 4, 1971, p. 2. The resolution was adopted by a vote of 5,073,000 to 1,032,000.

26. Agence EUROPE October 13, 1971, p. 2. The vote was 2,274 to 324.

27. Agence EUROPE, October 29, 1971, p. 2.

28. Ibid.

29. Out of 326 Conservatives, 282 voted for and 39 against entry; out of 289 Labourites, 69 voted for and 199 against the resolution; five out of six Liberals voted with the government. Ibid.

30. The vote was 451 to 58—a majority of 393 in favor of British entry. Ibid.

31. Ibid.

32. Ibid. M. Jean Monnet, who was present at the voting in Parliament, also expressed his satisfaction with the results.

33. Agence EUROPE, February 19, 1972, no. 989. On July 13, 1972, the bill was finally approved by 301 to 284 (EUROPEAN COMMUNITY, October 1972, no. 159).

34. Agence EUROPE, May 13, 1972, no. 1045, p. 2.

35. THE NEW YORK TIMES, September 26, 1972.

36. THE NEW YORK TIMES, October 3, 1972.

37. EUROPEAN COMMUNITY, no. 153.

38. The MANCHESTER GUARDIAN WEEKLY, November 6, 1971, editorial.

39. Camps, EUROPEAN UNIFICATION, p. 220.

40. Pierre Drouin in LE MONDE-GUARDIAN, November 6, 1971, p. 16.

41. Harold van B. Cleveland speaking as a witness before the Foreign Economic Subcommittee of the US House of Representatives' Foreign Affairs Committee on July 20, 1971 (EUROPEAN COMMUNITY, September 1971, no. 148, p. 19). His view was supported by most witnesses, including Mr. John Schnittker, former US Undersecretary of Agriculture (ibid). However, representatives of national farmers organizations were sceptical with regard to the CAP (ibid).

42. Willis C. Armstrong, who became Deputy Undersecretary of State in 1972 (ibid).

43. Robert J. Schaetzel quoted in Agence EUROPE Document no. 638.

44. U.S. FOREIGN POLICY IN THE 1970s (1971 and 1972).

45. UNITED STATES FOREIGN POLICY 1971: A Report of the Secretary of State (Washington, D.C. GPO, 1971), p. viii.

46. Part 4 of the EEC Treaty.

47. THE FACTS, p. 24. The eighteen signatory states are: Burundi, Cameroon, Central African Republic, Chad, Congo-Brazzville, Congo-Kinshasa,

Dahomey, Gabon, Ivory Coast, Madagascar, Mali, Mauritania, Niger, Ruanda, Senegal, Somalia, Togo, and Upper Volta. Mauritius acceeded to the Convention in March 1972 (Agence EUROPE, no. 1002, March 9, 1972).

48. THE FACTS, p. 24.

49. Ibid.

50. The three East African countries are Kenya, Uganda, and Tanzania.

51. Ibid.

52. Ibid. When the new military regime took over in Greece in 1967, the association agreement with the EEC was temporarily suspended (until democracy is restored); operations are limited to the administration of current affairs only.

53. Agence EUROPE, December 22, 1970, no. 712.

54. Therefore, the American argument that this type of associate membership (which is based on economic rather than political considerations) is inconsistent with GATT rules, has some validity; this is also true in the case of preferential agreements (e.g., with Israel and Spain).

55. EUROPEAN COMMUNITY, February 1971, no. 142, p. 17.

56. EUROPEAN COMMUNITY, March 1972, no. 154, p. 4. The commission defended the planned trade agreements on the ground that the six countries involved account for only 3.6 percent of all US exports, while between 38-61 percent of their exports go to the enlarged European Community (THE MANCHESTER GUARDIAN WEEKLY, November 27, 1971, p. 12).

57. Statement by US deputy undersecretary for economic affairs (Agence EUROPE, April 29, 1972, no. 1037, p. 4).

58. For example, in 1970, 56.1 percent of Austria's total imports came from the EEC and 39.4 percent of the total exports went to the EEC (MONTHLY STATISTICS of Foreign Trade, Brussels, 1971, no. 6, p. 77).

59. The so-called Moscow Memorandum of spring 1955, concluded between an Austrian delegation and the Soviet government, contained an understanding between the parties that Austria would adopt a neutral status as soon as its independence was restored.

60. On July 24, 1970, for instance, Radio Moscow declared that "the rules of the Common Market seek to involve Austria in a dense network of commitments which would do away with the country's sovereignty. . . . " (EUROPEAN COMMUNITY, November-December, 1970, no. 140, p. 10).

61. EUROPEAN COMMUNITY, March 1972, no. 154, p. 15.

62. EUROPEAN COMMUNITY, February 1971, no. 142, p. 17.

63. Ibid.

64. However, Switzerland belongs to several Specialized Agencies of the UN and to the Council of Europe. During 1971, some Swiss officials even contemplated accession to the UN in view of the fact that many other neutral countries find UN membership compatible with their special status.

65. EUROPEAN COMMUNITY, February 1971.

66. Ibid.

67. EUROPEAN COMMUNITY, March 1972.

68. EUROPEAN COMMUNITY, February 1971.

69. Ibid.

70. Ibid., p. 16.

71. Agence EUROPE, no. 1094, July 25, 1972, p. 3-5. Tariff reductions will take place in five stages: on April 1, 1973, and on January 1, 1974, 1975, 1976, and 1977 (20% each year). The free trade already in force between the EFTA countries will be maintained (although EFTA is bound to "go out of business" by 1977).

72. Agence EUROPE, no. 1070, June 20, 1972.

73. Ibid.

74. Ibid.

75. EUROPEAN COMMUNITY, December 1971, no. 151, p. 3. Effective January 1, 1973, these privileges were extended to: Cuba, Bangla-Desh, Bhutan, Fiji, Bahrein and Quatar, Ras-al-Khaimah, Oman, Sikkim, Nauru, Western Samoa, and Tonga (Agence EUROPE, June 28, 1972).

Chapter 7
Alternative Political Structures for the New Europe

1. WEU, POLITICAL UNION OF EUROPE (Paris: June 1964), p. 29 ff.

2. WEU Assembly, 1961: A RETROSPECTIVE VIEW OF THE POLITI-CAL YEAR IN EUROPE. Paris, May 1962, p. 64-67. This draft treaty was submitted by France on Nov. 10, 1961.

3. EUROPEAN COMMUNITY, no. 141, January 1971, p. 18.

4. Editorial, Agence EUROPE, July 31, 1970, no. 623.

5. Ibid.

6. Agence EUROPE, September 13, 1971, no. 880. Originally, Commissioner Ralf Dahrendorf wrote under the pseudonym "Wieland" in DIE ZEIT; he subsequently defended his views as constructive criticism intended to enhance the status of the European Community.

7. Agence EUROPE, May 9, 1972, no. 1042.

8. Ibid. This proposal was reminiscent of the "Fouchet Plan" notion of a European Political Commission located in Paris.

9. WEU: MONTHLY NOTE NO. 1 (Paris: January 1971), p. 19-20.

10. WEU: MONTHLY NOTE NO. 3 (Paris: March 1971), pp. 11-13.

11. THE BULLETIN 19, no. 7 (Bonn, March 2, 1971).

12. LE MONDE, July 8-14, 1971. It should be noted that the leader of the CDU/CSU, Mr. Rainer Barzel also favors a gradualist approach to political unification as evidenced in his "four-stage plan" of 1971 (see Agence EUROPE, no. 627, June 3, 1971).

13. Ambassade de France: Service de Presse et d'Information, New York, May 1971.

14. Agence EUROPE, September 17, 1971, no. 884, p. 2.

15. Agence EUROPE, July 26, 1971, no. 856.

16. See his CHALLENGE AND RESPONSE: A PROGRAM FOR EUROPE (New York: Atheneum, 1970), p. 97.

17. Ibid.

18. See his: OLD WORLD, NEW HORIZONS (Cambridge: Harvard Univ. Press, 1970), p. 73.

19. The WEU Treaty prohibiting atomic weapons (as well as bacteriological and chemical) for West Germany would have to be revised. Furthermore, the McMahon Act limiting American nuclear information to the United Kingdom would have to be amended by the US Congress.

20. François Duchêne, "A New European Defense Community," FOREIGN AFFAIRS 50 (October 1971): 80. "A West European defense organization would be a minimum security assurance against a breakdown in détente." (Ibid., p. 81.)

21. Among its 20-odd component groups are: the European Federalist Movement and the European Center for Federalist Action (which were merged in a joint committee on April 8, 1972), the Council of European Municipalities, European Union of Christian Democrats, European Movement of the Left, Liberal Movement for a United Europe, Association of European Journalists, European Association of Teachers, the Christian Democratic, Socialist, and Liberal Groups of the European Parliament, and the National Councils of the member organizations (governed by a Federal Council and an Executive Committee) YEARBOOK OF INTERNATIONAL ORGANIZATIONS, 1971, p. 813.

22. "Europe 1980 Program" (June 5, 1971) and Resolution of September 13, 1971 (Agence EUROPE DOCUMENTS, nos. 630, and 643).

23. Ibid.

24. Etienne Hirsch (former Euratom President), Agence EUROPE Documents, no. 639.

25. Henri Brugmans (former Rector of the College of Europe), ibid.

26. Altiero Spinelli (former head of the Italian Federalist Movement and member of the European Commission). BULLETIN OF THE EUROPEAN COMMUNITIES, 4, no. 5 (1971), p. 140.

27. For a three phase plan see the resolution of the Europa Union Deutschland, above. See also the agenda of the Paris Summit (Appendix D).

28. Agence EUROPE Documents no. 671, April 14, 1971.

29. Henry A. Kissinger, "Coalition Diplomacy in a Nuclear Age," FOREIGN AFFAIRS (July 1964), p. 143.

30. "The Common Market and Political Federation in Western European Public Opinion," INTERNATIONAL STUDIES QUARTERLY 14, no. 1 (March 1970): 57.

31. Ibid., p. 59. These findings were supported by a European analyst who reported that while 60 percent of Europeans favored a united Europe, only half that number favored a federation. See Jacques R. Rabier, L'OPINION PUBLIQUE ET L'EUROPE (Brussels, 1966), p. 23.

32. Karl W. Deutsch et al., FRANCE, GERMANY AND THE WESTERN ALLIANCE (New York: Scribner, 1967), p. 298.

33. "An End to European Integration?" AMERICAN POLITICAL SCIENCE REVIEW 61, no. 1 (March 1967): 91.

34. Carl Friedrich, EUROPE: AN EMERGENT NATION? p. 42.

35. "An Analysis of the Deutsch Sociocausal Paradigm of Political Integration," INTERNATIONAL ORGANIZATION 23, no. 2 (Spring 1969): 285.

36. EURATLANTICA, (Cambridge, Mass.: M.I.T. Press, 1969), p. 199.

37. Jacques R. Rabier, "The European Idea and National Public Opinion," GOVERNMENT AND OPPOSITION 2, no. 3 (April-July 1967): 446.

38. Ibid.

39. Annamaria Sternberg-Montaldi, LE RÔLE DE L'OPINION PUBLIQUE DANS LA COMMUNAUTÉ ATLANTIQUE (Leyde: A.W. Sythoff, 1963), p. 257.

40. Ronald Inglehart, "Public Opinion and Regional Integration," INTERNATIONAL ORGANIZATION 24, no. 4 (Autumn 1970): 774. These findings were corroborated by a public opinion survey in 1971 which showed that a substantial majority favors the development of the Common Market into a United States of Europe (EUROPEAN COMMUNITY, no. 156, May 1972, p. 3).

41. Ibid. See also his "Changing Value Priorities and European Integration," JOURNAL OF COMMON MARKET STUDIES, 10, no. 1 (Sept. 1971).

Chapter 8
Europe and the World

1. A successful European Security Conference and mutual, balanced force reductions in the 1970s might contribute to a further rapprochement between East and West Europe without producing a Pan-Europe under Soviet souzerainty. The pacification of Europe is indeed a *desideratum*.

2. This neo-Gaullist call for more independence from the United States is qualified—at least for the time being—by France's desire to remain a member of the Atlantic Alliance and to oppose the withdrawal of American troops from the European Continent. For a detailed analysis of European attitudes on the "third force" concept see Gerhard Mally, UNITED EUROPE AND THE ATLANTIC COMMUNITY (Ph.D. dissertation, University of Pennsylvania, 1964).

3. Agence EUROPE Document, no. 667.

4. CHALLENGE AND RESPONSE, (New York: Atheneum, 1970), p. 145.

5. THE BULLETIN (BONN: May 2, 1972), p. 119.

6. "Germany's Westpolitik," FOREIGN AFFAIRS 50, no. 3 (April 1972): 418, 425. His reelection (in Nov. 1972) assured continuity of the *Westpolitik*.

7. THE BULLETIN (Bonn: June 6, 1972), p. 153.

8. OLD WORLD, NEW HORIZONS, p. 75.

9. Agence EUROPE, no. 925, November 18, 1971, p. 3.

10. THE BULLETIN (Bonn: January 4, 1972), p. 5.

11. Ibid., p. 423.

12. THE BULLETIN, May 2, 1972 (German Information Service), p. 120.

13. Ibid., p. 84.

14. EUROPEAN COMMUNITY, no. 159, October 1972, p. 10. The participants in OECD Development Assistance Committee include: the European
Commission, Belgium, France, Germany, Italy, the Netherlands, Britain, Denmark, Norway, Austria, Sweden, Switzerland, Portugal, Canada, the United
States, Australia, and Japan. In 1970, they spent a total of $15,851.2 billion (or
0.80 of their GNP).

AID BY DAC MEMBERS* (in millions of dollars)

	1970	% of GNP–1970	1971	% of GNP–1971
Belgium	308.6	1.23	300.3	1.03
France	1,869.4	1.27	1,655.8	1.02
Germany	1,487.1	.80	1,915.2	.88
Italy	681.9	.73	861.5	.85
Netherlands	456.6	1.46	590.2	1.63
Community Total	4,803.6	–	5,323.0	–
United Kingdom	1,278.6	1.06	1,569.8	1.14
Denmark	85.6	.55	138.3	.80
Norway	66.7	.59	64.6	.51
United States	6,254.0	.64	7,045.0	.67
Other DAC	3,515.0	–	4,157.8	–
Total	15,851.2	.80	18,095.6	.83

Source: OECD Press Release, Paris, July 5, 1972.
*All 1971 figures are provisional.

15. THE US AND THE EUROPEAN COMMUNITY (New York: Manhattan
Publ. Co., 1971), p. 10.

16. William D. Eberle quoted in EUROPEAN COMMUNITY, no. 152,
January 1972, p. 11.

17. Ibid.

18. REPORT TO CONGRESS of February 9, 1972, p. 41.

19. Ibid.

20. EUROPEAN COMMUNITY, November 1971, no. 150, p. 16.

21. UNITED STATES FOREIGN POLICY (Washington, D.C.: G.P.O.,
1971), p. 8.

22. Ambassador Robert J. Schaetzel quoted in agence EUROPE Document no. 638, p. 4.

23. EUROPEAN COMMUNITY, September 1971, no. 148, p. 12. The Council of GATT had previously condemned the US surtax as incompatible with the rules of international trade, since art. 12 of GATT provides only for the imposition of import quotas in case of severe balance-of-payments deficits but not for any surtax (nevertheless, the US cited art. 12 to justify the surtax).

24. Ibid.

25. Agence EUROPE, no. 900, October 11, 1971, p. 5.

26. European Community Information Service, PRESS RELEASE of Sept. 24, 1971.

27. Agence EUROPE, September 14, 1971, no. 881, p. 4. France favored the smaller, Germany the wider margin. The leading monetary expert Professor Robert Triffin also favored greater flexibility of exchange rates and proposed to widen the official fluctuation margin from the existing official 1 percent up to 3 percent. (TIME MAGAZINE, October 4, 1971.)

28. Agence EUROPE, October 1, 1971, no. 894, p. 10.

29. THE NEW YORK TIMES, December 1, 1971.

30. Ibid. During these negotiations Treasury Secretary Connally gained the reputation of being at once partisan, tough and abrasive. European officials, for their part, were often "afflicted with a myopic preoccupation with intra-European problems [and] tend to react with defensive self-righteousness to outsider's criticisms of Community policies and scant consideration for their legitimate commercial interests" (EUROPEAN COMMUNITY, January 1972, no. 152, p. 12).

31. Agence EUROPE, December 14, 1971, no. 943, p. 2.

32. Agence EUROPE, December 20, 1971, no. 947, p. 5.

33. Ibid.

34. Agence EUROPE, December 21, 1971, no. 948, p. 8.

35. Ibid., p. 6.

36. Agence EUROPE, February 12, 1972, no. 984, p. 3.

37. The Senate approved devaluation in March, and the House in May, 1972.

38. Agence EUROPE, February 12, 1972, p. 3.

39. US FOREIGN POLICY FOR THE 1970s, (Washington, D.C.: G.P.O., 1972) pp. 69, 72, and 78.

40. Agence EUROPE, April 29, 1972, no. 1037, p. 4.

41. THE MILITARY BALANCE 1970-71. Institute for Strategic Studies (London, 1970).

42. Ibid.

43. WHITE PAPER 1971/72 published by the German federal government, 1971, p. 170.

44. US FOREIGN POLICY 1969-1970, p. 166.

45. Foreign Policy Report to Congress by President Nixon, 1972, p. 45.

46. Ambassador Schaetzel in EUROPE DOCUMENTS, no. 638. Since 1958 US Investments in the Common Market have increased fivefold and amounted to some $10.2 billion in 1971.

47. For the figures see Table I-A.

48. Schaetzel, Europe Documents, no. 638.

49. US FOREIGN POLICY 1969-1970, p. 166.

50. US FOREIGN POLICY FOR THE 1970s, p. 44.

51. John Newhouse, "US Troops in Europe: Issues and Alternatives," THE ATLANTIC COMMUNITY QUARTERLY, 9, no. 4 (Winter 1971-72): 473. It should be remembered that Senator Mansfield, supported by a sizable number of senators, repeatedly called for a substantial unilateral reduction of US troops in Europe. For details see: John Yochelson, "The American Military Presence in Europe: Current Debate in the United States," ORBIS 15, no. 3 (Fall 1971): 784 ff. See also Robert L. Pfaltzgraff, "NATO and European Security: Prospects for the 1970s," ORBIS 15, no. 1 (Spring 1971): 154 ff.

52. Nixon, Foreign Policy Report, 1972.

53. See MILITARY BALANCE 1970-71 (London: Institute for Strategic Studies, 1970) p. 91 ff.

54. Walter Lippmann UNITED STATES FOREIGN POLICY: SHIELD OF THE REPUBLIC (Boston: Little, Brown, and Co., 1943), p. 135.

55. Final Report of the Commission on Religion and Spiritual Values of the Conference on Atlantic Community (Bruges, 1957), Ernst Bieri et al., BASIC VALUES OF THE ATLANTIC COMMUNITY (London: The Pall Mall Press Ltd., 1962), pp. 129-30. This conference was sponsored jointly by the College of Europe and the University of Pennsylvania and held in Bruges (Belgium) in September 1957.

Statement of the ATLANTIC CONGRESS concerning the Moral and Spiritual Values of the Atlantic Community (London, June 1959):

1. The Atlantic Congress states that, in spite of differences in their cultural, political and spiritual outlook, the member countries of the Community must realize that they form a *moral unity* which expresses itself through common principles.

2. *Respect for human dignity* is the inalienable basis of civilization. The purpose of political and economic society is to create conditions enabling every human being freely to fulfill his destiny.

3. The guarantee of this dignity is, first, the recognition of objective spiritual values which cannot be altered by any human agency but are the expression of a *natural or transcendent law* governing communities and individuals alike.

4. Among the *fundamental rights* which every authority must recognize and guarantee and which are recognized in the UN Charter and in the Universal Declaration of Human Rights the following should be specifically mentioned:

a. The right to life; the worth of human being—in short, respect for the sanctity of human life.
b. The right to an inviolate personal life.
c. Freedom of speech, conscience, opinion, belief, religion and association.
d. The right of every man to work and receive his just reward.
e. The right of the family to stability and the right of parents over their children and their education.

5. The Atlantic Community recognizes that political and economic society is based indissolubly on the dual *principle of individual liberty and the common good*. It deplores selfish individualism as much as any form of totalitarianism. *It is*, moreover, *open to all political and economic regimes which respect its basic principles*.

6. The safeguards of both *rights and duties* of individuals and peoples must be *constitutionally expressed*. The Law is the essential instrument through which the principles of civilization are put into practice.

7. Respect due to every human being implies the duty to bring material and spiritual well-being progressively within the reach of all at both national and international levels.

8. Peace and unity among all men with justice and freedom are the highest expression of the application of those principles which the Community seeks to promote.

9. Civilization is the common product of all peoples. In particular, Africa, Asia and Oceania have a part to play side by side with the Western peoples. It is important to realize that the common values of civilization are differently expressed by different peoples according to their various traditions.

10. At a time when the future of the world is at stake, when the enslaved peoples are looking for hope, when the peoples of Africa, Asia and Oceania have a decisive choice before them, the Atlantic Community must put forward a constructive concept of civilization of the future, which is capable of winning everyone's support, and must demonstrate by its actions that it is determined to promote that idea. (Emphasis added.)

56. See: Robert Strausz-Hupé et al., BUILDING THE ATLANTIC WORLD (New York: Harper & Row, 1963); Robert L. Pfaltzgraff, THE ATLANTIC COMMUNITY: A COMPLEX IMBALANCE (New York: Van Nostrand, 1969); Burgess-Huntley, EUROPE AND AMERICA (New York: Walker, 1970); Deutsch, POLITICAL COMMUNITY AND THE NORTH ATLANTIC AREA, in International Political Communities, NY: Anchor 1966.
57. Deutsch, POLITICAL COMMUNITY, p. 168 ff.
58. Deutsch, K.W., R.C. Macridis, and R.L. Merritt, FRANCE, GERMANY AND THE WESTERN ALLIANCE, (New York: Scribner, 1967), p. 301.

59. Richard L. Merritt and Donald Puchala, WESTERN EUROPEAN ATTI-
TUDES ON ARMS CONTROL, DEFENSE, AND EUROPEAN UNITY,
1952-1963 (New Haven: Yale University Press, 1966), appendix 7.

60. See Ronald Inglehart, "An End to European Integration?" p. 104. This
internationalism is reinforced by the emergence of a cross-national, post-bour-
geois generation. See his "The Silent Revolution in Europe: Intergenerational
Change in Post-Industrial Societies," AMERICAN POLITICAL SCIENCE RE-
VIEW 65, no. 4 (December 1971): 991 ff.

61. EURATLANTICA, (Cambridge, Mass.: M.I.T. Press, 1969) p. 308-9.

62. Henry Kissinger, "What about the Future?" THE ATLANTIC COM-
MUNITY QUARTERLY 4, no. 3 (Fall 1966), p. 317.

63. Timothy Stanley, NATO, p. 76.

64. Henry A. Kissinger, AMERICAN FOREIGN POLICY (New York:
Norton, 1969), p. 68.

65. Charles W. Yost referring to the "New American Policy" of 1971 in THE
WASHINGTON POST, November 7, 1971, p. B6. In the opinion of a British
editorialist "the danger in Mr. Nixon's approach to the dollar's longstanding
problems is that it is self-evidently protectionist and as such invites retaliation"
(The London DAILY TELEGRAPH quoted in TIME Magazine, August 30,
1971).

66. James Richardson, "The Concept of Atlantic Community," JOURNAL
OF COMMON MARKET STUDIES 3, no. 1 (October 1964): 20.

67. François Duchène, BEYOND ALLIANCE (Paris: The Atlantic Institute,
1965) p. 34.

68. Joseph Kraft, THE GRAND DESIGN (New York: Harper & Row, 1962),
pp. 22-23.

69. Ibid., p. 39.

70. "What about the Future?" p. 328.

71. "America and Ourselves," THE ATLANTIC COMMUNITY QUAR-
TERLY, p. 341. This concept was also adopted by the influential Club Jean
Moulin in its declaration POUR UNE POLITIQUE ÉTRANGERE DE L'EU-
ROPE (Paris: Le Seuil, 1966).

72. EUROPEAN COMMUNITY (January 1972), no. 152, p. 17.

73. Report to Congress of February 25, 1971, p. 30.

74. Ibid.

75. Agence EUROPE, December 21, 1971, no. 948, p. 6.

76. The "Group of Ten" consists of France, Germany, Italy, Netherlands,
Belgium, Britain, Sweden, United States, Canada, and Japan.

77. The "Eurogroup" members are Belgium, Germany, Italy, Luxembourg,
the Netherlands, Britain, Denmark, Norway, Turkey and Greece.

78. Recent examples of such difficulties encountered by the participants in
the Atlantic dialogue are: (1) the obduracy of Congress to abolish the American
selling price, following an agreement between the executive branch and the

European Community; (2) the reluctance on the part of the Council of Ministers (due to French opposition) to institutionalize the Atlantic dialogue as proposed by the commission.

79. Pierre Uri, PARTNERSHIP FOR PROGRESS (New York-Evanston: Harper & Row, 1963), p. 102.

80. Ibid., p. 103.

81. DECLARATION of June 15, 1967 (Brussels), p. 5.

82. DECLARATION of February 24, 1971 (Brussels), p. 7.

83. Curt Gasteyer, EUROPE AND AMERICA AT THE CROSSROADS (Paris: The Atlantic Institute, 1972), p. 18.

84. Ibid., p. 49-50.

85. See Gerhard Mally, "Proposals for Integrating the Atlantic Community," ORBIS 9, no. 2 (Summer 1965): 378 ff. See also Joseph W. Harned and Gerhard Mally, ATLANTIC ASSEMBLY: PROPOSALS AND PROSPECTS (London: Hansard, 1965).

Chapter 9
The European Community in Perspective

1. See Etzioni, "The Epigenesis of Political Communities at the International Level," in James N. Rosenau, ed. INTERNATIONAL POLITICS, p. 351.

2. THE UNITING OF EUROPE, (Stanford, Cal.: Stanford University Press, 1958) p. 524 and 308.

3. Ibid., pp. 526-27.

4. Haas-Schmitter, in "Economics and Differential Patterns of Political Integration," p. 278.

5. See his "The Uniting of Europe," p. 327.

6. "The Study of Regional Integration," p. 635.

7. Ibid., p. 638.

8. Lindberg-Scheingold, EUROPE'S WOULD-BE POLITY, p. 32.

9. Ibid., p. 74.

10. Peter Hay, FEDERALISM AND SUPRANATIONAL ORGANIZATIONS (Urbana, Ill.: University of Illinois Press, 1966), p. 89.

11. Walter Hallstein, UNITED EUROPE: CHALLENGE AND OPPORTUNITY (Cambridge: Harvard Univ. Press, 1962), p. 11 ff.

12. EUROPE: AN EMERGENT NATION? pp. 213-14.

13. Karl Kaiser, "The Interaction of Regional Subsystems," p. 86.

14. Lindberg-Scheingold, p. 32.

15. Walter Yondorf, quoted in ibid., p. 307.

16. Ronn D. Kaiser, "Toward the Copernican Phase of Regional Integration Theory," JOURNAL OF COMMON MARKET STUDIES 10, no. 3 (March 1972): 231.

17. Donald J. Puchala, "Of Blind Men, Elephants, and International Integration," ibid., p. 267 ff.

18. Yondorf, in Lindberg-Scheingold, EUROPE'S WOULD-BE POLITY, p. 307.

19. EUROPEAN UNIFICATION IN THE SIXTIES (New York: McGraw-Hill, 1966), p. 220.

20. John Pinder and Roy Price, EUROPE AFTER DE GAULLE: TOWARDS THE UNITED STATES OF EUROPE (London: Penguin, 1970), p. 129-130.

21. Sérvan-Schreiber, THE AMERICAN CHALLENGE, p. 107.

22. William Pickles. "The Bourbons of Europe," JOURNAL OF COMMON MARKET STUDIES 9, no. 2 (December 1970): 181-82.

23. John Lambert, BRITAIN IN A FEDERAL EUROPE (London: Chatto & Windus, 1970).

24. Karl W. Deutsch, NATIONALISM AND ITS ALTERNATIVES, p. 124.

25. Henry A. Kissinger in AGENDA FOR THE NATION, p. 595.

26. Quoted in Sampson, ANATOMY OF EUROPE, p. 47.

27. Jordan, ed., EUROPE AND THE SUPERPOWERS, pp. 231 and 252.

28. Resolution of the "Congress of Europe" at the Hague, Netherlands, adopted on May 10, 1948. Robertson, EUROPEAN INSTITUTIONS, p. 11.

29. Alexandre Marc, EUROPE TERRE DÉCISIVE (Paris: La Colombe, 1959), p. 24.

30. Preamble to the Treaty establishing the EEC. Robertson, EUROPEAN INSTITUTIONS p. 317.

31. Ibid., p. 299.

32. Arnold J. Zurcher, THE STRUGGLE TO UNITE EUROPE, 1940-1958 (Washington Square, N.Y.: New York University Press, 1958), p. xix.

33. Carol A. Cosgrove and Kenneth J. Twitchett, eds., THE NEW INTERNATIONAL ACTORS: THE U.N. AND THE E.E.C. (New York: St. Martin's Press, 1970), p. 11.

34. Ibid., p. 38. This conclusion seems reinforced by the comparative size of the budget of these two international organizations: United Nations budget for 1971: $183,974,800 (EUROPA YEARBOOK, 1971, p. 7); European Community budget for 1971: $2,764,000,000 (see Chapter 5).

35. For an analysis of rule-making in various IGOs, see Paul A. Tharp, ed., REGIONAL INTERNATIONAL ORGANIZATIONS: STRUCTURES AND FUNCTIONS (New York: St. Martins Press, 1971).

36. Inis L. Claude. EUROPEAN ORGANIZATION, p. 31-32.

37. Inis L. Claude. SWORDS INTO PLOWSHARES: THE PROBLEMS AND PROGRESS OF INTERNATIONAL ORGANIZATION (New York: Random House, 1964), p. 104.

38. Ibid., p. 105.

39. Amitai Etzioni, POLITICAL UNIFICATION, p. 230.

40. Bruce M. Russett, "Interdependence and Capabilities for European Cooperation," p. 149.

41. Karl W. Deutsch, THE ANALYSIS OF INTERNATIONAL RELA-TIONS, p. 190.

42. Frans Alting von Geusau, BEYOND THE EUROPEAN COMMUNITY, p. 8.

43. Henri Brugmans "From Political Defense to World Leadership," ATLAN-TIC COMMUNITY QUARTERLY 2, no. 2 (Summer 1964): 203.

44. James N. Rosenau, "Adaptive Polities in an Interdependent World," ORBIS 16, no. 1 (Spring 1972): 169.

45. This *pragmatic* approach was adopted by the leaders of the New Europe at the Paris Summit in October 1972. On that occasion they agreed to strengthen the institutions of the Community in order to advance the goal of an "Economic and Monetary Union," and to intensify political cooperation in an effort to promote the "European Union" targeted for 1980 (See Appendix D, page 282).

Selected Bibliographies

Official Documents:
  Annual Reports (Commission)
  Bulletin of the European Communities
  Journal Officiel
  Monthly Statistics
  Parliamentary Reports
  Proceedings of the Court of Justice
  Treaties:
    Acts of Accession (1972)
    "Merger Treaty" (1965)
    ECSC Treaty of Paris (1951)
    EEC-Euratom Treaties of Rome (1957)

Yearbooks:
  Europa Yearbook (London)
  European Yearbook (The Hague)
  The Political Year (Paris)

Periodicals:
  Agenor
  Atlantic Community Quarterly
  Common Market Law Review
  Economist, The
  Europa Archiv
  Europe (Agence Europe)
  European Community
  Foreign Affairs
  German Tribune, The
  Guardian-Le Monde
  International Organization
  Interplay
  Journal of Common Market Studies
  NATO Review
  OECD Observer
  Orbis

Suggested Reading*

Altin von Beusau, Frans A.M. BEYOND THE EUROPEAN COMMUNITY. Leyden: Sijthoff, 1969

*This selection complements the source material in the NOTES.

Armand, Louis and Michel Drancourt. THE EUROPEAN CHALLENGE. London: Weidenfeld and Nicolson, 1970.

Axline, W. Andrew. EUROPEAN COMMUNITY LAW AND ORGANIZATIONAL DEVELOPMENT. Dobbs Ferry, N.Y.: Oceana Publications, 1968.

Ball, George W. THE DISCIPLINE OF POWER. Boston: Atlantic-Little-Brown, 1968.

Bliss, Howard. ed. THE POLITICAL DEVELOPMENT OF THE EUROPEAN COMMUNITY: A DOCUMENTARY COLLECTION. Waltham, Mass.: Blaisdell, 1970.

Bloes, Robert. LE PLAN FOUCHET ET LE PROBLÈME DE L'EUROPE POLITIQUE. Bruges, Belgium: College of Europe, 1970.

Bromberger, Merry and Serge. JEAN MONNET AND THE UNITED STATES OF EUROPE. New York: Coward-McCann, 1969.

Buchan, Alastair. EUROPE'S FUTURES, EUROPE'S CHOICES. London: Chatto & Windus, 1969.

Burgess, Randolph W. and James R. Huntley. EUROPE AND AMERICA. New York: Walker, 1970.

Calleo, David P. EUROPE'S FUTURE: THE GRAND ALTERNATIVES. New York: Horizon Press, 1965.

Calleo, David P. THE ATLANTIC FANTASY. Baltimore: Johns Hopkins Press, 1970.

Calmann, John. WESTERN EUROPE: A HANDBOOK. New York: Praeger, 1967.

Camps, Miriam. EUROPEAN UNIFICATION IN THE SIXTIES. New York: McGraw-Hill, 1966.

Clark, Hartley W. THE POLITICS OF THE COMMON MARKET. Englewood Cliffs, N.J.: Prentice-Hall, 1967.

Cleveland, Harlan. NATO: THE TRANSATLANTIC BARGAIN. New York: Harper & Row, 1970.

Deutsch, Karl et al. FRANCE, GERMANY AND THE WESTERN ALLIANCE. New York: Scribner, 1967.

Deutsch, Harold et al. THE CHANGING STRUCTURE OF EUROPE. Minneapolis: Univ. of Minnesota, 1970.

Etzioni, Amitai. POLITICAL UNIFICATION. New York: Holt, Rinehart & Winston, 1965.

Feld, Werner J. THE EUROPEAN COMMON MARKET AND THE WORLD. Englewood Cliffs, N.J.: Prentice-Hall, 1967.

Friedrich, Carl J. EUROPE: AN EMERGENT NATION? New York: Harper & Row, 1969.

Gasteyger, Curt. EUROPE AND AMERICA AT THE CROSSROADS. Paris: The Atlantic Institute (The Atlantic Papers 4), 1971.

Graubard, Stephen (ed.). A NEW EUROPE? Boston: Houghton-Mifflin Co., 1964.

Green, Andrew W. POLITICAL INTEGRATION BY JURISPRUDENCE: THE WORK OF THE COURT OF JUSTICE OF THE EUROPEAN COMMUNITIES IN EUROPEAN POLITICAL INTEGRATION. Leyden: A.W. Sijthoff, 1969.

Haas, Ernst B. THE UNITING OF EUROPE. Stanford, Cal.: Stanford Univ. Press, 1958.

Henig, Stanley. EXTERNAL RELATIONS OF THE EUROPEAN COMMUNITY. London: Chatham House, 1971.

Héraud, Guy. LES PRINCIPES DU FÉDÉRALISME ET AL FÉDÉRATION EUROPÉENNE. Paris: Presses d'Europe, 1970.

Jordan, Robert S. (ed.) EUROPE AND THE SUPERPOWERS. Boston: Allyn & Bacon, 1971.

Laqueur, Walter. THE REBIRTH OF EUROPE. New York: Holt, Rinehart-Winston, 1971.

Kissinger, Henry A. THE TROUBLED PARTNERSHIP. New York: McGraw-Hill, 1965.

Kitzinger, U.W. THE POLITICS AND ECONOMICS OF EUROPEAN INTEGRATION. New York: Praeger, 1963.

Kohnstamm, Max. THE EUROPEAN COMMUNITY AND ITS ROLE IN THE WORLD. Columbia: Univ. of Missouri Press, 1964.

Krause, Lawrence B. EUROPEAN ECONOMIC INTEGRATION AND THE UNITED STATES. Washington, D.C.: Brookings Institution, 1968.

Lerner, Daniel and Morton Gorden. EURATLANTICA. Cambridge, Mass.: M.I.T. Press, 1969.

Lichtheim, George. THE NEW EUROPE. New York: Praeger, 1964.

Lindberg, Leon N. THE POLITICAL DYNAMICS OF EUROPEAN ECONOMIC INTEGRATION. Stanford, Cal.: Stanford Univ. Press, 1963.

Lindberg, Leon N. and Stuart A. Scheingold. EUROPE'S WOULD-BE POLITY. Englewood Cliffs, N.J.: Prentice-Hall, 1970.

Liska, George. EUROPE ASCENDENT. Baltimore: Johns Hopkins Press, 1964.

Marc, Alexandre. EUROPE: TERRE DÉCISIVE. Paris: La Colombe, 1959.

Maynaud, Jean and Dusan Sidjanski. L'EUROPE DES AFFAIRES: ROLES ET STRUCTURES DES GROUPES. Paris: Payot, 1967.

Mayne, Richard. THE RECOVERY OF EUROPE. New York: Harper & Row, 1970.

Mayne, Richard, ed. EUROPE TOMORROW. London: Collins & Co., 1972.

Merritt, Richard L. and Donald T. Puchala, eds. WESTERN EUROPEAN PERSPECTIVES ON INTERNATIONAL AFFAIRS. New York: Praeger, 1968.

Monnet, Jean. LES ETATS UNIS D'EUROPE ONT COMMENCÉ. Paris: Laffort, 1955.

Munk, Frank. THE ATLANTIC DILEMMA: PARTNERSHIP OR COMMUNITY. Dobbs Ferry, N.Y.: Oceana Publ., 1964.

Newhouse, John. DE GAULLE AND THE ANGLO-SAXONS. New York: Viking Press, 1970.

Newhouse, John et al. US TROOPS IN EUROPE. Washington, D.C.: Brookings, 1971.

Nye, Joseph S. PEACE IN PARTS. Boston: Little, Brown & Co., 1971.

Nye, Joseph (ed.). INTERNATIONAL REGIONALISM. Boston: Little, Brown & Co., 1968.

Oudenhove, Guy Van. THE POLITICAL PARTIES IN THE EUROPEAN PARLIAMENT. Leyden: Sijthoff, 1965.

Palmer, Michael and John Lambert (eds.). EUROPEAN UNITY: A SURVEY OF EUROPEAN ORGANISATIONS. London: Allen & Unwin, 1968.

Patijn, S., ed. LANDMARKS IN EUROPEAN UNITY. Leyden: A.W. Sijthoff, 1970.

Pfaltzgraff, Robert L. THE ATLANTIC COMMUNITY: A COMPLEX IMBALANCE. Princeton, N.J.: Van Nostrand, 1969.

Pinder, John & Roy Pryce. EUROPE AFTER DE GAULLE: TOWARDS THE UNITED STATES OF EUROPE. London: Penguin, 1970.

Robertson, Arthur H. EUROPEAN INSTITUTIONS. New York: Praeger, 1966.

Rougemont, Denis de. THE MEANING OF EUROPE. New York: Stein & Ray, 1965.

Sampson, Anthony. ANATOMY OF EUROPE. New York: Harper & Row, 1969.

Serfaty, Simon. FRANCE, DE GAULLE AND EUROPE. Baltimore: Johns Hopkins University Press, 1968.

Sérvan-Schreiber, Jean J. THE AMERICAN CHALLENGE. New York: Atheneum, 1968.

Sidjanski, Dusan, ed. MÉTHODES QUANTITATIVES ET INTÉGRATION EUROPÉENNE. Geneva: Institut Universitaire d'Etudes Européennes, 1970.

Spinelli, Altiero. THE EUROCRATS. Baltimore: Johns Hopkins Univ. Press, 1966.

Stanley, W. Timothy and Darnell M. Whitt. DETENTE DIPLOMACY: UNITED STATES AND EUROPEAN SECURITY IN THE 1970s. New York: Dunellen, 1970.

Stein, Eric and Petery Hay. LAW AND INSTITUTIONS IN THE ATLANTIC AREA. Indianapolis: Bobbs-Merrill, 1967.

Strausz-Hupé, Robert et al. BUILDING THE ATLANTIC WORLD. New York: Harper & Row, 1963.

Uri, Pierre. PARTNERSHIP FOR PROGRESS. New York: Harper & Row, 1963.

Van der Beugel, Ernst. FROM MARSHALL PLAN TO ATLANTIC PARTNERSHIP. Amsterdam: Elsevier Publ., 1965.

Wilcox, Francis O. and Field R. Haviland, eds. THE ATLANTIC COMMUNITY: PROGRESS AND PROSPECTS. New York: Praeger, 1963.

Walsh, A.E. and J. Paxton. THE STRUCTURE AND DEVELOPMENT OF THE COMMON MARKET. New York: Taplinger, 1968.

Warnecke, Steven J. ed. THE EUROPEAN COMMUNITY IN THE 1970s. New York: Praeger, 1972.

Zaring, J.L. DECISION FOR EUROPE. Baltimore: Johns Hopkins Univ. Press, 1969.

Zellentin, Gerda. INTERSYSTEMARE BEZIEHUNGEN IN EUROPA. Leyden: A.W. Sijthoff, 1970.

Index

About the Author

Gerhard Mally holds a law degree from the University of Vienna. He received the M.A. and Ph.D. from the University of Pennsylvania, where he was the recipient of a Penfield Fellowship.

Dr. Mally has served on the research staff of the Foreign Policy Research Institute (Philadelphia), and of the Atlantic Institute (Paris) where he also was associate editor of *Atlantic Studies*. He has taught political science at Penn Morton College, at the University of Virginia, at Georgetown University, and at Southwestern at Memphis. He spent a year in the federal government under a Ford Foundation program entitled "Washington Internships in Education."

Dr. Mally is a lecturer at the Foreign Service Institute of the Department of State, and a member of the Committee on Atlantic Studies which is affiliated with the Atlantic Council of the United States and composed of scholars specializing in research on European-American relations.

He is the author of *Britain and European Unity* and of several monographs and articles on European politics and Atlantic relationships.